# THEORY OF INTERNATIONAL TRADE

# THE CAMBRIDGE ECONOMIC HANDBOOKS

*General Editors*

# THEORY OF INTERNATIONAL TRADE

## A dual, general equilibrium approach

*by*

## AVINASH DIXIT

UNIVERSITY OF WARWICK

*and*

## VICTOR NORMAN

NORWEGIAN SCHOOL OF ECONOMICS AND BUSINESS ADMINISTRATION

JAMES NISBET & CO. LTD
*Digswell Place, Welwyn*
CAMBRIDGE UNIVERSITY PRESS

*First published 1980*
*by James Nisbet and Company Limited*
*Digswell Place, Welwyn, Herts.*
*and the Cambridge University Press*

SBN 0 7202 0315 5 Board
SBN 0 7202 0314 7 Paperback

For use in the United States of America and Canada:

SBN 0521 29969 1 Cased
SBN 0521 23481 6 Paperback

局版臺業字第〇八五二號

發行人：張　澤雲

發行所：台北市羅斯福路四段六號

總經銷：雙葉書店

雙葉書廊有限公司

地址：台北市羅斯福路四段六號

電話：三四一四一九八

郵政劃撥：七一一二六號

中華民國七十二年　月　日

Printed and bound in Great Britain by
William Clowes (Beccles) Limited, Beccles and London

# PREFACE

An addition to the large stock of books on trade theory calls for strong justification. We believe we have one, although not in any novelty of basic aims. On the contrary, we claim that previous treatments fail, often in not pursuing their own avowed aims far enough, and almost always in not pursuing them by the most efficient means.

It is always said that trade theory is a showcase for the theory of general economic equilibrium. Too much of it, however, usually considers only a part of the whole equilibrium, namely the comparative statics of production in one country. This occurs in some discussions of the effects of changes in factor endowments or technologies and of tariffs, but most importantly in dealing with factor-price equalization. The usual way to pose that question is as one of determining factor prices given output prices, or assuming diversified production. Both of these assumptions should really be a part of the whole equilibrium being studied. It turns out that the usual partial insights are very misleading when it comes to such a complete equilibrium of trading countries.

Secondly, when generalizing the simple two-by-two model, trade theorists often forget the lessons to be learnt from general microeconomic theory as to the right questions to be asked. The long and fruitless pursuit of wrong questions has led to much pessimism about the use of the basic model of comparative advantage. General equilibrium theory should have told us long ago that it is pointless to expect general results concerning changes in individual prices and quantities, but that we can deduce simple and instructive correlations between price and quantity changes from revealed preference arguments.

Finally, there is the matter of technique. The use of 'dual' or 'indirect' functions has proved very useful in general equilibrium theory and its applications, notably public finance and growth theory. Trade theory has long used unit cost functions to examine whether output prices determine factor prices, but the gain from consistent use of dual methods has not been realized. The revenue

v

function, which is arguably the most natural way of modelling production in each country, has been rarely used.

We offer progress in all these respects, without pretending to break totally fresh ground in any. In particular, it is a pleasure to acknowledge Samuelson's innovations in all three aspects. He pioneered the use of revealed preference in comparative statics long ago. He also used cost and revenue functions, and emphasized the importance of treating factor-price equalization in a truly general equilibrium setting. We hope that our consistent application of these ideas will be something of a tribute, coming so close to the silver jubilee of his important article on this subject.

We would like to emphasize in the strongest possible terms that our objective is not one of providing a comprehensive treatment of trade theory, so that 'the rest would be silence'. On the contrary, we only aim to show the readers the usefulness of the approach, and to give them some facility in handling the techniques, so that they can go on to develop the numerous extensions and generalizations that are conceivable. Notes at the end of each chapter point the way. We believe our aim will be best promoted by keeping the technical aspects as simple as possible, and have accordingly omitted all generality that would be spurious to each point being considered. Issues of welfare inherently need analyses with many consumers, and those of effective protection, many firms. But elsewhere we have often used models with one representative firm and one representative consumer, leaving the simple extensions to the readers.

Some knowledge of introductory trade theory will help the readers grasp the background to some issues, but the main pre-requisite is a working knowledge of modern micro-economics. Mathematical requirements are modest—multivariate calculus, elementary vector and matrix algebra, convexity, homogeneity, and constrained maximization—and are sketched in an Appendix. Readers familiar with the material can also benefit from a quick glance through the Appendix to get used to the notation.

The plan of the book is as follows. Chapter 1 contains a brief survey of introductory trade theory, with emphasis on issues and methodology. Chapter 2 establishes the basic properties of revenue and cost functions that are used throughout. In Chapters 3–5, we analyse trade in a Walrasian equilibrium, establishing its properties and deriving comparative static results. Chapter 6 is devoted to issues of taxation and trade policy. In Chapters 7 and 8 we discuss questions relating to exchange rates and the balance of payments, using a model of temporary equilibrium with and without flexible prices. Finally, Chapter 9 considers trade with imperfect competition.

The interrelations among the chapters are shown below:

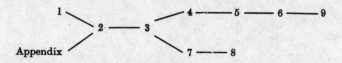

Vidar Christiansen discussed most of the issues with us in the formative stages of the work. Richard Cornes gave us very detailed comments on an earlier draft, and brought to our attention a great deal of previous work. Frank Hahn, the editor of the series, also provided very detailed comments, and proved a most valuable taskmaster in trying to make us improve the exposition. We are happy to thank all three, and also Peter Neary, Geoff Renshaw, Agnar Sandmo, Alasdair Smith and Knut Sydsæter for comments on earlier drafts. We are also grateful to Jan Haaland for his help in preparing the bibliography and the index. The work began when Victor Norman was visiting the University of Warwick, and he would like to thank the department for its hospitality. Finally, Grethe Didrichsen, Kirsten Herstad, Ann Sampson, and Liz Thompson deserve our gratitude for their prompt and efficient typing.

*July 1979*                                                      A.D.
                                                                 V.N.

# CONTENTS

ix

# CHAPTER 1

# THE THEORY OF INTERNATIONAL TRADE

There are two broad themes in the theory of international trade. One is qualitative, being concerned with the pattern of trade, i.e. which country will export which good. The standard theory relates this to comparative advantage, i.e. to international differences in relative opportunity costs, and then tries to explain comparative advantage in terms of differences in technologies, factor supplies, etc. This theme is also concerned with the way in which trade in return affects such determinants of comparative advantage. The other theme is more quantitative, and seeks to explain the terms of trade, i.e. relative prices of exports and imports in a trading world. It also examines how they are affected by changes in data such as factor supplies or technology, and policies such as tariffs. While we have stated the themes as descriptive, it is clear that normative analyses will have to be based on, and will benefit from, a proper understanding of them. Questions of the state of the balance of payments, or of determination of exchange rates, can also be seen as elaborations and extensions of the same basic ideas.

In developing these themes, one should bear in mind two important points. The first is that the very concepts of trade theory—relative costs and relative prices—call for consistent use of general equilibrium analysis. This need not always be Walrasian competitive analysis, but in a problem with several goods and factors, and several producing and coṇṣuming units, an approach which constantly reminds us of their mutual relationships is essential if errors of oversight are to be avoided. While obvious, this is sometimes forgotten. We shall see that two important debates in trade theory—the one about the impact of tariffs on domestic income distribution, and the discussion of how trade affects domestic factor prices when there are more goods than factors—arose because some of the discussants forgot that a trading equilibrium is a general, rather than a partial, equilibrium. The second point is that micro-economic theory tells us a great deal about general equilibria, and we should simplify our task in trade theory by making full use of such knowledge. For example, consider a Walrasian competitive case, which will be the focus of the first five chapters. We can regard each country as being

1

in a general equilibrium, treating its trade pattern as if it were a fixed vector of endowments and liabilities. Such an equilibrium is known to be Pareto efficient. In particular, treating market prices as parametric, (a) the production vector maximizes the value of net output, (b) the value of consumption equals that of net output, and (c) subject to this budget constraint, the consumption vector maximizes some increasing function of the consumers' utilities. This information can, and should, be used when we develop the themes. It points the way ahead, and helps us avoid sidetracks, by suggesting parallels from other applications of general micro-economic theory. This simplifies the analysis of a trading equilibrium to the extent that further *ad hoc* simplifications, such as an assumption of two goods and two factors, are in most cases unnecessary. It also suggests the techniques best suited to the purpose, but that is anticipating the work of later chapters.

In this chapter we give a brief summary of the major themes of trade theory, from a micro-economic point of view. In fact only the most basic concepts and tools are used—budget lines, revealed preference, input coefficients and price–cost relations. Even less previous knowledge of trade theory is assumed—the chapter or two on comparative advantage and on effects of tariffs that can be found in any good elementary economics textbook should suffice. If readers with this minimal knowledge are sometimes left wondering why the debates we mention should ever have arisen, so much the better.

In subsequent chapters we will develop more sophisticated techniques, and use them to treat in greater depth these and other issues. The basic insights gained from this introduction will prove useful in grasping that material more easily.

## 1. COMPARATIVE ADVANTAGE

Although perhaps the area of economics least understood by laymen (and, alas, many undergraduates), the theory of comparative advantage is essentially very simple: If two countries engage in trade, each will have incentives to increase production, and reduce consumption, of goods in which it has the lower *relative* marginal cost *prior to trade* than the other. Thus we may conjecture that in a free trade equilibrium, each country will export such goods. That is the first, oldest, and most basic proposition in the theory of international trade.

A quick recapitulation will provide a gentle beginning. Suppose Britain in isolation has competitive equilibrium prices of £300 per television set and £4 per bottle of whisky, and let the corresponding magnitudes for Japan be 100,000 and 2,000 yen respectively. For expository convenience, neglect complications like excise taxes. Then prices equal marginal costs. If Britain were to produce one television set less, this would release a package of resources that could be redeployed to produce another (300/4 = ) 75 bottles of whisky. Similarly, Japan could produce one more television set by diverting resources engaged in making 50 bottles of whisky. It is clearly to their mutual advantage to do both these things, and achieve an extra output of 25 bottles of whisky. In technical terms, the pre-trade relative price of a television set is 50 bottles of whisky in Japan, and 75 bottles in Britain. Thus Japan has an inducement to expand television production and export sets to Britain, importing whisky in return. The presumption is that after trade has commenced, the common relative price will settle somewhere between 50 and 75; the extent of trade depends on other aspects like demand conditions and the sizes of the countries.

Note that the above argument is valid irrespective of any absolute productivity levels: Japan may be better at making both goods than Britain, but it still benefits from trade, and its overall superiority is simply reflected in its higher standard of living. Likewise, the exchange rate, i.e. the price of a pound in terms of yen, is immaterial for the validity of the basic gain from trade. The sole purpose of the exchange rate is to translate comparative advantage into an actual lower cost for consumers in the other country. For example, at an exchange rate of 500 yen to the £, Japan will be able to under-sell Britain in TV sets while matching them in whisky; at $333\frac{1}{3}$ yen/£, Britain will be able to undersell Japan in whisky and just compete in TV sets. For equilibrium in trade, the exchange rate must settle somewhere between these extremes.

We must next ask why relative marginal costs in autarky should differ between countries. In principle, such differences could arise from any differences in the underlying exogenous entities in the equilibrium of each: consumers' tastes, production technologies, or factor supplies. The first does not produce any particularly interesting analyses in competitive equilibrium models; the observation that, other things being equal, a country will import goods for which domestic consumers have stronger preferences than foreign con-sumers, is rather trivial. With imperfect competition and product diversity, however, consumer tastes could have a more important effect on trade. We consider this case in Chapter 9. The second aspect—differences in production technology—is at the heart of Ricardo's model with one input, which is expounded at length in elementary textbooks. Beyond illustrating in a simple way how comparative, rather than absolute, advantage matters for trade, the simple Ricardo model is not very enlightening. A modification of it —the Ricardo–Viner model—is very instructive in that it embodies both differences in technology and differences in factor endowments as determinants of trade.

That brings us to the last aspect, namely differences in factor endowments. This has proved the most enlightening explanation of comparative advantage, in that it yields the greatest variety of testable propositions. The idea is that in each country, the factor which is relatively abundant will be relatively cheaper, and then the good which uses this factor relatively more intensively in its production will be relatively cheaper, too. Therefore we should expect a country to have its comparative advantage in goods relatively intensive in the use of those factors which are in relatively abundant supply there. This proposition is associated with the names of Eli Heckscher and Bertil Ohlin. We shall reserve the term 'the Heckscher–Ohlin model' for the special case of two goods and two factors, and shall refer to the general proposition more simply as the factor-abundance hypothesis. It is the second important hypothesis regarding comparative advantage.

In our example, we would say that whisky is relatively more capital-intensive than television sets (remember all the time it takes to mature whisky, as against all the labour it takes to rig up the connections to a silicon chip). Therefore comparative advantage in making whisky resides with the country where capital is cheaper, being relatively more abundant, than labour. We have taken this to be the case in Britain.

The third proposition is, in a sense, a corollary to the first two. If trade is due to the existence in autarky of differences in relative costs, then free trade should eliminate such differences, so that, at the margin, no country has a comparative advantage anywhere. In the case where comparative advantage derives from differences in factor endowments, therefore, one should expect the manifestations of such differences, namely the differences in domestic factor prices, to be eliminated by trade. This conjecture is the factor price equalization hypothesis.

Let us illustrate this using our simple example again. As Britain expands whisky production at the expense of television production, the relative factor demands shift in favour of capital, which is used relatively more intensively in the expanding industry, and against labour. This acts to relieve the scarcity of labour in Britain, which by assumption was the more acute. Wage rates fall relative to

· interest rates, and Britain's comparative advantage in whisky production diminishes. The opposite changes take place in Japan, reducing its comparative advantage in television production. In the final trading equilibrium, there is nothing to be gained from a further shift in production, i.e. there is no comparative advantage left at the margin. Note that the relative factor scarcities could be relieved directly by Britain exporting capital or importing labour from Japan, but the same object is being indirectly promoted by the trade in goods.

Even though these three propositions are simple and plausible in the light of elementary economic intuition, it is far from trivial to establish them rigorously. In part, this is because the concepts involved are imprecise. Only the first proposition is immediately meaningful; the other two involve notions of factor intensity and factor abundance that have yet to be defined precisely. Further difficulties arise from the fact that none of these propositions are valid without qualifications. Even within the context of reasonably simplified models, the propositions are only valid over a limited range of parameter values, or only in a vague general sense.

To see the nature of the problems involved, let us look back on the three propositions and sum up their basic content. The first asserts a relation between pre-trade product prices and the pattern of trade. The second goes further, and relates the pre-trade product price differences to factor price or factor supply differences. The third conjectures a particular property for different countries' prices of factors when they trade goods. We know from general microeconomic theory that such detailed characterizations or comparative statics of general economic equilibria are very hard to come by. Some such results need restrictive assumptions concerning demand (e.g. homotheticity) or supply (e.g. constant returns and no joint production); others are valid only in simple models with two or three commodities. So it is with trade. To acquire a preliminary understanding of what is possible, it is instructive to look at traditional cases with two goods or two factors or both, emphasizing questions rather than answers, and trying to see why the results may fail to generalize. An added advantage is that it is possible to do so with minimum use of mathematics. We therefore devote much of the rest of this chapter to this programme.

## 2. THE PATTERN OF TRADE

The first of the above propositions, stating that the pattern of trade is governed by differences in relative product prices in pretrade

Walrasian equilibria, is generally true in the two-good case. To see this, consider a one-consumer economy producing and trading two goods at a price ratio $(p_1/p_2)$. If the economy is competitive, we know that the allocation of resources will be such as to maximize the consumer's utility, given production constraints and the condition that there be no trade deficit. (We do allow for free disposal, and thus for a trade surplus; but a non-satiated consumer will never leave consumption possibilities unused.) As the no-trade allocation satisfies this condition, autarky is always a feasible choice; so any relative prices that generate foreign trade must give an allocation that is at least as attractive to the consumer as the autarky allocation. By the same token, of course, the no-trade equilibrium must be preferred to any other allocation that is feasible given the relative prices in autarky. Let the slope of the line $b^a b^a$ in Figure 1.1 indicate relative prices in autarky, so that the set $S^a$ gives the feasible trades given autarky prices. Then the origin must correspond to an allocation which is preferred to allocations corresponding to any other point in $S^a$, and (in the absence of satiation) the origin must be strictly preferred to any allocation not on the frontier of $S^a$. This means that for relative prices above $(p_1/p_2)^a$, such as the relative price $(p_1/p_2)^1$ and the corresponding trade-balance line $b^1 b^1$, trades in the south-east quadrant are ruled out, as all such trades are inferior to the no-trade situation. It follows that for $(p_1/p_2) > (p_1/p_2)^a$, the country will export good 1 and import good 2, and conversely for $(p_1/p_2) < (p_1/p_2)^a$.

The relationship between comparative advantage and trade is then immediate. Consider two countries with different autarky price ratios. Any relative prices below the lower of the two autarky price ratios, or above the higher of the two, must be ruled out as candidates for equilibrium prices, as such price ratios would make both countries export the same good. The equilibrium price ratio must therefore lie between the two autarky price ratios; in which case it is obvious that the country with the lower relative price of good 1 in autarky will export that good, and vice versa.

The underlying line of reasoning here is obviously not dependent on there being only two goods, so it should be possible to establish a similar result for the general case. Such a general result must, however, be weaker than the two-good case might suggest. An example illustrates why. Suppose there are three goods, with prices $p_1$, $p_2$, and $p_3$; and with quantities imported to the country in question of $m_1$, $m_2$, and $m_3$. Let good 3 be the numeraire, i.e. let all prices be reckoned in units of good 3. Letting superscript 'a' denote autarky value, the kind of result one could establish through the line of

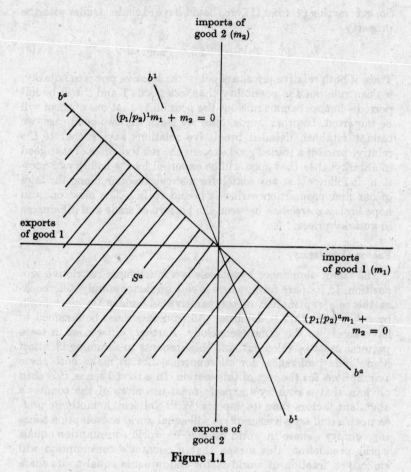

Figure 1.1

reasoning employed in the two-good case, would be that trades such that

$$p_1^a m_1 + p_2^a m_2 + m_3 \leq 0 \qquad (1)$$

could be excluded—i.e. that trades that would be feasible given autarky prices could be ruled out. At the same time, we would know that actual trades, evaluated at actual prices, would balance—i.e.

$$p_1 m_1 + p_2 m_2 + m_3 = 0 \qquad (2)$$

So, subtracting (2) from (1), we should have excluded trades with the property

$$(p_1^a - p_1)m_1 + (p_2^a - p_2)m_2 \leq 0 \qquad (3)$$

Thus, if both relative prices are below the relative prices in autarky, we can rule out the possibility that *both* goods 1 and 2 will be imported—but we cannot rule out the possibility that *one* of them will be imported. In other words, once we leave the two-good case, we cannot establish detailed predictive relations saying that if. the relative price of a traded good exceeds the relative price of that good in autarky, then that good will be exported by the country in question. It follows that any search for a *strong* theorem along the lines of our first proposition earlier is bound to fail. The most one can hope for is a *correlation* between the pattern of trade and differences in autarky prices.

### Factor abundance

The factor abundance hypothesis is a much more restrictive proposition. In its pure form, where it sets up factor supply differences as the sole explanation of comparative advantage, it must begin by ruling out other possibilities. All countries must be assumed to have access to the same technology. Further, differences in taste patterns must be ruled out, and this amounts to assuming identical homothetic preferences for all countries. Let us make both these assumptions for the rest of this section. In a trivial sense, it is then obvious that a country's exports must use more of the country's abundant factors than its imports. With uniform, homothetic preferences, a country's consumption will equal world consumption times the country's share in world income. As world consumption equals world production, this means that a country's consumption will embody a fraction of world factor endowments equal to its share in world income. At the same time, its production will obviously embody its own factor endowments. As its net exports equal its production less its consumption, this means that its net exports will embody domestic factor endowments less its income share times world factor endowments. Thus, if the country is abundantly endowed with a particular factor, in the sense that its share of the factor exceeds its share of world income, its exports must embody more of that factor than its imports.

If it is to provide insight into the characteristics of a trading equilibrium, however, the factor abundance hypothesis must be something more than an accounting triviality. In particular, if it is to have any predictive content, it must be capable of establishing a relationship between relative factor abundance and pre-trade relative output prices. It has already been suggested that a link might be provided through the concept of relative factor intensities. In fact there are two ways to proceed, for we might interpret the idea of relative factor abundance in its physical sense of quantities or in its economic sense of scarcity values, i.e. prices. The vague, intuitive treatment of the previous section treated these as one and the same. However, we have just seen how problems can arise in relating prices to quantities for outputs, and the same is true for factors. There are some important cases where factor supply differences can be negatively correlated with factor price differences, but this is not strong enough save in the case of two factors. We shall therefore investigate the two notions separately. From an empirical point of view, factor quantities are more easily observed than autarky factor prices. From a conceptual point of view, too, factor quantities can be seen as primary data while factor prices are merely endogenous variables in the full equilibrium system. However, relations between product prices and factor prices are easy to establish, and provide useful techniques for later use.

## Product prices and factor prices

We begin with such relations in the case of two factors producing two goods. We will assume that there are constant returns to scale, and no joint production. To start with, we will also suppose that the technology defines fixed input coefficients. Let $(p_1, p_2)$ be the output prices, $(w_1, w_2)$ the factor prices, and $b_{ij}$ the input coefficients denoting the amount of factor $j$ required for unit output of good $i$, for $i$ and $j$ ranging over $(1, 2)$. In a competitive equilibrium, each output price must equal its marginal cost, which under constant returns to scale equals the average cost. Therefore we have the equations of production equilibrium:

$$p_1 = b_{11}w_1 + b_{12}w_2$$
$$p_2 = b_{21}w_1 + b_{22}w_2 \tag{4}$$

Now define the relative prices $\pi = p_1/p_2$ and $\omega = w_1/w_2$. Dividing the first of the above equations by the second, we have a functional relation between relative output prices and relative factor prices:

$$\pi = (b_{11}\omega + b_{12})/(b_{21}\omega + b_{22}) \tag{5}$$

To see whether this function is increasing or decreasing, take logarithms of both sides and differentiate. This yields

$$\frac{1}{\pi}\frac{d\pi}{d\omega} = \frac{b_{11}}{b_{11}\omega + b_{12}} - \frac{b_{21}}{b_{21}\omega + b_{22}}$$

$$= \frac{1}{\omega + b_{12}/b_{11}} - \frac{1}{\omega + b_{22}/b_{21}}$$

$$= \frac{b_{22}/b_{21} - b_{12}/b_{11}}{(\omega + b_{12}/b_{11})(\omega + b_{22}/b_{21})} \tag{6}$$

Therefore a higher $\omega$ corresponds to a higher $\pi$ if and only if $b_{22}/b_{21} > b_{12}/b_{11}$, i.e. production of good 2 requires a relatively greater input of factor 2. This is the same as saying $b_{11}/b_{12} > b_{21}/b_{22}$, i.e. that production of good 1 requires a relatively greater input of factor 1. It is natural to make this relation between the factor inputs our definition of relative factor intensity: in the above case we will say that good 2 is relatively factor 2 intensive, or good 1 is relatively factor 1 intensive.

It is instructive to look at this in diagrammatic form. In Figure 1.2, the line $B_1B_1$ is the set of factor prices consistent with unit cost = price for good 1; i.e. the combinations of $w_1$ and $w_2$ giving $b_{11}w_1 + b_{12}w_2 = p_1$. Its slope will equal the factor input ratio in the production of good 1; i.e. $(b_{11}/b_{12})$. Similarly, the line $B_2B_2$ gives the combinations of factor prices giving unit cost = price for good 2. Its slope is $(b_{21}/b_{22})$. If both goods are to be produced, we must have unit cost = price for both; so factor prices must be given at the intersection point $A$.

Using Figure 1.2, we can easily find the relationship between factor prices and product prices. Set $p_1 = 1$. All possible factor price combinations are then given by the $B_1B_1$-line. If any point on $B_1B_1$ is to be an equilibrium in which both goods are produced, a line such as $B_2B_2$ must pass through it. For example, if $A'$ is to be an equilibrium, $p_2'$ must be such that the line $b_{21}w_1 + b_{22}w_2 = p_2$ passes through $A'$; so $p_2$ must equal $p_2'$. Obviously, then, a higher $(w_2/w_1)$ must correspond to a higher $(p_2/p_1)$.

Now consider two countries with identical technologies, i.e. the same input coefficients $b_{ij}$. In the autarky equilibrium of each, the same equations (4) will be valid, but the magnitudes of the prices will be different. Choosing labels so that good 1 is factor 1 intensive, the country with the higher relative price of factor 1 will also have the higher relative price of good 1. The factor abundance hypothesis in this form is therefore verified for this model.

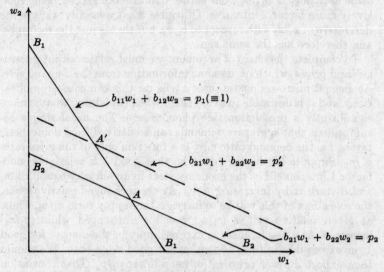

**Figure 1.2**

It will have struck the reader that such a monotonic relationship also entails a reverse link—output prices to factor prices—and this has an obvious bearing on our third proposition, the factor price equalization hypothesis. We shall return to this point in the next section; here we continue with the other aspect of the factor abundance hypothesis, which is concerned with factor quantities.

## Production and factor supply

We maintain the assumptions of constant returns to scale, no joint production, and fixed input coefficients. In addition, we assume full employment for both factors. Then we have, writing $(v_1, v_2)$ as the factor supplies and $(x_1, x_2)$ as the output quantities,

$$v_1 = x_1 b_{11} + x_2 b_{21}$$
$$v_2 = x_1 b_{12} + x_2 b_{22} \tag{7}$$

A relation between the ratios is easy to establish. We have

$$v_1/v_2 = (b_{11}(x_1/x_2) + b_{21})/(b_{12}(x_1/x_2) + b_{22}) \tag{8}$$

This is formally quite similar to (4), save for an occasional interchange of subscripts. We can easily verify that the derivative of $v_1/v_2$ with respect to $x_1/x_2$ is positive if $b_{22}/b_{12} > b_{21}/b_{11}$, which is the same as $b_{22}/b_{21} > b_{12}/b_{11}$, our earlier definition of good 2 being relatively more factor 2 intensive. Of course what we really want is the derivative of $x_1/x_2$ with respect to $v_1/v_2$, but that is just the reciprocal and therefore has the same sign.

To complete the chain of argument we must relate output quantities and prices, which needs some information from the demand side. As general micro-economic theory tells us, this can cause complications, and it is desirable to avoid them when explaining what is more significantly a production side phenomenon. The usual simple assumption is that aggregate demands can be derived from homothetic tastes, i.e. the demand ratio $c_1/c_2$ is a function only of the price ratio $p_1/p_2$. Suppose labels are chosen so that good 1 is relatively more factor 1 intensive. Let the economy start in an autarky equilibrium, and disturb it by increasing $v_1/v_2$. At an unchanged relative price, the sole effect of this will be to increase the supply ratio $x_1/x_2$. Thus, at given relative prices, $(c_1/c_2)$ remains unchanged while $(x_1/x_2)$ increases. As a result, there is excess supply in the market for good 1, or excess demand in the market for good 2, or both. We should then expect a lower price ratio, i.e. a lower $p_1/p_2$. That conclusion presupposes that the equilibrium is stable in the sense that excess demands are decreasing functions of relative prices in the neighbourhood of the equilibrium, so that a tâtonnement process restores the initial equilibrium if it is disturbed. In the two-good case, stability in this sense is uncomplicated. In later chapters, we shall encounter cases where stability is non-trivial.

An increased relative factor supply ratio $v_1/v_2$, therefore, will result in a lower $p_1/p_2$. We can interpret this comparative static result as comparing two closed economies with identical technologies and tastes of the kind assumed here; then the economy with the relatively higher quantity of factor 1 will have the relatively lower pre-trade price of good 1, thus confirming this form of the factor abundance hypothesis.

Incidentally, we are sometimes interested in the absolute and not merely the relative changes in quantities. This is easily examined by taking total differentials in (7):

$$dv_1 = dx_1 b_{11} + dx_2 b_{21}$$
$$dv_2 = dx_1 b_{12} + dx_2 b_{22}$$

These are easy to solve, yielding

$$dx_1 = (b_{22}\, dv_1 - b_{21}\, dv_2)/(b_{11}b_{22} - b_{12}b_{21})$$
$$dx_2 = (-b_{12}\, dv_1 + b_{11}\, dv_2)/(b_{11}b_{22} - b_{12}b_{21})$$

$$(9)$$

The partial derivatives $\partial x_i / \partial v_j$ may be read off from the coefficients on the right-hand sides. Note that the denominator in (9) can be written as

$$b_{12}b_{22}\left(\frac{b_{11}}{b_{12}} - \frac{b_{21}}{b_{22}}\right)$$

so that the signs of the partial derivatives are directly related to our factor intensity condition. In particular, if good 1 is factor 1 intensive, an increased supply of factor 1 will lead to increased production of good 1, and reduced production of good 2. That result, known as the Rybczynski theorem, is useful in many contexts. This can be illustrated diagrammatically in much the same way as Figure 1.2; we leave this to the reader. Conversely, once a unit of account is chosen, we can obtain algebraic relations between absolute prices of factors and goods. The readers can easily verify that an increase in $p_1$ with $p_2$ held constant will increase $w_1$ and reduce $w_2$. This is known as the Stolper–Samuelson theorem.

### Input substitution

We must next ask how far the simple case above can generalize. Begin by allowing choices of input mixes. Now the $b_{ij}$ are no longer constant, but can be chosen from a list of technical possibilities so as to minimize the cost of production. This choice depends on $\omega$, the factor–price ratio, and the properties of this functional dependence will be discussed in detail in Chapter 2. For now we merely state that equation (6) remains valid with the local values of the coefficients. In other words, the effect of a small change in relative factor prices on relative output prices depends on which good is relatively more intensive in which factor at the initial point. Therefore this form of the factor abundance hypothesis is valid when the countries differ only slightly in their pre-trade factor prices. The same is true for small differences in factor quantities. Consider a small change in $v_1/v_2$, and examine what happens at the initial equilibrium level of $p_1/p_2$. The demand ratio $c_1/c_2$, being a function of the price ratio alone, is unchanged. From (5), we see that the factor–price ratio $w_1/w_2$ cannot change either, so long as the two goods do not happen to be equal in their factor intensities at the initial point. Then the $b_{ij}$ remain fixed, and the argument following (8) is valid. The only effect is therefore an increase in $x_1/x_2$. So long as the equilibrium is stable, the result must be a lower $p_1/p_2$.

Matters are different for large changes. When the $b_{ij}$ are functions of $\omega = w_1/w_2$, there is no reason why the comparison of relative factor intensities should remain invariant. We may have factor intensity reversals, i.e. cases where an interval of $\omega$ where good 2 is more factor 1 intensive is followed by one where it is factor 2 intensive, or vice versa, or indeed both. It is then impossible to find a global, monotonic relation between relative factor prices and relative product prices. Thus, suppose good 1 is factor 1 intensive for $\omega < \omega^*$, and factor 2 intensive for $\omega > \omega^*$. There will then be a positive relationship between $\omega$ and $\pi$ for $\omega < \omega^*$, and a negative one beyond $\omega^*$. If we compare two countries, one with $\omega < \omega^*$ and one with $\omega > \omega^*$, therefore, we cannot a priori tell which will have the lower relative price of good 1. As a result, we cannot say which country will have a comparative advantage in good 1.

As an illustration, consider our example of trade in whisky and television sets between Britain and Japan. Suppose there is only one way of producing whisky, but several alternative modes of production for TV sets (ranging from manual assembly to fully automated production runs). It could then well be that at British factor prices, TV production is more capital intensive than whisky production; while the opposite is true in Japan. Knowing that Britain has a comparative advantage in capital intensive production (TV sets), and Japan a comparative advantage in labour intensive production (TV sets), clearly is insufficient for us to know which country will export TV sets in a trading equilibrium. Factor abundance differences still provide the reason for any trade, but they do not a priori suffice to determine the pattern of trade.

### Several goods and factors

The issue of factor intensity reversals has received much attention; some would say too much attention. In fact, another problem is potentially more serious. This is the attempt to generalize the factor abundance hypothesis to a world with many goods and factors. The case of any, but equal, numbers of goods and factors is not too difficult. If the common number is $n$, we have $n$ equations like (4), and then $(n - 1)$ equations relate the difference in output prices to that in factor prices. Similarly, from $n$ equations like (7) we can obtain $(n - 1)$ equations connecting relative factor supply changes to relative output supply changes. Similarly we can generalize (9) for absolute changes. All these obviously involve more complicated expressions and interpretations of relative factor intensities, but retain the property that factor intensities are defined in terms of technological factor input coefficients alone.

More serious problems arise if $n$, the number of goods, does not equal $m$, the number of factors. First suppose $n < m$. Now (7) gives us $m$ equations in $n$ unknowns, which is in general an overdetermined system. The point is that inter-industry substitution, i.e. changing the output mix, is not by itself sufficient to ensure full employment of all factors, or to maintain it in the face of changes in factor supplies. If the technology has fixed coefficients, there is no more to be said; some factors will remain unemployed, and we can disregard them so long as our comparisons do not cross from a regime where they are unemployed to one where they are fully employed. With intra-industry substitution possible by changing the factor mix, there is the possibility of full employment. However, changes in factor supplies will now entail changes in the input coefficients to preserve this state of affairs. The derivatives $\partial x_j/\partial v_i$ will then have to take into account such induced changes in the $b_{ji}$, and (8) cannot be differentiated by analogy with (6). We could simply define the properly computed derivatives $\partial x_j/\partial v_i$ as our notions of factor intensity; good $j$ is relatively intensive in its use of factor $i$ if the derivative is positive. This notion of factor intensity is, however, no longer a property of the technology, but of the whole equilibrium including the factor supplies. This makes the definition tautological and non-operational.

The problem is even worse when $n > m$. Now the analogues of (7) are an underdetermined system. In other words, the supply side of the economy is insufficient to determine quantities produced. The simple case of a constant returns economy with two goods and one factor serves to suggest what goes wrong. In such an economy, the production possibility frontier is a straight line, and for relative prices equal to the rate of transformation, supplies are indeterminate. When the $x_j$ are not single-valued functions of the $v_i$, one cannot hope to differentiate them.

Even under the restrictive assumptions of identical technology and homothetic preferences, therefore, the factor-abundance hypothesis does not seem very robust. To hold in the general case, it must involve definitions of factor intensity based on general-equilibrium derivatives rather than easily observable factor input coefficients; and even then it may not be valid when there are more goods than factors. That does not mean that a study of the hypothesis is uninteresting—in many ways a hypothesis of limited validity is more instructive than an all-encompassing theorem. It does, however, mean that a search for general theorems on the relationship between factor endowments and trade patterns is not worth while.

## 3. FACTOR PRICE EQUALIZATION

Our third proposition—the factor price equalization hypothesis—provides a perfect illustration of how instructive it can be to study a hypothesis that, at best, is valid for a limited set of parameter values. The basic assumptions behind the hypothesis are very strong indeed: all countries must have access to the same, linearly homogeneous technology, and free trade must lead to complete equalization of output prices. The latter, in particular, makes the hypothesis virtually irrelevant from an empirical point of view, as any Scandinavian in Oxford Street knows. Nevertheless, a study of the hypothesis is rewarding, not only because it illustrates the relationship between markets for traded and non-traded goods, but also because it serves to clarify important issues regarding the pattern of specialization in a free trade equilibrium.

The essence of the hypothesis is that, when two countries engage in trade, resources in each country will tend to be shifted away from sectors in which the country has a comparative cost disadvantage, and to sectors in which it has a comparative cost advantage. As relative costs reflect relative factor prices, this means that resources are shifted away from sectors that use expensive factors intensively, and to sectors that are intensive in the use of relatively cheap factors. Consequently, the effective scarcity of relatively scarce factors should be reduced, as should the effective abundance of relatively abundant factors. Moreover, this process should continue until relative production costs are the same in both countries, or until each country has stopped producing the goods in which it still has a comparative cost disadvantage. In other words, we shall either have some measure of production specialization, or reduction of international factor price differences to the point where relative costs are the same in both countries.

### The two-by-two case

In the two-good, two-factor case, the various possible outcomes are easily found. The actual (technologically determined) relationship between relative factor prices and relative costs is important in this context. Our examination of the right-hand side of (5) showed what can happen. One possibility, illustrated in Figure 1.3a, is that relative factor prices $(w_1/w_2)$ map uniquely into relative product prices $(p_1/p_2)$ *and vice versa*. This corresponds to the case where good 1 is intensive in factor 1 regardless of factor prices—i.e. where there are no factor intensity reversals. The other possibility, shown in Figure 1.3b, is that more than one factor–price ratio may be consistent with a particular ratio of unit costs. That corresponds to the case where factor intensities are reversed—i.e. where good 1 is intensive in factor 1 over some ranges of relative factor prices

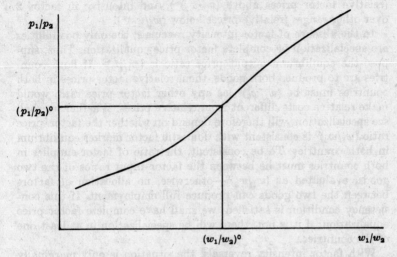

**Figure 1.3a**

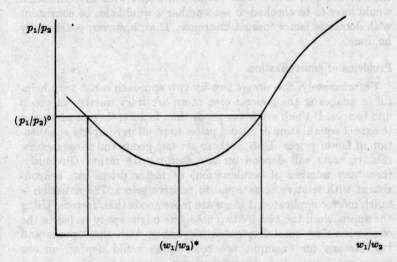

**Figure 1.3b**

(relative factor prices above $(w_1/w_2)^*$), and intensive in factor 2 over other ranges (relative prices below $(w_1/w_2)^*$).

In the absence of factor intensity reversals, the only possibilities are specialization or complete factor price equalization. Thus, suppose the equilibrium output–price ratio is $(p_1/p_2)^0$. If both countries are to produce both goods, then, relative factor prices in both countries must be $(w_1/w_2)^0$, as any other factor–price ratio would make relative costs different from relative prices. Whether we shall see specialization, will therefore depend on whether the factor–price ratio $(w_1/w_2)^0$ is consistent with domestic factor market equilibrium in both countries. To be consistent, the ratio of factor supplies in both countries must lie between the factor–input ratios of the two goods, evaluated at $(w_1/w_2)^0$—otherwise, no allocation of factors between the two goods can produce full employment. If this consistency condition is satisfied, we shall have complete factor price equalization; if it is not, there will be specialization in at least one of the countries.

With factor intensity reversals, the situation is only marginally more complex. Thus, in Figure 1.3b, there are two factor–price ratios consistent with relative costs equal to $(p_1/p_2)^0$, so the *possibility* that there may be diversification without factor price equalization certainly exists. To determine whether we shall see a diversified equilibrium with *equal* factor prices, a diversified equilibrium in which factor price *differences* persist, or a specialized equilibrium, each of the two factor–price ratios consistent with diversification would have to be checked to see whether it would also be consistent with domestic factor market clearance. That, however, could easily be done.

### Problems of generalization

Unfortunately, the simple two-by-two approach is not very helpful in analysing the general case of an arbitrary number of goods and factors. If there are fewer goods than factors, there is no reason to expect equalization of output prices to result in complete equalization of factor prices. Thus, if there are two goods and three factors, relative costs will depend on two factor–price ratios. Obviously, then, any number of combinations of factor prices can be consistent with relative costs equal to relative prices. The situation is much more complicated if there are more goods than factors. Using the approach of the two-by-two case, one might easily be led to the conclusion that specialization is inevitable: with three goods and two factors, for example, *two* cost ratios would depend on *one* factor–price ratio. For arbitrarily given output–price ratios, factor price equalization is then only possible if we are able to solve two equations (the two cost ratios equal to the two price ratios) in one unknown (the factor–price ratio)—and as a general proposition, that is impossible. Now it might be argued that if we happen to find an equilibrium in which both countries are producing all three commodities, the two equations will happen to be consistent, and then there will be no less reason to expect factor price equalization than before. Whether such an equilibrium will occur is, however, itself a question endogenous to trade theory, so this argument is incomplete at best. On the contrary, it can be argued that for generally specified output prices, it being impossible to satisfy both relevant equations, an equilibrium without specialization will be unlikely and therefore so will factor price equalization. This argument suffers from the same flaw, for the equilibrium magnitudes of output prices are themselves of endogenous interest to trade theory. It is incumbent upon us to examine the possibility of equilibria where the one factor–price ratio satisfies both cost–price equations. The conclusion must be that the two-by-two case is too simple-minded, rather than that the factor price equalization hypothesis is in general false. To find out, we must examine a completely specified general equilibrium model of a trading world. This we do in Chapter 4.

## 4. WELFARE AND THE TERMS OF TRADE

The relationship between the theory of comparative advantage and the theory of the terms of trade is in many respects similar to the relationship between physics and engineering. The theory of comparative advantage is concerned with 'ultimate' causes of trade and basic interrelations between markets for tradeables and non-tradeables; whereas the theory of the terms of trade takes all this for granted, being concerned simply with the pragmatic issue of how certain parameters—including policies a trading country might pursue—affect the terms of trade. Underlying this concern is the presumption that the terms of trade are a relevant measure of the welfare of a trading country—but that is usually taken for granted.

### Welfare implications

In fact, one can easily establish the relationship between relative prices and national welfare. The essence of the argument is illustrated in Figure 1.4. Suppose a country trades at relative prices $(p_1/p_2)^0$, exporting $OA$ of good 1, and importing $OB$ of good 2.

Consider an improvement in the terms of trade, i.e. an increase in the relative price of the exported good, to $(p_1/p_2)^1$. We then see that the original trade vector $(OA, OB)$ is a feasible trade given the new terms of trade. As domestic equilibrium is a Pareto-optimum, this means (i) that in the one-consumer case, the new terms of trade must give an allocation that is at least as attractive as the old one from the consumer's point of view, and (ii) that in the many-consumer case, there must exist a set of lump-sum transfers domestically such that the new allocation is Pareto-superior to the old one. In that sense, therefore, there is a one-to-one correspondence between the terms of trade and the level of national welfare, appropriately defined. A similar result can be derived for a many-consumer economy even if lump-sum transfers are impossible, if the government pursues a policy of optimum redistribution through a complete set of indirect taxes. The presumed relationship between the terms of trade and welfare therefore seems fairly robust.

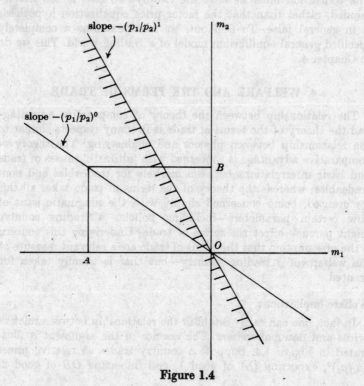

**Figure 1.4**

Relative prices in general equilibrium will depend on all under-lying parameters of demand and supply, so relative prices in a trading world will depend on factor endowments, technology, preferences, ownership distribution, and any distortive taxes or subsidies (including trade taxes). Four determinants seem of par-ticular interest. The first concerns the relationship between the *international* distribution of income and the terms of trade—how will international income transfers affect relative prices? The second concerns the relationship between economic growth and relative prices—i.e. the effect of increases in domestic factor supplies on the terms of trade. The third, closely related to the second, is the impact of international factor movements on relative prices. And the fourth is the relationship between trade policies and trading terms. None of these relationships can be found except by setting up explicitly the general equilibrium model and carrying out comparative static analyses. At this point, therefore, all we can do is to suggest some of the issues involved, and indicate preliminary conjectures regard-ing the relationships. For that purpose, it is useful to think in terms of two goods and (when necessary) two factors.

### Income transfers

If income is transferred from one country to another, demands will change in both countries. The effect on international prices will depend on what happens to aggregate world demand for the different goods, and that will depend on the difference between the income derivatives of the demand functions in the two countries—i.e. on the difference between the marginal propensity to demand the various goods in the receiving and the donating country. All possi-bilities are therefore open. One possibility, in particular, is that world demand for the receiving country's exports declines. That will happen if the marginal propensity to demand the receiving country's export good is lower with the receiver than with the donor. That possibility is interesting because it suggests that the price of the receiving country's export good may fall, relative to the price of its import good, as the result of a transfer—i.e. that the donor country may find its terms of trade improved as the result of making a gift.

This raises the question of whether it is possible for a country, by making a gift to another country, to achieve a sufficiently large improvement in the terms of trade to make the country better off than it was before—i.e. whether the induced improvement in the terms of trade can compensate the donor completely for the cost of his gift. It would seem strange if it could, and it turns out that this possibility can be ruled out by stability conditions for a trading equilibrium. The donor may reap some benefits from making a gift, through improved terms of trade, but not sufficiently large ones to make giving a profitable proposition.

## Factor supply changes

Even though a country will always benefit from receiving a gift of purchasing power, however, it need not benefit from getting more abundantly endowed with factors of production. This possibility, of so-called immiserizing growth, provides one of the best illustrations of how parameter changes affect the terms of trade. As an example, let us consider the simple two-by-two model in which the factor abundance theory of comparative advantage holds. Suppose, within the context of such a model, that a country experiences an increase in the endowment of its relatively abundant factor. This will, for given output prices, have two effects. One is that national income rises. If both goods are normal, that will lead to increased domestic demand for both goods. The other effect—given by the general-equilibrium derivatives $(\partial x_i / \partial v_j)$ discussed earlier—is that domestic production of the good intensive in the abundant factor increases, while domestic production of the other good goes down; in other words, that production of the export good increases and production of the import good decreases. Thus, the country's excess demand for the imported good will increase. By the balance-of-trade condition, the country's excess supply of the export good must then also increase. But increased supply of exports, and increased demand for imports, should normally result in less favourable terms of trade. Moreover, in this case there are no obvious bounds to the induced change in the terms of trade; so there is no reason to expect the utility loss caused by less favourable trading terms to be smaller than the direct utility gain of a more abundant factor endowment. Consequently, the possibility of immiserizing growth is a real one.

After the above analysis, one can easily handle the effects of international factor movements, at least in the case where the factor income also moves and is spent in accordance with the demand pattern of the destination country. This is simply the sum of the effects of a factor supply increase in one country and a corresponding factor supply reduction elsewhere. These two effects will tend to counteract one another, as is apparent if we think of the factor endowment increase in the preceding paragraph as being the result of a transfer of factors from the rest of the world. In the rest of the world we should then expect the opposite effects on supply and demand—i.e.

the rest of the world will then produce more of the home country's imports, and demand less of them. Thus, the increase in the home country's excess demand for the imported good will be counteracted by an increase in the excess supply of that good from the rest of the world. Any terms of trade effects of factor movements must therefore be due to the differences between countries in marginal propensities to demand, or in the effects of factor endowment changes on outputs (i.e. differences in factor intensities across countries). All one can hope to get out of an analysis of factor movement effects, therefore, are formulae that can be useful in particular empirical applications.

## Tariffs and terms of trade

The last question regarding the determinants of the terms of trade concerns the relationship between trade policies and relative prices in a trading equilibrium. In a Walrasian equilibrium, we can always find a tariff which would have the same effect as a quota or any other trade restriction. The impact of trade policies can therefore be found simply by studying the effects of tariffs on the terms of trade. In general, changes in the level of tariffs will involve both income and substitution effects—substitution effects because relative prices are changed, and income effects because tariffs, as distortions, cause production and consumption inefficiencies. In general, therefore, it would seem impossible to predict the impact of tariffs on excess demands without an additional assumption of normality.

Surprisingly, that is not so. A simple argument—illustrated in Figure 1.5—shows why. Consider a one-consumer economy. Suppose the country in question under free trade exports good 1 and imports good 2, trading at relative prices $(p_1/p_2)^0$ to the point $A$. Let us consider the shift in excess demands—i.e. the changes in export supply and import demand *at constant world prices*—that would be brought about by the introduction of a tariff, at rate $t$, on the imported good. The new trade vector would still have to satisfy the balance-of-trade condition, so it would have to be somewhere along the line $b^0b^0$. Suppose it were at a point north-west of $A$, such as $B$. The budget line as perceived by domestic consumers, however, would seem to allow for any trade along $b^1b^1$, a 'budget' line with slope $(p_1^0/(p_2^0 + t))$ and an intercept equal to the tariff revenue generated by the trade vector $B$. As domestic equilibrium is a Pareto-optimum, this means that the allocation corresponding to $B$ is revealed preferred to any allocation corresponding to another point on the $b^1b^1$-line. In particular, then, it is revealed preferred to

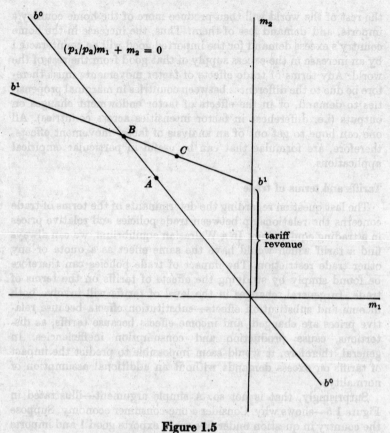

**Figure 1.5**

the allocation corresponding to the point $C$. But the point $C$ must give an allocation that is strictly preferred to the allocation at $A$, as $C$ allows for higher domestic consumption of both goods than $A$. Thus, we must have $B$ strictly preferred to $A$. But that involves a contradiction, as $B$ is a feasible trade without tariffs, and $A$ is revealed preferred to any other feasible, free trade. Consequently, the introduction of tariffs must shift excess demands to a point on $b^0 b^0$ south-east of $A$. In other words, tariffs must result in lower import demand, and lower export supply, than free trade at the same world prices. If the country is a significant buyer in world markets, and these markets are stable, it is then immediate that tariffs will improve the terms of trade of the home country.

An immediate corollary is that tariffs imposed by a country will always lower welfare in the rest of the world. On the other hand, it is by no means certain that the country levying tariffs will gain from so doing, as the utility gain from improved terms of trade is counteracted by the deadweight loss arising because tariffs distort the allocation of resources. For a 'small' tariff, the deadweight loss will be of second order of magnitude, so a 'small' tariff cannot be detrimental to the home country. For large tariffs, however, both effects will be of first order, so the question of whether protection is attractive or not involves weighing the marginal gain from improved terms of trade against the marginal loss from consumption and production inefficiencies. That is the question of optimum tariffs.

### Tariffs and income distribution

Related to the question of how tariffs affect domestic welfare is the question of how they affect the domestic income distribution. As a normative question, one could argue that this is a non-issue, as trade restrictions are neither first-best nor second-best means of achieving domestic distributional goals. As a purely positive issue, however, it serves to illustrate interesting general-equilibrium effects. Essentially, the issue illustrates two quite different effects. One is the effect that tariffs have on *domestic* prices, the other how changes in domestic prices affect the distribution of income. The latter issue involves finding the effect of price changes on factor rewards— intuition suggesting that an increase in the price of a good should raise the price of factors used intensively in the production of that good. That conjecture is correct, the result being the Stolper–Samuelson theorem, although the problems involved in defining factor intensities in the case of an arbitrary number of goods and factors makes it a rather weak proposition in the general case.

When it comes to the effect of tariffs on domestic prices, however, the intuitive conclusion—that tariffs will raise the domestic price of protected goods relative to the price of unprotected ones—is not generally true. As we have already seen, tariffs will improve the terms of trade, so the *international* prices of protected goods should tend to fall relative to other prices. Whether domestic prices of imports will rise (in real terms) will therefore depend on whether the terms of trade improvement can offset the price-raising effect of tariffs completely. As it turns out, it can—even when all goods are normal. This means that the effect of tariffs on domestic prices, and thus the effect of tariffs on the domestic distribution of income, cannot be predicted *a priori*.

## 5. A REMARK ON THE BASIC MODEL

The preceding discussion has taken us about as far as one can get without specifying in detail a complete general-equilibrium model of international trade. We hope the examples have shown that the conclusions one might derive from incomplete models—such as models of domestic factor market equilibrium taking output prices as given, or models of tariff effects on income distribution that ignore the terms of trade effect of protection—can be highly misleading. Only by taking the trouble to trace out the complete set of general-equilibrium effects can one hope to derive robust conclusions. And if such a procedure carries one to the conclusion that no generalization is possible, then so be it. At least one will have shown how to derive specific conclusions for special cases.

We also hope that the preceding discussion has illustrated the usefulness of revealed-preference arguments in trade theory. That is why a dual approach, where revealed preference is 'built in', seems a promising approach to trade issues. The following chapter provides an introduction to dual concepts, and shows how these can be used in formulating a general-equilibrium model of international trade.

A methodological point remains before such a model can be formulated. That is the question of what the appropriate *format* of a model of trade is. Obviously, any model of trade must capture the determination of prices in international markets. At the same time, however, the existence of transport costs, institutional constraints, and information barriers makes the number of truly international markets small—most goods and services being sold in national, regional, or local markets—and we should want the model to capture the resulting interaction between international and domestic transactions. We have already seen that this interaction is an essential feature (some would say *the* essential feature) of trade theory. In fact, one could argue that it is the explicit analysis of multi-market equilibrium in a hierarchical market structure that sets trade theory apart from abstract general-equilibrium analysis. In other words, trade theory can be claimed to be the application of general-equilibrium theory to a setting where some commodities are sold in international markets, some in national ones, some in regional ones, etc.

The particular hierarchy ordinarily used in trade theory is very simple. It derives from an assumption of a fundamental asymmetry between goods and factors: goods enter consumers' utility functions directly, are elastically supplied and demanded, and can be traded internationally at zero transportation cost. Factors only affect utility through the income that they generate, they are in fixed supply domestically, and they cannot be traded at all. This gives a hierarchy of domestic factor markets and international product markets, in which factor market equilibrium can be used to establish each country's supply of goods as a function of international product prices and domestic factor supplies, and where each country's demand for goods will be determined by product prices and the income levels corresponding to particular product prices and factor endowments.

One can object to the empirical relevance of this particular representation—after all, transport costs *are* important for goods as well as for factors, there *is* international movement of factors, the supply of labour and other inputs *does* depend on prices, and so forth. Most objections of this sort could be taken care of by clever reinterpretations of the model. Transport costs could be handled by interpreting one of the goods as transportation services, and by letting all other product prices be inclusive of freight to some international market 'place'. The question of factor mobility could be met simply by defining as a good anything that can be traded. Elastically supplied factors, and non-traded goods, could be eliminated by using the domestic market clearing conditions to 'net them out'. In this fashion, the simple trade model could be taken as an abstract, reduced form of a more complete and empirically relevant model. One would, however, pay a high price for this disguised 'realism', in that reduced form equations and parameters do not directly reflect behaviour. Therefore to interpret results derived using the simple model, one would in practice need the entire, structural form of the complete model.

We prefer to take the simple model literally—as the simplest possible representation of a general equilibrium system in which some markets are international and some national. The lack of realism in some of the explicit assumptions clearly calls for refinement through subsequent analysis of more complex models; but as a first approximation of a general equilibrium model with a hierarchical market structure, the simple trade theory model is sufficient. In fact, the simple model is surprisingly rich when it comes to illustrating interactions between domestic and international markets, and it enables one to analyse most questions one might ask about the determinants of international product prices and the pattern of trade, about the effects of trade on the prices of non-traded goods and factors, about the welfare economic implications of trade and trade policies, and about issues relating to exchange rates and the balance of payments. It is this richness we hope to illustrate in the following chapters.

## NOTES

It would be pedantic to retrace the history of the subject back to Ricardo and beyond. An elementary discussion of the basic concepts of the determinants of trade, and of its implications for factor prices, can be found in Samuelson (1976, ch. 34). At an intermediate level, Caves and Jones (1977, chs. 2, 3, 5–7) and Södersten (1971, chs. 1–7) give good and thorough treatments of the conventional approaches to the theory of comparative advantage. The order and emphasis is often different from ours; in particular, we postpone a full discussion of welfare aspects. At a more advanced level, Takayama (1972) discusses the subject using conventional production function methods and making some contact with dual cost functions.

Several important articles on the subject are collected in Caves and Johnson (eds.) (1968). For the material of this chapter, Robinson (1956), Samuelson (1949), Rybczynski (1955), and Johnson (1957) are particularly relevant.

There are also some survey articles. Bhagwati (1964, sections I, II) covers the issues raised in this chapter. Chipman (1965a, b, 1966) is for the more ambitious, and examines in detail issues of corner solutions, multiple equilibria, etc.

# CHAPTER 2

# SUPPLY AND DEMAND USING DUALITY

The relation of this chapter to trade theory proper is the same as that of the usual micro-economic chapter on consumer and producer behaviour to overall equilibrium theory. In other words, we develop here the models for supply and demand in one country, while the following chapters fit these into a trade equilibrium model and study its properties.

The analogy is valid in some other respects. One is the technical aspect of choosing the most convenient model. As the ultimate objective of equilibrium theory is to examine how the actions of different price-taking agents fit together, the natural building blocks should use prices as independent variables. This is best done using duality; i.e. modelling consumer behaviour by means of expenditure or indirect utility functions, and producer behaviour by means of cost, revenue or profit functions. The same choices prove convenient for modelling each country in international trade.

The second parallel is in the choice of simplifying assumptions to help us state the vital points with clarity and emphasis. In general equilibrium theory this often involves the use of 'representative' firms and consumers. We will sometimes use these constructs, and begin by commenting on them.

In an economy with several price-taking firms, so long as there are no distortions within the production sector, it is rigorously legitimate to treat the supply as coming from one vertically integrated price-taking firm. The point is simply that profit is a linear expression in the quantities of outputs and inputs, and the sum of its maxima for individual firms equals the maximum over the sum of the firms. Note that we do not give any monopoly power to this single firm, since it really stands for the collection of several small ones. The country as a whole may have monopoly power in trade, but it is for the government to exploit it by suitable use of tariffs.

When analysing production distortions we will not be able to use such a construct, and the study of effective protection will require us to go behind the veil and look at individual production units in detail.

For consumers, distortions are not so important as income and

29

taste differences. Welfare aspects clearly need a careful analysis with heterogeneous consumers, and we shall provide this notably in Chapters 3 and 6. In particular, we will establish that for redistribution purposes, tariffs are third-best policies, being inferior both to domestic lump-sum transfers and to domestic commodity taxation. Redistributive effects of tariffs are therefore of interest only if these superior policies are unavailable. To show how our approach can be used in handling such situations, we provide an example in Chapter 5.

When considering positive aspects such as the characterization and comparative statics of trading equilibria, heterogeneous consumers usually only present algebraic complications. Where a one-consumer analysis would involve the marginal propensity to consume, for example, the more general expression would have a weighted sum of the different consumers' marginal propensities, with the marginal income shares as weights. We usually leave such extensions aside, as they do not contribute much to a basic understanding. Of course it is often important to recognize inter-country taste differences; examples of this occur particularly in Chapters 5 and 9.

We will make all the standard assumptions that ensure existence of equilibrium, notably ones of convexity of technology and preferences. In some cases, particularly in relation to issues like factor-price equalization, we shall also make the conventional assumption of constant returns to scale and no joint production. No general restriction is placed on the numbers of goods or factors, although we do look at various special cases. We limit ourselves to models with two countries except when we look at issues like customs unions; there is little to be gained from generality here. The countries are labelled, purely for convenience, as 'home' and 'foreign'. All variables and functions pertaining to the home country will be in lower case symbols, and those for the foreign country in the corresponding upper case ones. The following sections discuss production and demand for the home country; identical models will apply to the foreign country. These are the building-blocks of models of trade equilibrium that will be the main subject of later chapters.

## 1. PRODUCTION: THE REVENUE FUNCTION

As explained at the end of Chapter 1, we divide commodities *a priori* into goods and primary factors. Let $v = (v_1, v_2, \ldots, v_m)$ be the aggregate vector of net inputs of primary factors, and $x = (x_1, x_2, \ldots, x_n)$ the vector of total net outputs of goods. Technological considerations tell us which combinations $(x, v)$ are feasible. We rule out increasing returns to scale and all increasing marginal rates of substitution and transformation. In other words, we assume a convex technology, i.e. a convex set of feasible $(x, v)$. So long as domestic production distortions are absent, this formulation encompasses considerable generality; for example, it allows intermediate goods to exist and be netted out in vertical integration. The general presumption is that goods are tradeable and factors are not, but we later indicate some simple generalizations.

Production' decisions will maximize total profit. In particular, for given prices $p$ of tradeables and quantities $v$ of non-tradeables, the problem will be to choose a technologically feasible $x$ to maximize the value of output. This is the inner product $p.x$ or $p^T x$.

The optimum $x$ is clearly dependent on the specified $p$ and $v$; write it as a function $x = x(p, v)$. The corresponding maximized value of output also becomes a function of $p$ and $v$. This is called the *revenue function*, written

$$r(p, v) = \max_x \{p.x \mid (x, v) \text{ feasible}\}$$

$$= p.x(p, v) \tag{1}$$

This function embodies all relevant properties of the technology, and is particularly convenient for establishing some properties of output supplies and factor prices that we need. We summarize such properties here, giving only some simple supporting arguments in each case. Formal proofs can be found in the references cited in the notes at the end of the chapter.

## Output supplies

For a while we shall fix $v$, and consider revenue as a function of $p$ alone. The first point is that it is a convex function. The economic idea can be expressed simply: with the input vector fixed, technological feasibility of an output vector is unaffected by a price change. It is thus always possible to maintain a fixed output vector, and make revenue a linear function of price. If there is any possibility of changing output composition along a transformation frontier, this will be used for the purpose of maximizing revenue, and then revenue will increase faster than linearly as prices change. To put it a bit more precisely, let $p'$ be any price vector, and suppose the corresponding maximum revenue is attained by choosing an output vector $x'$. For any other price vector $p$, since $x'$ remains

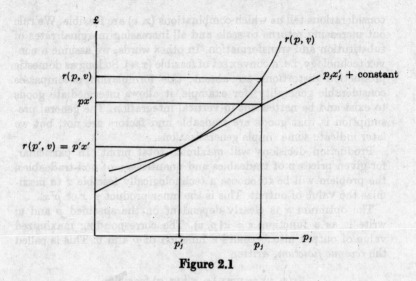

**Figure 2.1**

feasible, the maximum revenue can be no less than $p.x'$. So we have

$$r(p', v) = p'.x' \quad \text{and} \quad r(p, v) \ge p.x'$$

This can be rearranged into the form

$$r(p, v) - r(p', v) \ge (p - p').x' \tag{2}$$

Figure 2.1 shows the dependence of revenue on any one price, say the $j$th. In the compared $p.x'$, the only term involving $p_j$ is $p_j x'_j$, so the graph of that expression is a straight line with slope $x'_j$. The revenue function lies everywhere above this line, and the two coincide at $p'_j$. If $r$ has a $j$th partial derivative at this point, therefore, it must equal $x'_j$. If $r$ has a kink at this point, its slope on the left-hand side of $p'_j$ must be less than $x'_j$, and that on the right-hand side greater. Thus the linear function is a tangent in a generalized sense; call it a supporting line, or in many dimensions, a supporting hyperplane. The Appendix provides a somewhat more detailed treatment of this concept.

Collecting components, we have the result that if $r$ is differentiable at $p'$, then $r_p(p', v) = x'$. Since $p'$ could be any point, we can omit the prime and say that the optimally chosen supplies of goods are obtained by differentiating the revenue function with respect to their prices, i.e.

$$x(p, v) = r_p(p, v) \tag{3}$$

We will often assume differentiability of $r$ with respect to $p$, i.e. single-valued supply functions. However, there are important instances where this assumption is not valid, i.e. $r$ has a kink, the supporting hyperplane is not unique, and supply choices are not unique either. We shall return to this question when necessary.

Now let $p'$ and $p''$ be any two price vectors, and $x'$ and $x''$ corresponding revenue-maximizing choices. We have from (1) on taking $p = p''$ that

$$r(p', v) = p'.x' \quad \text{and} \quad r(p'', v) \geq p''.x'$$

On interchanging the roles of $p'$ and $p''$

$$r(p'', v) = p''.x'' \quad \text{and} \quad r(p', v) \geq p'.x''$$

From these, we see at once that

$$(p'' - p').(x'' - x') \geq 0 \tag{4}$$

In other words, price changes are non-negatively correlated with the resulting output supply changes. This is a natural multi-dimensional generalization of the familiar property that supply curves cannot be downward-sloping.

To conclude the study of $r$ as a function of $p$, we note that $r$ is homogeneous of degree 1 in $p$ for fixed $v$; this follows at once from the definition of $r$, since a proportionate change in all prices does not change the optimizing quantity choices. Now Euler's Theorem gives $\sum_j p_j \, \partial r/\partial p_j = r$, or

$$p.r_p(p, v) = r(p, v) \tag{5}$$

Next suppose $r$ is twice differentiable. Since it is a convex function, the matrix $r_{pp}$ of the second-order partial derivatives $\partial^2 r/\partial p_j \, \partial p_k$ must be positive semi-definite. Also, each $\partial r/\partial p_j$ is homogeneous of degree zero in $p$, therefore applying Euler's Theorem we have $\sum_k (\partial^2 r/\partial p_j \, \partial p_k)p_k = 0$, or, in matrix notation

$$r_{pp}(p, v)p = 0 \tag{6}$$

**Factor prices**

Now fix $p$, and study $r$ as a function of $v$ alone. We begin by showing that $r$ is a concave function of $v$: this is a natural extension of a concave production function for scalar output, and follows from our assumed convexity of the technology. Consider any two vectors $v'$, $v''$, and let $x'$, $x''$ be the corresponding optimum output choices. Since the set of feasible $(x, v)$ has been assumed convex, the average output $(x' + x'')/2$ is feasible given the average inputs $(v' + v'')/2$,

and therefore revenue $(r(p, v') + r(p, v''))/2$ is clearly attainable.
The best choice for $(v' + v'')/2$, whatever it might be, can yield no
less. The graph of the function in a diagram like that used earlier
must therefore appear as shown in Figure 2.2. Its slope at $v'$ can be
interpreted by a simple economic argument. The slope shows the
effect on the revenue of making available an extra unit of $v_i$ and
arranging production optimally. Since the original $v'$ was itself deployed optimally, the value of its marginal product in all uses has
been equalized. To first order, therefore, the same value is to be
had by employing the extra unit in any use, and thus the additional
revenue is simply this common value marginal product, which is
just the shadow price or demand price of the input. Employing this
argument for each component, and writing $w$ for the vector of the
shadow prices of the factors, we have

$$w(p, v) = r_v(p, v) \qquad (7)$$

If a vector $v$ of factor inputs is being used, a profit-maximizing user
will be willing to pay $w$ for further marginal quantities of these
factors, in accordance with (7). In other words, (7) gives us the
inverse demand functions for factors. To determine their equilibrium prices, we must introduce supply considerations. A particularly simple case is that of perfectly inelastic factor supplies.
In equilibrium, the fixed supply vector $v$ must equal the employment or input, and then the equilibrium factor price vector $w$ can
be found by using this $v$ in (7).

If $r$ is not differentiable with respect to $v$, the left- and right-hand
derivatives will provide bounds within which a non-unique $w$ must
lie. More important is the possibility of flat portions in the graph
of $r$ as a function of $v$, at least over some ranges. In such cases, over

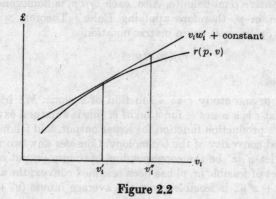

**Figure 2.2**

them, $w$ will be independent of $v$. This is an aspect of the question of factor price equalization that has received a great deal of attention, and we will examine it in greater detail shortly.

Since the graph of the concave function $r$ cannot lie above its tangent at $v'$, we have, using (7)

$$r(p, v'') \leq r(p, v') + (v'' - v').w'$$

Similarly, drawing the tangent at $v''$ and interpreting its slope as the shadow price $w''$ at that point, we have

$$r(p, v') \leq r(p, v'') + (v' - v'').w''$$

Adding these inequalities and simplifying, we find

$$(w'' - w').(v'' - v') \leq 0 \tag{8}$$

i.e. demand prices of factors are non-positively correlated with their quantities, which is a generalization of the normal idea that the derived demand curves for factors cannot slope upwards.

If there are constant returns to scale, we have two further results. First, $r$ is homogeneous of degree one in $v$ for each fixed $p$, and Euler's Theorem yields the familiar result of imputation of output into factor incomes:

$$v.r_v(p, v) = r(p, v) \tag{9}$$

Further, each $\partial r/\partial v_i$ is homogeneous of degree zero in $v$, and defining a matrix of second-order partial derivatives, we write

$$r_{vv}(p, v)v = 0 \tag{10}$$

## Cross effects

Finally, consider properties of $r$ taking into account both $p$ and $v$. If $r$ is twice differentiable, we can differentiate (3) with respect to $v$ and (7) with respect to $p$, and compare the result. We have for any $i$ and $j$,

$$\partial w_i/\partial p_j = \partial^2 r/\partial v_i\, \partial p_j = \partial^2 r/\partial p_j\, \partial v_i = \partial x_j/\partial v_i$$

or, letting $\partial w/\partial p$ be the matrix with elements $\partial w_i/\partial p_j$, etc.,

$$(\partial w/\partial p)^T = (r_{vp})^T = r_{pv} = \partial x/\partial v \tag{11}$$

It is clearly important to be able to say more about these effects of goods prices on factor prices and the related effects of factor supplies on goods supplies. To do so, we have to impose some specific structure on the production technology, and then it helps to supplement the revenue function with other mathematical tools. This analysis also makes us realize that we have to be careful about differentiability of the revenue function which we have assumed rather casually up to now. We return to these issues later in the chapter. We conclude this part by noting two more consequences of Euler's Theorem: $w$ is homogeneous of degree one in $p$, therefore

$$w = (\partial w/\partial p)p = r_{vp}p, \tag{12}$$

and, if there are constant returns to scale, $x$ is homogeneous of degree one in $v$, yielding

$$x = (\partial x/\partial v)v = r_{pv}v \tag{13}$$

### One-factor examples: The Ricardo model

We conclude this general discussion of revenue functions with some simple examples where several goods are produced using only one factor. This will illustrate some of the general points made above, and prepare the ground for later use of such functions in models of trade.

First consider the case where the factor has constant returns in the production of each good. In other words, the input requirement per unit output of good $j$ is constant, say equal to $a_j$. A production plan involving quantities $x_j$ requires a total factor input of $\sum a_j x_j$. The revenue maximization problem can then be written as

$$r(p, v) = \max_x \left\{ \sum p_j x_j \; \middle| \; \sum a_j x_j \leq v \right\} \tag{14}$$

The two-good case suffices to explain the issues. Suppose a fraction $\lambda$ of the factor quantity is allocated to good 1, and $(1 - \lambda)$ to good 2. Outputs are $x_1 = \lambda(v/a_1)$ and $x_2 = (1 - \lambda)(v/a_2)$, yielding

$$p_1 x_1 + p_2 x_2 = \lambda(p_1/a_1 - p_2/a_2)v + (p_2/a_2)v$$

First consider the case where $p_1/a_1 > p_2/a_2$. Clearly $\lambda$ will be set equal to 1, outputs will be $x_1 = v/a_1$ and $x_2 = 0$, and revenue $v(p_1/a_1)$. Since $p_j/a_j$ is simply the revenue yield per unit of factor use in the production of good $j$, this makes eminent economic sense. In this case, the marginal product of the factor is $p_1/a_1$; this must be its shadow price $w$. Similarly, if $p_1/a_1 < p_2/a_2$, we have $\lambda = 0$, $x_1 = 0$, $x_2 = v/a_2$, revenue is $v(p_2/a_2)$, and $w = p_2/a_2$.

If $p_1/a_1 = p_2/a_2$, let $\omega$ denote the common value of the ratio for the moment. Then all choices of $\lambda$ in the range of $0 \leq \lambda \leq 1$ yield the same revenue, equal to $\omega v$. Correspondingly, output choices are not unique: $x_1$ can lie in the range $0 \leq x_1 \leq v/a_1$ and $x_2$ in $0 \leq$

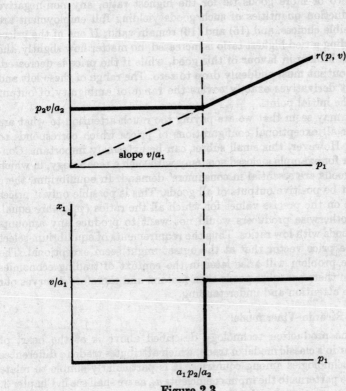

**Figure 2.3**

$x_2 \leq v/a_2$. This involves only one degree of freedom, since we must have $a_1x_1 + a_2x_2 = v$. The marginal product is $w = \omega$.

Figure 2.3 shows the revenue function and output of good 1 as functions of $p_1$. We see that the revenue function has a kink at $p_1 = p_2a_1/a_2$. The slopes of the function to the left-hand and right-hand sides at this point form the range in which the choice of $x_1$ there must lie. Where $r$ is differentiable, its slope equals the unique choice of $x_1$.

With several goods, the principle is the same. We seek the $j$ with the highest ratio $(p_j/a_j)$, and concentrate production on such a good, i.e. set $x_j = v/a_j$ and all other outputs zero. Then

$$r(p, v) = \max \left( v(p_j/a_j) \right) \qquad (15)$$

and

$$w(p, v) = \max \left( p_j/a_j \right) \qquad (16)$$

If two or more goods tie for the highest ratio, any non-negative production quantities of such goods yielding full employment are possible choices, and (15) and (16) remain valid. If one of the prices yielding a tied highest ratio is increased, no matter how slightly, the tie is broken in favour of this good, while if the price is decreased, the output must suddenly drop to zero. The range of these left and right derivatives exactly covers the range of ambiguity of output at the initial point.

It may seem that we are paying too much attention to what are after all exceptional configurations of prices which corresponds to ties. However, this small subset can be extremely important. Consider for example a closed economy with such a technology, in which all goods are essential in consumers' demand. In equilibrium, there must be positive outputs of all goods. This is possible only if prices take on the precise values for which all the ratios $(p_j/a_j)$ are equal, for otherwise producers would not want to produce any amounts of goods with low ratios. Thus the requirements of equilibrium select out a price vector that at the outset might seem exceptional. The same problem will arise later in the context of trading economies when there are more goods than factors, and therefore deserves our close attention and understanding.

### The Ricardo–Viner model

The production technology described above is at the heart of Ricardo's classic model of trade, which attributes trade to differences of technologies among countries. It is particularly simple to relate trade patterns to the input coefficients $a_j$, as we shall see in Chapter 3. However, the model is unsuitable for comparative statics. The phenomenon of multiple output choices with non-differentiable revenue functions makes it difficult to apply most standard techniques of analysis. For analyses which need single-valued supply choices, therefore, attention has shifted to a post-Ricardian model, often called the Ricardo–Viner model. Once again, we have several goods produced using only one factor, but this factor has diminishing returns in each use. Price changes then cause a smooth shift of the factor from one use to another.

As usual, diminishing returns can be attributed to the presence of fixed factors. Therefore the Ricardo–Viner technology can be thought of as producing $n$ goods using $(n + 1)$ factors, one of which is mobile across all uses, and the other $n$ are fixed, one to each use. If we take a Marshallian view of some factors being more easily shifted across uses than others, the same model can be used for depicting the short run where, for example, labour is mobile and capital specific to each sector. For the most part, we will not have to pay detailed attention to the quantities of the fixed factors; it will suffice to think of the aggregate rent accruing to each specific factor in its use. However, the analysis immediately yields further results where the quantities of such factors are explicitly accounted for, and we will append such results at the end of the discussion.

Suppose a total amount $v$ of the mobile factor is available, and its allocation to good $j$ is denoted by $v^j$, the superscript being used in order to avoid confusion with the notation for the components of a vector. Let the output of good $j$ be given by

$$x_j = f_j(v^j) \tag{17}$$

where each production function $f_j$ is increasing and strictly concave. The latter requirement reflects our assumption of diminishing returns. We also assume $f'_j(0) = \infty$ for each $j$. Then, for any positive prices, it is desirable to allocate at least a little of the mobile factor to each use, i.e. all output quantities are positive. The revenue maximization problem

$$r(p, v) = \max_{v^j} \left\{ \sum p_j f_j(v^j) \,\middle|\, \sum v^j = v \right\}$$

can then be solved by Lagrange's Method. The Lagrangean is

$$L = \sum p_j f_j(v^j) - w\left( \sum v^j - v \right)$$

where we have written the multiplier as $w$ since it is going to be the shadow price of the mobile factor. The first-order conditions are

$$p_j f'_j(v^j) = w \qquad \text{for all } j \tag{18}$$

In words, the value marginal products of the mobile factor in all its uses are equalized, and the common value is of course its shadow price. It will in the usual way equal its competitive market price. With $n$ goods, the $n$ equations in (18) together with the full employment constraint serve to determine the factor allocation and the factor price given $p$ and $v$. The output levels can then be calculated from (17). Finally $\pi_j$, the pure profits, or returns to specific factors in each sector, can be calculated as the residuals.

$$\pi_j = p_j x_j - wv^j = p_j\{f_j(v^j) - v^j f'_j(v^j)\} \tag{19}$$

Our aim is to determine how the endogenous magnitudes—the mobile factor allocations, the output levels, the price of the mobile factor, and the profits or prices of specific factors—depend on the

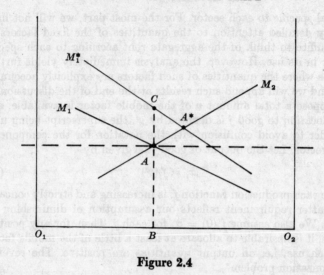

**Figure 2.4**

exogenous ones—output prices, the quantity of the mobile factor, and later, the quantities of the specific factors.

We outline the case of two goods, using a minimum of algebra. In fact the results generalize without too much difficulty. (See Jones (1975), Mussa (1974), Jones and Scheinkman (1977), Dixit and Norman (1979).)

Figure 2.4 juxtaposes the two value marginal product functions. The horizontal distance $O_1O_2$ is the total quantity of the mobile factor, with $v^1$ measured to the right from $O_1$ and $v^2$ to the left from $O_2$. The curves $M_1$ and $M_2$ show the value marginal products $p_1f_1'(v^1)$ and $p_2f_2'(v^2)$ as functions of the respective factor allocations. The two meet at $A$, so that the optimum allocations are $v^1 = O_1B$ and $v^2 = O_2B$, and the factor price $w$ is given by the vertical distance $BA$.

Now suppose $p_1$ rises. This shifts $M_1$ upwards equiproportionately with $p_1$, to a position such as $M_1^*$. The new intersection is at $A^*$, indicating an increase in $v^1$ and a decrease in $v^2$. Then $x_1$ rises and $x_2$ falls. There is also an increase in $w$, but since the vertical coordinate of $A^*$ is not as great as that of $C$, the rise in $w$ is of a smaller proportion than the increase in $p_1$.

To see what happens to the profits in the two sectors, note that each $\pi_j/p_j$ can be expressed solely in terms of $v^j$ from (19), and

$$\partial(\pi_j/p_j)/\partial v^j = -v_j f_j''(v^j) > 0 \qquad (20)$$

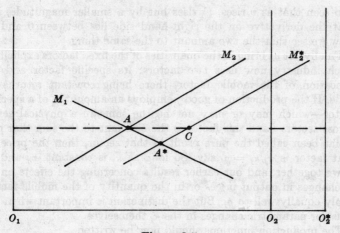

**Figure 2.5**

In response to the increase in $p_1$, therefore, we can say that as a result of the ensuing increase in $v^1$, $\pi_1/p_1$ will increase, i.e. that $\pi_1$ will increase by a greater proportion than $p_1$. Similarly, as $p_1$ increases, $v^2$ decreases and $\pi_2/p_2$ and therefore $\pi_2$ decrease.

Let us turn to the effects of an increase in $v$. This is shown in Figure 2.5 by shifting $O_2$ to the right to $O_2^*$, and $M_2$ to $M_2^*$ with it. We see that $A^*$ is to the right of $A$, so $v^1$ rises, but $A^*$ is to the left of $C$, so $v^1$ rises by a smaller amount than the increase in $v$. Therefore $v^2$ must rise as well. Accordingly, both output quantities rise. The price $w$ of the mobile factor falls. Finally, (20) shows that the profits in both sectors rise.

We can use general properties of the revenue function to relate two of these effects. We have

$$\partial w/\partial p_1 = \partial^2 r/\partial p_1 \, \partial v = \partial^2 r/\partial v \, \partial p_1 = \partial x_1/\partial v$$

But

$$\partial x_1/\partial v = f'_1(v^1) \, \partial v^1/\partial v = (w/p_1) \, \partial v^1/\partial v$$

Therefore

$$\frac{p_1}{w} \frac{\partial w}{\partial p_1} = \frac{\partial v^1}{\partial v} \tag{21}$$

We have seen that as $p_1$ rises, $w$ rises but by a smaller proportion, i.e. the elasticity on the left-hand side lies between 0 and 1. We have also seen that as $v$ rises, $v^1$ rises but by a smaller magnitude, i.e. that the derivative on the right-hand side lies between 0 and 1. Now we see that the two amount to the same thing.

Finally, let us bring in the quantities of the fixed factors explicitly. Each industry now uses two factors: its specific factor and its allocation of the mobile factor, there being constant returns to scale. If the production of good $j$ employs an amount $\kappa_j$ of a specific factor—which may or may not be the same in a physical sense across sectors—and this factor is the claimant to the sum that has so far been called the pure profit in that sector, then the price of that factor is $\pi_j/\kappa_j = \rho_j$ say. So long as $\kappa_j$ is constant, $\pi_j$ and $\rho_j$ move together, and our earlier results concerning the effects on $\pi_j$ of changes in output prices or in the quantity of the mobile factor apply equally well to $\rho_j$. But the distinction is important when we consider parametric changes in the $\kappa_j$ themselves.

The production functions should now be written

$$x_j = f_j(v^j, \kappa_j)$$

and the value marginal products are $p_j \, \partial f_j/\partial v^j$. There are constant returns to scale, so that each $f_j$ is homogeneous of degree one in $(v^j, \kappa_j)$. Then the marginal products, being partial derivatives of the production functions, are homogeneous of degree zero in these variables, and can therefore be expressed as functions of the ratio $v^j/\kappa_j$. In other words, if $v^j$ were to increase in proportion with $\kappa_j$, the value of the marginal product would not alter.

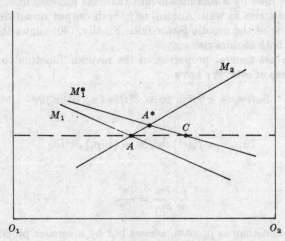

Figure 2.6

Figure 2.6 uses this fact to analyse the effects of an increase in $\kappa_1$. The curve $M_1$ showing the marginal product of $v^1$ shifts equiproportionately to the right. Using reasoning similar to that of the previous cases, we see that the optimum allocation $v^1$ increases but by a smaller proportion than the rise in $\kappa_1$. Then output $x_1$ must also rise but by a smaller proportion than $\kappa_1$. On the other hand, $v^2$ falls, and so does $x_2$. The price $w$ of the mobile factor rises. Since both output prices are held fixed, the prices of the specific factors $\rho_j$ must fall in both sectors. However, $\pi_1 = \rho_1\kappa_1$ may rise or fall.

Thus we have signed all the effects of changes in $p_1$, $p_2$, $v$, $\kappa_1$ and $\kappa_2$ on $v^1$, $v^2$, $x_1$, $x_2$, $w$, $\rho_1$ and $\rho_2$. The same can be done with several goods: the own effects, e.g. $\partial x_1/\partial p_1$, are as here, and the signs we have found for the cross effects, e.g. $\partial x_2/\partial p_1$, apply to all pairs of goods. Recalling how the various entities can be expressed in terms of the revenue function, we can summarize these results. Let $r(p, v, \kappa)$ be the revenue function, where $p$ is the vector of product prices, $v$ the scalar quantity of the mobile factor, and $\kappa$ the vector of the specific factor quantities. Then we have

$$x_j = \partial r/\partial p_j, \qquad w = \partial r/\partial v, \qquad \rho_j = \partial r/\partial \kappa_j$$

$$\partial^2 r/\partial p_j^2 > 0, \qquad \partial^2 r/\partial p_i\, \partial p_j < 0 \qquad \text{for all } i \neq j$$

$$w/p_j > \partial^2 r/\partial p_j\, \partial v > 0$$

$$\partial^2 r/\partial \kappa_j\, \partial p_j > \rho_j/p_j > 0$$

$$\partial^2 r/\partial \kappa_i\, \partial p_j < 0 \qquad \text{for all } i \neq j \tag{22}$$

$$\partial^2 r/\partial v^2 < 0, \qquad \partial^2 r/\partial \kappa_j\, \partial v > 0$$

$$x_j/\kappa_j > \partial^2 r/\partial \kappa_j\, \partial p_j > 0$$

$$\partial^2 r/\partial \kappa_i\, \partial \kappa_j < 0 \qquad \text{for all } i, j$$

The label (22) indicates all these relations collectively.

These riches of unambiguous comparative static results explain the attraction of the Ricardo–Viner model of production. We will have occasion to use several of these results in the context of trade later.

The relative simplicity of the analysis and the unambiguous results of the above examples are due to the fact that they involved only one factor which could be allocated to different uses. When more factors are mobile, we are forced to use alternative and sometimes more difficult techniques, and have to be content with less clear-cut results. That is the plan of the next two sections.

## 2. PRODUCTION: COST FUNCTIONS

Throughout this section, and later on when we use its formulations, we assume constant returns to scale, and the absence of joint production. Then for each good $j$, we have a production function relating its output $x_j$ to the vector of inputs $v^j = (v_1^j, \ldots, v_m^j)$, say $x_j = f^j(v^j)$, each $f^j$ being concave and homogeneous of degree one. Define the vector of inputs per unit of output $a^j = v^j/x_j$, so that $f^j(a^j) = 1$.

For efficient production, we should equate the marginal rates of input substitution in all sectors, i.e. the factor prices should be common to all of them. It is then advantageous to use a formulation which makes these factor prices the independent variables. This is done by observing that the economic optimum choice of input coefficients will minimize the unit cost of production. We therefore work with the unit cost function for each good, defined as

$$b^j(w) = \min_{a^j} \{w.a^j \mid f^j(a^j) = 1\} \tag{23}$$

This function has several useful properties. It is obviously homogeneous of degree one in $w$. Next, it is a concave function of $w$. The point should be familiar by now: as $w$ changes, it is always possible to leave $a^j$ unchanged at some feasible value once found, and thus secure a unit cost linear in factor prices. If there is no possibility of input substitution, this is all that can be done. If there is such a possibility, the input coefficients will be changed to minimize the unit cost, yielding a function that increases more slowly than the linear one, i.e. is concave. Finally, the optimum choice of input coefficients is given by the corresponding partial derivatives of the unit cost function. This is proved using the same argument as that used in deriving (3), and written using the vector notation introduced there

$$a^j(w) = b_w^j(w) \tag{24}$$

With constant returns to scale, the best choice of $v^j$ to produce output $x_j$ when factor prices are $w$ is simply $x_j a^j(w)$.

### An alternative form for the revenue function

Here we establish a relation between the revenue function and these unit cost functions. In particular, we show that

$$r(p, v) = \min_w \{w.v \mid b^j(w) \geq p_j \text{ for all } j\} \tag{25}$$

i.e. that production revenue can be found by finding the factor price vector which minimizes the value of factor endowments given that unit cost should not be lower than price for any good.

We prove this in an indirect manner, using optimality properties of a competitive equilibrium. Consider the competitive factor price vector, call it $\hat{w}$, and the competitive output vector, $\hat{x}$. (If the competitive equilibrium is not unique, we can take $(\hat{w}, \hat{x})$ as any pair of equilibrium factor prices and outputs.) The input coefficients chosen by firms will then be $b_w^i(\hat{w})$, so total employment of factor $i$ will be

$$\sum_j x_j b_i^j(\hat{w})$$

If this equals the factor supply $v_i$, we multiply the equation by $\hat{w}_i$. If this falls short of the supply of factor $i$, that factor will be a free good, i.e. $\hat{w}_i = 0$. We shall therefore have for all $i$,

$$\hat{w}_i \hat{v}_i = \sum_j \hat{x}_j b_i^j(\hat{w}) \hat{w}_i$$

So, summing over all $i$ and noting that

$$\sum_i b_i^j(\hat{w}) \hat{w}_i = b^j(\hat{w})$$

we have, defining a vector function $b$ with component functions $b^j$,

$$\hat{w}.v = b(\hat{w}).\hat{x}$$

But we also know that any good produced in a competitive equilibrium will have unit cost (= marginal cost) = price, while any good not produced must have unit cost above price (i.e. $b^j \geq p_j$). The competitive factor price vector will therefore satisfy the constraints in (25), and it will have the property that

$$\hat{w}.v = p.\hat{x}$$

As producers in a competitive equilibrium maximize their profit, moreover, we know that $p.\hat{x}$ must equal $r(p, v)$, so we have

$$\hat{w}.v = r(p, v)$$

Next, consider any other factor price vector $w'$ satisfying $b^j(w') \geq p_j$ for all $j$. We recall that, as the competitive equilibrium is feasible, we have

$$v \geq \sum_j \hat{x}_j b_w^j(\hat{w})$$

so we shall have

$$w'.v \geq \sum_i \sum_j \hat{x}_j b_i^j(\hat{w}) w_i' = \sum_j \hat{x}_j \sum_i b_i^j(\hat{w}) w_i'$$

But $b_w^j(\hat{w})$ is a feasible choice of input coefficients, and $b^j(w')$ is minimum unit cost over the set of feasible input coefficients when factor prices are $w'$, so we must have

$$b^j(w') \leq \sum_i b_i^j(\hat{w})w_i'$$

Thus

$$w'.v \geq b(w').\hat{x} \geq p.\hat{x} = \hat{w}.v$$

so among all factor price vectors giving unit cost greater than or equal to price for all goods, the competitive vector gives the lowest value of factor endowments. This, together with the fact that $\hat{w}.v = r(p, v)$, proves (25). Readers familiar with mathematical programming will recognize (25) as the dual to (1).

It is a simple application of the Sufficiency Theorem of the Appendix to verify that, for the minimization problem of (25), the Kuhn–Tucker conditions are sufficient as well as necessary. It is instructive to write these conditions explicitly, and interpret them as conditions of a competitive equilibrium. We must first introduce the multipliers. In doing so, it helps to keep their interpretation in mind. The multiplier on the constraint $b^j(w) \geq p_j$ gives the marginal effect on the objective of a relaxation of the constraint, i.e. $\partial r/\partial p_j$. But this is just the optimum output choice $x_j$. The multipliers on the factor quantity constraints are of course the factor prices. Then the Kuhn–Tucker conditions can be written

$$\sum_j b_i^j(w)x_j \leq v_i, \qquad \text{with equality if } w_i > 0 \qquad (26)$$

and

$$b^j(w) \geq p_j, \qquad \text{with equality if } x_j > 0 \qquad (27)$$

These are the standard complementary slackness properties: factors with positive shadow prices are fully employed (i.e. factors not fully employed have zero shadow prices), and activities in use break even (i.e. loss-making goods are not produced). It is common to assume that all the factors are fully employed, and this will indeed be the case irrespective of the relative numbers of factors and goods if there is enough possibility of substitution in production. We will usually work with this assumption, and state explicitly any exceptions we make. With regard to (27), however, it is not possible to have any presumption as to which goods will be produced. Even when the number of factors exceeds the number of goods, it will be optimum not to produce all the goods in a non-trivial subset of cases. We shall therefore leave this question open, to be examined in each instance.

## A geometric interpretation

We conclude this section by presenting a geometric interpretation of the cost-minimization problem (25) that will prove useful in comprehending several important properties of production and its comparative statics. The following section will continue the discussion.

In $w$-space we show the constraints $b^j(w) \geq p_j$. Since each $b^j$ is an increasing concave function, each constraint defines a convex set with a frontier to the south-west, formally much like an upper contour set of an ordinary utility function or production function. The feasible set is the intersection of such sets, one for each good. The function being minimized is linear, and its contours are parallel planes with the common direction perpendicular to them given by the vector $v$.

Figure 2.7 shows an illustrative case with two factors and three goods. The points $w$ satisfying each constraint $b^j(w) \geq p_j$ must lie on or above the corresponding contour. The feasible region therefore consists of the upper envelope of these contours and all points to the north-east; the boundary of this is shown shaded. The iso-factor-cost curves form a family of parallel straight lines, with $v$ as the common perpendicular direction. Only the line corresponding to the optimum is shown. This is a tangent in the generalized sense to the frontier of the feasible set, i.e. it supports the feasible set, at $A$.

The first two constraints are binding, so we have two equations to solve for $w_1$ and $w_2$. The third is slack, and therefore $x_3 = 0$, i.e., the third good is not produced. Then the conditions for full employment become

$$x_1 b_w^1(w) + x_2 b_w^2(w) = v \tag{28}$$

and with $w$ known, we have here two equations to determine the two output levels $x_1$ and $x_2$. This illustrates the principle of solution to (25).

Three useful inferences can be drawn from this picture. The first concerns the uniqueness of $w$. Multiple solutions will arise if the iso-cost line coincides with the frontier of a constraint. This requires a linear cost function $b^j$ in the relevant sector, which as we saw corresponds to there being no substitution possibilities there. But even if all the unit cost functions $b^j$ are linear, non-uniqueness of $w$ will

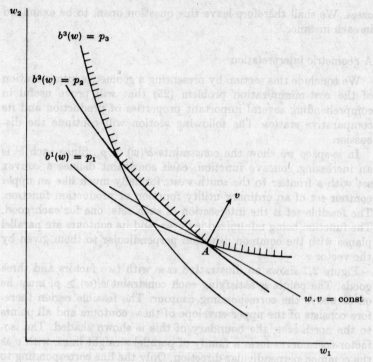

**Figure 2.7**

be rare, for linear programming theory now tells us that a minimum will typically occur at a corner. We will therefore ignore the problem of $w$ being non-unique, and thus assume the revenue function differentiable with respect to $v$.

The second point is that with minimal substitution possibilities, e.g. any non-zero constant elasticity of substitution, it can be shown that contours $b^j(w) = p_j$ cannot meet the axes at a positive angle. Then the solution will have $w$ strictly positive, i.e. full employment of factors. We therefore feel justified in treating this as the normal case.

Finally, we cannot say how many constraints will be binding, save in the linear programming case. In the non-linear case shown, there are whole ranges of values of $v$ for which the solution occurs on one of the curves on the frontier and not at a corner. Then only one of the three goods will be produced, even though there are two factors.

## 3. COMPARATIVE STATICS OF PRODUCTION

In this section we continue our study of production in one country, concentrating on how the endogenous variables—output quantities and factor prices—respond to changes in the exogenous ones—output prices and fixed factor endowments. The basic tool will be the minimum-factor-cost representation of the revenue function and its illustrative diagram. We will usually develop the arguments by means of geometric examples involving few goods and factors, followed by pertinent but not always fully rigorous algebra. We think that a basic understanding of the problems is best conveyed in this manner.

We begin with the best known case, with two goods and two factors, shown in Figure 2.8. We assume that the unit cost contour for good 1 is steeper than that for good 2 at their point of intersection; the significance of this will become clear shortly. Let $v^1$ be the direction perpendicular to the unit cost contour for good 1, and $v^2$ that for good 2, at that point. When $v$ lies between the limiting directions $v^1$ and $v^2$ shown in the figure, the solution occurs at the corner with both constraints binding and both goods produced. If $v$ lies outside this range, the solution is on one of the curves, with only

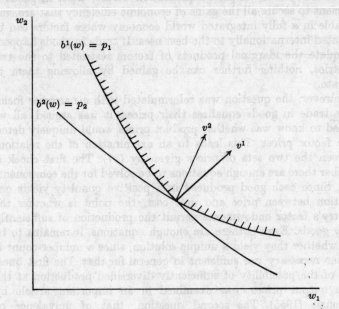

**Figure 2.8**

one constraint binding and only one good produced. We concentrate on the case where both goods are produced for the moment. The significant point is that over the range of its validity, the same value of $w$ occurs independently of $v$. It can be said that $w$ is determined by $p$ alone. We solve the equations

$$b^1(w_1, w_2) = p_1 \quad \text{and} \quad b^2(w_1, w_2) = p_2 \qquad (29)$$

to write

$$w_1 = w^1(p_1, p_2) \quad \text{and} \quad w_2 = w^2(p_1, p_2)$$

and the revenue function accordingly takes the form

$$r(p, v) = v_1 w^1(p_1, p_2) + v_2 w^2(p_1, p_2)$$

## Product prices and factor prices

This issue of invertibility, i.e. of whether factor prices can be determined from a knowledge of the prices of goods alone, is the focus of conventional discussions of factor-price equalization. As the name implies, the question was once a much broader one: when would two countries with identical technologies, trading in goods alone, end up with equal factor prices? This question is interesting because if such factor-price equalization occurs, trade in goods is sufficient to secure all the gains of economic efficiency that are conceivable in a fully integrated world economy where factors can be allocated internationally to the best uses. If trade in goods happens to equate the marginal products of factors restricted to the two countries, nothing further can be gained by allowing them to migrate.

However, the question was reformulated with a narrower focus. Since trade in goods equalizes their prices, it was argued, all we needed to know was whether product prices would uniquely determine factor prices. This leads to an examination of the relations between the two sets of prices given by (27). The first check is whether there are enough equations to be solved for the components of $w$. Since each good produced in a positive quantity yields one equation between price and unit cost, the point is whether the country's factor endowments permit the production of sufficiently many goods. Even if there are enough equations, it remains to be seen whether they yield a unique solution, since a number-count is neither necessary nor sufficient in general for that. The first question, of the possibility of sufficiently diversified production at the given output prices, was examined in an important article by McKenzie (1955). The second question, that of univalence or invertibility, has generated a great deal of mathematical research, culminating in Gale and Nikaido (1965), and also much controversy, notably between Samuelson and Pearce in the International Economic Review in 1966.

We have a serious objection to this whole line of reasoning, namely to the starting point of accepting given product prices. Surely trade theory should treat prices of traded goods as endogenous variables. By not doing so, the usual treatment makes factor-price equalization a question of production equilibrium in one country, rather than that of a trading equilibrium of two (or more) countries.

Now it might be argued that, given any product price vector, it is always possible to find countries with factor endowments and tastes which make this an equilibrium price vector. This is true, but such a construction gives us little idea of whether we have found an exceptional case or a likely one. In particular, what might seem to be exceptional price vectors, i.e. ones forming a very small subset of the product price space, turn out to be not at all exceptional as trading equilibria from the more fundamental point of view of possible factor endowments and preferences, i.e. a large subset of possible combinations of factor endowments and preferences yield such equilibrium prices. In a manner similar to that indicated in connection with the Ricardian model, seemingly exceptional price vectors are selected by the requirement of positive production in at least one of the countries. We will examine the general problem of factor-price equalization in Chapter 4, and point out how the conventional narrow question has led to misconceptions about the likelihood of its occurrence. This will build on work by Samuelson (1953), and Uzawa (1959), which has been neglected as a result of the subsequent concentration on the question of univalence. In the meantime, we illustrate points about diversification and invertibility using the unit cost contour diagrams. In view of our general criticism, we will not build elaborate models of details or general cases. For these, see Pearce (1970, ch. 12), Kuhn (1968) or Takayama (1972, ch. 18).

It is possible to show how both problems arise in the case of two goods and two factors. First examine Figure 8. For the given $p$, we have a range $(v^1, v^2)$ such that if the country has its factor endowment proportions within this range, it will produce both goods and have factor prices $w$ uniquely determined at the corner point of the feasible set. Outside the range, cost-minimization will occur on one of the two curved faces of the frontier, only one good will be produced, and $w$ will vary with $v$. Further, if $p$ changes, both constraints will shift, altering the range $(v^1, v^2)$.

Such a range of factor endowments is called a *diversification cone*. The concept is due to Lerner (1952) and McKenzie (1955); see Chipman (1966) and Woodland (1977a) for further details and alternative treatments. In the context of Figure 2.8, we can state when the assumption of diversification is valid: each country's factor endowments must lie in the diversification cone. Once this is ensured, factor-price equalization follows.

However, in other cases there may be several such cones for a given product price vector. This happens for two goods and two factors if the constraint curves intersect more than once, i.e. if two or more factor price vectors yield all unit costs equal to prices, i.e. if univalence fails. To understand this, let us see what the important assumption is behind the shapes of the curves in Figure 2.8. Using the Implicit Function Theorem, we can express the slope of the curve $b^1(w) = p_1$ at a point on it as a ratio of partial derivatives:

$$-dw_2/dw_1 = b_1^1(w)/b_2^1(w)$$

This is just the ratio of the cost-minimizing unit input coefficients in the production of good 1, or $b_{11}/b_{12}$ in the notation of Chapter 1. A similar expression can be found for the other curve. Our assumption that the first curve is steeper therefore amounts to the condition that the first good is relatively more factor-1 intensive. However, there is no reason in general why this should be so for all values of $w$. If the ranking of relative factor intensities can be reversed as $w$ changes, there arises the possibility of multiple intersections of constraint curves. Figure 2.9 shows a case with two intersections. At $A$, good 1 is relatively more factor-1 intensive, while at $B$ it is relatively more factor-2 intensive. It is now possible for there to be a trade equilibrium where both countries are producing both goods, but one happens to end up at $A$ and the other at $B$, so they have unequal factor prices. In other words, diversification does not guarantee factor-price equalization when univalence fails. In McKenzie's terminology, there are two distinct diversification cones for the one product price vector, one at $A$ and the other at $B$, as shown in the figure. For equality of factor prices, the two countries' factor endowment vectors must lie in the same cone. For diversification alone, it is acceptable for them to lie in different cones.

All this is conditional on the exogenous product prices. However, unless the two countries together are small in the whole trading world, product prices must be endogenously determined. Let us revert to the simple case of Figure 2.8. and let the two countries' factor endowment vectors lie in the diversification cone. Then their

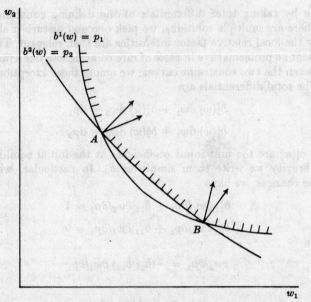

**Figure 2.9**

common factor prices are determined. We can use these in the factor-market clearing conditions (28) for each, and solve for their output quantities, finally summing to obtain the implied world supplies of goods. In general there is no reason why these should equal demand at the initially specified product prices. When we examine the complete general equilibrium problem in Chapter 4, we find that the requirements of endogenous determination of equilibrium product prices can place further restrictions on the sets of factor endowment vectors that are compatible with factor-price equalization.

In view of this more important difficulty, we shall not pursue the analyses of diversification cones and of univalence in the general context of many goods and factors. We merely note the importance of conditions concerning relative factor intensities for the problem of univalence. This has been discussed at length in previous literature, and we have nothing new to say about it. For a recent account, see Takayama (1972, ch. 18).

### Price and quantity derivatives

We continue with the case where two factors are producing two goods, and examine the effect on $w$ of a small change in $p$. This is done by taking total differentials of the defining equations (29). If there are multiple solutions, we pick one and disturb it slightly; only the local relative factor intensities are then relevant. This will present no problems save in cases of rare coincidences like a tangency between the two constraint curves; we ignore these exceptions.

The total differentials are

$$b_1^1(w)\,\mathrm{d}w_1 + b_2^1(w)\,\mathrm{d}w_2 = \mathrm{d}p_1$$

$$b_1^2(w)\,\mathrm{d}w_1 + b_2^2(w)\,\mathrm{d}w_2 = \mathrm{d}p_2$$

The $b_i^j(w)$ are the unit input coefficients at the initial equilibrium; for brevity we write them simply as $b_{ji}$. In particular, when $p_1$ alone changes, we have

$$b_{11}\,\partial w_1/\partial p_1 + b_{12}\,\partial w_2/\partial p_1 = 1$$

$$b_{21}\,\partial w_1/\partial p_1 + b_{22}\,\partial w_2/\partial p_1 = 0$$

Then

$$\partial w_2/\partial p_1 = -(b_{21}/b_{22})\,\partial w_1/\partial p_1$$

and

$$(b_{11} - b_{12}(b_{21}/b_{22}))\,\partial w_1/\partial p_1 = 1 \qquad (30)$$

Label the goods and factors so that at the initial equilibrium, good 1 is relatively more factor 1 intensive, i.e. $b_{11}/b_{12} > b_{21}/b_{22}$. Then the expression in the parentheses on the left-hand side of (30) is positive, yielding a positive $\partial w_1/\partial p_1$ and then a negative $\partial w_2/\partial p_1$.

A stronger conclusion is possible using the elasticity of $w_1$ with respect to $p_1$. We have $p_1 = b^1(w) = b_{11}w_1 + b_{12}w_2$ by Euler's Theorem. Therefore $p_1 > b_{11}w_1$, and using (30), we have

$$\frac{p_1}{w_1}\frac{\partial w_1}{\partial p_1} > \frac{b_{11}}{b_{11} - b_{12}(b_{21}/b_{22})} > 1 \qquad (31)$$

The conclusion is that an increase in $p_1$ raises the price of factor 1 (in which good 1 is relatively more intensive) by a greater proportion than itself, and lowers the price of factor 2.

These effects of product prices on factor prices were examined by Stolper and Samuelson (1941), and we will call such derivatives $\partial w_i/\partial p_j$ the Stolper–Samuelson derivatives. Their analysis was a part of an overall study of the effects of tariffs on factor prices. To complete the chain, we have to study the effects of tariffs on the equilibrium prices of goods. This will be done in Chapter 5.

Note the difference between (31), where the change in a factor price is a magnification of the change in the price of the good which uses it relatively more intensively, and the Ricardo–Viner case of (21), where the price of the mobile factor changes by a smaller proportion than the price of any good. This is because in the present case, an increase in $p_1$ causes some reallocation of factor 2 to good 1, thereby further raising the marginal product of factor 1 in that use. This is ruled out in the Ricardo–Viner case since other factors are immobile.

Dual to (31), we have the effects of factor quantities on output quantities. After Rybczynski (1955), the corresponding derivatives will be called the Rybczynski derivatives. Using the full employment condition, $v_1 = x_1 b_{11} + x_2 b_{21} > x_1 b_{11}$, and then

$$\frac{v_1}{x_1}\frac{\partial x_1}{\partial v_1} > \frac{b_{11}}{b_{11} - b_{12}(b_{21}/b_{22})} > 1 \tag{32}$$

while $\partial x_2/\partial v_1 < 0$.

The form (30) has a useful interpretation. Consider raising the price of factor 1 by one unit while lowering that of factor 2 in order to keep the unit cost of producing good 2 unchanged. Thus $dw_1 = 1$, and $b_{21}\,dw_1 + b_{22}\,dw_2 = 0$, i.e. $dw_2 = -b_{21}/b_{22}$. The unit cost of good 1 changes by $b_{11}\,dw_1 + b_{12}\,dw_2 = b_{11} - b_{12}(b_{21}/b_{22})$, which is precisely the expression in the parentheses on the left-hand side of (30). If this effect is positive, it is natural to say that factor 1 is more important in the production of good 1, or that good 1 is relatively more factor 1 intensive. This coincides with our earlier definition, and has the advantage of being capable of generalization. Consider a case where $n$ factors are producing $n$ goods, and take total differentials of the conditions of equality between all prices and the corresponding unit costs. Using obvious notation, we have

$$\sum_{k=1}^{n} b_{jk}\,dw_k = dp_j, \quad j = 1, 2, \ldots, n$$

Looking in particular at $\partial w_1/\partial p_1$, and letting $S$ denote the set of indices $2, 3, \ldots, n$, we can write

$$\begin{aligned} b_{11}\,\partial w_1/\partial p_1 + b_{1S}\,\partial w_S/\partial p_1 &= 1 \\ b_{S1}\,\partial w_1/\partial p_1 + b_{SS}\,\partial w_S/\partial p_1 &= 0 \end{aligned} \tag{33}$$

where $b_{1S}$ is a row vector of components $b_{1k}$ with $k = 2, 3, \ldots, n$, $b_{S1}$ is a column vector and $b_{SS}$ a matrix analogously defined, and $\partial w_S/\partial p_1$ is a column vector of derivatives $\partial w_k/\partial p_1$ for $k$ in $S$. Then, assuming $b_{SS}$ non-singular,

$$(b_{11} - b_{1S}\,b_{SS}^{-1}\,b_{S1})\,\partial w_1/\partial p_1 = 1 \tag{34}$$

The expression in the parentheses on the left-hand side tells us the effect of a unit increase in the price of factor 1 on the unit cost of good 1, when the prices of all other factors are changed suitably to keep the unit costs of all other goods unchanged. If this effect is positive, we say that good 1 is relatively more intensive in its use of factor 1 than the economy as a whole. If this is the case, $\partial w_1/\partial p_1$ is positive, and the corresponding elasticity is

$$\frac{p_1}{w_1}\frac{\partial w_1}{\partial p_1} > \frac{b_{11}}{b_{11} - b_{1s}b_{ss}^{-1}b_{s1}} > 1$$

otherwise $\partial w_1/\partial p_1$ is negative. It is useful to be able to extend the two-factor, two-good result so easily, but we shall see in a moment that problems arise when the number of factors does not equal the number of goods.

### Problems of generalization

We turn to a case where the number of fully employed factors, $m$, exceeds the number of goods being produced, $n$. Figure 2.10 shows the simplest case with two factors and one good. There is no problem concerning uniqueness, and the solution and its resulting value

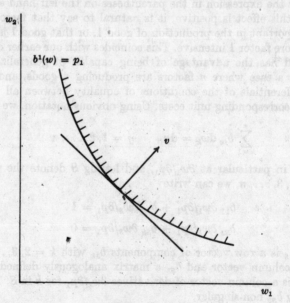

**Figure 2.10**

change only gradually as $p$ and $v$ change, so there is no problem concerning differentiability. However, $w$ is not invariant with respect to $v$ even in some small range. Therefore $r_{vp}$ also depends on $v$, and it is not possible to lay down conditions that govern the signs of $\partial w_i/\partial p_j$ by considering properties of the unit cost functions alone. The attraction of the two-by-two case, or its $n$-by-$n$ generalization above, was that the definition of factor intensity involved only the technology and not the factor endowments. To see what is going on, let us try to repeat our earlier exercise. In studying the effect of the price of factor 1 on that of good 1, we want to adjust the remaining factor prices to keep the unit costs of the remaining goods unchanged. Since there are $(m - 1)$ factor prices to adjust and maintain $(n - 1)$ unit costs fixed, there are degrees of freedom left over. Analogues of (33) would have multiple solutions for $\partial w_S/\partial p_1$. We might rescue the situation by considering the factor markets. Thus we might define good 1's intensity in factor 1 as the increase in its unit cost brought about by a unit increase in the price of factor 1, with accommodating changes in other factor prices and output quantities so as to maintain the unit costs for other goods unchanged and preserve equilibrium in all factor markets. If we denote this measure by $F_{11}$, we clearly still have

$$F_{11}\, \partial w_1/\partial p_1 = 1$$

and the Stolper–Samuelson derivatives are still related to a natural measure of factor intensity. But this measure has become a property of the whole general equilibrium of production. Therefore we might as well take the Stolper–Samuelson derivatives embodied in the matrix $r_{pv}$ directly as definitions of factor intensities: good $j$ is relatively more intensive in factor $i$ than the average if $\partial^2 r/\partial p_j\, \partial v_i$ is positive. The special interpretation in terms of unit costs is available for the $n$-by-$n$ case, and is consistent with the general definition.

Finally, consider the case where there are more produced goods than fully employed factors. Figure 2.11 shows a case with two factors and three goods. It may seem a rare accident that produces three constraint curves passing through the one point $A$, and indeed when $p_1$, $p_2$, and $p_3$ are all arbitrarily assigned, such an occurrence is unlikely. But when we consider a trading equilibrium, we have to take the matter back to the primary data such as the factor endowments of the two countries, and ask: is the occurrence of such a configuration of output prices itself unlikely? We shall consider this in Chapter 4, where the answer will be a resounding 'no'. This is one of the misleading ideas about the likelihood of factor price

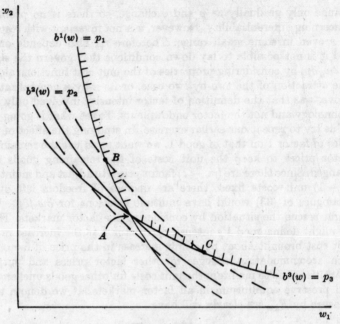

**Figure 2.11**

equalization that arise from the partial equilibrium study of production in one country. It also makes it important to understand the problems that arise in this case.

There is no special difficulty about the uniqueness of $w$, but an important indeterminacy in output quantities is introduced. The simplest way to see this is to study the effects on revenue of changes in $p$. If $p_2$ decreases, for example, the second constraint in Figure 2.11 moves to the lower dashed position. The constraint becomes redundant, the solution in $w$ does not change, and so neither does $r$. The derivative of revenue with respect to a decrease in $p_2$ is zero. If $p_2$ increases, the constraint moves to the upper dashed position, the feasible set shrinks, and the solution in $w$ moves to some point along $BC$. This affects $r$, and the derivative of $r$ with respect to the increase in $p_2$ is positive. As we saw earlier when establishing (3), $r$ is not differentiable, and any number between these two limiting derivatives serves as an optimizing choice of $x_2$ (taken along with suitable $x_1$ and $x_3$). To see this in the general case of $n$ produced goods and $m$ fully employed factors with $n > m$, turn to the defining equations (26) and (27). From (27) we select $m$ equations to solve for the factor prices; given our basic premise that the values of output prices happen to be just right, the equations are mutually consistent and it does not matter which ones we choose. Once $w$ is known, (26) provides $m$ full employment equations to solve for $n$ output levels, leaving $(n - m)$ degrees of freedom.

With $x$ indeterminate, $r_p$ does not exist, and it follows that $r_{pv}$ is not defined. This simply reflects the fact that factor intensities are ill-defined in this case. The three-by-two case serves as an illustration. With the notation for unit input coefficients as used before, at the initial equilibrium in Figure 2.11 we have arranged

$$b_{11}/b_{12} > b_{21}/b_{22} > b_{31}/b_{32}$$

Clearly good 1 is relatively intensive in factor 1, and good 3 in factor 2. Whether good 2 is intensive in factor 1 or in factor 2, however, depends on what linear combination of goods 1 and 3 we compare it with. As the production vector is indeterminate, however, a wide range of linear combinations is possible. Consequently, no unique relative factor intensity can be assigned to good 2: even its sign may be ambiguous. As to the other goods, even though their signs are clear, ambiguity applies to their magnitudes.

## 4. CONSUMPTION

Our treatment of demand also relies on duality, expressing the outcome of the consumer choice problem as a function of the underlying parameters. The models of this section apply in the first instance to one consuming unit, typically a household. However, when we assume in some special cases that the demand of all consumers of a country can be treated as if there were just one consumer, the same models will apply to a country as a whole.

### The expenditure function

For simplicity of exposition, we begin with the special case where utility does not depend on the quantities of factors supplied, i.e. where factors are in perfectly inelastic supply. Then we may omit them from the explicit discussion of consumer choice, although in later use the consumer's income will have to be related to his ownership of factors. Let $c$ denote the vector of consumption of goods, $p$ the vector of their prices, and $y$ money income. Let $f$ be the utility function, assumed to be strictly quasi-concave. The notation should not be confused with the production functions $f^j$ of section 2; and we will not have to use the two concepts together in any applications. In fact there are clear mathematical similarities between the cost functions which we derived in the case of production, and the expenditure function which will be defined shortly for the consumer.

The fundamental problem of consumer choice is

$$\max_{c} \{f(c) \mid p.c \leq y\}$$

and it yields the demand functions $d(p, y)$. As is well known, it proves useful to isolate the pure substitution effect of prices on demands, and this is done by considering a mirror image problem. Difficulties can arise if some of the goods have zero prices, but this is not of much interest in our applications, so we ignore them. We fix an indifference surface, and look for its tangency with an iso-expenditure plane, i.e. we seek to minimize the expenditure necessary to attain a target utility level at $u$ at the given prices $p$. The solutions to this problem are the Hicksian compensated demand functions $c(p, u)$. The corresponding expenditure $p.c(p, u)$, which of course equals the income that will have to be provided if utility $u$ is to be attained at prices $p$, is also a function of $(p, u)$. This is defined as the *expenditure function*, and written

$$e(p, u) = \min_{c} \{p.c \mid f(c) \geq u\} \qquad (35)$$

It will be noticed that the above problem is quite similar to that of cost-minimization which we considered before, in (23). However, since we assumed constant returns to scale in production, we could consider the cost of producing one unit of output, and then simply multiply that by the level of output. A similar decomposition exists for the present problem in the case of homothetic tastes, but in general we will have to work with the general form.

If we model the consumer using the expenditure function, while the true datum of the problem for this decision is the money income, then we have to say how the level of utility in the expenditure function is obtained. This is simply the consistency condition that the money income $y$ just suffices to achieve the utility level, i.e.

$$y = e(p, u) \qquad (36)$$

Now we consider some properties of the expenditure function. First fix $p$ and consider $e$ as a function of $u$ alone. It is clearly an increasing function. This establishes a one-to-one relation between $u$ and $y$ defined by (36). It can then be inverted to give $u$ as a function of $p$ and $y$; this is the maximum utility that is attainable at prices $p$ with income $y$, and is called the indirect utility function.

Differentiating (36) with respect to $y$ holding $p$ fixed, we have

$$1 = e_u(p, u) \, \partial u / \partial y,$$

i.e. $1/e_u(p, u)$ gives the marginal utility of money income. Since the consumer's choice problem depends only on the ordinal aspect of the utility function, it does not at this stage make sense to impose any convexity or concavity on $e$ as a function of $u$, or equivalently to say whether the marginal utility of money income should be increasing or decreasing. When considering the welfare aspects we will sometimes have to choose particular cardinalizations, and then we shall impose the relevant restriction. This will usually involve a decreasing marginal utility of money income, and then $e$ will be a convex function of $u$.

## Demand functions

Now fix $u$ and consider $e$ as a function of $p$. This is obviously increasing and homogeneous of degree one. More importantly, it is a concave function. The argument should by now be familiar. If indifference curves are L-shaped, there will be only one non-wasteful way of attaining utility $u$, say by using a particular consumption vector $c'$. Then we will have $e(p, u) = p \cdot c'$ for all $p$, and the function will be linear. If some substitution is possible, $c'$ will be the best choice for some particular $p'$, yielding $e(p', u) = p' \cdot c'$ but $e(p'', u) \leq p'' \cdot c'$ for all $p''$. Then

$$e(p'', u) \leq e(p', u) + (p'' - p') \cdot c' \tag{37}$$

Arguing as we did in the case of revenue or cost functions, this shows that $e$ is concave at $p'$, and that if it is differentiable there, the vector $e_p$ of its partial derivatives is simply $c'$. Since $p'$ could be any vector, we have proved that $e$ is concave in $p$, and have also obtained expressions for the compensated demand functions as the price partial derivatives of the expenditure function

$$c(p, u) = e_p(p, u) \tag{38}$$

This yields several well known properties very simply. If $e$ is twice differentiable, we have from the $j$th component equation $c_j = \partial e / \partial p_j$ that $\partial c_j / \partial p_j = \partial^2 e / \partial p_j^2$. This is $\leq 0$ since $e$ is concave. Now $\partial c_j / \partial p_j$ shows the effect of $p_j$ on the Hicksian compensated demand for good $j$, i.e. the own substitution effect for this good, so we have proved that own substitution effects are non-positive. The multi-dimensional generalization is the result that the Slutsky–Hicks substitution matrix

$$c_p(p, u) = e_{pp}(p, u) \tag{39}$$

is negative semi-definite, since $e$ is concave. However, since $e$ is homogeneous of degree one in $p$, each compensated demand is homogeneous of degree zero, and therefore the matrix is singular:

$$c_p(p, u)p = e_{pp}(p, u)p = 0 \qquad (40)$$

Even if $e$ is not twice differentiable, we can obtain results concerning substitution effects, simply by writing an equation similar to (37) with the roles of $p'$ and $p''$ reversed, and writing $c''$ for the choice at $p''$. Adding the two and simplifying, we have

$$(p'' - p') . (c'' - c') \le 0 \qquad (41)$$

i.e. price changes are non-positively correlated with the resulting changes in compensated demands. This is similar in form and substance to the earlier result (4) concerning supply, but is now restricted to compensated changes.

Next we consider the relation between the compensated demand functions $c(p, u)$ and the ordinary uncompensated demand functions $d(p, y)$. For positive prices the two will coincide if the income level in $d(p, y)$ is just right to attain the utility level in $c(p, u)$, i.e. if $y$ and $u$ are related as in (36). In other words,

$$c(p, u) = d(p, e(p, u)) \qquad (42)$$

Differentiate the $j$th component of (42) with respect to $p_k$, using the Chain Rule on the right-hand side. This yields

$$\partial c_j / \partial p_k = \partial d_j / \partial p_k + (\partial d_j / \partial y)(\partial e / \partial p_k)$$
$$= \partial d_j / \partial p_k + (\partial d_j / \partial y)d_k \qquad (43)$$

when $y$ and $u$ are related as in (36), and $\partial e / \partial p_k = c_k = d_k$ by (42). This is the Slutsky–Hicks equation relating the income and substitution effects of a price change to its total effect. In matrix notation, it becomes

$$c_p(p, u) = d_p(p, y) + d_y(p, y)\, d(p, y)^T \qquad (44)$$

We can also express the pure income effect in terms of the expenditure function. This is done by differentiating (42) with respect to $u$. Then $c_u = d_y e_u$, while $c = e_p$ gives $c_u = e_{pu}$. Thus

$$d_y(p, y) = e_{pu}(p, u)/e_u(p, u) \qquad (45)$$

It must be remembered that the $y$ on the left-hand side and the $u$ on the right are related as in (36).

One special case will have some prominence in Chapter 3: this is where tastes are homothetic. As shown in the Appendix, this corresponds to a multiplicatively separable expenditure function

$e(p, u) = \psi(u)\bar{e}(p)$ where $\psi$ is an increasing function, while $e$ is increasing, homogeneous of degree one, and concave. When only ordinal utility matters, we can take $\psi(u)$ itself as the indicator of utility, and then relabel it $u$. Thus in the case of homothetic tastes, we have the expenditure function of the form

$$e(p, u) = u\,\bar{e}(p) \qquad (46)$$

Using (45), we can then verify that with homothetic preferences, all income elasticities of demand equal one.

### Variable factor supplies

Now consider the more general case where utility can also depend on factor supplies. If the basic function is $f(c, v)$, we can write the expenditure function as

$$e(p, v, u) = \min_{c} \{p.c \mid f(c, v) \geq u\} \qquad (47)$$

This will have the same properties with respect to $p$ and $u$ as above, but there will be additional effect of $v$ to be considered. Most importantly, the partial derivatives $e_v$ will tell us the trade-off between factor supplies and the expenditure necessary on commodities while maintaining utility constant. These are just the amounts of additions to income that will elicit further supplies of the factors at the margin, i.e. the supply prices of the factors. To find equilibrium in the factor markets, it will only be necessary to equate them to the demand prices, which are the values of marginal products, i.e. the corresponding derivatives of the revenue function.

If factor supplies are chosen optimally, therefore, we have

$$e_v(p, v, u) = w \qquad (48)$$

which yields the factor supplies $v(p, w, u)$. Substituting this into the partial expenditure function $e(p, v, u)$ we get a general expenditure function $e^*(p, w, u)$ which gives us the minimum *lump-sum* income needed to achieve utility $u$ when product prices are $p$ and factor prices are $w$. In other words, the general expenditure function can be found as

$$e^*(p, w, u) = \min_{c, v} \{p.c - w.v \mid f(c, v) \geq u\} \qquad (49)$$

This formulation will prove convenient when we discuss the welfare economics of trade.

The properties of $e^*$ can be deduced in the same way as those of the earlier dual or envelope functions, and we merely list them: $e^*$ is increasing in $p$, decreasing in $w$, concave and homogeneous of degree one in $(p, w)$ jointly. It is increasing in $u$, but any concavity here is irrelevant. The compensated demand functions for goods and supply functions for factors are the partial derivatives

$$c(p, w, u) = e_p^*(p, w, u) \qquad (50)$$

and

$$v(p, w, u) = -e_w^*(p, w, u) \qquad (51)$$

In fact, (48) and (51) give the same information in terms of the two formulations $e$ and $e^*$. It is also possible to derive Slutsky–Hicks equations involving $e^*$, but we shall not have occasion to use them.

## NOTES

The micro-economics that should be known to the readers of this book, or at least acquired in parallel by them, is well covered by Baumol (1977). Varian (1978) provides a more modern approach emphasizing duality, but is mathematically more demanding. Our mathematical requirements are outlined in the Appendix, and covered in detail in the references cited there.

The general concept of dual functions, with economic applications, is outlined at an elementary level by Dixit (1976, chs. 3, 7), and more thoroughly by Diewert (1974, 1978).

The revenue function, sometimes called a restricted profit function, or the national product function, was introduced for the purpose of comparative statics of a country in trade, by Samuelson (1953). For details of its general properties and other applications, see Diewert (1974) and McFadden (1978). The structure of the revenue function in the two-by-two case is explored in great detail by Chipman (1972). For the case of one mobile factor, see Dixit and Norman (1979).

Woodland (1977a) obtains the equivalent expression for the revenue function as the minimum factor cost, but his use of this form is largely confined to the two-by-two case.

The cost function appears in Samuelson (1947, pp. 68–69), and has come a long way in theoretical developments and micro-economic applications. See Diewert (1974, 1978) for historical notes, and Uzawa (1964) for a compact treatment. In trade theory, the classic article by Jones (1965) used a formally identical approach to discuss the two-by-two model. In analyses of the univalence problem, it has been used a great deal; Pearce (1970, ch. 12), Kuhn (1968), and Takayama (1972, ch. 18) study this problem, and provide further references.

# CHAPTER 3

# INTERNATIONAL EQUILIBRIUM AND THE GAINS FROM TRADE

In this chapter we begin to make use of the analytical techniques developed in the previous one. Our aim is to establish some of the most basic propositions concerning the pattern of trade and the gains from trade. To this end, we first set up models for one country in autarky, and in a trading equilibrium. Simple 'revealed preference' comparisons allow us to prove the results concerning gains from trade. Then we consider a model of two countries in a trading equilibrium, which gives some insights into the reasons for trade, and the patterns of trade. Finally, we derive various well-known models as special cases, and compare their properties. The general model will be the workhorse for later chapters, where we study some further properties of trade equilibria, and carry out some comparative statics and policy analyses.

The exposition will proceed from very simple models to successively more complex ones: from one consumer to many, from inelastic factor supplies to variable ones, and from all goods being tradeable to some being non-tradeable. The simpler models serve to introduce concepts and techniques in settings where they are more easily understood; this familiarity will then make the more complex and more realistic cases easier to grasp. In later chapters, we sometimes revert to simpler models for similar reasons; when the complication is not material to the particular purpose, allowing it only confuses the issue.

All models of this chapter, and those of Chapters 4–7, share two important underlying assumptions: (1) each agent, consumer or producer, is a price-taker, (2) prices adjust instantaneously to levels which clear all markets. Such settings will be called Walrasian, or perfectly competitive, general equilibria. These assumptions are ubiquitous in international trade theory, and we feel compelled to emphasize them only because in Chapters 8 and 9 we consider other kinds of equilibria. In Chapter 9, we have differentiated products whose sellers individually possess and exploit some monopoly power. There are many such products, and free entry is allowed, so the

65

resulting equilibria are Chamberlinian with monopolistic competition. The other assumption is altered in Chapter 8, where some or all prices are fixed in the short run, and the corresponding equilibria are achieved through quantity adjustment. The case of Keynesian unemployment is prominent there. In the meantime, we proceed to study Walrasian equilibria in some detail.

In order to ensure the existence of a competitive equilibrium, we have to rule out increasing returns to scale and non-convex isoquants and transformation frontiers. This is briefly stated by requiring the set of all technologically feasible input–output vectors to be convex. We also require each consumer to have preferences with convex indifference curves; the general assumption we make is that each consumer has a strictly quasi-concave utility function.

# 1. AUTARKY

We begin with models of equilibrium in one country. Here we ignore domestic production distortions. Then, as explained in Chapter 2, and using the notation established there, production decisions can be modelled using a revenue function $r(p, v)$. We consider different cases on the consumer side, starting with the simplest.

## One consumer, fixed factor supply

Here we may model the consumer by means of an expenditure function $e(p, u)$. The equilibrium is then very easily characterized; we have

$$e(p, u) = r(p, v) \tag{1}$$
$$e_p(p, u) = r_p(p, v) \tag{2}$$

The former expresses equality of national income and product, or an overall budget constraint arising from the fact that all income generated through production ultimately flows to the sole consumer. The second is a vector equation, being simply the market-clearing condition for goods. We do not need to model factor markets explicitly. The supplies are fixed at $v$, the revenue function being evaluated for this amount already subsumes the factor market equilibrium, and if desired, we can find the factor prices as $w = r_v(p, v)$.

If there are $n$ commodities, we have $(n + 1)$ unknowns in $u$ and the components of $p$, while (1) and (2) provide the same number of equations. However, as is usual in general equilibrium theory, this is slightly deceptive. Only relative prices matter: if the vector $p$ is changed in scale, both sides of (1) change in the same scale, while (2) remains unaltered. Thus there are only $n$ relevant unknowns: $u$ and $(n - 1)$ relative prices. Correspondingly there is one redundant equation: by Walras's Law we can drop one market-clearing equation as being implied by the rest, or we can take the inner product of (2) with $p$, and $p.e_p = p.r_p$ becomes (1) on account of homogeneity. In any event, there are only $n$ independent equations. This is only an informal check. We shall not worry about the formal problem of existence of equilibrium; well-known general theorems apply to all the models of Walrasian equilibria we consider. We shall also leave open the question of the scale of prices, and in each application make the choice that is most convenient.

In writing (2), we have implicitly assumed $r$ to be differentiable with respect to prices, i.e. the supply choices to be unique. However, in Chapter 2 we pointed out the possibility that at crucial points, the revenue-maximizing output choice may be non-unique and $r$ non-differentiable. In the present context, that is not a problem. We can simply interpret $r_p$ as the entire range of possible output choices, and (2) as stating that the demand vector $e_p$ should lie in this range. The same applies to all the models in this chapter. Where the multiplicity of output choices is a vital part of the story, as in the next chapter, we will discuss the issue in detail. Later, when considering comparative statics by calculus methods, we will follow the traditional route and assume unique supply choices.

There is another way to model equilibrium in this case, and it proves useful in later models of trade. Suppose the country were given the gift of a vector $m$ of goods (negative components representing gifts to the rest of the world). If the country now produces $x$ from its own factor endowments $v$, it can consume $c = x + m$. The production choice will be made from among all feasible $x$ to maximize the utility $u = f(c)$ to the consumer. The outcome depends on the given values of $m$ and $v$; we can therefore define an envelope function. For simplicity of exposition, suppose production feasibility is expressed by a constraint $g(x, v) \leq 0$, where $g$ is a convex function, increasing in $x$ and decreasing in $v$. Then the envelope function $\phi$ is defined by

$$\phi(m, v) = \max_x \{f(x + m) \mid g(x, v) \leq 0\} \tag{3}$$

We call $\phi$ the Meade utility function, in recognition of the geometric treatment of indifference curves defined on net trades by Meade (1952, ch. II).

We now examine the properties of $\phi$. It is clearly an increasing function. If greater quantities of net imports were made available, or if factor endowments increased, it would always be feasible to leave the production plan unchanged. Any changes can only increase utility.

More interestingly, $\phi$ is quasi-concave in $m$. To see this, let $m'$ and $m''$ be any two net gift vectors, and let $x'$ and $x''$ be the corresponding optimum production plans, so that $\phi(m', v) = f(x' + m')$ and $\phi(m'', v) = f(x'' + m'')$. By convexity of the technology, outputs $\frac{1}{2}(x' + x'')$ are feasible, and therefore

$$\phi(\tfrac{1}{2}(m' + m''), v) \geq f(\tfrac{1}{2}(x' + x'') + \tfrac{1}{2}(m' + m'')) \qquad \text{by definition of } \phi$$

$$= f(\tfrac{1}{2}(x' + m') + \tfrac{1}{2}(x'' + m'')) \qquad \text{rearranging arguments}$$

$$\geq \min\,(f(x' + m'), f(x'' + m'')) \qquad \text{by quasi-concavity of } f$$

$$= \min\,(\phi(m', v), \phi(m'', v))$$

Thus $\phi$ has the essential properties of a utility function.

Derivatives of $\phi$ can be interpreted using the envelope theorem. To do so, note first that a producer with the technology defined by the function $g$, and facing prices $p$ for outputs and $w$ for inputs, would maximize $p.x - w.v$ subject to $g(x, v) \leq 0$. The first-order conditions for this are $p = \theta g_x$ and $w = -\theta g_v$ where $\theta$ is the Lagrange multiplier. We can therefore interpret $g_x$ and $-g_v$ as producer prices omitting the common scale factor. Similarly, $f_c$ will be the vector of the consumer's marginal utilities, proportional to the consumer prices.

The Lagrangean for the problem in (3) is

$$L = f(x + m) - \mu g(x, v)$$

where $\mu$ is the multiplier. The first-order conditions are

$$f_c(x + m) = \mu g_x(x, v)$$

i.e. the consumer and producer prices should differ at most by a common scale factor. This is the standard optimality condition equating marginal rates of substitution and transformation for all pairs of goods. Then, by the envelope theorem, the derivative of $\phi$ with respect to any of its arguments equals the partial derivative of the Lagrangean with respect to that argument, evaluated at the optimum. This yields

$$\phi_m(m, v) = f_c(x + m) \tag{4}$$

$$\phi_v(m, v) = -\mu g_v(x, v) \tag{5}$$

The first says that the marginal effects of net gifts on achievable utility are simply the marginal utilities of consumption, and hence proportional to prices. A change in the net gift vector induces a change in the production plan, but the plan having been chosen to maximize utility, the effect of a small change is of the second order of smalls. The marginal effects of factor endowments on achievable utility are similarly proportional to factor prices.

Although we have spoken of $m$ as a net gift, we have the usual by-product of the maximization problem: the marginal effect on utility, $\phi_m$, tells us the maximum payment that will be offered for a marginal increase in net imports if they are not a gift. Hence the function $\phi$ later proves useful in discussions of trade.

It also enables us to find autarky prices very easily. In autarky we have $m = 0$. Therefore to find prices we need only evaluate the appropriate partial derivatives of $\phi$ at this point. Prices of goods are then proportional to $\phi_m(0, v)$, those of factors to $\phi_v(0, v)$.

## Many consumers, fixed factor supplies

Let consumer $h$ have the expenditure function $e^h(p, u^h)$. Assume that there are constant returns to scale. This is quite harmless in this context; if there are diminishing returns to scale generating pure profits, we simply define artificial factors which are repositories for such profits, and then there are constant returns to scale in genuine and artificial factors taken together. This device can alter things when the *number* of factors matters, but here it does not. Then let consumer $h$ own amounts $v^h$ of factors, with $v = \sum v^h$. Since factor prices are $r_v(p, v)$, the income of consumer $h$ is $r_v(p, v).v^h$. Then we can easily write down the equilibrium conditions:

$$e^h(p, u^h) = r_v(p, v).v^h \qquad \text{for all } h \tag{6}$$

$$\sum_h e^h_p(p, u^h) = r_p(p, v) \tag{7}$$

One equation is again redundant by Walras's Law, and the rest serve to determine the relative product prices and the utilities of all consumers.

These differ from the corresponding equations for the one-consumer case only in their algebraic complexity. The same applies to several comparative static results for the two cases. Where a small change in (2) would involve the consumer's marginal propensities to spend on various goods, for example, (7) would yield an average of all consumers' marginal propensities weighted by their marginal income shares. Where general results can be obtained by such minor but sometimes messy exercises in algebra, we will usually leave the task to the reader and confine the exposition to the simple case.

We will look at the generalizations of the Meade utility function to the case of many consumers in Chapter 6, where the relevant domestic distributive policies will be introduced in conjunction with trade.

## One consumer, variable factor supplies

The only new feature is the determination of equilibrium quantities as well as prices for factors. To model factor supply, we saw in Chapter 2 that we could use two forms of expenditure functions: $e(p, v, u)$ (giving the total income necessary to achieve utility $u$ when factor supplies are $v$, which yields supply prices $e_v$ for factors), and $e^*(p, w, u)$ (giving the transfer income over and above factor income that is needed to achieve utility $u$ when factor prices are $w$ and quantities optimally set at $-e_w^*$). In equilibrium, the former must equal the total revenue, and the latter the pure profit. Thus we have the equilibrium conditions in the first formulation:

$$e(p, v, u) = r(p, v)$$
$$e_p(p, v, u) = r_p(p, v)$$
$$e_v(p, v, u) = r_v(p, v) \qquad (= w) \tag{8}$$

while in the second formulation, assuming constant returns to scale as explained before

$$e^*(p, w, u) = 0$$
$$e_p^*(p, w, u) = r_p(p, v)$$
$$-e_w^*(p, w, u) = v \tag{9}$$
$$w = r_v(p, v)$$

The reader should check the numbers of independent equations and unknowns in each case.

We can also define a Meade utility function

$$\phi(m) = \max_{x, v} \{f(x + m, v) \mid g(x, v) \le 0\} \tag{10}$$

The first-order conditions extend the proportionality of consumer and producer prices to factors:

$$f_c(x + m, v) = \mu g_x(x, v), \qquad -f_v(x + m, v) = -\mu g_v(x, v)$$

and by the envelope theorem, we have $\phi_m(m) = f_c(x + m)$ at the optimum.

The reader should be able to construct many-consumer models with variable factor supplies in the same way as above. The next section will involve some elements of such models; corresponding Meade functions will appear in Chapter 6.

## 2. GAINS FROM TRADE

Now let the economy be opened to international trade in goods, and a Walrasian trading equilibrium established. To determine the prices in such an equilibrium, we will have to write down conditions equating the net excess demands for goods from this country to the net excess supplies from the rest of the world. However, for the purpose of this section, it will not matter how the equilibrium prices of goods are arrived at. We will be able to derive all the results by examining the consumption and production decisions in the one country in response to the equilibrium prices.

The aim is to prove that free trade, and certain kinds of restricted trade, can be no worse than autarky. We consider a succession of models of increasing technical difficulty.

### The one-consumer case

First consider the case where factor supplies are fixed. Suppose that the autarky consumption, production and utility are $c^a$, $x^a$ and $u^a$ respectively, with $c^a = x^a$ for equilibrium. Let $p^1$ be the equilibrium price vector in free trade, and $u^1$ the corresponding utility. Equating total expenditure and income, we have $e(p^1, u^1) = r(p^1, v)$. Then

| | |
|---|---|
| $e(p^1, u^a) \leq p^1.c^a$ | by definition of the expenditure function |
| $= p^1.x^a$ | by condition of autarky equilibrium |
| $\leq r(p^1, v)$ | by definition of the revenue function |
| $= e(p^1, u^1)$ | by the income-expenditure equality |

Since $e$ is increasing in the utility level, it follows that $u^1 \geq u^a$.

This line of reasoning highlights the traditional separation of the gains from trade into consumption and production gains. The first inequality shows how consumers at trade prices can attain autarky utility more economically, while the second shows how producers can generate a greater value of output. The two put together imply that the consumers can then use the higher income to achieve greater utility. In the rigorous formulation of the general case, all these inequalities must be weak ones. As an extreme case, trade prices might happen to equal autarky prices, when there will be zero gains. Even with a distinct trade price vector, if the indifference curves or the production frontiers have kinks at the relevant points, it may be impossible to change the consumption or production patterns to take advantage of the changed prices. But otherwise we would expect the inequalities to be strict. The same remarks apply to all the analyses of gains from trade that follow.

While it is useful to understand the gains from trade in terms of the consumption and production components, it is often easier to handle the problem in a model where the two aspects are merged together. This is done using the Meade utility function. We have already seen that in autarky, the utility level is $\phi(0)$. Suppose that the set of choices available in trade includes one where the net import vector is zero. Then the trade equilibrium level of utility can be no less than $\phi(0)$; this follows merely from the definition of a maximum, and from the fact that the trade equilibrium, being Pareto efficient for the single consumer, must maximize his utility subject to the technological and trading constraints.

This direct reasoning enables us to make some further comparisons. We discuss the most general of these. Suppose the alternative to autarky is not free trade, but trade under some system of tariffs, subsidies or even quantity controls. The ultimate outcome of all these is to make the vector of prices of goods faced by domestic producers and consumers, $p^1$, different from the vector $\hat{p}$ prevailing in the rest of the world. If $m^1$ is the resulting equilibrium vector of net imports, then an amount of net revenue $t = (p^1 - \hat{p}) . m^1$ is generated by the trade restrictions. This includes the net revenue of the system of tariffs and subsidies, and also the rent accruing to the importers of items subject to quantity restrictions. Ultimately, the whole of this accrues to the one consumer. Thus the national income identity must be modified to $e(p^1, u^1) = r(p^1, v) + t$. Examining the effect of this on our earlier chain of inequalities, we see that the chain is strengthened provided only that $t \geq 0$. In other words, provided only that the system of modifications to free trade generates non-negative net revenue, the resulting equilibrium is preferable to autarky. If the net revenue is negative, it is possible that the implied resource transfer to the rest of the world outweighs the gains from modification of the consumption and production plans to suit the new prices, and no general conclusion is possible.

The argument is illustrated in Figure 3.1. At relative prices $(\hat{p}_1/\hat{p}_2)$, trades are restricted to the balance-of-trade line $bb$. Suppose the actual trade is at $A$, generating tariff revenue $OB$ in terms of good 2. The budget line as perceived by the consumer is then $cc$, and the allocation corresponding to the trade $A$ is revealed preferred to any allocation corresponding to any other trade on or below this line. Obviously, $A$ is revealed preferred to the origin, and thus the actual trade is revealed preferred to autarky. The reader can verify, by redrawing the diagram, that a similar argument can *not* be made if there is negative tariff revenue, e.g. if there are export subsidies. In that case the line $cc$ will cut the vertical axis below the origin,

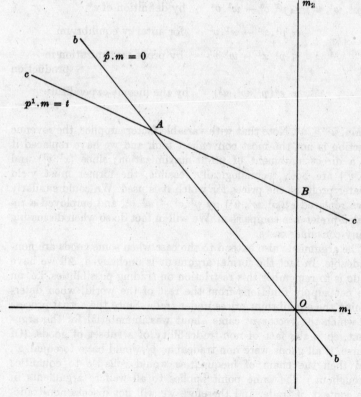

**Figure 3.1**

and a general comparison of such trade with autarky will not be possible.

In the single-consumer case, therefore, only trade subsidies can prevent trade from being preferable to no trade. Note that this is true regardless of whether the country is a price-taker in international trade: the price vector used in the argument above is whatever emerges as an equilibrium price vector in trade. That may well depend on domestic supply and demand.

All the above arguments extend easily to the case where factors are in variable supply. We illustrate the simplest case. To modify the argument at the beginning of this section, we have to use the expenditure function $e^*$. Let $w^1$ be the equilibrium vector of factor prices in trade, and $v^a$ and $v^1$ the factor quantity vectors in autarky and trade respectively. Then

$$e^*(p^1, w^1, u^a) \leq p^1.c^a - w^1.v^a \qquad \text{by definition of } e^*$$

$$= p^1.x^a - w^1.v^a \qquad \text{for autarky equilibrium}$$

$$\leq p^1.x^1 - w^1.v^1 \qquad \text{by profit-maximization in production}$$

$$= e^*(p^1, w^1, u^1) \qquad \text{by the income-expenditure equality.}$$

Again, $u^1 \geq u^a$. Note that with variable factor supplies, the revenue function is not the most convenient tool, and we have replaced it by a direct statement of profit-maximization: since $(x^1, v^1)$ and $(x^a, v^a)$ are both technologically feasible, the former must yield greater profit at the prices for which it is used. We could similarly have replaced $e^*(p^1, w^1, u^1)$ by $p^1.c^1 - w^1.v^1$, and employed a revealed preference comparison. We will in fact do so when discussing many-consumer cases.

The arguments also extend to the case when some goods are non-tradeable. In fact the formal argument is unchanged. All we have to do is to remember this restriction on trading possibilities, i.e. on the net supply functions from the rest of the world, when determining the equilibrium prices under trade. Since the actual process by which the vector $p^1$ came about was immaterial for the argument, so is the fact of non-tradeability of a subset of goods. (Of course, if all goods were non-tradeable, $p^1$ would have to equal $p^a$, and then the chain of inequalities would collapse to equalities throughout.) The same point applies to all welfare arguments in the context of trade, and therefore we will not discuss non-tradeables explicitly when dealing with this aspect. Problems of com-

parative statics with non-tradeables are important, and will be
dealt with when they arise.

## Many consumers, general issues

In the more realistic case of many consumers, it is possible that
a move from autarky to free trade, unaccompanied by any redistributive measures, benefits some consumers and harms others.
A simple example is provided by the two-good, two-factor production model discussed in Chapter 2. Suppose the labels are chosen so
that good 1 is relatively more factor-1 intensive. Then we know
that an increase in the relative price of good 1 will increase the price
of factor 1 measured in terms of either good, and lower that of factor 2 measured in terms of either good. Suppose that one consumer,
or a group of consumers, derive income solely from factor 1, and
the rest solely from factor 2. When trade changes relative prices,
the owners of one factor will be clear gainers, and the owners of the
other factor will be clear losers. Trade will allow production gains
as before, but their distribution among consumers will be extremely
unequal. If we are to ensure that trade benefits all consumers, i.e.
that it is Pareto superior to autarky, we will have to employ some
redistributive measures.

Now it may not be necessary to ensure Pareto superiority of
trade to conclude that it is preferable to autarky. A Bergson–
Samuelson social welfare function with its interpersonal comparisons
may be the standard employed, and it may judge the gains of some
consumers to outweigh the losses of others. However, Pareto
superiority will be clearly very strong evidence of the desirability
of trade relative to autarky. We therefore investigate the alternative
redistributive measures that can ensure this.

A very general conclusion is possible from competitive equilibrium
theory. Free trade being a competitive equilibrium for the whole
world, it is Pareto efficient. If lump sum transfers could be deployed
freely, they would enable us to trace out the entire Pareto efficient
frontier for all the consumers in the world. In particular, a point
which is Pareto superior to the autarky equilibrium from the point
of view of the consumers in any one country could be so realized.
However, this is a very weak result. It needs lump sum transfers
at an international level, and neglects the consumers in other
countries. Lump sum transfers within one economy are difficult
enough to achieve; those across countries and raising the possibility
that consumers in some countries may be harmed by them seem
out of the question. We must therefore go beyond the general

results of competitive equilibrium theory and look for arguments specific to the context of trade.

The first step towards realism will be to allow lump sum transfers, but within the confines of the country in question. We will see that such policies are able to achieve a trade equilibrium that is Pareto superior to autarky. The next step is to restrict domestic policies to taxation of goods and factors; we find that even this more limited set of instruments suffices to make free trade Pareto superior to autarky. Conversely, even the most powerful set of domestic policies, lump sum transfers, cannot make autarky superior to free trade in the Pareto sense. This set of results constitutes a powerful argument in favour of trade, and is developed over the rest of this section.

### Lump-sum transfers

We begin by describing the autarky equilibrium. Suppose that consumer $h$ consumes a vector $c^{ha}$ of goods and supplies a vector $v^{ha}$ of factors in autarky, the superscript $h$ indicating the consumer and $a$ indicating the autarky value. Similarly, let the output of goods be $x^a$ and the employment of factors $v^a$. For equilibrium, we have

$$\sum c^{ha} = x^a, \qquad \sum v^{ha} = v^a \qquad (11)$$

where the summations are taken over the set of all consumers. The autarky prices are immaterial for our purpose. Let $u^{ha}$ be the utility of consumer $h$ in the autarky equilibrium.

We want to show that, using domestic lump sum transfers, it is possible to achieve a free trade equilibrium where each consumer has the same utility level as in autarky. This establishes the Pareto superiority of free trade in the weak sense; as explained before, it will usually be possible to strengthen this to obtain strict Pareto superiority.

Suppose that, at prices $p$ for goods and $w$ for factors, consumer $h$ is to attain utility $u^{ha}$. He must be given the amount

$$y^h = e^*(p, w, u^{ha}) \qquad (12)$$

of lump-sum income. This may be positive or negative. The total disbursement of such transfers is $\sum y^h$, and therefore the net revenue to the government organizing such a scheme is $-\sum y^h$. We will show that, in a free trade equilibrium, the net revenue is nonnegative. Let the government spend it on goods according to some simple rule such as one of equal expenditures. Then the demand for goods from the government is given by

$$g_j(p, w) = -\sum_h e^*(p, w, u^{ha})/(np_j) \tag{13}$$

where $n$ is the total number of goods in the economy. Since each $e^*$ is homogeneous of degree one in $(p, w)$, (13) shows that government demands are homogeneous of degree zero in these prices.

The consumers' demand for goods is $c^h = e_p^*(p, w, u^{ha})$, and their supply of factors is $v^h = -e_w^*(p, w, u^{ha})$. Profit-maximization by producers at prices $(p, w)$ yields their output supply $x$ and factor demand $v$. Under constant returns, these are as usual indeterminate up to a scale factor.

· Under free trade, relative prices of goods will be the same in all countries. The net demand from the rest of the world can then be written as a function of $p$, say $M(p)$. This will be homogeneous of degree zero, and will satisfy $p.M(p) = 0$ reflecting the absence of international lump sum transfers.

Now consider the system of excess demands in the world markets for goods and the domestic markets for factors. All are functions of $(p, w)$, satisfying continuity, homogeneity, and Walras's Law. Standard arguments as in Arrow and Hahn (1972, ch. 5) ensure the existence of equilibrium. The free trade prices $(p, w)$ are then determined from the market-clearing conditions

$$\sum c^h + g - x + M = 0 \tag{14}$$

$$\sum v^h - v = 0 \tag{15}$$

All that remains to be done is to verify that the government revenue is non-negative, thus ensuring that it is not being required to hand out quantities of goods out of nowhere. This follows from simple arguments of the revealed preference type.

Consumer $h$ gains equal utilities from the plans $(c^h, v^h)$ and $(c^{ha}, v^{ha})$, while the former is optimum at prices $(p, w)$. Therefore the latter must require no less lump sum income at these prices, i.e.

$$y^h = p.c^h - w.v^h \le p.c^{ha} - w.v^{ha} \tag{16}$$

Similarly, $(x, v)$ and $(x^a, v^a)$ are both technologically feasible, but the former is optimum at prices $(p, w)$, and yields zero profit under our assumption, harmless in this context, of constant returns to scale. Therefore

$$0 = p.x - w.v \ge p.x^a - w.v^a \tag{17}$$

Adding (16) for all consumers and subtracting (17) from the result, we have

$$\sum y^h = p \cdot \left( \sum c^h - x \right) - w \cdot \left( \sum v^h - v \right)$$

$$\leq p \cdot \left( \sum c^{ha} - x^a \right) - w \cdot \left( \sum v^{ha} - v^a \right)$$

$$= p \cdot (c^a - x^a) - w \cdot (v^a - v^a)$$

$$-\sum y^h \geq p \cdot (x^a - c^a) = 0 \qquad (18)$$

by the equilibrium condition for domestic product markets in autarky. This is the desired result. Incidentally, note from (18) that the net revenue from the transfer scheme equals the excess of the value of domestic output over that of the domestic consumers' demand, i.e. the trade surplus of the private sector of the country. This is a natural consequence of various budget balance conditions, or of Walras's Law, and it enables us to give an alternative formulation of the feasibility condition for the transfer scheme.

Once again, the formal proof only establishes weak Pareto superiority of trade. But we see at once what is needed for strict Pareto superiority. If the government in the above scheme obtains strictly positive net revenue, then it will be feasible to increase the lump-sum transfers to all consumers and thus attain a new free trade equilibrium in which they all have utilities higher than the autarky levels. What we need is a strict inequality somewhere in (16) and (17). As in the one consumer case, this will obtain if there is some substitution possibility in consumption or production and if the free trade price vector does not happen to coincide with that in autarky.

The generalization of this result to the case where trade is restricted by a scheme of tariffs and subsidies having non-negative net revenue is straightforward, and is left to the reader.

Having established that trade can be made Pareto-superior to autarky, it follows that the converse cannot be true: If it were, we could start at one autarky equilibrium and employ two sets of lump-sum transfers in succession to arrive at another autarky equilibrium Pareto-superior to the first. This is impossible since each autarky equilibrium is Pareto efficient under the constraint, common to the two, that there be no trade. The reader can verify the impossibility directly by trying to carry out the compensating procedure above starting from a position of free trade. He will then find that net transfer revenue will be negative.

## Commodity taxes

Now suppose that lump-sum transfers are impossible, so the domestic redistributive instruments are taxes and subsidies on goods and factors. Let the autarky equilibrium have quantities $(c^{ha}, v^{ha})$ for consumers and $(x^a, v^a)$ for producers, and utilities $u^{ha}$, as before. The aim is to find a free trade equilibrium where each consumer achieves the same utility level as in autarky. Having seen the manner in which the existence of equilibrium can be checked when treating lump sum transfers, we will not repeat the same argument. We will merely take the equilibrium prices that emerge, and verify that the government's net revenue is non-negative, or equivalently, that the private sector has a non-negative trade surplus. This will establish the practical feasibility of the trade equilibrium.

Let $(p^a, w^a)$ be the autarky consumer prices for goods and factors. We arrange matters (set commodity taxes) in such a way that consumers go on facing the same prices in the free trade case. Therefore they make the same choices $(c^{ha}, v^{ha})$, and attain the same utility levels $u^{ha}$. Total factor supply is $v^a = \sum v^{ha}$. Domestic producers in free trade face the same prices for goods as those prevailing in the rest of the world. Let $p$ be the equilibrium price vector for goods, and $w$ the producer factor price vector. The specific commodity tax rates are then implicitly defined. The vector of tax for goods is $(p^a - p)$, and that for factors is $(w - w^a)$.

There being no lump-sum transfers, we have the consumer budget conditions for each $h$:

$$0 = p^a . c^{ha} - w^a . v^{ha} \tag{19}$$

Producers must use $v^a$ in both equilibria, but their output plans can change in response to the prices. Let $x$ be the output vector under free trade. Since both $x$ and $x^a$ are feasible given factor quantities $v^a$, while $x$ is chosen under trade, we must have

$$0 = p . x - w . v^a \geq p . x^a - w . v^a \tag{20}$$

The government's net tax revenue is

$$(p^a - p) . \sum c^{ha} + (w - w^a) . \sum v^{ha}$$

$$= -p . \sum c^{ha} + w . \sum v^{ha} \quad \text{using (19)}$$

$$= -p . x^a + w . v^a \quad \text{from autarky equilibrium}$$

$$\geq -p . x + w . v^a = 0 \quad \text{using (20)}$$

which proves the result.

In conclusion, it can be said that we have established quite strong results concerning the superiority of free trade over autarky. These results are clearly stronger than the general statements that come from competitive equilibrium theory and require international lump-sum transfers. They are also stronger than the traditional treatments of gains from trade, which remain content with proving that autarky could not be Pareto superior to free trade (see Ohyama (1972)). They are further strengthened by the fact that domestic redistributive instruments weaker than lump sum transfers are shown to suffice for the purpose.

There is only one qualification that needs to be made. If constant returns to scale are achieved by artificially defining factors, the pure profits of different firms will accrue to different factors. Our assumption of complete commodity taxation entails the ability to tax the incomes of factors at arbitrary rates, which in this context amounts to the ability to tax the profits of different firms at different rates. This is in general not achieved by a uniform profits tax. In this sense, the requirement of commodity taxation is more stringent than usual.

## 3. INTERNATIONAL EQUILIBRIUM

The discussion so far has concentrated on one country. Even when we considered a trade equilibrium, the focus was on one country, and the rest of the world was summarized by its net demand for goods. Now we describe trade equilibria taking full account of all countries. In fact for most of our purposes it suffices to consider two countries, which for convenience are distinguished by the labels home and foreign. All variables pertaining to the home country will be denoted by lower case letters, and those for the foreign country by the corresponding upper case letters. The models of production and consumption for one country have been developed at length in Chapter 2 using the home country notation, and the foreign country has exactly similar models. It only remains to put the pieces together.

In this section, we consider only the simplest model, where each country has one consumer, all goods are tradeable, and factor supplies are fixed. Generalizations in all these respects are in principle quite easy, and are postponed until the next section in order to convey the basic points in the simplest possible setting.

Equilibrium is characterized by a national income identity for each country, and market-clearing equations for the goods for the two countries taken together. Thus

$$e(p, u) = r(p, v) \tag{21}$$

$$E(P, U) = R(P, V) \tag{22}$$

$$e_p(p, u) + E_P(P, U) = r_p(p, v) + R_P(P, V) \tag{23}$$

Factor prices in the two countries are then given by $w = r_v(p, v)$ and $W = R_V(P, V)$.

In free trade the two countries have the same relative prices for goods, i.e. $p$ and $P$ differ only by a scale factor. But this factor of proportionality can be chosen arbitrarily, since the equilibrium conditions go on being satisfied if the equilibrium values of $p$ and $P$ are changed by independent scalar multiples. This is simply a reflection of the fact that in our non-monetary model of trade, the issue of exchange rates is not of any significance. Once again we leave this question of scale, i.e. of normalization of prices, open, to be settled in each case according to convenience. Now we have $(n + 1)$ unknowns, namely the $(n - 1)$ relative prices and the two utility levels. Correspondingly, of the $(n + 2)$ equations in (21)–(23), any one can be dropped using Walras's Law.

As before, existence is guaranteed by standard theorems. We will usually also assume uniqueness of the free trade price and utility levels. However, there might be inherent features of non-uniqueness in the output quantities. We saw in Chapter 2 that the revenue function may fail to be differentiable at certain crucial points, and then the symbols in (23) must be interpreted as a selection from among the range of possible revenue-maximizing output choices. It is then possible to have non-unique selections for $r_p$ and $R_P$ separately, adding up to the right demand quantities. This is the case in certain equilibria when there are more goods than factors, and in the next chapter we will return to the issue in our analysis of specialization and factor prices.

Having stated the basic model, we give a brief summary of the uses to which it is going to be put in later chapters. First we have some questions of *characterization*: Which country will export which goods? How will production patterns and factor prices change when trade opens up? These will be the subject of Chapter 4. Next comes *comparative statics*: If some underlying parameters change, or if some policy variables are introduced, how will the trade equilibrium change? This is discussed in Chapter 5. Closely related is the issue of *welfare* or *policy*, which we study in Chapter 6. The basic model must be augmented or at times simplified to deal with these different aspects in the best way, but its general structure will remain common to all three chapters.

Here we outline various special cases that have been used as 'workhorse' models in the long tradition of international trade theory. All of them can be said to stem from one general concern. To understand it, suppose for a moment that the two countries treated separately in autarky happen to have a common equilibrium price vector except possibly for the arbitrary choice of a scale factor. Then the same vector will also serve as an equilibrium price vector when trade in goods is allowed. We see this by inspection: if (1) and (2) and the corresponding equations for the foreign country are satisfied for the same $p$, then that $p$ also satisfies (21)–(23). In fact the goods markets happen to balance within each country, i.e. there is no trade even when it is allowed.

Trade can therefore be said to be explained by differences in the two countries' autarky prices; a point which will be pursued in more detail in Chapter 4. Such differences in turn can be explained by differences in the underlying data for the two countries: their tastes, technologies, or factor endowments. Various special models have been built by taking particular differences into account and ignoring others.

All the standard models ignore taste differences; in fact most of them assume identical and homothetic preferences in the two countries. We will not have to make this extreme assumption except when explicitly stated. However, we agree that the most interesting features of international trade are to be found in differences in production possibilities among countries. We outline some well-known models which capture particular aspects of these; later chapters will use them as illustrative examples for the general results.

### Ricardo's model

Here the focus is on differences of technology between the two countries. In fact it is possible to allow differences in factor endowments and tastes as well, but the particular form of the technologies makes these other differences secondary for several issues. Each country is assumed to be capable of producing several goods using just one factor. Constant returns are assumed, and with just one factor this amounts to assuming constant input coefficients in the production of each good. The values of these differ between the countries.

Suppose the home country requires $a_j$ units of the factor to produce a unit of good $j$, and has a total endowment of $v$ units of the factor. The corresponding entities for the foreign country are $A_j$

and $V$. The forms of the revenue functions were studied in detail in Chapter 2; equation (15) there gives

$$r(p, v) = \max_j (v p_j / a_j), \qquad R(P, V) = \max_j (V P_j / A_j) \qquad (24)$$

Unit cost functions are also simple, given by the product of the factor price and the unit factor requirement:

$$b^j(w) = a_j w, \qquad B^j(W) = A_j W \qquad (25)$$

Output determination was studied in conjunction with the revenue function in Chapter 2, and was seen to involve non-uniqueness associated with kinks in the revenue function at some crucial prices. We can alternatively learn something about output choices by using the unit cost functions. Production equilibrium conditions in those terms were fortuitously, equations (26) and (27) in Chapter 2. In this example, they become:

$$a.x = v, \qquad A.X = V \qquad (26)$$

$$
\begin{aligned}
a_j w \geq p_j & \quad \text{with equality if } x_j > 0 \\
A_j W \geq P_j & \quad \text{with equality if } _j > 0
\end{aligned}
\qquad (27)
$$

As for demand, we only need to assume that all goods are essential in each country. Then, in autarky, all goods must be produced in positive quantities in each. Autarky prices are determined by (27) without any further details concerning demand being required:

$$p^a = wa, \qquad P^a = WA \qquad (28)$$

where $a$ and $A$ are vectors with components $a_j$ and $A_j$ respectively. The scalar factors $w$ and $W$ affect only the normalization of prices. Relative prices only depend on the relative magnitudes of the input coefficients; thus $p_1^a/p_2^a = a_1/a_2$ etc. This has important implications for trade patterns. In particular, differences between the two sets of autarky relative prices are explained by differences between the two countries' relative input coefficients. This was in fact the first formulation of the concept of comparative advantage.

Now let trade commence, and let an equilibrium price vector $p$ for goods be established. (This is the right point to explain that when the two countries share some economic variable in common, we will use the home country or lower case symbol for the common value. This may be called the imperial convention—the rest of the world is like us—in contrast to the more modest convention—we are like the rest of the world.) To determine the production and trade patterns, begin by observing that if good $j$ is produced in the home country and good $k$ in the foreign country, we have

$$a_j w = p_j \leq A_j W$$

and

$$a_k w \geq p_k = A_k W$$

Dividing, we have $a_j/a_k \leq A_j/A_k$, i.e. $a_j/A_j \leq a_k/A_k$. In a weak sense, each country has a lower relative input coefficient for the good it produces. We shall rule out cases where two or more of these ratios are tied, as unlikely coincidences for exogenous input coefficients. With all the ratios $a_j/A_j$ distinct, we can write strict inequalities in the above argument. Also, the two countries can produce at most one good in common, for if both are producing goods $j$ and $k$, we have $a_j w = p_j = A_j W$ and $a_k w = p_k = A_k W$, implying $a_j/A_j = a_k/A_k$.

Rank the goods in increasing order of the ratios $a_j/A_j$. Then the production pattern is clear. The home country will produce goods with low numbers and the foreign country will produce goods with high numbers. There may be a good in the middle which is produced by both countries, or there may not. That depends on the precise specification of demand and factor endowments. With two goods, for example, if one country is very large, it may produce both goods while the other produces only one. However, with several goods this question is of minor importance.

The trade pattern also is almost entirely clear: the home country must be exporting goods which are not produced in the foreign country, and vice versa. With several goods, if one good is produced in both countries, whether it is exported or imported depends on demand conditions. With two goods, even that ambiguity is not possible. For example, the large country which produces both goods must be exporting the one which is not produced in the small country, and therefore must be importing the other.

Everything thus far hinges on the relative input coefficients. Absolute advantage, in the form of lower input coefficients for all goods, does not matter as far as the pattern of trade is concerned. It does affect the real income of factors. This is most easily seen in the case where one good, say $j$, is produced in both countries. Then we have

$$w/p_j = 1/a_j, \qquad W/p_j = 1/A_j$$

i.e. the country with the lower input coefficient (higher productivity) for this good has a higher factor price in terms of it. In general, we have to consider an index for deflating money wages, and the comparison depends on the choice of index.

## Factor abundance models

We turn to two models which allow a more complicated technology, but where the technology is common to the two countries. Differences in production possibilities arise due to differences in their factor endowments. Let $r$ be the common revenue function, and $v$, $V$ the factor endowments in the respective countries. Then the home supply functions are $r_p(p, v)$ and the foreign ones $r_p(P, V)$. Even with identical demands, the autarky equilibrium prices in the two countries will be different.

In the most general case of many goods, it is not possible to establish clear systematic relations between factor endowments and autarky prices. We will examine the problems, and the limited results that are available, in Chapter 4. Here we consider two particular models that are commonly used in trade-theoretic literature. Each of these allows two goods, and assumes identical and homothetic demands in the two countries. They differ in their treatment of production.

We begin by establishing the general line of reasoning of these models. The supplies of the two goods are given by $x_j = \partial r / \partial p_j$, and each being homogeneous of degree zero in $(p_1, p_2)$, can be expressed as a function of the ratio $p_1/p_2$. Then so can the ratio $x_1/x_2$. With homothetic preferences, the demand ratio $c_1/c_2$ is also a function of the ratio $p_1/p_2$. When the demand ratio is equal to the supply ratio, we must have equality of demand and supply for each good, for by Walras's Law we could not have equiproportionate excess demands (or supplies) for both goods. This allows us to determine the equilibrium relative price. The demand ratio is independent of the factor endowments, but the supply ratio is affected by them. The relative price in autarky in each country can then be found by using its factor endowments in the equilibrium condition.

Suppose that, at fixed prices, the supply ratio $x_1/x_2$ is increased if the point of evaluation for factor endowments is changed from $v$ to $V$. Then, at the home country's autarky equilibrium prices, the foreign country has too high a supply ratio, which must mean that it has an excess supply of good 1 and an excess demand for good 2. Assuming stability of equilibrium, then, the foreign country must have a lower relative price of good 1 in autarky. This gives us a simple way of determining, where possible, how the two countries' autarky price ratios differ.

The simplest application of this occurs in the case where we have two factors producing two goods in separate 'industries' without joint production and with constant returns to scale. The numbering of goods and factors can be chosen so that good 1 is relatively more intensive in its use of factor 1. Reversals of factor intensities are assumed to be absent. This is the well-known basic *Heckscher–Ohlin* model, and properties of production in this case were studied in Chapter 2. It was found that, at constant output prices, an increase in the relative supply of the first factor raises the output of good 1 relative to that of good 2. The relations between the two countries' factor endowments and autarky prices are then clear: if $V_1/V_2 > v_1/v_2$, then $P_1^a/P_2^a < p_1^a/p_2^a$. With only two goods, we saw in Chapter 1 that trade patterns could be simply related to autarky price differences: the country with the lower relative autarky price of good 1 would export that good in free trade. Thus we see that, in the Heckscher–Ohlin model, with good 1 relatively more factor 1 intensive, the country with the relatively greater abundance of factor 1 will export good 1.

Next consider the *Ricardo–Viner* model, where there are three factors, one mobile between the two uses and the others specific, one in the production of each good. In Chapter 2, the set of equations (22) summarized the properties of the revenue function, and we can use them to examine how the supply ratio depends on the factor endowments.

For example, for a change in the quantity $\kappa_1$ of the first specific factor,

$$\frac{1}{x_1/x_2} \frac{\partial(x_1/x_2)}{\partial \kappa_1} = \frac{1}{x_1} \frac{\partial x_1}{\partial \kappa_1} - \frac{1}{x_2} \frac{\partial x_2}{\partial \kappa_1}$$

$$= \frac{1}{x_1} \frac{\partial^2 r}{\partial \kappa_1 \, \partial p_1} - \frac{1}{x_2} \frac{\partial^2 r}{\partial \kappa_1 \, \partial p_2}$$

$$> 0$$

Therefore, if the two countries differ only in the foreign country having a greater amount of the specific factor involved in the production of good 1, it will have a lower relative autarky price of that good. The analysis of a change in $\kappa_2$ is similar. If it is the quantity of the mobile factor $v$ that differs between the two countries, however, the relevant expression is

$$\frac{1}{x_1} \frac{\partial^2 r}{\partial v \, \partial p_1} - \frac{1}{x_2} \frac{\partial^2 r}{\partial v \, \partial p_2}$$

in which both terms are positive, and the net result ambiguous. The point is that an increase in $v$ is shared out between the sectors, and the relative output response depends on which sector benefits more at the margin. That depends on further properties of the technology, including substitution possibilities between the mobile factor and the specific factor in each sector. We do not pursue the details here; the interested reader can refer to Dixit and Norman (1979). It will suffice to note that in the Ricardo–Viner model, factor abundance considerations take us only part of the way in determining autarky prices and trade patterns.

## Pure exchange

This is a case of differences in technology in a trivial sense. There is no actual production; each country merely has a fixed endowment of goods, $\bar{x}$ in the home country and $\bar{X}$ in the foreign country. In autarky, each country's equilibrium is found simply by setting its consumption equal to its endowment, and the prices are the marginal utilities. If $f(c)$ and $F(C)$ are the respective utility functions, we thus have

$$p^a = f_c(\bar{x}), \qquad P^a = F_c(\bar{X}) \qquad (29)$$

omitting the arbitrary factors of normalization. In some simple cases, (29) gives further information. For example, with two goods, and identical homothetic preferences in the two countries, it can be seen that the country with the relatively greater endowment of good 1 has a lower relative price of that good in autarky, and therefore exports it in free trade.

## Intertemporal trade

General equilibrium theory handles problems of resource allocation over time by treating goods and factors available at different dates as different commodities, and considering marginal substitution and transformation possibilities among them. Their prices are to be interpreted as payments or receipts in forward markets, all transactions taking place at the outset. For example, if commodity 1 is wheat available this year and commodity 2 is wheat available next year, $(p_2/p_1)$ is the number of units of wheat of this year that must be paid to secure the promise of delivery of one unit of wheat next year. Equilibrium in such markets can be established in the usual way, and has Pareto efficiency properties interpreted in the intertemporal sense. This structure is explained in detail by Bliss (1975).

We can use the same idea to model trade involving time. For simplicity of exposition, suppose there is only one good at each date, and the suffix numbering the good denotes its date of availability. In autarky, each country's consumption at each date must equal its output. In trade, this need no longer be the case. Consumption and output must match at each date for the world as a whole, but one country may consume less than its production at one date and more at another. The discrepancies may be termed its current account surpluses or deficits at the appropriate dates. The overall trade balance condition $p.x = p.c$ is an intertemporal budget constraint. Since the prices $p$ are all in comparable, or present value, terms, any discounting that is necessary is already implicit in them.

On the side of production, there will be some factor specificities arising in a natural way due to dating. For example, the labour available at each date will be specific to the output of that date (although storage possibilities may get around this to some extent). As an interesting possibility, if the stock of a natural resource can be allocated over production at different dates in each country, but is not tradeable between them, we have the precise formal structure of the Ricardo–Viner model.

In fact we will not find this the best way of modelling balance of payments problems. In this approach, today's trade surplus corresponds to future excess demands, already determined in the forward markets in the form of claims to deliveries of specific goods at specific dates. It is much more realistic to introduce generalized stores of purchasing power, i.e. financial assets, in terms of which such claims can be held, and translated into specific goods only in spot markets at later dates. Such a formulation will be developed in Chapter 7; in the meantime we leave the intertemporal aspects of trade aside.

## 4. SOME EXTENSIONS

In the interests of simplicity of exposition, the basic model of international equilibrium above assumed that demand in each country could be modelled as if it arose from the choice of a single consumer, factor supplies were fixed exogenously, and all goods were assumed to be tradeable. Now we show how the model can be generalized in all these respects.

Bringing in several consumers is as easy as it was in autarky. Just as (1) and (2) for the one-consumer case were modified to (6) and (7) for the many-consumer case, (21)–(23) can be altered to give

$$e^h(p, u^h) = r_v(p, v).v^h \qquad \text{for all } h \qquad (30)$$

$$E^H(P, U^H) = R_V(P, \dot{V}).V^H \qquad \text{for all } H \tag{31}$$

$$\sum_h e_p^h(p, u^h) + \sum_H E_P^H(P, U^H) = r_p(p, v) + R_P(P, V) \tag{32}$$

where $h$ and $H$ index the consumers in the two countries, and $v = \sum v^h$ and $V = \sum V^H$ are the total factor supplies. When considering the characterization of equilibria and carrying out comparative statics, we will usually leave such simple generalizations to the reader. The distributive policy analyses in Chapter 6 will of course use several-consumer models explicitly.

Accordingly, we revert to the one-consumer case. The next new feature is to allow variable factor supplies. In the context of autarky, we devised two ways of doing so. The first defined an expenditure function involving factor quantities, $e(p, v, u)$, and the partial derivatives $e_v$ gave us the supply prices of factors $v$. The second defined an expenditure function involving factor prices, $e^*(p, w, u)$, and the optimum factor supplies could be found as $-e_w^*$. Here we adopt the former procedure. The foreign country has the corresponding upper case variables, and factor markets in each country are cleared by setting the supply price equal to the demand price. Thus the full set of equilibrium conditions is

$$e(p, v, u) = r(p, v) \tag{33}$$

$$e_v(p, v, u) = r_v(p, v) \qquad (= w) \tag{34}$$

$$E(P, V, U) = R(P, V) \tag{35}$$

$$E_V(P, V, U) = R_V(P, V) \qquad (= W) \tag{36}$$

$$e_p(p, v, u) + E_P(P, V, U) = r_p(p, v) + R_P(P, V) \tag{37}$$

Finally, consider the case where some goods are not tradeable. In fact, we could regard a factor with a minus sign as a good, so the variable factor supply case can be subsumed in the case of some goods non-tradeable, and the following may be seen as an alternative way of handling it. Let us suppose this done, and leave only fixed factors in the explicit form. To state the equilibrium conditions, we simply add a set of domestic market-clearing conditions for non-traded goods to the set of world market-clearing equations for the traded goods. Let $p$ denote the price vector for traded goods, and $q$ the price vector for non-traded ones. Further, let corresponding subscripts on the expenditure and revenue functions indicate the vectors of partial derivatives. Then the full set of equilibrium conditions is

$$e(p, q, u) = r(p, q, v) \tag{38}$$

$$e_q(p, q, u) = r_q(p, q, v) \tag{39}$$

$$E(P, Q, U) = R(P, Q, V) \tag{40}$$

$$E_Q(P, Q, U) = R_Q(P, Q, V) \tag{41}$$

$$e_p(p, q, u) + E_P(P, Q, U) = r_p(p, q, v) + R_P(P, Q, V) \tag{42}$$

Note the similarity in structure to (33)–(37). In free trade, the price vectors for traded goods, $p$ and $P$, are equal, to within a scalar multiple, but of course $q$ and $Q$ can differ in general, just as $w$ and $W$ could differ in general.

We proceed to examine in some detail another feature of the model with non-tradeable goods. Suppose we use the domestic market-clearing conditions for such goods first to determine their prices in terms of those of traded goods, e.g. solve (39) for $q$ in terms of $(p, u, v)$ and similarly (41) for the foreign country. Substituting these solutions in (38), (40), and (42), we would obtain a system remarkably like (21)–(23), the set of equilibrium conditions for the case where all goods are tradeable. In this sense, the simpler model could be interpreted as the reduced form of the more general model. The question is to what extent this interpretation is valid or helpful.

To understand this, we look at (21)–(23) in a slightly different way. Define the compensated import demand functions for the home country as

$$m(p, v, u) = e_p(p, u) - r_p(p, v) \tag{43}$$

These are the price partial derivatives of $e - r$, which can be thought of as a net expenditure or excess expenditure function, defined as

$$\tilde{e}(p, v, u) = e(p, u) - r(p, v)$$

Recalling the separate definitions of $e$ and $r$, from Chapter 2 equations (35) and (1), we can write this explicitly as

$$\tilde{e}(p, v, u) = \min_{c, x} \{p \cdot (c - x) \mid f(c) \geq u, (x, v) \text{ feasible}\} \tag{44}$$

This has all the properties of an expenditure function: it is increasing in $u$, homogeneous of degree one and concave in $p$. In terms of it, and a corresponding function for the foreign country, (21)–(23) can be written as

$$\tilde{e}(p, v, u) = 0 \tag{45}$$

$$\hat{E}(P, V, U) = 0 \tag{46}$$

$$\tilde{e}_p(p, v, u) + \hat{E}_P(P, V, U) = 0 \tag{47}$$

When non-tradeables are introduced, we have the obvious extension of (44), remembering that consumption must equal output for these goods within the country. Denote by $z$ the vector of quantities of non-tradeables. We then define

$$\tilde{e}(p, v, u) = \min_{c, x, z} \{p.(c - x) \mid f(c, z) \geq u, (x, z, v) \text{ feasible}\} \tag{48}$$

In this the economic optimum choice of the quantities of non-tradeables is explicitly introduced. This could alternatively be done by using prices to induce consumers and producers to optimize separately, and then setting prices at levels which clear markets. In other words,

$$\tilde{e}(p, v, u) = e(p, q, u) - r(p, q, v) \tag{49}$$

when $q$ satisfies (39).

Once again, $\tilde{e}$ has all the relevant properties of an expenditure function. It is obviously increasing in $u$ and homogeneous of degree one in $p$. By the first result on convexity of envelope functions in the Appendix, it is concave in $p$. By the envelope theorem, its partial derivatives are the compensated import demand functions for tradeables. Together with the corresponding function for the foreign country, it can therefore be used to write the equilibrium conditions as

$$\tilde{e}(p, v, u) = 0 \tag{50}$$

$$\tilde{E}(P, V, U) = 0 \tag{51}$$

$$\tilde{e}_p(p, v, u) + \tilde{E}_P(P, V, U) = 0 \tag{52}$$

The analogy with the simple model of (45)–(47) is now exact.

This provides formal justification for our earlier claim that non-tradeables can always be netted out of the model by using their domestic equilibrium conditions, leaving a 'reduced form' model in which all goods are tradeable. We will have occasion to use this wide interpretation of the simple model, particularly when we discuss the balance of payments in Chapter 7. However, when we are interested in details concerning non-tradeables themselves, for example when studying the possibility of factor-price equalization, we must use the general 'structural form' with non-tradeables explicit.

There is another drawback. The function $\tilde{e}$ is the outcome of imposing equilibrium in non-tradeables on the decisions of individuals. Its properties therefore combine both features, and do not relate in a simple way to individual choice parameters. The price and income effects on compensated import demand functions for tradeables are complicated expressions involving demand and supply responses for all commodities. We shall have to spell these out when we need them.

All the extensions considered thus far have maintained the assumption of free trade, reflected in the fact that the two countries' price vectors for tradeable goods are allowed to differ at most by a scale factor. Tariffs, or other distortions, will introduce differences of relative prices between the countries. This is formally quite easy to handle. We incorporate into the equilibrium conditions the relations specifying how the two price vectors are allowed to differ, and modify each country's national income identity by including any tariff revenue on the income side. We leave the detailed formulation and analysis of such equilibria to the chapters on comparative statics and policy.

## NOTES

The conventional treatment of gains from trade consists of a rigorous demonstration that autarky could not be made Pareto superior to free trade. Superiority of free trade to autarky is not rigorously proven, and is often cast in terms of hypothetical compensation. Kemp (1969, ch. 12) provides the most succinct account. Our treatment is greatly influenced by Ohyama (1972); he shows awareness of what needs to be done to prove that free trade can be made Pareto superior to autarky. The result that it is possible to do so using domestic commodity taxation alone is, to the best of our knowledge, new. The comparison of trade restricted by taxes yielding non-negative net revenue and autarky is due to Ohyama.

The Ricardian and Heckscher–Ohlin models of trade are discussed in most textbooks; see Södersten (1971, chs. 1–7) or Takayama (1972, chs. 2–4). The Ricardo–Viner model is relatively new. A textbook exposition and comparison with the Ricardian model can be found in Caves and Jones (1977, chs. 5–7); for the Ricardo–Viner treatment of comparative advantage and factor prices, see Samuelson (1971) and Dixit and Norman (1979).

For trenchant comments on the treatment of non-traded goods through reduced form models, see Pearce (1970, pp. xxiii–xxvi).

# CHAPTER 4

# TRADE, SPECIALIZATION, AND FACTOR PRICES

If two countries have the same relative prices of commodities in autarky, and trade is allowed to open up, there is a general equilibrium with zero imports and exports. In the case of a unique equilibrium, therefore, comparative advantage—meaning differences in autarky relative prices—is the basis for trade. However, this is a trivial point, and the theory of comparative advantage goes beyond it to postulate a systematic relationship between the pattern of comparative advantage and the commodity composition of trade. In the first part of this chapter, we examine whether such a systematic relationship exists.

The hypothesis that the pattern of trade reflects comparative advantage is meaningful in the sense that we *could* test it by computing autarky prices for the countries and comparing them with the observed trade pattern. However, this is hardly in the realm of practical empirical work. Propositions relating trade patterns to easily observable variables are, therefore, much more attractive. That is why the factor abundance hypothesis merits careful consideration: it is the only hypothesis regarding the commodity composition of trade that requires only limited information about demand patterns and production technologies. We therefore look closely at this hypothesis. First we look at the relationship between factor abundance and autarky relative prices. Then we examine some properties of a free trade equilibrium in which the countries differ only in their factor endowments. Under this heading we here study the effect of trade on international factor price differences, and the question of the extent of production specialization induced by trade. We illustrate the general results using the special examples of the Ricardo–Viner and the Heckscher–Ohlin models.

In our preliminary look at these issues in Chapter 1, we stressed the limitations of several simple conjectures in this area. There, and again in Chapter 2, we emphasized the importance of studying the questions in a full general equilibrium model of trade. We do not repeat these warnings in detail; we simply concentrate on establishing the results that are valid.

93

## 1. COMPARATIVE ADVANTAGE AND TRADE PATTERNS

The hypothesis that trade is governed by comparative advantage involves a comparison of prices in one equilibrium (autarky) with quantities in another (free trade). The only reason such a comparison is possible, is that the free trade equilibrium is at least as good as no trade. This means that the free trade vector of net imports must be at most barely attainable at autarky prices. First consider the one-consumer case. Writing $m$ for the net import vector in free trade, and $p^a$ for the vector of autarky prices, we must have

$$p^a . m \geq 0 \tag{1}$$

with strict inequality if trade is strictly preferred to no trade. We can see this in more detail by considering an arbitrary price vector $p$, and the corresponding utility level $u$, demands $e_p(p, u)$, and supplies $r_p(p, v)$. As quantities produced at prices $p$ must be feasible, we must have

$$p^a . r_p(p, v) \leq r(p^a, v) \qquad \text{by definition of } r \tag{2}$$

By the same token, we must have

$$p^a . e_p(p, u) \geq e(p^a, u) \qquad \text{by definition of } e \tag{3}$$

But we already know that the utility level corresponding to an arbitrary price vector $p$ must be at least as great as utility in autarky. This can be written as

$$e(p^a, u) \geq e(p^a, u^a) \tag{4}$$

Substituting (4) into (3) and subtracting (2), we therefore get

$$p^a . \{e_p(p, u) - r_p(p, v)\} \geq e(p^a, u^a) - r(p^a, v) = 0 \tag{5}$$

which gives us (1), as $(e_p - r_p)$ is the import vector.

Next, allow several consumers, and suppose that domestic lump-sum transfers or commodity taxes are deployed in the manner explained in Chapter 3, to make free trade Pareto superior to autarky. Then we can add the revealed preference inequalities like (4) for all consumers, and obtain (1) for the aggregate net import vector in free trade.

The inequality (1) holds for both countries in a free trade equilibrium, so if lower case letters denote the home country and upper case ones the rest of the world, we have

$$p^a . m \geq 0 \qquad P^a . M \geq 0$$

But in a free trade equilibrium, $m + M = 0$, so $M = -m$. Substituting that into the latter of the two inequalities, we can then add the two to obtain

$$(p^a - P^a).m \geq 0 \qquad (6)$$

This establishes a positive correlation between autarky price differences and imports. Although (6) might give the impression that *absolute* price differences matter, a moment's reflection will make clear that this is not so: (6) is the sum of the two inequalities above, and is thus the sum of two positive numbers. The choice of numeraire in the two countries will affect the exact values of these numbers, but it will not affect their signs; so (6) will hold regardless of what numeraires are chosen. Thus (6) confirms the comparative advantage hypothesis, in that a country will tend to import goods that are relatively more expensive there than in the rest of the world in autarky, and export goods that are relatively cheap at home in a no-trade equilibrium.

The result above is, however, only a very weak version of the comparative advantage hypothesis, as it only establishes a *correlation* between comparative advantage and the pattern of trade. It would have been nice if one could prove the stronger conjecture that a country will export each good in which it has a comparative advantage. Unfortunately, that conjecture is false. This should not surprise any micro-economics student; without some very strong assumptions like gross substitutes or severe limitations on income effects, only very weak results concerning comparisons of general equilibria are valid, and these are usually only correlations like the one established above from revealed preference considerations. Just to complete the argument, we offer an example which makes the point explicitly.

## A counter-example

There are three commodities, of which the first will be chosen as the numeraire in all settings. Production in the home country consists simply of using fixed endowments, with $x_1 = 240$, $x_2 = 264$, and $x_3 = 240$. Demands are given by

$$c_1 = c_2 = \tfrac{1}{2}y/(1 + p_2), \qquad c_3 = \tfrac{1}{2}y/p_3$$

where $y = 240 + 264p_2 + 240p_3$ is the income, i.e. value of endowments. It is then easy to verify that the home autarky equilibrium has $p_2^a = 0$ and $p_3^a = 1$.

The foreign country has a transformation surface

$$2X_1 + X_2 + 4X_3 = 700$$

and demands are in fixed proportions, i.e.

$$C_1 = C_2 = C_3 = Y/(1 + P_2 + P_3)$$

where $Y$ is the foreign country's income, which equals the value
of its output. For all three commodities to be produced, the autarky
equilibrium must have prices $P_2^a = \frac{1}{2}$ and $P_3^a = 2$. Then producers
are indifferent as to their choice on the transformation surface, and
no matter what their choice, $Y = 350$. Demands are $C_1 = C_2 =
C_3 = 100$, and producers do not mind complying with these, so
yielding an equilibrium.

Since $p_2^a < P_2^a$ and $p_3^a < P_3^a$, the strong comparative advantage
conjecture would be that in free trade the home country would
export both commodities 2 and 3. However, we can compute the
trade equilibrium explicitly and show that the conjecture is false.

Try prices $p_2 = \frac{1}{2}$ and $p_3 = 2$. For the home country, $y = 852$,
and $c_1 = c_2 = 284$, $c_3 = 213$. The foreign producers are again indifferent as to their choice, and $Y = 350$, $C_1 = C_2 = C_3 = 100$. If
equilibrium is to obtain, the foreign production pattern must be
$X_1 = 144$, $X_2 = 120$ and $X_3 = 73$. These are all non-negative and
compatible with the producer's choice. A general trading equilibrium is therefore established, and the home country's net imports
are seen to be $m_1 = 44$, $m_2 = 20$ and $m_3 = -27$. It exports commodity 3, but imports commodity 2. The inner product of the
expression in (6) amounts to 17, so the correlation is verified. The
weak form of the comparative advantage hypothesis is checked, but
its strong form is not valid.

This counter-example may seem rather special. However, it is
not difficult to construct others of apparently greater generality.
They only involve more complicated calculations and expressions.

We reassert that, even though there will be a systematic correlation between comparative advantage and the trade pattern, it is
not possible to predict the exact commodity composition of trade
on the basis of autarky price ratios alone.

## 2. COMPARATIVE ADVANTAGE AND FACTOR
## ENDOWMENTS

It is impossible to say anything about the relationship between
comparative advantage and factor endowments without further
restrictions on supply and demand. In particular, as differences in
autarky prices might reflect differences in income levels, preferences,
or technology rather than differences in factor supplies, we need
restrictions that eliminate such sources of autarky price differences.

The simplest way to do that is by assuming that both countries
have access to the same technology, so that the revenue function
is the same for both countries (although, of course, it will be evaluated
at different points); and by assuming that preferences are uniform
and homothetic, so that the expenditure function is separable in
prices and utility, and is the same for both countries (but again,
evaluated at different points).

With homothetic preferences, we recall, the expenditure function
can be written as $e(p, u) = u\,\bar{e}(p)$, so the conditions for a no-trade
equilibrium in the home country can be written as

$$u^a\,\bar{e}(p^a) = r(p^a, v) \tag{7}$$

$$u^a\,\bar{e}_p(p^a) = r_p(p^a, v) \tag{8}$$

With the same preferences and production technology in the rest
of the world as in the home country, the autarky price vector and
utility level for the rest of the world are determined by

$$U^a\,\bar{e}(P^a) = r(P^a, V) \tag{9}$$

$$U^a\,\bar{e}_p(P^a) = r_p(P^a, V) \tag{10}$$

As before (7)–(10) only determine prices up to scalar multiples,
so we are free to choose numeraires for the two countries. It is convenient to choose price levels in such a way that we get

$$\bar{e}(p^a) = \bar{e}(P^a) = 1 \tag{11}$$

With this choice of numeraire, we see that $u^a = r(p^a, v)$ and $U^a =
r(P^a, V)$. But we already know that any other price vector, being a
possible free-trade equilibrium price vector, is preferable to the
autarky price vector. This means that we must have $r(p, v) \geq
r(p^a, v)$ for any price vector satisfying $\bar{e}(p) = 1$. In particular, then,
we must have

$$r(P^a, v) \geq r(p^a, v) \tag{12}$$

and similarly

$$r(P^a, V) \leq r(p^a, V) \tag{13}$$

Combining these, we have

$$(r(p^a, v) - r(P^a, v)) - (r(p^a, V) - r(P^a, V)) \leq 0 \tag{14}$$

which is a general relationship between autarky prices and factor
endowments in the two countries. It permits us to compute the
range of autarky prices that are conceivable given particular factor
endowments. In this respect, (14) could be called the most general

statement of the factor abundance hypothesis. However, it leaves two things to be desired. It does not quite relate factor abundance to trade patterns, but we have already seen the weakness in the next link in the chain, namely, that connecting autarky prices to trade patterns. Secondly, the form of (14) makes it rather hard to relate it to entities for which economists have an intuition. Much of the conventional theory on this subject can be seen as an attempt to cast (14) in a more easily comprehensible form.

The simplest approach is to think of the left-hand side of (14) as a kind of second difference of the function $r$ between the points $(P^a, V)$ and $(p^a, v)$. If these two are sufficiently close together, we may approximate this by the second-order terms in a Taylor expansion of $r$, and write

$$(p^a - P^a)^T r_{pv} (v - V) \leq 0 \qquad (15)$$

To interpret this inequality, recall that in Chapter 2 we related the signs of the elements of the matrix $r_{pv}$ to the relative factor intensities of the goods. In the two-by-two case with constant returns to scale and no joint production, these could be shown to be equivalent to the elementary notions of relative factor intensities. In the $n$-by-$n$ generalization, there was a natural generalization involving a comparison of the intensity of one good in using one factor and that of the economy as a whole. With more factors than goods, we argued that the signs of elements in $r_{pv}$ gave us the only obvious definition of factor intensities available. What (15) says, therefore, is that an abundant supply of a factor tends on the average to give a low (relative) price in autarky of goods intensive in that factor, i.e. that factor endowment differences are negatively correlated with autarky price differences. Thus, the inequality can be taken as confirmation of a weak version of the factor abundance hypothesis.

### Problems of generalization

Large changes are more difficult. One case where something can be said is that of constant returns to scale and no jointness in production. In such a case, recall that the revenue function can be written as

$$r(p, v) = \min_{w} \{w.v \mid b^j(w) \geq p_j \text{ for all } j\}$$

This means that

$$r(p^a, v) = w^a.v \qquad r(P^a, V) = W^a.V \qquad (16)$$

Moreover, as $w^a$ obviously satisfies the constraints $b^j(w) \geq p_j^a$ (all $j$), it also means that

$$r(p^a, V) \leq w^a . V \qquad (17)$$

Similarly, as $W^a$ satisfies $b^j(w) \geq P_j^a$,

$$r(P^a, v) \leq W^a . v \qquad (18)$$

Therefore, combining (12), (16), and (18), we have

$$w^a . v = r(p^a, v) \leq r(P^a, v) \leq W^a . v \qquad (19)$$

Similarly, from (13), (16), and (17),

$$W^a . V = r(P^a, V) \leq r(p^a, V) \leq w^a . V \qquad (20)$$

Adding the extremes in (19) and (20) and simplifying

$$(v - V) . (w^a - W^a) \leq 0 \qquad (21)$$

i.e. autarky factor price differences are negatively correlated with endowment differences.

The next step is to relate autarky factor prices to autarky output prices. If each country produces all goods in autarky, we have the price–cost equations of production equilibrium satisfied in each case:

$$b^j(w) = p_j \qquad \text{for all } j \qquad (22)$$

Assuming an equal number of goods and factors, these are $n$ equations in $n$ unknown factor prices and $n$ unknown product prices. It might therefore seem that we could use (22) to solve for any combination of $n$ factor and product prices in terms of the rest; and, in particular, that we could solve for the factor prices in terms of the product prices. Unfortunately, it is not obvious that the unit cost functions are invertible—i.e. that (22) defines a unique factor price vector for an arbitrary vector of product prices. This *univalence* problem is closely related to the problem of factor intensity reversals—in fact, non-uniqueness of the mapping from $p$ to $w$ can be seen as the $n$-by-$n$ generalization of the two-by-two notion of reversals of factor intensities. As in the two-by-two case, very severe restrictions are needed to ensure univalence.

If we assume the unit cost functions to satisfy the univalence condition, however, we can use (22) to solve for the factor price vector in terms of the product price vector alone, to obtain $w = w(p)$. In that case, then, we must have $w^a = w(p^a)$, $W^a = w(P^a)$, so (21) becomes

$$(v - V) . (w(p^a) - w(P^a)) \leq 0 \qquad (23)$$

We can apply the mean-value theorem to the scalar-valued function $(v - V).w(P)$, and express (23) in terms of price differences as

$$(v - V)^T w_p(\tilde{p}) (p^a - P^a) \leq 0 \qquad (24)$$

for some 'intermediate' price vector $\tilde{p}$. Since $w_p = r_{vp} = r_{pv}^T$, this is like (15), and has the same interpretation of there being a negative correlation between factor supply differences and autarky price differences when computed via the factor intensity matrix. The new aspect is that (24) is valid for large changes.

It should be noted that the scale of factor supplies does not matter, economically because homothetic preferences and constant returns to scale imply that a proportional change in factor endowments will leave relative prices unchanged, and formally because (21) can be seen as the sum of (19) and (20), each of which is invariant to the scaling of factor quantities. Thus the inequality confirms, for the special case under discussion, the factor abundance hypothesis.

In general, however, we must be content with the non-linear relation (14). It embodies all the information we can hope to obtain without specifying and examining the exact equilibrium that would obtain under free trade, or without restricting the scope of the problem by further assumptions of particular functional forms.

## 3. CHARACTERISTICS OF A FREE TRADE EQUILIBRIUM

So far in this chapter we have examined the implications for trade of various aspects of each country's autarky equilibrium. Now we turn to the trade equilibrium itself. The countries will be assumed to have identical technologies with constant returns to scale and no joint production, but different factor endowments. Identical homothetic tastes are often not required, but will be assumed when necessary. Comparative statics and welfare aspects are the topics of the next two chapters; here we concentrate on describing one equilibrium. The endogenous variables are the common output prices, and the separate factor prices and output quantities, for the two countries. Two questions are of particular interest, one of the extent to which factor prices are brought closer together by trade, and the other of the extent to which production patterns become specialized as a result of trade. The two are in fact closely linked together.

### Factor price differences

Begin with factor prices. One result follows without any special assumptions concerning demand. Observe that in each country the factor markets equilibrate given the common trade equilibrium commodity price vector $p$. Let $r$ be the common revenue function, and $v$, $V$ the factor supplies. Then the factor prices are $w = r_v(p, v)$ and $W = r_v(p, V)$. We saw in Chapter 2 equation (8) that relating factor endowments to their shadow prices at fixed output prices, i.e. considering derived demand curves for factors, there was a non-positive correlation between quantity and price changes.

Formally the same comparison is involved between the two countries here; they have the same technology, and trade equalizes product prices. Therefore,

$$(v - V).(w - W) \leq 0 \qquad (25)$$

This is the usual correlation between quantity and price differences for factors when we compare two trading countries. A similar line of reasoning can say something about how a movement from autarky to trade affects factor prices, but only partial answers are available, and those only in special cases. Let tastes be homothetic and identical for the two countries, and as in section 2 choose the normalization rule to make the value of the function $\bar{e}$ equal to 1 at all relevant prices. The utilities in the free trade equilibrium are $u = r(p, v)$ and $U = r(p, V)$, and since free trade is revealed preferred to autarky for each, we have

$$w^a.v = r(p^a, v) \leq r(p, v) = w.v \qquad (26)$$

$$W^a.V = r(P^a, V) \leq r(p, V) = W.V \qquad (27)$$

Next, $w$ and $W$ both satisfy the constraints that no good can be produced at a pure profit given the trade equilibrium output prices. Therefore the factor-cost minimization definition of the revenue function implies

$$r(p, v) \leq W.v \quad \text{and} \quad r(p, V) \leq w.V \qquad (28)$$

Now compare (26) and (27) as completed by (28), with (19) and (20). If it were the case that

$$W.v \leq r(P^a, v) \quad \text{and} \quad w.V \leq r(p^a, V) \qquad (29)$$

i.e. if each country could enjoy greater national product from being given the other country's autarky commodity prices than it could have national income from being given the other's trade factor prices, then we would have complete chains,

$$w^a.v \leq w.v \leq W.v \leq W^a.v$$

$$W^a.V \leq W.V \leq w.V \leq w^a.V$$

These would imply

$$(v - V).(w^a - W^a) \leq (v - V).(w - W) \leq 0 \qquad (30)$$

i.e. the negative correlation between factor quantity and factor price differences would be numerically smaller after trade than in autarky. The question of whether trade would reduce factor price differences, in the sense that $w$ would be closer to $W$ than $w^a$ to $W^a$, is often posed. The concept of distance is usually taken to be the Euclidean one, which has no special claim to attention in this instance. The natural economic issue should be whether there is a smaller negative correlation with factor endowment differences, i.e. whether (30) is satisfied. We now see that it is not possible to have a general result of this kind. The step (29), which fails to be generally valid, shows us precisely where the difficulty lies.

Lacking a general result, we consider special examples which illustrate different possibilities and the forces involved.

### The Ricardo–Viner model

The first special example we consider is the two-good Ricardo–Viner model. This was discussed in Chapter 2, where the form of the revenue function was at stake, and again in Chapter 3, where the relation between autarky prices and factor endowments was studied. Recall that there are three factors, one mobile between the two uses and available in quantity $v$, and the other two factors available in quantities $\kappa_1$ and $\kappa_2$, specific to the production of goods 1 and 2 respectively. For efficient allocation of the mobile factor we equate its marginal product in use $j$ to $w/p_j$. Since the marginal product is a decreasing function of $v^j/\kappa_j$, we can solve this for the allocation $v^j$ to use $j$ in the form

$$v^j = \kappa_j \, g_j(w/p_j) \qquad (31)$$

where $g_j$ is a decreasing function inverse to the marginal product function. The condition of equilibrium in the market for the mobile factor is to set the sum of the factor demands determined by (31) equal to the supply $v$. Choose good 2 as the numeraire, and write $p_1 = p$ for simplicity. Then we have

$$\kappa_1 \, g_1(w/p) + \kappa_2 \, g_2(w) = v. \qquad (32)$$

This determines a relation between $w$ and $p$, as the locus of all points compatible with equilibrium in the market for the mobile factor. Call this the factor market equilibrium locus for brevity.

Note that as $p$ rises, $w$ must rise (else the left-hand side of (32) would increase through an increase in each $g_j$), but by a smaller proportion (else the left-hand side of (32) would fall). This is a simple recapitulation of the general result in Chapter 2 that the elasticity of $w$ with respect to the price of any one good lies between 0 and 1. From the other results summarized in the set of equations (22) in Chapter 2, we know that at fixed product prices, $w$ rises as any $\kappa_j$ rises, and falls as $v$ rises. If we depict (32) in $(p, w)$ space, therefore, an increase in $\kappa_1$ or $\kappa_2$ will shift the locus upwards, and an increase in $v$ will shift it downwards.

Next we examine the determination of output prices. Write the output supply ratio $x_1/x_2$ as $\xi$. It is a function of $p$, $v$, $\kappa_1$, and $\kappa_2$. Further, our earlier analysis shows that it is increasing in $p$, decreasing in $\kappa_2$, increasing in $\kappa_1$ and in general ambiguous with respect to $v$. Assuming homothetic tastes, the demand ratio $c_1/c_2 = \gamma$ is a decreasing function of $p$, and independent of other variables. Product market equilibrium is given by

$$\xi(p, v, \kappa_1, \kappa_2) = \gamma(p) \qquad (33)$$

For fixed factor endowments, this defines a particular value of $p$, which can be shown as a vertical straight line in $(p, w)$ space. If $\kappa_2$ rises at fixed $p$, the left-hand side of (33) will fall, making it necessary to raise $p$, and restore equilibrium. Thus the locus shifts to the right as $\kappa_2$ increases. Similarly, it shifts to the left as $\kappa_1$ increases, while the shift in response to an increase in $v$ is in general ambiguous.

The intersection of (32) and (33) defines the full equilibrium for the economy. This allows us to consider two countries differing in their factor endowments, and study the effect of trade on the price of the mobile factor. Different cases must be distinguished.

Figure 4.1 shows the case where the two countries differ only in the endowment of the second specific factor, the foreign country having more of it. The factor-market equilibrium loci are $HH$ for the home country and $FF$ for the foreign country. Note that along each locus, as $p$ rises, $w$ rises, but $w/p$ (which is the slope of the line joining a point on the curve to the origin) falls, in accordance with our deductions following (32). Similarly, $FF$ lies above $HH$. Turning to autarky equilibria in the product market, assume that the two countries have identical homothetic taste patterns, i.e. the same function $\gamma$. Then, following the argument of (33), the foreign country's relative autarky price $P^a$ is higher than that of the home country, $p^a$. These price lines are shown in Figure 4.1, and the resulting autarky equilibria are $H^a$ for the home country and $F^a$ for the foreign country.

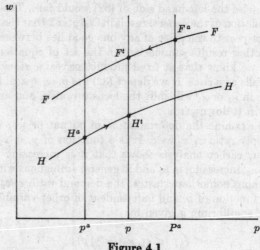

**Figure 4.1**

In the two-good case, we know that in free trade in goods, the equilibrium relative price of goods must settle somewhere between the two countries' autarky levels. Suppose that $p$ as shown is the free trade price of good 1 in terms of good 2. The two countries' trade equilibrium points can then be read off as the intersections of the vertical line at $p$ and their respective factor market equilibrium loci, i.e. the points $H^t$ and $F^t$ as shown.

When trade commences, therefore, the home country's equilibrium point in $(p, w)$ space moves from $H^a$ to $H^t$, and the foreign country's from $F^a$ to $F^t$. It can be said that trade has brought the prices of the mobile factor closer together.

However, this need not always be so. Figure 4.2 shows a case where the two countries differ only in the foreign country having more $\kappa_1$. The locus $FF$ is still above $HH$, but the ranking of the autarky product prices is reversed. In this case, trade pushes the prices of the mobile factor further apart.

Perhaps even more surprising is the case shown in Figure 4.3. Here the foreign country has more of the mobile factor than the home country, the amounts of the specific factors being equal in the two. Thus $FF$ lies below $HH$. Further, it is easy to have cases where the supply ratio is independent of $v$; this happens, for example, if the production functions in the two sectors are both Cobb–Douglas with equal elasticities with respect to the mobile factor employed there. In such a case, the two countries will have equal

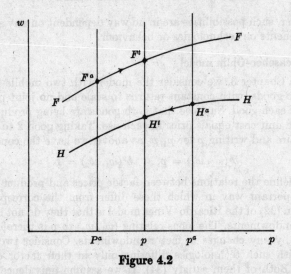

**Figure 4.2**

autarky relative prices, and the free trade price must also have the same value, i.e. there will be no trade in goods even when it is allowed. Thus the opening of trade will have no effect on factor prices.

The conclusion must be that in the Ricardo–Viner model, any kind of change in factor prices as a result of trade is conceivable.

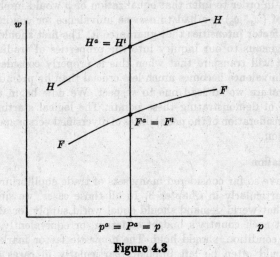

**Figure 4.3**

Moreover, such possibilities are in no way dependent on any strange requirements on technologies or behaviour.

### The Heckscher–Ohlin model

As in Chapter 3, we consider the model with two mobile factors and two goods, with constant returns to scale and no joint production for each good. Suppose that both goods are being produced, so that the unit cost equals price in each use. Taking good 2 to be the numeraire and writing $p$ for $p_1/p_2$ as above, we have the conditions

$$b^1(w_1, w_2) = p, \qquad b^2(w_1, w_2) = 1 \qquad (34)$$

These define the relations between factor prices and product prices. The important way in which these differ from the corresponding equation (32) of the Ricardo–Viner model is that they do not involve factor endowments. The locus relating $(w_1, w_2)$ to $p$ is therefore not shifted by any changes in factor endowments. Consider two countries with such technologies differing only in their factor endowments. Both of them satisfy (34). If we assume univalence, trade between them, by equalizing $p$, will equalize $(w_1, w_2)$. There will be *complete* equalization of factor prices.

The difference between the two models is further explored and placed in the context of the history of the subject by Samuelson (1971). We do not pursue it further for reasons which should by now be obvious. In order to write (34), we had to *assume* that both goods were being produced in positive quantities, i.e. diversification. Further, in order to infer that equalization of $p$ would imply equalization of $(w_1, w_2)$, we had to *assume* univalence, or conditions on relative factor intensities that guarantee it. The first should clearly be endogenous to our inquiry into the properties of trading equilibria. It will transpire that when this is properly considered, the role of univalence becomes much less crucial than its prominence in the literature would lead one to suspect. We now begin the programme of demonstrating these points. The logical starting point is the consideration of the possibilities of diversified versus specialized production.

### Specialization

We have so far considered many sets of trade equilibrium conditions, particularly in Chapter 3. In all those cases, we simply required that world demand should equal world supply for all goods, and that each country's budget equation, or equivalently a trade balance condition, should hold. The domestic factor market equilibria could often be left implicit, particularly in cases of fixed endowments. Therefore we did not worry about domestic factor demands and prices too much. In doing so, however, we begged a number of questions. In particular, we did not consider the possibility that the equilibrium could involve some measure of production specialization in the countries. Nor did we consider the possibility that supply functions might not be single-valued, i.e. that an individual country's supply might be indeterminate. Both problems were mentioned, and they must be allowed in the present context since they turn out to be of considerable importance for the question of factor prices. Therefore we must consider a more complete description of simultaneous equilibrium in international product markets and domestic factor markets. We shall retain some simplifications: we shall assume that each good is produced in at least one of the countries, that there are no free goods and that all available factors are fully employed in both countries. Constant returns to scale and non-jointness prevail in production.

The only complications are therefore the ones in which we are interested, namely that there might be some production specialization and that output choices might not be unique. Accordingly, we write equilibrium conditions in a form that allows these possibilities. The usual rules of general equilibrium under constant returns to scale apply: pure profit is ruled out, any good produced in positive quantity has price equal to unit cost, and any good for which unit cost exceeds price is not produced. For the home country, for example, for each $j$, we must have

$$b^j(w) \geq p_j \quad \text{and} \quad x_j \geq 0$$

with at least one equality. We shall denote this by

$$b(w) \geq p, \quad x \geq 0 \quad \text{with complementary slackness}$$

the last phrase indicating that of each pair of component inequalities, not both can be slack (i.e. hold as strict inequalities).

The input coefficient matrix can be expressed in terms of $w$ as $a(w) = b_w(w)^T$, i.e. $a_{ij} = \partial b^j / \partial w_i$. The factor requirements for an output vector $x$ are then $a(w)x$.

The factors located in the home country will be owned by consumers indexed by $h$ in amounts $v^h$. They will have incomes $y^h = w . v^h$ and demand functions $d^h(p, y^h)$. At this stage nothing needs to be assumed about these beyond homogeneity, continuity and Walras's law.

As usual, all the variables and functions pertaining to the foreign country, where they are distinct from those for the home country, will be denoted by the corresponding upper case letters. With this set-up, we have the following equilibrium conditions: for brevity we shall refer to them collectively as $(T)$.

For production equilibrium in the two countries,

$$b(w) \geq p, \qquad x \geq 0 \qquad \text{with complementary slackness} \qquad (35)$$

$$b(W) \geq p, \qquad X \geq 0 \qquad \text{with complementary slackness} \qquad (36)$$

For factor market equilibrium in the two countries,

$$a(w)x = v \tag{37}$$

$$a(W)X = V \tag{38}$$

For output market equilibrium in the world,

$$x + X = \sum_h d^h(p, w.v^h) + \sum_H D^H(p, W.V^H) \tag{39}$$

As an informal check, note that $(T)$ comprises $3n + 2m$ equations, where $n$ is the number of goods and $m$ that of factors. (Each component pair in (35) and (36) contributes one equation.) We have the same number of unknowns, viz. the components of $p$, $w$, $W$, $x$, and $X$. With the usual deduction of one unknown to reflect the choice of normalization and of one equation made redundant by Walras's Law, we have a determinate system. The standard rigorous existence proofs apply, so we do not need to worry about that. In fact, to avoid tedious qualifying statements that are not of primary interest, we shall assume equilibrium prices to be unique.

## Factor prices and factor mobility

The question of factor price equalization is: under what conditions will the solution to $(T)$ have the property that $w = W$? We shall approach this through the back door, stipulating such a solution and seeing what it entails. This will provide suggestions for completing the reverse chain of reasoning that really interests us.

Let $\hat{w}$ be the common factor price vector in such an assumed equilibrium. Since all goods are produced somewhere, the appropriate selection from (35) and (36) determines all output prices as $\hat{p} = b(\hat{w})$. We can substitute this in the demand functions and express world demand as a function of the common factor prices alone, say $\hat{d}(\hat{w})$. Since we shall keep factor ownerships by consumers fixed throughout there is no need to mention them explicitly. Let $\hat{x}$ denote the world output vector. Then we have

$$b(\hat{w}) = \hat{p} \tag{40}$$

$$a(\hat{w})\hat{x} = v + V \tag{41}$$

$$\hat{x} = \hat{d}(\hat{w}) \tag{42}$$

Of these, (40) and (42) are clear; (41) is obtained by adding (37) and
(38). Call this set $(\hat{T})$. It is immediate that these are the equations
of equilibrium for a *fully integrated world economy* i.e. one in which
*factors as well as goods are mobile*: (40) are just the zero pure profit
conditions, written as price–cost equations since all goods are produced somewhere, and (41) and (42) are respectively conditions for
clearance of the world factor and goods markets. In other words,
we have shown that any equilibrium of trade in which factors are
immobile but factor prices happen to be equalized must be an
equilibrium of trade where the factors can move as well.

Incidentally, this result provides a formal demonstration that if
trade in goods happens to equalize factor prices, nothing further
remains to be gained by allowing factor mobility as well. All the
benefits to international production possibilities that could be
conceived from reallocation of factors are in fact secured through
the trade in goods.

The reverse argument should now be clear. Suppose we calculate
the equilibrium $\hat{w}$, $\hat{p}$, and $\hat{x}$ for $(\hat{T})$, the fully integrated case with
factors as well as goods mobile. This ensures satisfaction of the
first parts of (35) and (36). Any split $\hat{x} = x + X$ into non-negative
parts also satisfies (39). It remains to be seen if such a split is possible
satisfying (37) and (38). The answer is also obvious: this will be
possible if and only if the equations

$$a(\hat{w})x = v, \qquad 0 \leq x \leq \hat{x} \qquad (43)$$

have a solution in $x$. If they do, we only have to set $X = \hat{x} - x$.
Conversely if (37) and (38) can be satisfied with $w = \hat{w}$ and non-
negative $x$ and $X$, then $x = \hat{x} - X \leq \hat{x}$, so (43) is satisfied.

We have shown the following. Let $\hat{w}$, $\hat{p}$, and $\hat{x}$ denote solutions to
the fully integrated equilibrium $(\hat{T})$. If (43) has a solution, then a
trade equilibrium with goods mobile and factors immobile exists,
having goods prices $\hat{p}$, common factor prices $\hat{w}$, and production
levels $x$ and $X = \hat{x} - x$ in the two countries. If (43) has no solution,
then factor price equalization is ruled out.

With this background, we can formulate the question of the
'likelihood' of factor price equalization as follows. Consider a collection of two-country world economies, all with the same total
factor endowment $\hat{v}$, the same division of this total among the
owner-consumers, and consequently the same aggregate demand
functions. Only the location of the factors as regards production
in the two countries, i.e. the split of the given $\hat{v}$ into $v + V$, differs
for different economies in our collection. Then the collection can be
shown geometrically by means of an $m$-dimensional rectilinear box,

with the lengths of its sides given by the components of $\hat{v}$. The point $v$ in this box represents an economy where the vector $v$ of factors engages in production in the home country, and $V = \hat{v} - v$ in the foreign country. Calculate the fully integrated equilibrium, for which of course the split of $\hat{v}$ is immaterial. Assume that both the prices $(\hat{w}, \hat{p})$ and the world outputs $\hat{x}$ in this equilibrium are unique. Let $a(\hat{w})$ be the corresponding input coefficient matrix. Define the set

$$\mathscr{V} = \{v \mid v = a(\hat{w})x, 0 \le x \le \hat{x}\} \tag{44}$$

For all of the economies from our collection lying in $\mathscr{V}$, there will be an equilibrium with equal factor prices even when only the goods are mobile. For points of the box outside $\mathscr{V}$, there will not. The likelihood of factor price equalization can therefore be measured as the size of $\mathscr{V}$ relative to the box.

Note that in our collection, the physical location with respect to production of a factor does not directly affect the demand of a consumer who derives income from it. In other words, demands are specific to consumers, and not to the sources of their income as such. This is the standard procedure in micro-economic theory. However, in this respect our treatment differs from that of Uzawa (1959), who changes demands with the split $v + V$.

Secondly, our limited comparison can easily be extended to allow varying total factor supplies $\hat{v}$, and changing parameters of the demand functions. That simply makes a higher dimensional problem, of which our box and the set $\mathscr{V}$ are cross-sections perpendicular to the axes representing these other variables. Considerations such as whether $\mathscr{V}$ is of zero measure relative to the box are the basis for similar issues in the more general problem where such cross-sections are stacked on top of one another.

Finally, note that we do not say what actually happens in economies outside $\mathscr{V}$. This will depend on detailed properties of the technology and demands; we will consider some illustrative examples in the next section.

## 4. FACTOR PRICE EQUALIZATION

We begin by considering some general properties of the set $\mathscr{V}$ that yields equilibria with equal factor prices. First a trivial point. Since $\hat{v} = a(\hat{w}) \hat{x}$, for $0 \le \lambda \le 1$, $\lambda\hat{v} = a(\hat{w})(\lambda\hat{x})$ is in $\mathscr{V}$. This is the diagonal of our box. In other words, if the two countries have all factors in the same proportions, there will be factor price equalization.

To understand the structure of $\mathscr{V}$ in more detail, let $a^j(\hat{w})$ be the $j$th column of the matrix $a(\hat{w})$. This is an $m$-dimensional vector giving the unit factor requirements of the $j$th commodity in the fully integrated equilibrium. Then we can write

$$a(\hat{w})x = \sum_{j=1}^{n} a^j(\hat{w})x_j \qquad (45)$$

If we allowed $x$ to range over the whole $n$-dimensional space, (45) would yield all linear combinations of the columns $a^j(\hat{w})$. This is a subspace of $m$-dimensional real space, or at most all of it. Call it the subspace *spanned* by the $(a^j(\hat{w}))$. Since $\mathscr{V}$ is found from (45) as $x$ ranges over a more restricted $n$-dimensional set, it is a part of this subspace. Different possibilities arise, depending on the relative numbers of goods and factors.

## More factors than goods

If the number of factors $m$ exceeds the number of goods $n$, we have only $n$ columns in (45) and they can span at most an $n$-dimensional subspace of the totality of the factor endowment space. Since $\mathscr{V}$ is a part of this subspace, it is also at most $n$-dimensional. Relative to the $m$-dimensional box, it must have zero measure. In this sense, factor price equalization is unlikely. This applies to the Ricardo–Viner model, since it has $n$ goods, and $(n + 1)$ factors altogether including the specific ones. We shall return to the issue of factor prices in this model later, after some familiarity with the technique of using the box and the set $\mathscr{V}$ has been earned.

## Equal numbers of goods and factors

If the number of goods equals the number of factors, then the number of columns $a^j(\hat{w})$ equals the dimension of the factor space. The columns could be linearly dependent, and therefore span a smaller space. In the two-by-two case, this happens if $a_{11}/a_{12} = a_{21}/a_{22}$, which is the case of equal factor intensities. Linear dependence in the $n$-by-$n$ case is a simple generalization of this idea. If we rule it out as coincidental for general technologies, however, the columns will span the full space. Correspondingly, the set $\mathscr{V}$ will have the same dimension as the box, and will therefore have positive measure. Factor price equalization will not be unlikely, but its numerical probability will depend on details of the technology and the demand functions.

The two-by-two case will illustrate this. In Figure 4.4 we have the box $OB_1O'B_2O$ representing the given total factor endowments $\hat{v}$.

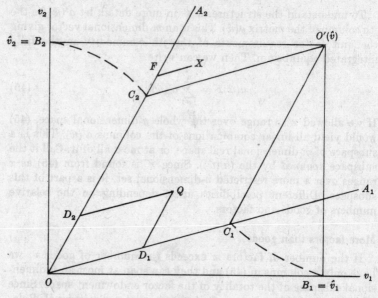

**Figure 4.4**

Having found the equilibrium factor prices $\hat{w}$ for the fully integrated world economy, we can show the rays $OA_1$ and $OA_2$ along which the factor input vectors of goods 1 and 2 must respectively lie. We know that the world factor endowment lies inside the cone defined by these rays, since the equilibrium entails a non-negative solution to (41). With full employment, the world factor use vector must be the whole of $\hat{v}$. Then we can mark off lengths $OC_1 = a^1(\hat{w})\hat{x}_1$ and $OC_2 = a^2(\hat{w})\hat{x}_2$ along the respective rays, representing the factor requirements for the equilibrium output levels of the two goods. Their vector sum is $0'$, i.e. $OC_1O'C_2O$ is a parallelogram. If $v$ is a point inside this, we can decompose it into components parallel to $OC_1$ and $OC_2$ which correspond to outputs in the home country between the limits of 0 and $\hat{x}$, leaving non-negative amounts to be produced in the foreign country with factors $V = \hat{v} - v$. At $Q$ shown in the figure, for example, we have components $OD_1 = \frac{1}{2}OC_1$ and $OD_2 = \frac{1}{3}OC_2$. With this share of the factors, therefore, the home country can produce half the world output of good 1 and. a third that of good 2, leaving the rest to the foreign country. This is not possible for points outside the parallelogram. At $X$, for example, we have $FX/OC_1$ times the world output of good 1, and $OF/OC_2$

times that of good 2. But $OF > OC_2$, so the home country with factor endowment at $X$ would have to produce more than the entire world demand for good 2, leaving a negative amount to the foreign country. This is not a feasible decomposition of the integrated equilibrium into separate country equilibria. The same conclusion can be verified for any other point outside the parallelogram. In other words, the parallelogram is the set $\mathscr{V}$ in this case. For home factor endowments measured relative to $O$ (and, if desired, foreign factor endowments simultaneously shown relative to $O'$) lying inside this parallelogram, we will have factor price equalization. Outside it, we will not.

It may seem strange that we have said nothing about factor intensity reversals in this context, since much of the literature on factor price equalization in the $n$-by-$n$ case is concerned with this issue in its relation to univalence. However, by posing the question as we have done, we have been able to side-step the univalence problem. The usual approach assumes an equilibrium with diversification, and asks whether it will show equal factor prices. We have searched for the set of factor allocations that are consistent with factor price equalization *directly*, without going through an assumption of diversification. In fact we see that inside the parallelogram we have diversified production, i.e. positive outputs of both goods in each country, and on its boundaries one country just reaches specialization in one commodity. Whether there are other regions of the box where diversification is compatible with unequal factor prices is beside the point. If the univalence condition is not satisfied, as in the two-by-two case and when there are factor intensity reversals, there will be such regions, and we shall illustrate this in a moment. We believe that our direct approach has greater economic appeal. The univalence analysis which assumes diversification is thereby leaving an important endogenous aspect of the whole trade problem unanalysed, while it emerges as a part of our discussion starting from the basic data.

In order to be able to say what actually happens outside the factor price equalization region, we need more information concerning the technology and the demand functions. Even when the former does not pose problems like factor intensity reversals, the latter can make matters very complicated. However, in the case conventionally used by trade theorists, with identical homothetic tastes, as illustrated in Figure 4.4 there would be two symmetrically placed boundary curves, one joining $C_1$ to $B_1$ and the other joining $C_2$ to $B_2$. These would divide the portion of the box outside the parallelogram into four regions, all with unequal factor prices. In $OC_1B_1$

the home country would be producing only commodity 1, while the foreign country would produce both commodities. The reader can similarly infer the production patterns in the other regions.

Matters are much more complicated when there are factor intensity reversals, even when identical homothetic tastes are assumed. To make this point, we have computed all possible equilibria in a world with two goods and two factors, when there are fixed proportions in the production of one of the goods, and a unit elasticity of substitution for the other. The particular parametrization used has cost functions

$$b^1(w) = w_1^{1/2}w_2^{1/2}, \qquad b^2(w) = 2w_1 + w_2$$

Taking ratios of partial derivatives of these, the factor proportions used by the two goods can be written as

$$b_2^1/b_1^1 = w_1/w_2, \qquad b_2^2/b_1^2 = \tfrac{1}{2}.$$

Therefore the first good is more factor 1 intensive for $w_1/w_2 < \tfrac{1}{2}$, and more factor 2 intensive otherwise, i.e. factor intensity reversals are possible. Demands are homothetic, arising from a unit expenditure function

$$\bar{e}(p) = p_1^{1/2}p_2^{1/2}$$

Factor supplies for the world are $\hat{v}_1 = 1\cdot4$ and $\hat{v}_2 = 1$.

Figure 4.5 shows all possibilities. The parallelogram $A$ gives the allocations that have diversification and factor price equalization. Areas $B$ and $B'$ have diversification but unequal factor prices, and the remaining areas $C$, $C'$, $D$, $D'$ have specialization in one of the countries, and correspondingly unequal factor prices.

## More goods than factors

This last case is in many ways the most interesting, and one about which most misconceptions persist. The difficulty has been that the conventional approach, which concentrates on the price–cost equations, is not suited to handle the issues. On one hand, it might appear that we have too many equations, one for each good, in too few unknowns, the factor prices. This raises the danger of inconsistency. On the other hand, it might appear that, at fixed output prices, optimum production choices must involve specialization, thereby removing any guarantee that the two countries produce sufficiently many goods in common, which is the basis of the univalence discussions. The trouble with both these points is that no account is taken of the fact that the product price vector that is relevant to the discussion is the trade equilibrium one.

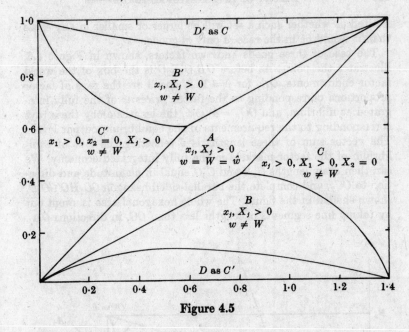

$D'$ as $C$

$B'$
$x_j, X_j > 0$
$w \neq W$

$C'$
$x_1 > 0, x_2 = 0, X_j > 0$
$w \neq W$

$A$
$x_j, X_j > 0$
$w = W = \hat{w}$

$C$
$x_j > 0, X_1 > 0, X_2 = 0$
$w \neq W$

$B$
$x_j, X_j > 0$
$w \neq W$

$D$ as $C'$

**Figure 4.5**

In an integrated world equilibrium with factors and goods mobile, provided only that all goods are essential in demand, all will be produced in positive quantities. The product price vector $\hat{p}$ and the factor price vector $\hat{w}$ corresponding to such an equilibrium therefore satisfy the condition $b(\hat{w}) = \hat{p}$. Thus there is no insurmountable obstacle to finding $m$ factor prices to satisfy $n$ equations even with $n > m$. Furthermore, at these prices, production of all goods exactly breaks even in both countries. Although one or the other might specialize, there is no reason why all goods should not be produced in both, if this is compatible with the clearing of factor markets in each. We have already verified that such compatibility exists provided the home factor endowments lie in the set $\mathcal{V}$. It remains to study the structure of it in more detail in the present case.

As we have posed the problem, with $n$ goods and $m$ factors and $n > m$, the $n$ columns $a^j(\hat{w})$ are in general capable of spanning the $m$-dimensional space. We can even allow some linear dependence among the columns; so long as some subset of $m$ of them is linearly independent, there is no problem. Assuming this, the set $\mathcal{V}$ is of full dimension in the box, i.e. factor price equalization is a non-trivial possibility. Moreover, dimensional considerations alone do not tell us whether such a set will be larger or smaller in any sense than it would be in the case of only $m$ goods.

The case of three goods and two factors, shown in Figure 4.6, illustrates the point. As before $OB_1O'B_2O$ is the box of the world factor endowments, $OA_j$ for $j = 1, 2$, and 3 are the rays of factor proportions corresponding to the factor prices $\hat{w}$ of the fully integrated equilibrium, and $OC_j = a^j(\hat{w})\hat{x}_j$ the lengths along these rays corresponding to the requirements of the equilibrium output levels. The vector sum of these lengths is $\hat{v}$ reflecting the fact of equilibrium of the factor markets in the fully integrated economy. We can then draw lengths $C_1H$ and $C_3G$ equal in magnitude and direction to $OC_2$, and complete the parallel-sided hexagon $OC_1HO'GC_3O$, shown shaded in the figure. The whole hexagonal area is swept out by taking line segments of lengths less than $OC_j$ in directions $OA_j$,

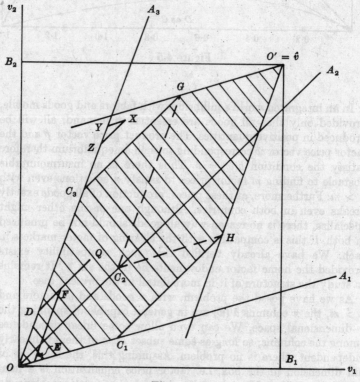

**Figure 4.6**

and taking the vector sum of these. In other words, the hexagon is just the set $\mathscr{V}$ for this case. To put this the other way around, any factor endowment $v$ inside the hexagon can be fully employed through a production plan $x$ in the range $0 \le x \le \hat{x}$, leaving $\hat{v} - v$ to be fully employed by $\hat{x} - x$. For example, the $Q$ shown can be fully employed through the production plan given by $ODQ$ involving production of goods 2 and 3 (and through a number of other plans, for example $OEFQ$ involving production of all three goods). On the other hand, any allocation outside the hexagon can be fully employed only by violating the constraint $0 \le x \le \hat{x}$. For example, consider the point $X$. If we try to produce goods 1 and 3 to employ the factor endowment represented by it, we will have to produce $YX/OC_1$ times the world demand for good 1 and $OY/OC_3$ times that for good 3. The latter exceeds unity, requiring the foreign country to produce a negative amount of that good. Thus a non-negative assignment of outputs to countries is not possible along these lines. If we try to employ $X$ in the home country producing goods 2 and 3, the home outputs relative to world demands will be the ratios $ZX/OC_2$ and $OZ/OC_3$; again the latter exceeds unity. Any attempt to employ $X$ through the production of all three goods will require the factor use in the production of good 3 to lie somewhere between $Y$ and $Z$; again that corresponds to an output level greater than the world demand for that good. Finally, $X$ cannot be employed through the production of goods 1 and 2 alone, since it does not lie in the cone spanned by $OA_1$ and $OA_2$. Readers can similarly verify the impossibility of non-negative assignments of goods to countries if the factor endowment point is anywhere outside the hexagon. Incidentally, it is easy to guess that with four goods and two factors the factor price equalization region will be an octagon, and in the general case of more goods than factors, it will be polyhedral.

In showing how a factor endowment inside our hexagon could be fully employed by a production plan inside the prescribed limits, we stumbled upon an important point: such a decomposition is in general not unique when there are more goods than factors. The basic point is that, of the $n$ column $a^j(\hat{w})$ in $m$-dimensional space, at most $m$ can be linearly independent. Even assuming maximal independence, some $(n - m)$ of them can be expressed in terms of the remaining $m$. For example, suppose

$$a^{m+1}(\hat{w}) = \sum_{j=1}^{m} \xi_j\, a^j(\hat{w})$$

Then $a(\hat{w})\xi = 0$, where $\xi$ is a vector with the first $m$ components $\xi_j$ found above, $\xi_{m+1} = -1$, and any remaining components zero.

Doing the same for the remaining columns, we find an $(n - m)$-dimensional space of vectors $\xi$ such that $a(\hat{w})\xi = 0$. If $x$ satisfies $a(\hat{w})x = v$, then, so does $x + \xi$ for any $\xi$ from this space. With $X = \hat{x} - x$ and $V = \hat{v} - v$, we need only change $X$ to $X - \xi$ to preserve $a(\hat{w})X = V$, the full employment condition in the foreign country, while maintaining the world output level at $\hat{x}$. Thus there are $(n - m)$ degrees of freedom in choosing the decomposition. We must not choose the magnitude of $\xi$ so large that some components of $x + \xi$ or $X - \xi$ become negative, and this may pose a one-sided constraint if some components of $x$ or $X$ are already zero. But subject to this caution, considerable freedom remains. It should be made clear that the ambiguity is in no way inconsistent with our assumption of uniqueness of equilibrium in the integrated economy: the world full employment condition (41) will have multiple solutions in $\hat{x}$, but only one of them will be assumed to be compatible with demand, i.e. (42). The situation is analogous to that of industry equilibrium under competition and constant returns to scale: industry output is uniquely determined by demand, but the output of any individual firm is indeterminate.

This means that it is impossible to predict the pattern of trade in the factor price equalization region with more goods than factors. We illustrate this using Figure 4.6. With factor endowments in the home country of $Q$, the home country's share of world production of good 2 can be anything from 0 to $DQ/OC_2 = \frac{1}{2}$. We have chosen $v_1 = \hat{v}_1/4$ and $v_2 = \hat{v}_2/3$ at $Q$. For illustration, take $\hat{v}_1 = \hat{v}_2 = 1$, and $\hat{w}_1 = 4$ and $\hat{w}_2 = 3$. Then the home country's share of world income will be $\frac{2}{7}$, and with homothetic identical preferences, this will also be its share of world demand for each good. Thus the home country's trade in good 2 can range from importing $\frac{2}{7}$ of world output to exporting $\frac{3}{14}$. Not only are the exact quantities of trade impossible to predict; so is the qualitative pattern of trade.

What happens outside the hexagon, when factor prices are not equalized, again depends on the specific demand and cost functions. In the simplest case of three goods and two factors with Cobb–Douglas cost and demand functions, however, the obvious first guess is valid. We show this in Figure 4.7. The hexagon of factor price equalization is $A$. When labels are chosen so that the relative factor 1 intensity decreases from good 1 to 2 to 3, regions $B$, $C$, and $D$ have partially specialized patterns of production as indicated, and $B'$, $C'$, and $D'$ the corresponding patterns with the country labels interchanged.

With factor intensity reversals, much more complicated patterns can arise. In particular, it is even possible to have regions where each

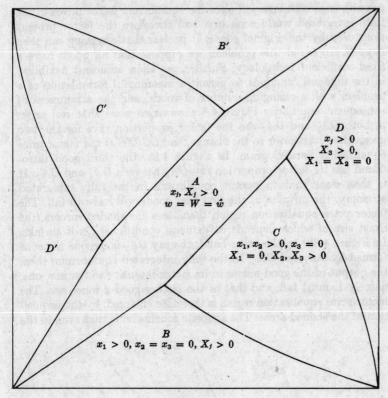

$$B'$$

$$C'$$

$$D$$
$$x_j > 0,$$
$$X_3 > 0,$$
$$X_1 = X_2 = 0$$

$$A$$
$$x_j, X_j > 0$$
$$w = W = \hat{w}$$

$$C$$
$$x_1, x_2 > 0, x_3 = 0$$
$$X_1 = 0, X_2, X_3 > 0$$

$$D'$$

$$B$$
$$x_1 > 0, x_2 = x_3 = 0, X_j > 0$$

**Figure 4.7**

country is producing positive amounts of all three goods, but factor prices differ. In such a case the ambiguity in production and trade patterns mentioned above will arise again. As a result, even outside the region of factor price equalization one cannot prove general theorems regarding trade patterns in a world with more goods than factors. In this sense, it appears that it is the factor price equalization hypothesis and not the factor abundance theory that is more robust when there are more goods than factors.

### Adding more goods

Finally, we consider starting with a case of equal numbers of goods and factors, and ask whether the introduction of another good will make factor price equalization more likely or less likely. In general, such a change will alter the equilibrium factor prices in the fully integrated world economy, and therefore the factor proportions used by the original goods. It is clear that anything can then happen. To avoid this problem, we suppose that all goods have a fixed-coefficient technology. Further, we allow sufficient flexibility in the demand functions to permit a meaningful formulation of a problem with a changing number of goods, and the attainment of subsequent equilibria. Figure 4.8 shows two cases that can arise; in both $OA_1$ and $OA_2$ are the factor proportion rays for the two goods that exist prior to the change, and $OC_1O'C_2O$ the factor price equalization parallelogram. In Figure 4.8a, the third good introduced has its factor proportion ray $OA_3$ between $OA_1$ and $OA_2$. It is then clear that to permit equilibrium in the fully integrated economy, the outputs of the first two goods will have to fall. The factor price equalization region then loses the shaded corners (the exact size of which depends on demand conditions) i.e. it shrinks. In Figure 4.8b, on the other hand, the ray $OA_3$ is outside the cone formed by $OA_1$ and $OA_2$. In the fully integrated equilibrium, then, the output of the good nearer in its factor intensity to the new one, namely 1, must fall, and that of the farther good 2 must rise. The factor price equalization region is therefore enlarged, by the acquisition of the shaded areas. The agnostic conclusion is that even in the

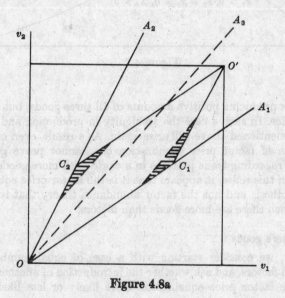

Figure 4.8a

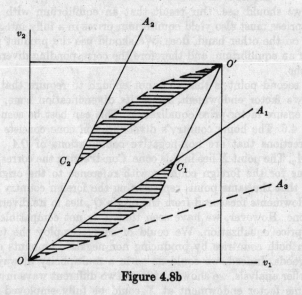

**Figure 4.8b**

case most favourable to the existence of a clear-cut result, we cannot say whether the introduction of additional goods will make factor-price equalization more likely or less likely, without specifying further details of the technologies.

## Relation to Diversification Cones

In Chapter 2, we referred to the work of McKenzie (1955), dealing with the question of whether the factor endowments of a country were compatible with the production of all goods in non-negative quantities when product prices were exogenously specified. An affirmative answer required the factor endowment to lie in a diversification cone, generated by the factor input vectors for all the goods. The construction of our factor-price equalization set $\mathscr{V}$ has involved some similar ideas, and we comment on the relation between this work and McKenzie's.

The first point is one that we have constantly emphasized, and it concerns the importance of regarding product prices as endogenous. We saw in a simple two-by-two example in Chapter 2 that the range of factor endowments compatible with diversified production shifts as product prices changes, i.e. the diversification cone depends on the product price vector. If we set out to analyse factor prices in two trading economies with given factor endowment, the conventional method would not tell us which of the possible diversification cones we should use. Our result that an equilibrium with equal factor prices must also yield equilibrium prices in a fully integrated world, on the other hand, does. We should use the product prices of such an equilibrium, and therefore the corresponding diversification cone.

The second point is that it is not enough to require that each country's factor endowment lies in its diversification cone, if we are to ensure factor-price equalization. This can best be seen from Figure 4.6. The home country's diversification cone consists of all the directions that are non-negative combinations of $OA_1$, $OA_2$, and $OA_3$. The point $X$ lies in this cone. Constructing the corresponding cone for the foreign country with reference to the origin $O'$, we see that the same point, representing the foreign country's factor endowments measured from the origin $O'$, lies in its diversification cone. However, we have seen that $X$ is not compatible with factor-price equalization. We could of course employ the factors fully in both countries by producing non-negative amounts of the three goods. Indeed, we could do so in a multiplicity of ways. In our earlier analysis, we showed at least two different ways in which the home factor endowment at $X$ could be fully employed while producing goods 1 and 3, or 2 and 3. Similar remarks apply to the foreign country. The problem is that such choices could not be compatible with the world demand for goods, which we can calculate from the fully integrated equilibrium. Those demands correspond to factor use vectors $OC_1$, $OC_2$, and $OC_3$, and we have seen that any home plan for using $X$ involves a greater production of good 3 than entailed by $OC_3$. Thus we must take into account the product market equilibrium requirements, as well as the factor proportion requirements of the diversification cones. It was the purpose of the analysis of Figure 4.6 to do precisely this, and the outcome was the hexagon of factor-price equalization, an area smaller than the diversification cone method would have led one to suppose.

### The Ricardo–Viner model

We have already mentioned that factor-price equalization is unlikely in the Ricardo–Viner model, since it has $n$ goods and $(n + 1)$ factors. However, the special structure of this model allows us to obtain some sharper results. It also serves to illustrate further uses of the geometric technique we have developed above.

Consider the two-good, three-factor case. The box of world factor endowments is now three-dimensional. Figure 4.9 gives a representation of it. The two countries' factor quantities are measured from the diagonally opposite corners $O$ and $O'$. The mobile factor is along

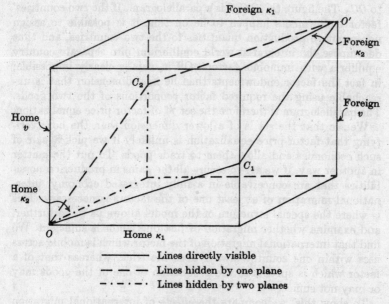

Lines directly visible
— — —  Lines hidden by one plane
— · — · —  Lines hidden by two planes

**Figure 4.9**

the vertical axis, the home quantity being measured upwards from $O$, and the foreign quantity downwards from $O'$. The factor specific to the production of good 1 is along the horizontal axis, with the home quantity to the right from $O$ and the foreign quantity to the left from $O'$. The factor specific to good 2 is in the third direction, extending backward from the page. The home quantity is measured going to the rear from $O$, the foreign quantity coming forward from $O'$.

Now suppose the prices and quantities in the equilibrium of the integrated world economy have been computed. The factor use vector for good 1, relative to the origin $O$, must lie entirely in the front face of the box: by definition, good 1 uses none of the specific factor 2. Similarly, that for good 2 must lie entirely along the left face. The output of good 1 must be such that the total factor requirement in its production is $OC_1$, where $C_1$ is the point at which its factor proportion direction meets the right edge of the front face, in order to ensure full employment of the first specific factor. Similarly, if $C_2$ is the point where the factor proportions direction for good 2 meets the rear edge of the left face, $OC_2$ gives the total factor employment in the production of good 2. Then $C_2O'$ is parallel and equal in length to $OC_1$, while $C_1O'$ stands in the same relation

to $OC_2$. The figure $OC_1O'C_2O$ is a parallelogram. If the two countries'
factor endowments happen to lie on this, it is possible to assign
non-negative production quantities to the two countries, and thus
decompose the integrated world equilibrium into separate country
equilibria with immobile factors. Off it, this is clearly impossible;
in fact the factor endowments then lie in a dimension that is un-
reachable using the required factor proportions of the two goods.
The parallelogram is therefore the set $\mathcal{V}$ of factor-price equalization.

We see that the set is of a lower dimension than the box, veri-
fying that factor-price equalization is unlikely if we pick a pair of
such economies and allow them to trade goods. To put the matter
in another way, if we are to secure all the gains in production possibilities that are conceivable in a fully integrated economy, international migration of at least one of the factors is necessary. This
is where the special structure of the model allows us to go further,
and examine whether migration of just one factor is sufficient. We
find that international migration of the factor which is mobile across
uses within one country always does the trick, whereas that of a
factor which is specific to the production of one of the goods may
or may not suffice.

To show this, we compare the effects of international migration
of the mobile factor with that of the first specific factor, while
holding the two countries' quantities of the second specific factor
unchanged. To do this, we must take a cross-section of the box in

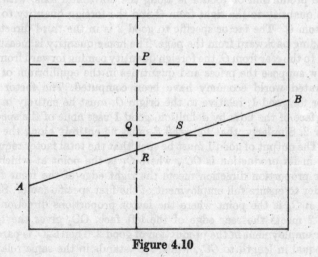

**Figure 4.10**

Figure 4.9, passing through the particular initial point, and perpendicular to the axis of the second specific factor, i.e. parallel to the plane of the paper. Figure 4.10 shows such a section, taken about a third of the way down, i.e. from an initial point where the foreign country has about twice as much of the second specific factor as the home country. The trace of the factor-price equalization parallelogram on this section is the line $AB$. Let $P$ be the initial point. International migration of the mobile factor would correspond to vertical movements from $P$, while that of the first specific factor would be captured by horizontal movements. We see that the former can place the two countries on the line $AB$, and thus equate factor prices, while the latter cannot. If the initial point had been $Q$ instead, we see that migration of either factor would have sufficed. The two types of migration would lead to different points on $AB$, with migration of the mobile factor giving $R$ and that of the first specific factor giving $S$. But this merely corresponds to different assignments of production in the two countries, all prices and total output quantities remain those of the fully integrated equilibrium at both points.

# NOTES

This chapter continues and deepens the discussion of matters introduced in Chapter 1, and the works cited there are also relevant here. Only a few additions need be mentioned specifically.

Chipman (1965a, b) discusses production and trade patterns with identical homothetic tastes under different conditions of technology. He points to the difficulties in obtaining generally valid results on the details of trade equilibria, but does not consider the possibility of results in the form of revealed preference correlations.

On factor price equalization in a complete general equilibrium of trading countries, the most important contribution is clearly that of Samuelson (1953). He saw through the whole problem, and we think that if he had filled out some of the asides and terse remarks he makes, he would have developed the argument much as we have done here. Uzawa (1959) also considered the whole equilibrium, but as noted in the text, he treated demand in a way which seems to us contrary to micro-economic practice.

The question of the relative likelihood of factor price equalization with different numbers of goods and factors is discussed in a vague way by many people: see Chipman (1966) for a summary. Land (1959) and Johnson (1967) develop more specific models, but do not consider a full general equilibrium. The case of three goods and two factors is considered by Melvin (1968), who does point out the importance of determining product prices endogenously. Factor prices in the Ricardo–Viner model are discussed by Samuelson (1971) and Dixit and Norman (1979).

# CHAPTER 5

# COMPARATIVE STATICS

A number of important questions regarding international trade relate to the effects of changes in the parameters that determine equilibrium prices. Is it necessarily true that a transfer of goods leads to higher welfare for the recipient country? Or could a transfer lead to a deterioration in the recipient's terms of trade sufficient to offset the direct gain from the transfer? Is it necessarily to the advantage of a country to get better production technology, or could this induce terms of trade changes making the country worse off? Is economic growth, in the sense of growth in factor endowments, to the advantage of a country, or is so-called immiserizing growth possible? Is economic growth in one country to the advantage of other countries? Is it to the advantage of both countries to move a factor from a country where its marginal productivity is low to a country where its marginal productivity is higher? To show how answers to such questions can be provided, we must show how parameter changes affect equilibrium prices and utility levels. That is what we do in this chapter. The method is the standard microeconomic one: We take total differentials of the equilibrium equations and solve for changes in prices and utility levels. It will be seen that the formulations adopted in Chapters 2 and 3 make this task much simpler than one might expect.

To avoid unnecessary complications, we shall stick to the simplest version of the catalogue of models set out in Chapter 3. In other words, we shall stick to a model with one consumer in each country, with inelastic factor supplies, and with no non-traded goods. Generalizations follow the lines indicated in that chapter, and are usually left to the reader. Even within our simple framework, it turns out that there are very few clear results. Often, however, one can derive specific results for the case of two goods, and these specific results can serve to illustrate the principle involved in the general formulae. For each change that we consider, therefore, we first look at the general case, and then interpret this in terms of the two-good example. We should stress, however, that one should avoid drawing general conclusions from the two-good results. The moral, if any, in this chapter is that one cannot say much about the

127

general equilibrium effects of changes in parameters without knowing the exact values of the parameters and the exact characteristics of demand and supply functions. If the theory is to be applied, therefore, it should be done by putting numerical values into the general formulae; not by applying qualitative results from the two-good case directly.

We begin by considering the simplest problem, namely the transfer of commodities from one country to another. This also provides a useful easy setting to introduce some general issues such as the normalization of prices. Moreover, some of the conditions governing the effects of a transfer prove useful later, when we discuss effects of changes in factor supplies and technology (sections 2 and 3), and when we look at the implications of factor movements (section 4). In section 5 we consider the question of how trade taxes (tariffs) affect equilibrium prices and utility levels. In section 6 we depart from the assumption of one-consumer economies to look at some effects of trade taxes on income distribution. The final section introduces intermediate inputs explicitly, and examines the concept of effective protection.

Throughout, we shall make the important simplification of assuming that the revenue functions are differentiable with respect to prices, i.e. that the output vectors in each country are uniquely determined. If that is not so, we know that a range of output vectors solves the problem of revenue maximization, but only one extreme point of the range will do if we want to estimate the first-order change in revenue as prices change, and a different selection is needed for different price changes. Since there is no reason why the actual level of production should coincide with such extreme points, we would have to work with inequalities for revenue changes in doing comparative statics. Further difficulties would arise for factor movements, when we need the second-order derivatives $r_{pv}$ and $R_{PV}$. Fortunately, we can argue that the problem of indeterminacy of output was seen to arise with more goods than factors in the region of factor price equalization, where the question of factor movements between countries loses much of its interest.

## 1. TRANSFER OF GOODS

The model we shall consider is the one set out in Chapter 3, section 3. We recall that the equilibrium in this model is given by

$$e(p, u) = r(p, v)$$
$$E(P, U) = R(P, V)$$
$$e_p(p, u) + E_P(P, U) - r_p(p, v) - R_P(P, V) = 0$$

In the absence of any trade taxes, $p$ is proportional to $P$, but the two can be independently normalized by separate choices of units of account in the two countries. For the present purpose, it is simplest to choose a common normalization. To simplify the accompanying notation, we adopt the following practice: Let the total number of goods be $(n + 1)$. Select one good and label it 0; this will be the numeraire in both countries. Let $p$ and $P$ be the respective price vectors in the home and foreign country for goods $1, 2, \ldots, n$. Thus the full price vectors are $(1, p)$ and $(1, P)$, and in the absence of any trade taxes, we have $p = P$. Indicate the derivatives with respect to the price of good 0 by a subscript 0 (if desired this can be interpreted as an equiproportionate opposite change in the prices of all other goods), and the vector of derivatives with respect to the other prices by the subscript $p$ or $P$ as appropriate. Then we can rewrite the equilibrium conditions as

$$e(1, p, u) = r(1, p, v) \tag{1}$$

$$E(1, P, U) = R(1, P, V) \tag{2}$$

$$e_0 + E_0 - r_0 - R_0 = 0 \tag{3}$$

$$e_p + E_P - r_p - R_P = 0 \tag{4}$$

The arguments of the functions in (3) and (4) are omitted for brevity. By Walras's law, one market-clearing condition can be derived from the rest and is therefore redundant; of course, we drop the one for the numeraire. In the absence of trade taxes, $p = P$, and as a quick check we have in (1), (2), and (4) just the right number of equations, $(n + 2)$, to determine the $n$ relative prices and the two utility levels.

### Effects of a transfer

Now suppose the foreign country transfers a vector $(g_0, g)$ of goods as a gift to the home country. Since this is a competitive trade model, we can regard the home country as placing these on the market and buying back whatever it wishes. Accordingly, we change (1) to

$$e(1, p, u) = r(1, p, v) + g_0 + p \cdot g \tag{5}$$

and (2) to

$$E(1, P, U) = R(1, P, V) - g_0 - P \cdot g \tag{6}$$

The vector of imports of the non-numeraire goods for the home country is $m = e_p - r_p - g$, and the corresponding import vector for the other country is $M = E_P - R_P + g$. Of course, we have $(m + M) = 0$ by (4).

Take total differentials in (4), (5), and (6). Since $P = p$, we have $dP = dp$, and according to our established 'imperial' convention we use only the latter. From (5) we find

$$e_p . dp + e_u \, du = r_p . dp + dg_0 + p . dg + g . dp$$

so using $m = e_p - r_p - g$, we have

$$m . dp + e_u \, du = d\xi \tag{7}$$

where $d\xi = dg_0 + p . dg$ is the value of the incremental physical transfer at the initial equilibrium prices. We take this to be positive, so the home country is the recipient at the margin. Similarly, from (6) we can write

$$M . dp + E_U \, dU = -d\xi \tag{8}$$

Finally, we differentiate (4) to obtain

$$(e_{pp} + E_{PP} - r_{pp} - R_{PP}) \, dp + e_{pu} \, du + E_{PU} \, dU = 0$$

or

$$S \, dp + e_{pu} \, du + E_{PU} \, dU = 0 \tag{9}$$

where

$$S = e_{pp} + E_{PP} - r_{pp} - R_{PP} \tag{10}$$

is the matrix of derivatives of the compensated world excess demands for the non-numeraire goods with respect to the non-numeraire prices. The corresponding matrix including the numeraire would be negative semi-definite. So will (10). If there is some substitutability in demand or production between the numeraire good and other goods, however, (10) will be negative definite. To see that, consider the two-good case. $S$ is then simply the own compensated price derivative of the excess demand for good 1, so it is a scalar. We know that $e_{pp}$ must be non-positive. Moreover, if there is any degree of substitutability between good 1 and the numeraire, the compensated cross-price derivative $e_{p0}$ will be strictly positive. But compensated demands are homogeneous of degree zero in all prices, so $e_{pp}p = -e_{p0}$. If $e_{p0}$ is strictly positive, therefore, $e_{pp}$ must be strictly negative. The same goes for $E_{PP}$, and similar arguments can be made for $r_{pp}$ and $R_{PP}$. With substitutability somewhere, $S$ will be strictly negative; or, in the many-goods case, negative definite. We take that to be the case.

We can then use (7), (8), and (9) to solve for $dp$, $du$, and $dU$. We have

$$dp = -S^{-1}e_{pu}\,du - S^{-1}E_{PU}\,dU \qquad (11)$$

Substituting in (7) and (8), and using $M = -m$, we therefore get

$$-m.S^{-1}e_{pu}\,du - m.S^{-1}E_{PU}\,dU + e_u\,du = d\xi$$

$$m.S^{-1}e_{pu}\,du + m.S^{-1}E_{PU}\,dU + E_U\,dU = -d\xi$$

These can be simplified by noting that $e_p = c$, the home demand vector, and therefore $e_{pu} = c_u = c_y y_u = c_y e_u$ where $y$ is an abbreviation for money income. Similarly for the foreign country $E_{PU} = C_Y E_U$. Then we can collect terms and write in matrix form

$$\begin{bmatrix} 1 - m.S^{-1}c_y & -m.S^{-1}C_Y \\ m.S^{-1}c_y & 1 + m.S^{-1}C_Y \end{bmatrix} \begin{bmatrix} e_u\,du \\ E_U\,dU \end{bmatrix} = \begin{bmatrix} d\xi \\ -d\xi \end{bmatrix} \qquad (12)$$

The determinant of the matrix on the left-hand side will be denoted by $D$. It is easy to check that

$$D = 1 + m.S^{-1}(C_Y - c_y) \qquad (13)$$

and then

$$\begin{bmatrix} e_u\,du \\ E_U\,dU \end{bmatrix} = \frac{1}{D} \begin{bmatrix} 1 + m.S^{-1}C_Y & m.S^{-1}C_Y \\ -m.S^{-1}c_y & 1 - m.S^{-1}c_y \end{bmatrix} \begin{bmatrix} d\xi \\ -d\xi \end{bmatrix}$$

which simplifies to

$$\begin{bmatrix} e_u\,du \\ E_U\,dU \end{bmatrix} = \frac{1}{D} \begin{bmatrix} d\xi \\ -d\xi \end{bmatrix} \qquad (14)$$

In other words, the recipient benefits from the transfer (and the donor loses so far as the utility from consumption is concerned, leaving out any satisfaction from the act of the transfer itself) if and only if $D$ is positive.

This is essentially a stability condition. To see this in its simplest setting, suppose there are only two goods, so $S$ is simply a negative scalar. Then $D$ is positive if and only if

$$S + m(C_Y - c_y) < 0$$

or, written out in full with prices and quantities pertaining to commodity 1,

$$\left\{ \frac{\partial c}{\partial p}\bigg|_{u\,\text{const}} - \frac{\partial x}{\partial p} \right\} - (c - x)\frac{\partial c}{\partial y}$$

$$+ \left\{ \frac{\partial C}{\partial P}\bigg|_{U\,\text{const}} - \frac{\partial X}{\partial P} \right\} - (C - X)\frac{\partial C}{\partial Y} < 0$$

This is just the price derivative of the world market excess demand for the non-numeraire commodity, and in a two-commodity world this is the condition for Walrasian stability of the equilibrium.

We can substitute (14) back in (11) to find the price change

$$\mathrm{d}p = S^{-1}(C_Y - c_y)\,\mathrm{d}\xi/D.$$

This is not of great interest on its own. More useful is the question of the terms of trade. In a model with many commodities, we must interpret this carefully. The general idea is that terms of trade improve if the world prices of exports go up relative to those of imports. The natural generalization with many commodities is to form a price index, with net exports as the weights. Thus terms of trade for the home country improve if $-m.\mathrm{d}p$ is positive, and they deteriorate if this is negative. We can note that this is a straightforward application of the general notion of compensation for price changes: A consumer is better off in the face of a slight change in the price vector if, and only if, his initial consumption bundle is cheaper at the new prices than at the old. Similarly, a country's terms of trade have improved if the initial import vector ($m$) is cheaper at the new prices than at the old—i.e. if $m.\mathrm{d}p$ is negative.

We see that

$$-m.\mathrm{d}p = \frac{-m.S^{-1}(C_Y - c_y)}{1 + m.S^{-1}(C_Y - c_y)}\,\mathrm{d}\xi \tag{15}$$

Assuming the condition for the transfer to be beneficial to the recipient, terms of trade will improve for this country if

$$m.S^{-1}(C_Y - c_y) < 0$$

In the two-good case, where $S$ is a negative number, this is a simple comparison of income effects: $m(C_Y - c_y) > 0$. Thus, if the home country is a net importer of the non-numeraire commodity, its terms of trade improve if it has a smaller marginal propensity to spend on this commodity. This makes obvious economic sense: At unchanged terms of trade, the transfer of purchasing power leads to a smaller *increase* in demand for the non-numeraire good in the home country than the corresponding *decrease* in demand in the rest of the world. Thus, world demand should fall. Provided the appropriate stability conditions are satisfied, therefore, the world price of the non-numeraire good should fall if the marginal propensity to spend on that good is lower at home than abroad. Clearly, then, the terms of trade will improve for the home country if it imports the non-numeraire commodity.

This whole discussion was carried out assuming that there were no trade taxes or other distortions affecting trade. However, a generalization in this regard is in principle not difficult. We have deliberately set up the basic system (1), (2), and (4) in such a way that any prescribed difference between $p$ and $P$ due to tariffs or other distortions can be appended as an extra set of equations. We can then proceed as before, now maintaining the necessary distinction between $dp$ and $dP$. This is left as an exercise for interested readers.

## 2. FACTOR SUPPLY CHANGES

Now suppose the initial equilibrium as described by (1), (2), and (4) above is disturbed by an exogenous change in the factor endowment of the home country. This has repercussions on prices and utilities; in particular we have the possibility that an adverse shift in the terms of trade will outweigh the benefit from added output potential and leave the home country worse off, well known as the case of immiserizing growth. We investigate this general issue by comparative static methods, and extend the usual diagrammatic analyses by considering the whole world equilibrium and not just one country's transformation locus.

When $v$ changes by $dv$, total differentials of (1), (2), and (4) are

$$e_p.dp + e_u\,du = r_p.dp + r_v.dv$$
$$E_P.dP + E_U\,dU = R_P.dP$$

and

$$e_{pp}\,dp + e_{pu}\,du + E_{PP}\,dP + E_{PU}\,dU$$
$$- r_{pp}\,dp - r_{pv}\,dv - R_{PP}\,dP = 0.$$

Note that the vectors of non-numeraire imports are $m = e_p - r_p$ and $M = E_P - R_P$, with $m + M = 0$, and that $dP = dp$. Then defining $S$ as in the previous section, we have

$$m.dp + e_u\,du = r_v.dv \qquad (16)$$

$$M.dp + E_U\,dU = 0 \qquad (17)$$

$$S\,dp + e_{pu}\,du + E_{PU}\,dU = r_{pv}\,dv \qquad (18)$$

These are similar to (7), (8), and (9), differing only in the right-hand sides, and we solve them by similar methods. Writing

$$dp = -S^{-1}e_{pu}\,du - S^{-1}E_{PU}\,dU + S^{-1}r_{pv}\,dv$$

substituting in (16) and (17) and collecting terms, we have the matrix form

$$\begin{bmatrix} 1 - m.S^{-1}c_y & -m.S^{-1}C_Y \\ m.S^{-1}c_y & 1 + m.S^{-1}C_Y \end{bmatrix} \begin{bmatrix} e_u \, du \\ E_U \, dU \end{bmatrix} = \begin{bmatrix} r_v.dv - m.S^{-1}r_{pv}dv \\ m.S^{-1}r_{pv} \, dv \end{bmatrix}$$

yielding the solution

$$\begin{bmatrix} e_u \, du \\ E_U \, dU \end{bmatrix} = \frac{1}{D} \begin{bmatrix} 1 + m.S^{-1}C_Y & m.S^{-1}C_Y \\ -m.S^{-1}c_y & 1 - m.S^{-1}c_y \end{bmatrix}$$

$$\times \begin{bmatrix} r_v.dv - m.S^{-1}r_{pv} \, dv \\ m.S^{-1}r_{pv} \, dv \end{bmatrix}$$

which simplifies to

$$\begin{bmatrix} e_u \, du \\ E_U \, dU \end{bmatrix} = \frac{1}{D} \begin{bmatrix} (1 + m.S^{-1}C_Y)r_v.dv - m.S^{-1}r_{pv} \, dv \\ (-m.S^{-1}c_y)r_v.dv + m.S^{-1}r_{pv} \, dv \end{bmatrix} \tag{19}$$

## Effects on the home country

Assume $D > 0$, the condition for a goods transfer to be beneficial to the recipient. Then from (19) the home country gains from the change in its factor endowment if

$$(1 + m.S^{-1}C_Y)r_v.dv - m.S^{-1}r_{pv} \, dv > 0 \tag{20}$$

To see what this involves, consider the case of two goods, and let the endowment of just one factor increase. $r_v \neq w$ is the price of that factor, and $r_{pv} = (\partial w/\partial p)$ is the Stolper–Samuelson effect on the price of that factor of a change in the price of the non-numeraire good, so $r_{pv}$ is positive if the non-numeraire good uses the factor in question intensively. As $S$ is a scalar in the two-good case, we can multiply through (20) by $S$, recalling that $S$ is negative. We can then write (20) as

$$\{(S + mC_Y)w - m(\partial w/\partial p)\} \, dv < 0$$

so an increase in the endowment of a factor is beneficial to the home country if the term in parentheses is negative. But we can note that $m = -M$, so

$$(S + mC_Y) = S - MC_Y$$

$$= E_{PP} - R_{PP} - MC_Y + e_{pp} - r_{pp}$$

$$= (E_{PP} - R_{PP} - MC_Y) + (e_{pp} - r_{pp} - mc_y) + mc_y$$

But $(e_{pp} - r_{pp} - mc_y)$ and the corresponding expression for the other country are simply the uncompensated price derivatives of the import demand functions for the non-numeraire good. Writing these as $m_p$ and $M_P$, we therefore have $(S + mC_Y) = M_P + m_p + mc_y$. Using this, we see that the condition for factor growth to be beneficial becomes

$$(M_P + m_p + mc_y)w - m(\partial w/\partial p) < 0$$

Without loss of generality, we can choose the numeraire so that the ·non-numeraire good is exported by the home country. We therefore take $m$ to be negative. Dividing through by $m$, and multiplying by $p/w$, the condition then becomes (recalling that $m = -M$)

$$-M_P(P/M) + m_p(p/m) + pc_y - (\partial w/\partial p)(p/w) > 0$$

The first term here is the price elasticity of imports for the foreign country. The second term is the price elasticity of exports from the home country. The third term is the marginal propensity to consume the export good at home. And the last term is the Stolper–Samuelson factor price elasticity. The first three terms will all be positive if good 1 is normal in demand. Thus, the only possibility for growth to be harmful arises if the last term is positive—i.e. if an increase in the price of exports raises the domestic price of the factor in increased supply.

If we relate that to the alternative models of trade sketched in Chapter 3, we note that in the Ricardo–Viner model, $(\partial w/\partial p)(p/w)$ is always positive, but less than one. In that model, therefore, immiserizing growth is always a possibility. Whether it will happen, depends on the exact numerical values of the price elasticities of imports and exports, and on the marginal propensity to consume the export good at home. A sufficient condition for growth to be advantageous is that $pc_y > (\partial \log w/\partial \log p)$, but all we know about these is that they are both positive and less than one under assumptions of normality, so this sufficient condition does not really bring us any further.

In the Heckscher–Ohlin model, we must specify whether the factor in increased supply is used intensively in the export sector. If it is not, we know that $(\partial w/\partial p)$ will be negative, so the condition for growth to be beneficial is automatically satisfied. In other words, an increased endowment of the factor used intensively in import-competing production will always be beneficial. Relating that to the Heckscher–Ohlin hypothesis regarding trade patterns, it suggests that a country should always gain from an increased supply of a factor which is in relatively scarce supply domestically. It could lose from an increase in the supply of the factor which is already in relatively abundant supply there. Whether that would happen, would again depend on the exact numerical values of demand and supply elasticities. Note that in this case, $(\partial \log w / \partial \log p)$ is greater than one, so $pc_y$ close to one is insufficient to rule out immiserizing growth.

### Effects on the foreign country

More interesting than the possibility of immiserizing growth is the possibility that growth in one country can be harmful to the other. We should note at once that growth cannot be harmful to *both* countries: By (16) and (17), we see that $e_u \, du + E_U \, dU = r_v . dv$, so as long as $r_v . dv$ is positive, $du$ and $dU$ cannot be simultaneously negative. When we pose the question of whether trade at home can harm the rest of the world, therefore, we are really asking whether trade can give the home country an extra gain from growth, over and beyond the value of the increased factor supply. In other words, we are asking whether growth can cause changes in the terms of trade that are advantageous to the home country, and thus harmful to the rest of the world.

From (19) we see that a change $dv$ in the domestic supply of resources will be advantageous to the other country (i.e. make $E_U \, dU$ positive) if and only if

$$(-m . S^{-1} c_y) r_v . dv + m . S^{-1} r_{pv} \, dv > 0 \qquad (21)$$

With two goods, we can multiply through by $S$ (which is negative), to give the condition for an increase $dv$ in one factor to be advantageous:

$$-m c_y w + m (\partial w / \partial p) < 0$$

so, again choosing labels such that the home country exports the non-numeraire good, we get the condition

$$pc_y - (\partial w / \partial p)(p/w) < 0$$

which is the opposite of the sufficient condition discussed for the home country. In the Ricardo–Viner model we saw that we could not get prior restrictions on the left-hand side here. In the Heckscher–Ohlin model we can. We know that $(\partial w / \partial p)(p/w)$ is negative if the export sector does *not* use the factor in question intensively, while it is positive if that factor *is* used intensively in the export sector. In either case, it is greater than one in absolute value, while $pc_y$ is positive but less than one when both goods are normal. Thus, factor growth in the home country benefits the foreign country if the factor in question is used intensively in export production, while it harms the foreign country if it is the import-competing sector which uses the factor in increased supply intensively.

## 3. CHANGES IN TECHNOLOGY

Next, let us consider the effects of technological change on trade and utility. Technological shifts can easily be handled in the basic model, by introducing a shift parameter $\theta$ in the revenue function, to get $r(p, v, \theta)$. We shall first establish the general formulae for the effects of changes in such an arbitrary shift parameter. Thereafter, we look at particular cases—factor-augmenting technical change, product-augmenting change, and factor-augmenting change limited to one sector.

### General effects

To see how technical change in the home country affects prices and utility levels, we recall the general equilibrium conditions

$$e(1, p, u) = r(1, p, v, \theta) \tag{22}$$

$$E(1, P, U) = R(1, P, V) \tag{23}$$

$$e_p + E_P = r_p + R_P \tag{24}$$

$$p = P \tag{25}$$

Differentiating (24) totally, we get

$$S\,dp + e_{pu}\,du + E_{PU}\,dU = r_{p\theta}\,d\theta \tag{26}$$

while (22) and (23) give us

$$e_u\,du + (e_p - r_p).dp = r_\theta\,d\theta \tag{27}$$

$$E_U\,dU + (E_P - R_P).dp = 0 \tag{28}$$

Recalling that $m = (e_p - r_p)$ and $M = (E_P - R_P)$, this gives us

$$e_u\,du + m.dp = r_\theta\,d\theta \tag{29}$$

$$E_U\,dU + M.dp = 0 \tag{30}$$

We see that (26), (29), (30) are formally like (18), (16), and (17), differing only in the right-hand sides. Using the analogy, we can write down the solution at once:

$$\begin{bmatrix} e_u\,du \\ E_U\,dU \end{bmatrix} = \frac{1}{D} \begin{bmatrix} (1 + m.S^{-1}C_Y)r_\theta\,d\theta - m.S^{-1}r_{p\theta}\,d\theta \\ -m.S^{-1}c_y r_\theta\,d\theta + m.S^{-1}r_{p\theta}\,d\theta \end{bmatrix} \tag{31}$$

To see what this implies, we must specify the precise nature of the change in technology.

## Product augmenting change

First consider technical change in the production of particular products. Suppose this to be purely product augmenting—i.e. suppose we can write the production function for good $i$ as

$$x_i = \theta_i f^i(v^i)$$

In that case, a change in technology will be formally equivalent to a price change: An increase in $\theta_i$ means that we get correspondingly higher production value for a given vector of factor inputs. We can therefore write the revenue function as $r(\theta_1 p_1, \ldots, \theta_n p_n, v) = r(\theta p, v)$, where $\theta p$ is a vector with elements $\theta_i p_i$. Obviously, then, a one per cent change in $\theta_i$ has the same effect on revenue as a one per cent change in $p_i$, so

$$\theta_i(\partial r/\partial \theta_i) = p_i(\partial r/\partial p_i)$$

It then follows that

$$\theta_i(\partial^2 r/\partial \theta_i \partial p_j) = \delta_{ij}(\partial r/\partial p_i) + p_i(\partial^2 r/\partial p_i \partial p_j)$$

where $\delta_{ij}$ is the Kronecker delta ($\delta_{ij} = 1$ for $i = j$, and 0 otherwise). Choosing units in such a way as to make all initial prices equal to one, and letting the initial values of $\theta_i = 1$, we then have

$$r_\theta = r_p \qquad r_{p\theta} = r_{pp} + \text{diag}(r_p) \qquad (32)$$

where $\text{diag}(r_p)$ denotes a matrix with $(\partial r/\partial p_i)$ along the diagonal and zeros elsewhere. We can then substitute (32) into (31) to obtain the effects of product augmenting technical change.

Again, let us look at the special case of two goods. We assume that there is technical progress at home in the production of the non-numeraire good, so $d$ refers to a change in technology for the non-numeraire good only. By (32) we then have

$$r_\theta = x \qquad r_{p\theta} = x + (\partial x/\partial p)$$

Concentrating on the foreign country, we then see from (31) that

$$E_U dU = (1/DS)\{-mc_y + m(x + (\partial x/\partial p))\}d\theta$$

so

$$E_U dU = (1/DS)m\{x(1 - c_y) + (\partial x/\partial p)\}d\theta \qquad (33)$$

Since $S < 0$ and $(1 - c_y)$ is positive so long as both goods are normal, this means that

$$\text{sign}(dU/d\theta) = \text{sign}(-m)$$

so the foreign country is bound to benefit from technical progress in the home country's export industry.

This result has a simple economic interpretation. For a given factor allocation, a unit increase in $\theta$ raises the home country production of the non-numeraire good by $x$ units. It also raises domestic income by $x$, a fraction $c_y$ of which is spent on the good in question. For a given factor allocation, therefore, the home country net supply increases by $x(1 - c_y)$. In addition, the improved technology induces a reallocation of factors to the good with improved technology, causing a further increase of $(\partial x/\partial p)$ in supply. Obviously, the total effect is an outward shift in the home country net supply curve, and thus a lower relative price, for the good with improved technology. That is to the advantage of the foreign country if it is a net buyer of the good, and vice versa.

As usual, the home country gain is the direct gain $(r_\theta)$ less the foreign gain. The reader can work out the exact expression.

## General factor augmentation

If technical progress simply augments factor endowments, we can write the revenue function as $r(p, \theta v)$. A change in $\theta$ will then be formally equivalent to a change in the factor endowment in the home country. We see this more clearly if we measure the (fixed) factor endowment in such a way that $v_i = 1$, and set the initial values of $\theta_i = 1$. In that case, we get

$$r_\theta = r_v \qquad r_{p\theta} = r_{pv}$$

Substituting these into (31), we see that (31) becomes identical to (19).

This means that the results on factor growth hold for factor-augmenting technical progress as well. For example, a country experiencing technical progress that augments its abundant factor, could find its terms of trade deteriorating to such an extent that it is worse off with the new technology than with the old.

## Product-specific factor augmentation

As a last possibility, consider the effect of factor-augmenting technical change in a particular industry; as, for example, the effect of labour-augmenting technical progress in the production of labour-intensive goods in a labour-abundant economy. The general results for this case are not very illuminating, so we consider only the two-good, two-factor case with constant returns to scale.

In particular, suppose the unit cost functions in the numeraire and non-numeraire sectors are, respectively

$$b^0(w_1, w_2) \qquad b(w_1/\theta, w_1)$$

From Chapter 2, we recall that the revenue function can be found by minimizing the value of factor endowments subject to the constraints that unit cost be greater than or equal to price for all goods. In particular, therefore, $r(1, p, v, \theta)$ is given by

$$r(1, p, v, \theta) = \min_{w_1, w_2} w_1 v_1 + w_2 v_2$$

subject to $b^0(w_1, w_2) \geq 1$, $b(w_1/\theta, w_2) \geq p$.

Let $\mu$ be the Lagrangean multiplier corresponding to the unit cost = price constraint for the non-numeraire good. Then $r_p = \mu$, and $r_\theta = \mu(w_1/\theta^2)b_1$, where $b_1$ denotes the partial derivative of $b$ with respect to its first argument. Thus, using $\mu = r_p = x$, we have

$$r_\theta = x b_1 w_1/\theta^2$$

and

$$r_{p\theta} = r_{\theta p} = (1/\theta^2)\{b_1 w_1(\partial x/\partial p) + x(\partial w_1 b_1/\partial p)\}$$

or, in terms of elasticities

$$r_{p\theta} = \left(\frac{1}{\theta^2}\right)x\left(\frac{w_1 b_1}{p}\right)\left\{\left(\frac{\partial \log x}{\partial \log p}\right) + \left(\frac{\partial \log w_1 b_1}{\partial \log p}\right)\right\}$$

so evaluated at $\theta = 1$, we have

$$r_\theta = x w_1 b_1 \tag{35}$$

$$r_{p\theta} = x\left(\frac{w_1 b_1}{p}\right)\left\{\left(\frac{\partial \log x}{\partial \log p}\right) + \left(\frac{\partial \log w_1 b_1}{\partial \log p}\right)\right\} \tag{36}$$

Before considering this in the general case, let us look at the special case where the production function in the non-numeraire sector is Cobb–Douglas. Then cost shares are constant, so

$$\frac{\partial \log w_1 b_1}{\partial \log p} = 1$$

so we get simply

$$r_{p\theta} = \left(\frac{r_\theta}{p}\right)\left(\frac{\partial \log x}{\partial \log p}\right) + \left(\frac{r_\theta}{p}\right)$$

That gives the surprisingly strong result that the rest of the world is bound to benefit from factor-augmenting technical progress in the home country's export industry. To see this, substitute for $r_{p\theta}$ and $r_\theta$ in (31) to get

$$E_U\, \mathrm{d}U = -\left(\frac{1}{DS}\right) m\left\{c_y - \frac{1}{p}\left(\frac{\partial \log x}{\partial \log p}\right) - \frac{1}{p}\right\} r_\theta\, \mathrm{d}\theta \qquad (37)$$

As $r_\theta > 0$ and $DS < 0$, the condition for $\mathrm{d}U/\mathrm{d}\theta > 0$ can therefore be written as

$$-m\left\{(1 - pc_y) + \left(\frac{\partial \log x}{\partial \log p}\right)\right\} > 0 \qquad (38)$$

But we know that the price elasticity of production is positive, and we know that $(1 - pc_y)$ is positive (and less than one) if both goods are normal, so the term in brackets is positive. The foreign country will therefore benefit provided $m < 0$, i.e. provided technical progress occurs in the home country's export industry.

That result is only valid for the special case of a Cobb–Douglas technology in the non-numeraire sector, and it serves primarily to illustrate the dangers of using specific parameterizations when doing comparative statics exercises. In the more general case, the effect of factor augmenting technical progress in a particular industry will depend on which factor is augmented, and on the elasticity of substitution between factors in the non-numeraire industry. To see that, recall from (36) that $r_{p\theta}$ depends on $(\partial \log w_1 b_1/\partial \log p)$. But from production theory, it can be shown that

$$\frac{\partial \log w_1 b_1}{\partial \log p} = 1 + \left(1 - \frac{w_1 b_1}{p}\right)(1 - \sigma) \frac{\partial \log (w_1/w_2)}{\partial \log p} \qquad (39)$$

where $\sigma$ is the elasticity of substitution between the factors in the non-numeraire industry. This expression will be greater than one if the non-numeraire industry uses factor 1 intensively and the elasticity of substitution is less than one, but it will also be greater than one if both of these comparisons go the other way. The implication is that the foreign country is sure to benefit from factor augmentation in the home country's export industry if the factor in question is used intensively in that industry, and the elasticity of substitution is less than one. It is also certain to benefit from augmentation of the factor that is *not* used intensively in the export industry if the elasticity of substitution there is greater than one.

Again, the effect on the home country is a direct gain, less whatever gain the foreign country receives, so effects on the home country are just as ambiguous as the effects on the foreign country. So long as the outcome depends on the elasticity of substitution, we cannot derive general propositions regarding the effects of factor-augmenting technical change in import or export industries.

## 4. FACTOR MOVEMENTS

In this section we consider the movement of factors from one country to another. It is tempting to do this simply by putting together two shifts of the kind considered in section 2, one for each country. This may be appropriate if we are discussing a gift of factors, and readers can easily deal with this case. But there are other kinds of factor movements which are of greater practical interest and which introduce some new features. The simple approach implicitly assumes that the income accruing to the moving factor stays in the country to which it has moved, that the income is spent in accordance with the demand pattern of this country, and that it contributes to its total utility which is the relevant measure of welfare. Some or all of these need to be changed in important cases. The income accruing to direct investment will be received in the investing country. In practice this may not happen at once, but then our equilibrium model should distinguish commodities by dates of availability and consider the whole intertemporal equilibrium, where the income is received at once as far as the planning date is concerned. The case of migration of labour poses other problems. Migrants may repatriate some income to their country of origin, and may retain their demand patterns. Even in the absence of these complications, however, we must recognize that the magnitude of utility per capita in each country now acquires some interest. We may assume that the marginal migrant is revealing his preference for one utility level in his country of destination over another in his country of origin, but the effect of this on the per capita utilities of other residents in both countries needs to be calculated.

### Direct investment

Suppose the home country starts with a vector $v^0$ of factor endowments, and the foreign country starts with $V^0$. Then the home country invests a vector $\zeta$ in the foreign country, yielding factor inputs to production of $v = v^0 - \zeta$ and $V = V^0 + \zeta$ in the two countries. The home country's income is the value of its own output, $r(1, p, v)$, plus the income $W . \zeta$ earned by its direct investment in the foreign country, $W = R_V(1, P, V)$ being the vector of factor prices there. The income of the foreign country is the value of its output, $R(1, P, V)$, minus the amount $W.\zeta$ paid for the services of factors $\zeta$. This yields the equilibrium conditions

$$e(1, p, u) = r(1, p, v) + W.\zeta \tag{40}$$

$$E(1, P, U) = R(1, P, V) - W.\zeta \tag{41}$$

$$e_p(1, p, u) + E_P(1, P, U) - r_p(1, p, v) - R_P(1, P, V) = 0 \tag{42}$$

with the definitions $v = v^0 - \zeta$, $V = V^0 + \zeta$, and $W = R_V(1, P, V)$. Consider a slight change $\mathrm{d}\zeta$ in $\zeta$. Taking total differentials,

$$e_p.\mathrm{d}p + e_u\,\mathrm{d}u = r_p.\mathrm{d}p + r_v.\mathrm{d}v + W.\mathrm{d}\zeta + \zeta.\mathrm{d}W \tag{43}$$

$$E_P.\mathrm{d}P + E_U\,\mathrm{d}U = R_P.\mathrm{d}P + R_V.\mathrm{d}V - W.\mathrm{d}\zeta - \zeta.\mathrm{d}W \tag{44}$$

$$\begin{aligned} e_{pp}\,\mathrm{d}p + e_{pu}\,\mathrm{d}u + E_{PP}\,\mathrm{d}P + E_{PU}\,\mathrm{d}U \\ - r_{pp}\,\mathrm{d}p - r_{pv}\,\mathrm{d}v - R_{PP}\,\mathrm{d}P - R_{PV}\,\mathrm{d}V = 0 \end{aligned} \tag{45}$$

These can be simplified using the expressions for factor prices $w = r_v$ and $W = R_V$, those for imports $m = e_p - r_p$ and $M = E_P - R_P$, the earlier definition of $S$, and the relations $\mathrm{d}P = \mathrm{d}p$ and $\mathrm{d}V = \mathrm{d}\zeta = -\mathrm{d}v$. Further, we begin by considering the special case where the initial value of $\zeta$ is zero. Then we have

$$m.\mathrm{d}p + e_u\,\mathrm{d}u = (W - w).\mathrm{d}\zeta \tag{46}$$

$$M.\mathrm{d}p + E_U\,\mathrm{d}U = 0 \tag{47}$$

$$S\,\mathrm{d}p + e_{pu}\,\mathrm{d}u + E_{PU}\,\mathrm{d}U = (R_{PV} - r_{pv})\,\mathrm{d}\zeta \tag{48}$$

Again, these are formally like (16), (17), and (18), differing only in the right-hand sides. We therefore have the solution:

$$\begin{bmatrix} e_u\,\mathrm{d}u \\ E_U\,\mathrm{d}U \end{bmatrix} = \frac{1}{D} \begin{bmatrix} (1 + m.S^{-1}C_Y)(W - w).\mathrm{d}\zeta - m.S^{-1}(R_{PV} - r_{pv})\,\mathrm{d}\zeta \\ -m.S^{-1}c_y(W - w).\mathrm{d}\zeta + m.S^{-1}(R_{PV} - r_{pv})\,\mathrm{d}\zeta \end{bmatrix} \tag{49}$$

The interesting point to note is a difference between private and social desirability of direct investment. The former is governed by the sign of $(W - w).\mathrm{d}\zeta$; if each factor is capable of independent variation we can assume $(W_i - w_i)\,\mathrm{d}\zeta_i$ positive for each $i$ where such investment occurs. But this leads to induced changes in outputs depending on the differences in factor intensities between the countries, and these in turn affect prices and therefore utility levels. The outcome is summarized in (49). If the home country's government takes this into account, it may wish to control direct foreign investment.

There is an element of coincidence of private and social desirability at the world level: adding (46) and (47) we have

$$e_u \, du + E_U \, dU = (W - w).d\zeta$$

Therefore if direct investment is privately desirable, both countries cannot simultaneously lose by it, and it is possible that they both gain. Once again we see from (47) that the foreign country gains if and only if the terms of trade shift in its favour, i.e. against the home country.

As usual we illustrate (49) in the case where there are only two goods, and only one factor is moving from the home country to the foreign country. Assuming $D > 0$, and private desirability i.e. $(W - w) > 0$, we have the condition for the home country to benefit

$$S + m\left\{ pc_y - \frac{p}{W - w} \frac{\partial (W - w)}{\partial p} \right\} < 0$$

while for the foreign country to benefit we need

$$m\left\{ pC_Y - \frac{p}{W - w} \frac{\partial (W - w)}{\partial p} \right\} > 0$$

These do not lend themselves to simple interpretations except under additional restrictive assumptions. Let us consider one extreme set of simplifying assumptions just to illustrate the difficulties involved in making general assessments. Suppose there are two goods and two factors, both goods produced under constant returns to scale, and both goods being produced in both countries. Suppose, moreover, that production functions are the same in the two countries, apart from a scalar multiple reflecting a general technological advantage in the foreign country. With these assumptions, free trade will result in equalization of *relative* factor prices, but not of absolute factor rewards, so we shall have $W > w$. Relative factor proportions will, however, be the same in the two countries, reflecting the similarity of production functions and the equalization of relative factor prices. Using the expression for the Stolper–Samuelson derivatives in the two-by-two case derived in Chapter 2, equation (30), it will then be seen that $\partial W/\partial p$ will be proportional to $\partial w/\partial p$, the factor of proportionality being the relative technological advantage of the foreign country. Assuming the foreign country to be $\alpha$ times more productive than the home country, therefore, we have

$$W = \alpha w \qquad \frac{\partial W}{\partial p} = \alpha \left( \frac{\partial w}{\partial p} \right)$$

Using these, we see that the condition for the foreign country to benefit from direct investment there is

$$m \left\{ pc_y - \frac{p}{w} \frac{\partial w}{\partial p} \right\} > 0$$

But that is exactly the opposite of the condition we derived for economic growth in the home country to be beneficial to the foreign country, so we can apply the same reasoning. Letting the non-numeraire good be the good exported by the home country (so $m$ is negative), direct investment is beneficial to the host country if and only if the term in parenthesis is positive. In the Heckscher–Ohlin model $(\partial \log w / \partial \log p)$ is positive if the non-numeraire good is intensive in the mobile factor, and it is negative and greater than one in absolute value if the non-numeraire good is intensive in the other factor. In this particular example, therefore, the host country will gain if the mobile factor is used intensively in the other country's exports, and it will lose if the opposite is the case.

That conclusion is intuitively appealing, but it does not generalize. That is easily understood if we modify the example slightly. Suppose there are still only two goods and two factors, and constant returns; but suppose now that the foreign country has a technological advantage in only one of the goods. If that is the case, relative factor prices will not be equalized, so relative factor proportions will not be the same in the two countries. Depending on the elasticities of substitution between the factors in the two industries, $\partial(W - w)/\partial p$ could then have either sign, so no general inferences could be drawn. Again, therefore, we are left without clear qualitative conclusions. Calculations of effects of direct investment would have to be made for specific cases, using the formula (49).

The situation is even more complex if the initial level of direct investment is non-zero. Using (43) and (44), and noting that

$$dW = R_{VP} \, dP + R_{VV} \, dV$$

we get

$$(m - \zeta . R_{VP}) \, dp + e_u \, du = (W - w) . d\zeta + \zeta . R_{VV} \, d\zeta \quad (50)$$

$$(M + \zeta . R_{VP}) \, dp + E_U \, dU = -\zeta . R_{VV} \, d\zeta \quad (51)$$

These differ from (46) and (47). The additional terms represent the income effects of changes in the earnings of the intramarginal units of investment and their repercussions on prices. As an example, if $d\zeta$ is proportional to $\zeta$, i.e. if the home country is simply expanding its scale of investment in the foreign country, then $\zeta . R_{VV} \, d\zeta$ will be non-positive since $R_{VV}$ is a negative semi-definite matrix. The detailed calculations of the ultimate consequences of these effects do not yield anything particularly illuminating, and are therefore left as an exercise in the technique. A useful application is the calculation of the optimum direct investment.

## Migration of labour

We turn to the problem of labour migration. In this discussion we keep all other factors (which are constant throughout the exercise) in the background. Therefore in the notation previously introduced, $v = v^0 - \zeta$ and $V = V^0 + \zeta$ are both scalars. We have already discussed the problems involved in modelling preferences and repatriation of income in connection with consumer migration. We confine ourselves to a special case which is the simplest one to handle (although it conflicts with our treatment of factors in Chapter 4): We assume that migrants do not repatriate any income to their country of origin, and adopt the demand patterns of their country of destination. Let $e(1, p, u)$, $E(1, P, U)$ now stand for the expenditure functions for each worker in the home and the foreign country respectively. The equilibrium conditions become

$$v \, e(1, p, u) = r(1, p, v) \tag{52}$$

$$VE(1, P, U) = R(1, P, V) \tag{53}$$

$$ve_p(1, p, u) + VE_P(1, P, U) - r_p(1, p, v) - R_P(1, P, V) = 0 \tag{54}$$

Let a further marginal shift of $d\zeta$ occur, so that $dV = d\zeta = -dv$. Then

$$ve_p . dp + ve_u \, du + e \, dv = r_p . dp + r_v \, dv$$

$$VE_P . dP + VE_U \, dU + E \, dV = R_P . dP + R_V \, dV$$

$$ve_{pp} \, dp + ve_{pu} \, du + e_p \, dv + VE_{PP} \, dP + VE_{PU} \, dU$$
$$+ E_P \, dV - r_{pp} \, dp - r_{pv} \, dv - R_{PP} \, dP - R_{PV} \, dV = 0$$

To simplify these, note that the import vectors are now $m = ve_p - r_p$ and $M = VE_P - R_P$. Next, $e_p$ and $E_P$ are the respective home and foreign consumption vectors per capita; write them as $c$ and $C$.

The expression for $S$, the overall substitution derivative matrix for the non-numeraire commodities, naturally becomes

$$S = ve_{pp} + VE_{PP} - r_{pp} - R_{PP} \tag{55}$$

Finally, note that

$$e - r_v = r/v - r_v = (r - vr_v)/v$$

which is the non-wage income per capita in the home country; denote this by $k$. Similarly write $K$ for $E - R_V$ in the foreign country. Using all this, the total differentials become

$$m.dp + ve_u \, du = k \, d\zeta \tag{56}$$

$$M.dp + VE_U \, dU = -K \, d\zeta \tag{57}$$

$$S \, dp + ve_{pu} \, du + VE_{PU} \, dU = (R_{PV} - r_{pv} - C + c) \, d\zeta \tag{58}$$

These have a strong family resemblance to the form we have considered several times, so we simply write down the solution

$$
\begin{bmatrix} ve_u \, du \\ VE_U \, dU \end{bmatrix} = \frac{d\zeta}{D}
$$

$$
\times \begin{bmatrix} (1 + m.S^{-1}C_Y)k - m.S^{-1}C_YK - m.S^{-1}(R_{PV} - r_{pv} - C + c) \\ -m.S^{-1}c_y k - (1 - m.S^{-1}c_y)K + m.S^{-1}(R_{PV} - r_{pv} - C + c) \end{bmatrix}
\tag{59}
$$

Although the solution does not need much effort, what emerges is quite complicated, reflecting the numerous different forces involved. Let us simply note some of these, looking at the host country of immigrants. We can use (59) to write

$$VE_U \, dU = (d\zeta/D)[-K + m.S^{-1}[(R_{PV} - r_{pv}) - \{(C - c_yK) - (c - c_yk)\}]]$$

The first term, $-K$, reflects the fact that income per capita automatically falls as a result of immigration: At constant prices, income per capita $(R/V)$ changes by

$$\frac{d(R/V)}{dV} = -\frac{1}{V}\left(\frac{R}{V} - R_V\right) = -\frac{K}{V} \tag{60}$$

Thus, the direct effect on utility per capita in the host country must be negative. The remaining terms reflect induced changes in the terms of trade, caused by shifts in supply and demand curves. World supply of the non-numeraire good increases by $(R_{PV} - r_{pv})$. As usual, nothing can be said about the sign of this except in very special cases, like that discussed in relation to direct investment above. To understand the effect on world demand, we can look at the last term, i.e. at

$$(C - c_y K) - (c - c_y k)$$

This term is the shift in world demand for the non-numeraire good caused by migration. The shift is due (i) to the change in per capita income at home and abroad caused by migration, (ii) to the change in the immigrant's income, and (iii) to the change in the immigrant's tastes. To get a bit further, let us assume that preferences are uniform and homothetic. Then there is no change in tastes, and we can relate $(C - c)$ to the difference in per capita income at home and abroad. In particular, we can approximate $C - c$ by $c_y(Y - y)$, where $Y$ and $y$ are the per capita income levels in the two countries. Thus, the demand shift becomes

$$c_y\left(\frac{R}{V} - K - \frac{r}{v} + k\right) = c_y(W - w)$$

so in that case there will be an increase in world demand for the non-numeraire good if migrants move from low-wage to high-wage countries.

This gives rise to an interesting special case which can highlight the dilemma of an immigrant country. Consider the special two-by-two model we looked at in the case of direct investment, where the foreign country has a general technological advantage over the home country, but where there is equalization of relative factor prices. In this 'Ricardian' Heckscher–Ohlin model, the foreign country will have a higher income level per capita, and a higher wage level, than the home country, so migration to the foreign country will seem attractive. Suppose, moreover, that the foreign country is relatively capital-abundant, so it has a comparative advantage in capital-intensive production. (It has an absolute advantage in all production.) Let the numeraire good be capital-intensive, so the non-numeraire good is labour intensive, and is imported by the foreign country.

With all these assumptions, we have

$$R_{PV} = \alpha r_{pv} = \alpha(\partial w/\partial p) \qquad W = \alpha w$$

$$VE_U \, dU = \left(\frac{d\zeta}{D}\right)\left[-K + \left(\frac{1}{S}\right)m\left\{(\alpha - 1)\left(\frac{\partial w}{\partial p}\right) - c_y(\alpha - 1)w\right\}\right]$$

$$= \left(\frac{d\zeta}{D}\right)\left[-K + \left(\frac{1}{S}\right)m\left(\frac{w}{p}\right)(\alpha - 1)\left\{\frac{\partial \log w}{\partial \log p} - pc_y\right\}\right]$$

where the assumptions imply $m < 0$, $(\alpha - 1) > 0$, $(\partial \log w / \partial \log p) > 1$, so the term following $S$ is negative. As $S$ is negative, that means that the host country benefits from migration through improved terms of trade. The idea is that, under the special assumptions of the example, a movement of labour to the labour-scarce, technologically advanced economy increases world output of the labour-intensive good by more than it increases world demand for that good. The rich country importing the labour-intensive good will therefore experience an improvement in the terms of trade following immigration. That must be weighted against the direct effect in the form of lower per capita income in determining whether or not immigration is to the net advantage of the host country.

While the example may serve to illustrate the dilemma of a selfish immigrant country, therefore, it also serves to illustrate that there are no clear cut answers as to the net effects of migration on the country of origin and the country to which a person migrates. There seems to be only one very simple inference that is possible in the general case. Adding (56) and (57) we find

$$ve_u \, du + VE_U \, dU = (k - K) \, d\zeta$$

This provides certain one-sided tests. If the residents of the home country and the foreign country all benefit from the marginal migration, i.e. $du$ and $dU$ are both positive, we must have $k > K$. To put the matter in another way, if $k < K$, i.e. the non-wage income per head in the foreign country exceeds that in the home country, then someone (other than the marginal migrant who must be presumed to have gained) must lose from further migration. Conversely, if $k > K$, someone other than the marginal migrant must gain from his action.

To interpret this economically, note from (60) that $K/V$ is the reduction of income per capita in the foreign country, and similarly $k/v$ will be the increase of income per capita in the home country, as a result of a person moving from the latter to the former. Leaving this marginal migrant aside, $(k - K)$ is the total increase in the real income of the others. If this is positive, someone must gain. Casual empiricism suggests implications for the way in which one should look at migration in the world today, but we leave these to the reader.

## 5. TARIFFS AND THE TERMS OF TRADE

The next shift of the equilibrium that we shall consider is that due to trade taxes. We suppose that only one country (the home country) levies such taxes, thus abstracting from problems of retaliation. Our treatment owes as much to recent developments in the theory of commodity taxation in public finance as to the usual treatment of tariffs in the theory of international trade. One important lesson that carries over from the theory of commodity taxation is that there is a degree of arbitrariness about the tax rates themselves. When producer prices and consumer prices can be normalized independently, tax rates can be specified only if we relate these normalizations in a particular way, such as by cho sing a particular commodity to be untaxed. There is in general no natural choice of this kind. On the other hand, it does not matter much. What matters is not the tax rates themselves, but the impact that taxes have on the physical allocation of resources—i.e. on consumption and production; and these impacts are invariant to the choice of normalizations.

This carries over to tariffs. We saw in Chapter 3 that we can normalize prices in the two countries independently. This implies an arbitrariness about tariff or subsidy rates. In the two-good case, for example, it does not matter whether we levy a tariff on the imported good (thus taxing domestic consumption and subsidizing domestic production of that good) or levy a tax on exports (thus taxing domestic production of the export good, and subsidizing domestic consumption of it). The effects on the vector of net import demands are the same in the two cases, and it is that effect which is of economic interest. That is generally true—the only effect of tariffs that is of economic interest is the marginal impact on the quantities traded. We start this section by looking at a problem which highlights this aspect—namely, the question of how the home country can use tariffs to improve the vector of goods sold to it by the rest of the world. That is the question of optimum tariffs. It is of considerable interest in its own right, and it serves to clarify questions of trade tax normalizations. It therefore serves as a useful introduction to a discussion of the more general effects of tariffs.

### The optimum tariff

A small country facing fixed world prices cannot through any action of its own affect those prices, so for a small country tariffs are of interest only in relation to the domestic equilibrium. If we are to discuss tariffs in the context of international equilibrium, therefore, we should consider a country whose net purchases *have* an impact on world prices. When that is the case, it is useful to think of trade taxes in terms of the world market prices that they imply. Through its choice of tariff rates, the home country can affect world market prices, so in a sense we can cast the problem of choosing tariff rates as one of choosing international market prices.

Let us start out by using that approach. Suppose the home country presents the foreign country with a price vector $P$. The foreign country then attains an equilibrium in the manner described in Chapter 2: Its utility is given by $E(P, U) = R(P, V)$, and its net demands are then given by $M = E_P(P, U) - R_P(P, V)$. Ultimately, therefore, $M$ is a function of $P$, satisfying $P . M(P) = 0$, and homogeneous of degree zero. $M$ is the vector of imports to the foreign country, so $-M$ is the vector of exports to the home country, i.e. the supply functions facing the home country in international markets. Thus the home country treats $-M(P)$ as the vector of net import quantities and attains its own equilibrium. This is now easily characterized by means of the Meade utility function defined on net trades: Home utility is $u = \phi(m)$ at $m = -M(P)$; and with $p$ (the home price vector) proportional to $\phi_m(m)$. This implicitly defines trade taxes in specific form as $t = p - P$. We have an import tax on commodity $j$ if $t_j > 0$ and $m_j > 0$, an export tax if $t_j < 0$ and $m_j < 0$, and analogously for subsidies. The arbitrariness is clear, since $p$ and $P$ can be multiplied by independent positive scalars without changing the equilibrium. In the two-good case that is the well-known symmetry between import and export taxes pointed out earlier.

Now consider the effect of changing the price vector $P$. A change $dP$ leads to a change $-dM = -M_P(P)\,dP$ in the foreign net supply. The change in home utility is

$$du = \phi_m(-M(P)) . dm = -\phi_m(-M(P)) . dM = \alpha p . (-dM)$$

where $\alpha$ is a positive scalar, reflecting the choice of normalization of home prices. This immediately gives us the first order condition for the home country's optimum trade policy: It should contrive to leave the foreign country facing such a price vector $P$ that for any feasible departure $dP$, the inner product of the corresponding change in foreign supply and the domestic price vector should be zero. In other words, it should choose $P$ such that for any change $dP$, the corresponding change $dM$ in net trades should be orthogonal to the home price vector $p$. Since $p$ itself is orthogonal to the home country's trade indifference surface, i.e. proportional to $\phi_m(m)$, this stipulates a tangency between this indifference surface and the surface consisting of the foreign country's net trade offers. With two goods, therefore, the optimum tariff is defined by tangency between the trade indifference curve and the foreign offer curve—

a result that should be familiar. The above condition is a direct generalization of this.

Substituting for $dM$, we have $du = -\alpha p . M_P(P)\, dP$. The co-efficient of $dP$ is the gradient vector of $u$ when expressed as a function of $P$. For the optimum choice of $P$, the first-order condition is that the vector be zero. Since the inner product of a vector and a matrix is not defined, we have to use the transpose of $p$ when writing the coefficient on its own. Thus the condition is

$$p^T M_P(P) = 0 \tag{61}$$

To cast this in another familiar form, note that on differentiating the balanced-trade condition $P^T M(P) = 0$, we find $P^T M_P(P) + M^T = 0$. But we know that domestic prices are foreign prices plus tariffs, i.e. $p = P + t$, so (61) can be written as $(P + t)^T M_P(P) = 0$. Using $M^T = -P^T M_P(P)$, we therefore have the optimum condition

$$t^T M_P(P) = M^T \tag{62}$$

This looks like a formula involving the elasticity of the foreign offer curve. The connection can be established properly with a bit of care about normalization. As was done at the beginning of this chapter, let us suppose that there are $(n + 1)$ goods, number 0 being the common numeraire in the two countries, so there is no trade tax on that good. Writing $t$ for the vector of tariffs for the non-numeraire goods, $-M$ for their net supply from the foreign country, and $M_P$ for the matrix of derivatives of $M$ with respect to the prices of the non-numeraire goods, equation (62) remains valid. Thus, (62) defines the optimum tariff rates in terms of the price derivatives (elasticities) of the trade offers from the foreign country.

In the two-good case, (62) is simply the familiar inverse elasticity formula. To see this, write it as $(t/P)PM_P(P) = M$. The supply of the non-numeraire good from the foreign country is $-M$, so the elasticity of supply is $(-M_P P)/(-M) = PM_P/M$. The percentage tariff on the non-numeraire good should therefore be

$$\frac{t}{P} = \frac{1}{PM_P/M} \tag{63}$$

i.e. the inverse of the foreign country's supply elasticity.

### Price effects of tariffs

Implicit or explicit acceptance of an untaxed numeraire is common practice, and once it is done, questions such as the effects of tax rates on the home and foreign price vectors can be posed. To answer these, it is simpler to revert to the formulation used in previous sections. It must, however, be modified to take account of tariffs and tariff revenue. As all tariff revenue ultimately accrues to consumers, the domestic budget constraint then is that consumption expenditure should equal the value of production plus the net revenue from trade taxes. This revenue is $t.m$, where $t = p - P$ naturally pertains only to the non-numeraire goods, and $m$ is the vector of net imports of non-numeraire goods. In equilibrium the import vector can be written either as $e_p - r_p$, regarded from the point of view of the home country, or as $R_P - E_P$ on shifting the focus to the foreign country.

With no trade taxes in the foreign country, the equations defining the equilibrium are

$$e(1, p, u) = r(1, p, v) + t.m \tag{64}$$

$$E(1, P, U) = R(1, P, V) \tag{65}$$

$$e_p + E_P - r_p - R_P = 0 \tag{66}$$

where we have $p = P + t$.

We now want to find out how a change in the tariff vector affects prices at home and abroad. In the two-good case, the type of question we shall be interested in is whether a tariff lowers the international price of imports and raises the domestic price of the imported good. The latter is necessary if a tariff is to have the factor price effects predicted by Stolper and Samuelson. As we shall see, there is no reason to expect this to be the case. In the general case, we shall look at the effects of tariffs on the terms of trade. Taking total differentials, we have

$$e_p.dp + e_u\,du = r_p.dp + t.dm + m.dt$$

$$E_P.dP + E_U\,dU = R_P.dP$$

$$e_{pp}\,dp + e_{pu}\,du + E_{PP}\,dP + E_{PU}\,dU - r_{pp}\,dp - R_{PP}\,dP = 0$$

Using $m = e_p - r_p$ and $dp = dP + dt$, these simplify to

$$m.dP + e_u\,du = t.dm \tag{67}$$

$$M.dP + E_U\,dU = 0 \tag{68}$$

$$S\,dP + e_{pu}\,du + E_{PU}\,dU = -s\,dt \tag{69}$$

where $S$ is the world substitution matrix defined before, and $s$ is the part pertaining to the home country, $s = e_{pp} - r_{pp}$.

Some simple inferences can be drawn from these: (68) relates the foreign utility to the terms of trade in the manner that should by now be familiar, while (67) can be thought to give a decomposition of the effect on home utility into a volume of trade effect and a terms of trade effect:

$$e_u \, du = t.dm - m.dP$$

We can also derive the optimum tariff formula. Recalling that $m = -M$ which can be expressed as a function of $P$, the first-order condition $du = 0$ can at once be written in the form (62). It is also immediate that for a price-taking country, $P$ is constant and $dP = 0$, so the condition is satisfied at $t = 0$.

We can solve (67)–(69) fully for the utility changes in the case of a small departure from free trade. If the initial equilibrium has $t = 0$, then the equations are exactly in the general form like (7)–(9) that has been solved many times in this chapter, the only difference being in the right-hand sides. Therefore we can write down the solution directly

$$\begin{bmatrix} e_u \, du \\ E_U \, dU \end{bmatrix} = \frac{1}{D} \begin{bmatrix} m.S^{-1}s \, dt \\ -m.S^{-1}s \, dt \end{bmatrix} \tag{70}$$

Terms of trade changes are found at once, since with $t = 0$, (67) and (68) give

$$-m.dP = M.dP = e_u \, du = -E_U \, dU$$

Assuming the condition $D > 0$ for a transfer to be beneficial to the recipient, the condition for a small tariff $dt$ to be beneficial to the home country is $m.S^{-1}s \, dt > 0$.

Multiplying (69) by $S^{-1}$ and using (70), we can also find the effect of the tariff on world prices, and then its effect on domestic prices:

$$dP = -\frac{1}{D} S^{-1}s \, dt \tag{71}$$

and

$$dp = \left[ I - \frac{1}{D} S^{-1}s \right] dt \tag{72}$$

As usual, these reduce to familiar forms in the two-good case. Now $S$ and $s$ are both negative scalars, so from (71) the transfer condition, which as we saw reduces simply to a market stability condition, guarantees that a tariff on the non-numeraire good lowers its foreign relative price. Its home price rises if $1 - s/(SD)$ is positive, i.e. if $SD - s < 0$. Recalling the definition of $D$, we have

$$SD - s = S - m(C_Y - c_y) - s$$

$$= E_{PP} - R_{PP} + MC_Y - Mc_y$$

$$= -Mc_y + \partial M/\partial P$$

where we have used the Slutsky–Hicks equation to obtain the uncompensated derivative of the foreign excess demand of the non-numeraire good. The condition is therefore, taking $m = -M > 0$,

$$\frac{p}{M} \frac{\partial M}{\partial p} > p c_y \tag{73}$$

But we saw previously that $PM_P/M$ is the foreign supply elasticity, so we get that the foreign elasticity of net supply of the non-numeraire good should exceed its home marginal propensity to consume. If this holds, we can be sure that the tariff will increase the relative price of the imported good in the home country, and therefore that it will raise the price of the factor more intensive in the production of that good there, according to the Stolper-Samuelson theorem. 'Paradoxical' possibilities arising from the failure of the condition were pointed out by Metzler, but as (73) shows these are not exceptional in a rigorous sense.

Remember that the above exercises were performed for small moves from an initial free trade equilibrium. In general the right-hand side of (67) is non-zero, and $dm$ there must be related to $dP$ via the foreign supply function. This makes the algebra a little more complicated, and yields slightly different conditions for stability and for normal incidence of the tariff on prices. We leave this extension to the readers. It is worth observing a simple implication of (67) and (68): adding them, we have

$$e_u \, du + E_U \, dU = t \cdot dm$$

so in a natural sense the world welfare effect of the tariff depends only on the allocative or volume of trade aspect.

## 6. TARIFFS AND INCOME DISTRIBUTION

In this section we relax our assumption that each country on the demand side effectively consists of one consumer. Instead we regard the recipient of each factor income as a separate consumer, thereby obtaining the effects of trade taxes on the functional distribution of income. We consider only a special example with two factors and two goods, and incomplete specialization in both countries. This has some intrinsic interest, and the method generalizes without difficulty.

Let us stress a well-known result, which was demonstrated in detail in Chapter 3 and will appear again in Chapter 6, that from a welfare point of view tariffs are inferior to lump sum taxes or indirect commodity taxes in a redistributive role. Our present exercise has a twofold purpose. First, there may be genuine circumstances in which the better policies are not available, and it becomes necessary to examine whether tariffs can prove to be of some use. It is therefore helpful to know how the methods we have been employing can be adapted to handle such problems. Although each such problem of devising a third-best redistributive policy may need to be solved afresh given its own peculiar circumstances and constraints, an illustration will help the readers achieve an understanding of the general approach. Secondly, the example chosen gives us an opportunity to show the paces of the two-by-two 'workhorse' model of trade theory. The diagrammatic treatment of it is thoroughly examined in all textbooks, and algebraic formulations are also becoming well known. We have therefore felt it unnecessary to devote much space to it. However, the application here is somewhat novel, both in the questions asked and the formulation adopted.

The basic idea is simple. Choose labels so that the home country is importing commodity 1, which is relatively factor 1 intensive. Suppose the home country levies an import tariff, and take the case of 'normal' incidence, when the relative price of good 1 rises at home and falls abroad. By the Stolper–Samuelson result this raises the price of factor 1 relative to that of either commodity at home, and lowers it abroad. This benefits factor 1 at home and factor 2 abroad; the two others are harmed. However, there is a further effect arising from the tariff revenue. Suppose this is given to the factor 2 at home; with inelastic factor supplies it does not matter whether this is done in a lump sum or by a negative income tax specific to that factor. If various elasticities and marginal propensities are in suitable ranges to be determined, it is possible for the income effect of the tariff revenue to outweigh the Stolper–Samuelson price effect for factor 2. Thus we can secure a Pareto improvement at home even in the absence of any other redistributive tools, and factor 1 abroad is the only one harmed in the final reckoning. As a somewhat provocative case, suppose the UK becomes an importer of capital intensive goods from Japan, and levies a tariff and redistributes the proceeds to the workers. If the other good is sufficiently highly labour intensive, and if UK workers have a sufficiently low marginal propensity to consume the imported good, then the tariff can benefit both workers and capitalists in the UK, and also benefit workers in Japan, leaving the capitalists in Japan as the only losers. We hasten to add that there will typically be better ways of achieving this end.

We turn to the formal model. Good 2 will be chosen as the numeraire in both countries, i.e. $p_2 = P_2 = 1$. The home country is importing good 1, i.e. $m_1 > 0$, and levies a tariff $t_1$ expressed as a specific tax on it, i.e. $p_1 = P_1 + t_1$. The tariff revenue is an addition to the income $w_2 v_2$ of the second factor at home.

A production equilibrium with incomplete specialization will be given by equalities between prices and the corresponding unit costs:

$$p_1 = b^1(w_1, w_2), \qquad p_2 = b^2(w_1, w_2) \tag{74}$$

and

$$P_1 = B^1(W_1, W_2), \qquad P_2 = B^2(W_1, W_2) \tag{75}$$

On the demand side, in each country we now distinguish the recipients of incomes imputed to the two factors. Let $e^1$ and $e^2$ be the expenditure functions and $u_1$ and $u_2$ the utility levels at home for the respective owners of factors 1 and 2, and similarly in upper case letters for the foreign country. We have the consumer equilibrium conditions:

$$\begin{aligned} e^1(p_1, p_2, u_1) &= w_1 v_1 \\ e^2(p_1, p_2, u_2) &= w_2 v_2 + t_1 m_1 \end{aligned} \tag{76}$$

and

$$\begin{aligned} E^1(P_1, P_2, U_1) &= W_1 V_1 \\ E^2(P_1, P_2, U_2) &= W_2 V_2 \end{aligned} \tag{77}$$

Finally, we have two market-clearing conditions for the two goods. By Walras's Law, we need retain only one, and we use that for good 1. Writing $e_1^1 = c^1$ for the demand for this good from the owners of factor 1 in the home country, and similarly for the others, we have

$$e_1^1 + e_1^2 + E_1^1 + E_1^2 - r_1 - R_1 = 0 \tag{78}$$

Next we change the tariff by $dt_1$, and find the effect on the equilibrium by taking total differentials of the defining equations. Note that $dp_2 = dP_2 = 0$ and $dp_1 = dP_1 + dt_1$. From the production equations we find the Stolper–Samuelson derivatives as in Chapter 2, and from our factor intensity assumption we know that $\partial w_1/\partial p_1 > w_1/p_1$ while $\partial w_2/\partial p_1 < 0$, and similarly for the foreign country. Turning to (76),

$$e_1^1\,dp_1 + e_u^1\,du_1 = v_1\,dw_1 = v_1(\partial w_1/\partial p_1)\,dp_1$$

or

$$e_u^1\,du_1 = (v_1\,\partial w_1/\partial p_1 - c^1)\,dp_1$$

Now

$$v_1\,\partial w_1/\partial p_1 - c^1 > v_1 w_1/p_1 - c^1 > 0$$

abbreviate the expression by $\gamma_1$. Similarly for the other factor we have $\gamma_2$ which is negative, and for factors in the foreign country $\Gamma_1 > 0$, $\Gamma_2 < 0$. Also, since we start at an equilibrium without tariffs and consider the effect of a small initial tariff as usual, $d(t_1 m_1) = m_1\,dt_1$. Putting all this together, we have

$$
\begin{aligned}
e_u^1\,du_1 &= \gamma_1\,dp_1 \\
e_u^2\,du_2 &= \gamma_2\,dp_1 + m_1\,dt_1
\end{aligned}
\tag{79}
$$

$$
\begin{aligned}
E_U^1\,dU_1 &= \Gamma_1\,dP_1 \\
E_U^2\,dU_2 &= \Gamma_2\,dP_1
\end{aligned}
\tag{80}
$$

Finally, we turn to the market-clearing equation (78). From it,

$$e_{11}^1\,dp_1 + e_{1u}^1\,du_1 + e_{11}^2\,dp_1 + e_{1u}^2\,du_2 - r_{11}\,dp_1$$
$$+ E_{11}^1\,dP_1 + E_{1U}^1\,dU_1 + E_{11}^2\,dP_1 + E_{1U}^2\,dU_2 - R_{11}\,dP_1 = 0$$

Write $\sigma = r_{11} - e_{11}^1 - e_{11}^2$, the own substitution derivative of excess supply for good 1 in the home country, and define $\Sigma$ similarly for the foreign country. Next note that $e_{1u}^1/e_u^1$ is the derivative of the demand for good 1 by owners of factor 1 in the home country with respect to their money income; in keeping with our earlier notation for such derivatives write it as $c_y^1$. Finally, use (79) and (80) to substitute for the utility changes. This gives

$$-(\sigma - \gamma_1\,c_y^1 - \gamma_2\,c_y^2)\,dp_1 + m_1\,c_y^2\,dt_1$$
$$- (\Sigma - \Gamma_1\,C_Y^1 - \Gamma_2\,C_Y^2)\,dP_1 = 0$$

The expressions in the parentheses are just the uncompensated own price effects on the excess supply of good 1 in the two countries, when there are induced changes in factor prices to maintain unit costs equal to prices. Abbreviate these as $\lambda$ and $\Lambda$ respectively.

Walrasian stability requires $\lambda + \Lambda > 0$; in fact we shall soon make stronger assumptions.

Finally we can solve for the price changes:

$$dP_1/dt_1 = -(\lambda - m_1 c_y^2)/(\lambda + \Lambda) \qquad (81)$$

and

$$dp_1/dt_1 = (\Lambda + m_1 c_y^2)/(\lambda + \Lambda) \qquad (82)$$

Before we substitute these in (79) and (80) to examine the effects on the utilities of the four classes of income recipients, we note one relevant condition. Adding the two equations in (79), we have

$$e_u^1 du_1 + e_u^2 du_2 = (\gamma_1 + \gamma_2) dp_1 + m_1 dt_1$$

Now

$$\gamma_1 + \gamma_2 = v_1 \partial w_1/\partial p_1 - c^1 + v_2 \partial w_2/\partial p_1 - c^2$$
$$= \partial(v_1 w_1 + v_2 w_2)/\partial p_1 - c^1 - c^2$$

When $w_1$ and $w_2$ are expressed as functions of $p_1$ and $p_2$ from the unit cost equations, $v_1 w_1 + v_2 w_2$ is just the revenue function. The derivative is then the home output of good 1, and the right-hand side reduces to $-m_1$. Hence

$$e_u^1 du_1 + e_u^2 du_2 = m_1(dt_1 - dp_1)$$

If both factors at home are to benefit when the imported good is subjected to a small tariff, it is therefore a necessary condition that the price at home should rise by an amount smaller than the tariff, and correspondingly its price abroad should fall. This needs $\lambda > m_1 c_y^2$. Then $dP_1 < 0$, and from (80) we have $dU_1 < 0$ and $dU_2 > 0$.

For $du_1 > 0$, we need $dp_1 > 0$, i.e. $\Lambda + m_1 c_y^2 > 0$. Altogether we have required a completely 'normal' incidence of the tariff. Finally,

$$e_u^2 du_2 = [m_1 + \gamma_2(\Lambda + m_1 c_y^2)/(\lambda + \Lambda)] dt_1 \qquad (83)$$

The condition for $du_2 > 0$ is that the bracketed expression on the right-hand side be positive. Recalling that $\gamma_2$ is negative, we see that a small numerical value for it, or a small value of $c_y^2$, will prove conducive to fulfilment of this condition.

Incidentally, for a price-taking country, e.g. one facing an infinite $\Lambda$, we have $dp_1 = dt_1$, and then

$$e_u^1 du_1 + e_u^2 du_2 = 0$$

confirming that for such a country free trade will be Pareto efficient. In the absence of better instruments, it may be desirable to use tariffs to benefit one factor at the expense of the other.

## 7. EFFECTIVE PROTECTION

As we stated when introducing it in Chapter 2, the revenue function provides a very general tool for modelling production so long as there are no distortions. In particular, and contrary to popular belief, there is no need to restrict the analysis to the case where final goods are produced directly by primary factors. There may be any pattern of goods being used as inputs to the production of other goods; $r(p, v)$ simply gives the maximum value of *net* output of goods that can be achieved given the price vector $p$ for goods and the quantity vector $v$ of primary factors, and $r_p(p, v)$ gives the vector of *net* outputs that results when such optimum choices have been made. This has important implications for the response of production to price changes. Since $r$ is convex in $p$, each second-order derivative $\partial^2 r / \partial p_i^2$ is non-negative, i.e. an increase in any price raises the net output of that good. In a small country, therefore, an increase in any tariff raises the net output of that good. In this sense, tariffs do provide protection.

However, this approach does not tell us how the effect on net output is split into gross output changes and intermediate input changes. Nor do we know how the allocation of primary factors will shift across production activities. The theory of effective protection looks at production in greater detail in order to answer such questions.

The literature on this subject is very large, and often highly controversial. It is clearly beyond the scope of a general work such as this to go into the matter in any detail. Corden (1971) gives a thorough textbook treatment; Grubel and Johnson (eds) (1971) contain several articles expounding the advanced theory and controversial matters. We confine ourselves to looking at two aspects. Here we examine the effects of tariffs on gross outputs when intermediate goods have fixed input coefficients. In the following chapter, we examine the optimum policy response when there are constraints involving gross outputs; this helps clarify the welfare significance of effective protection.

### Tariffs and gross outputs

We assume a small economy with fixed supplies of primary factors. With domestic prices of goods given by $p$ and the world prices by $P$, tariffs are $(p - P)$. The new feature is an explicit account of intermediate inputs in production. Each good is produced using inputs of other goods as well as of primary factors. The special assumption we make is that fixed coefficients rule in determining inputs of goods in the production of goods. Let $a_{ij}$ be the amount of good $i$ required per unit of gross output of good $j$; let $A$ be the matrix with elements $a_{ij}$. Let $\xi$ denote the vector of gross outputs, and $x$ that of net outputs. The intermediate inputs of good $i$ used in the production process amount to $\sum_j a_{ij}\xi_j$. Thus $A\xi$ is the vector of intermediate inputs, and therefore $x = \xi - A\xi = (I - A)\xi$ where $I$ is the identity matrix. This should be very familiar from elementary input–output theory. If the system is capable of producing positive net outputs, the matrix $(I - A)$ must have an inverse, and this inverse must consist of non-negative entries; see Gale (1960, pp. 296–297). Then we can solve for $\xi$ in terms of $x$. Thus

$$x = (I - A)\xi, \qquad \xi = (I - A)^{-1}x \qquad (84)$$

We can think of the $\xi_j$ as the activity levels in different sectors of the economy. To specify the primary factor use, we write $v^j$ for the allocation of primary factors to sector $j$, and stipulate a transformation function

$$g^j(\xi_j, v^j) = 0 \qquad (85)$$

The allocations must be subject to the constraint imposed by the vector of total factor availability $v$; thus

$$\sum v^j = v \qquad (86)$$

Subject to (85) and (86), the chosen production plan will maximize the value of net output, i.e.

$$p^T x = p^T (I - A)\xi = \pi^T \xi \qquad (87)$$

where we define $\pi$ as

$$\pi = (I - A)^T p \qquad (88)$$

In particular, $\pi_i = p_i - \sum_j p_j a_{ji}$. Thus we subtract from the value of a unit of gross output of good $i$ the cost of intermediate inputs in its production in order to arrive at $\pi_i$. In other words, $\pi_i$ is the value added per unit of the activity level in sector $i$.

With this way of writing the objective function, we can forget about the structure of production for a moment, and think of 'outputs' $\xi$ produced in order to maximize value calculated at 'prices' $\pi$, subject to feasibility given factor endowments $v$. This is formally the same problem as that of Chapter 2, where the solution was called the revenue function. Let us define such a function $\rho(\pi, v)$, being the maximum of (87) subject to (85) and (86). This will be convex and homogeneous of degree one in $\pi$, and concave in $v$. If there are constant returns to scale, it will be homogeneous of degree one in $v$. Most importantly, the optimum choices of $\xi$ will be given by

$$\xi = \rho_\pi(\pi, v) \tag{89}$$

and the marginal contributions of primary factors to maximum value of net output, i.e. the competitive factor prices $w$, by

$$w = \rho_v(\pi, v) \tag{90}$$

To relate this to our earlier approach, we need only use the relation between $p$ and $\pi$ given by (88). Thus

$$r(p, v) = \rho((I - A)^T p, v)$$

Applying the Chain Rule of differentiation, we have

$$r_p = (I - A)\rho_\pi, \tag{91}$$

which is as it should be in the light of (84).

Our earlier work with the revenue function immediately tells us the effects of changing the vector of values added. We have $\partial \xi / \partial \pi = \rho_{\pi\pi}$, which is a positive semi-definite matrix. Thus an increase in the unit value added in any sector raises the activity level there. Moreover, this result takes given factor quantities, and allows equilibrium factor prices to be determined from (90). It is therefore a general equilibrium result.

The unit values added are not the immediate objects of control. To find the effect of changing the domestic prices, we simply use (88); differentiating (89) and (91) with respect to $p$, we have two equivalent expressions

$$\partial \xi / \partial p = \rho_{\pi\pi}(I - A)^T = (I - A)^{-1} r_{pp} \tag{92}$$

Neither of these matrices is symmetric, let alone positive semi-definite. Therefore the response of gross outputs to tariffs may produce seemingly paradoxical results. This is where the concept of effective protection comes in. The idea is that protection is provided to an activity by increasing the unit value added that it generates; this might for example be done by subsidizing inputs used there as well as levying tariffs on the goods it produces. Changes in effective protection are therefore measured by changes in $\pi$.

We can also calculate the response of factor prices to effective protection; we have

$$\partial w / \partial \pi = \rho_{v\pi} \tag{93}$$

This is subject to all the remarks in Chapter 2. In the Heckscher–Ohlin case, factor prices will respond to values added with a magnification effect; if a component of $\pi$ increases, the price of the primary factor which is used relatively intensively in this activity will rise by a greater proportion, while that of the other primary factor will fall. In the Ricardo–Viner model, we can draw several conclusions of a clear-cut nature. If a component of $\pi$ increases, (i) the price of the mobile factor will rise, but by a smaller proportion, (ii) the use of the mobile factor in this sector will rise and that in all other sectors will fall, (iii) the price of the specific factor for this sector will rise by a greater proportion than the rise in its unit value added, (iv) the prices of the factors specific to all other sectors will fall. In fact it might be argued that the interest in the concept of effective protection is primarily due to a concern for the pattern of resource use, and for the returns to factors employed in particular activities. In order to address these questions, the Ricardo–Viner model is the most natural one, and therefore these results have particular interest.

Again, the effects of changes in domestic prices add further complications; we have

$$\partial w/\partial p = \rho_{v\pi}(I - A)^T \tag{94}$$

and the sign patterns in this are hard to reduce to comprehensible rules even in simple models.

Needless to say, it is the assumption of fixed coefficients for intermediate inputs that is crucial in simplifying the above theory. If substitution among these inputs, and between them and primary inputs, is allowed, several complications can arise. It is then no longer possible in general to have a global measure of value added like the $\pi$ above. Further, it is possible that the effective protection given to an activity rises, but this induces such strong substitution of intermediate inputs for primary ones, that the primary factor use in that sector actually falls. For a discussion of these problems, and for a study of what can be salvaged under what conditions, see Jones (1971a) and Woodland (1977). For an alternative treatment of effective protection in the Ricardo–Viner model, see Jones (1975).

## NOTES

Questions of comparative statics are discussed in all the textbooks referred to earlier; in Caves and Jones (1976, ch. 4 and supplement to ch. 4), Södersten (1971, chs. 10, 11, 19, 25), and Takayama (1972, chs. 12, 13).

The transfer problem as posed here follows the approach of Samuelson (1952). More recently, a number of authors have examined the transfer problem in the context of models where non-traded goods are treated explicitly. Jones (1975) derives the condition for the terms of trade to deteriorate in such a context, and gives references to other papers on this.

The possibility of immiserizing growth was first discussed by Bhagwati (1958) and Johnson (1959). Johnson also looks at the effects of technological change. More recent literature focuses on a different but related question, viz. whether factor growth can be detrimental to a country facing fixed terms of trade. The answer is yes if there are domestic distortions, e.g. in the form of trade taxes. This was first pointed out by Johnson (1967). Bhagwati (1968) shows how the two types of immiserizing growth are related.

The effects of international capital movements are discussed by Kemp (1966) and Jones (1967). In both cases, the emphasis is on optimum taxes on direct investment, with or without (optimum) taxes on trade. Markusen and Melvin (1979) give a precise treatment of the effects of capital movements on welfare in the home and the host country. They also indicate how the analysis could be applied to international migration. Bhagwati and Rodriguez (1975) discuss migration in more general terms.

The classic reference on the effects of tariffs on the terms of trade is Metzler (1949). Bhagwati and Johnson (1961) discuss the terms of trade effects in a world with many consumers and elastic factor supplies, and where the government spends the tariff proceeds. Suzuki (1976) looks at the question in a model with three tradeables, generalizing a result by Gruen and Cordon (1970).

# CHAPTER 6

# WELFARE AND TRADE POLICY

We have looked at some questions of welfare in previous chapters. In Chapter 3 we established the gains from trade in single- and many-consumer economies. In Chapter 5 we looked at the welfare effects of income transfers, changes in technology, growth in factor endowments, and international factor movements—all in the context of one-consumer countries. We also saw how such a country could gain from the imposition of trade taxes if the world excess supply function facing it was less than perfectly elastic. Thus, we have already looked at a number of welfare implications of trade, and at some issues relating to trade policies. When we now turn to general questions of welfare and trade policy, therefore, it is merely a change in emphasis as compared to the previous chapters.

In particular, this chapter looks explicitly at the optimum formulation of trade policy from the point of view of a single country. By trade policy we shall mean the imposition of positive or negative trade taxes, i.e. specific departures from a policy of free trade. Such a departure could be rationalized on four grounds: (i) trade taxes could be used to affect world market prices, and thereby to achieve better terms of trade, (ii) trade taxes could be used to achieve an optimum domestic distribution of income, (iii) trade taxes could be used to achieve exogenously given targets for trade, production, or consumption at home, and (iv) trade taxes could be used to correct distortions due to market failure. We shall consider each of these separately. In so doing, however, one should take care to allow for other types of policy than trade policy. In our framework of Walrasian equilibria, quantitative restrictions— whether on trade, consumption, or production—can never achieve more than can be achieved by taxes or subsidies, as there will always be a shadow tax or subsidy implicit in a quantitative constraint. In addition to trade taxes, therefore, we only allow for domestic taxes on consumption or production of particular goods, or taxes on particular uses of factors. Subsidies are just taxes at negative rates, so if we allow for taxation, we allow for subsidies as well.

The country we look at is assumed to have a fixed trading environment, in the form of given net excess supply functions from the rest of the world. When we consider the special case of a small country, the excess supply function is perfectly elastic, so world prices are fixed. By assuming a fixed environment, we are unable to consider the problem of choosing tariffs when other countries retaliate. A proper treatment of that would require game-theoretic considerations that are outside our scope.

The criterion we shall use for evaluating policies is a standard Bergson–Samuelson welfare function, i.e. an increasing function of all the consumers' utility levels. Such a function incorporates inter-personal judgements, and thus enables us to find optimum policies for domestic redistribution. On the other hand, a Bergson–Samuelson welfare function makes it hard to rationalize targets for trade, consumption, or production of specific goods—such as targets for oil imports, consumption of tobacco or spirits, or self-sufficiency in food products. When it comes to evaluating policies to achieve such targets, therefore, we implicitly assume a lexicographic social preference ordering: such targets are given first priority; but once they are achieved, the Bergson–Samuelson function can be used to evaluate remaining questions of resource allocation and income distribution. The choice theoretic basis for such a lexicographic ordering is weak, but so is the very idea of quantitative targets, so we shall not worry about any axiomatic justification that our procedure might require.

The first substantive problem we shall look at is that of optimum tariffs, where we recapitulate the argument set out in Chapter 5 for the one-consumer case. We now look at it in the context of a many-consumer economy, where policy makers have access to domestic taxes as well as trade taxes. We then look at tax policies which maximize the social welfare function, given the constraints of technical feasibility, the constraints of the trading environment, and any constraints on the set of domestic taxes that can be employed. We first look at the first-best problem in which there are no con-straints on the types of taxes that can be levied, i.e. where both lump-sum and indirect taxation is possible. We find that trade taxes should only be used to secure improvements in the terms of trade, while domestic lump-sum transfers should be used to achieve an optimum distribution of income among domestic consumers. That is hardly a surprising result. Our next result is slightly more surprising. We there restrict domestic taxation to commodity taxes —i.e. taxes on consumption of goods or supplies of factors. It turns out that the same result holds under those circumstances: Inter-personal redistribution is best achieved by deploying domestic taxes, levying tariffs to secure improvements in the terms of trade.

The implication is that trade taxes should play a role in domestic redistribution only if a complete set of domestic commodity taxes cannot be implemented.

Given this very strong result, it is not very interesting to look at questions of distortions or quantity targets in the context of a many-consumer economy which can influence its terms of trade. When we turn to distortions and quantity targets, therefore, we concentrate on the case of a one-consumer, small country.

Distortions in the economy of the home country arise from various market imperfections concerning consumption, production, or factor use. In these cases, the best policy is the one well known from the general theory of welfare economics. Appropriate Pigouvian taxes or subsidies counteract the distortions directly, and restore the full first-best optimum. The implication is that trade taxes should be used only if trade is the source of the distortion. Applications are given in section 2.

Distortions which are capable of being fully corrected must be distinguished from constraints which make it impossible to attain the full optimum as measured by the social welfare function. A constraint which requires domestic production, consumption, or trade to be at levels other than those of the first-best optimum—and which might be rationalized on the lexicographic grounds suggested above—is one which cannot be overcome by any policy. The remainder of section 2 is devoted to the formulation of optimum policy subject to such constraints. The general principle that emerges is quite similar to that of the best responses to distortions: The optimum policy is one which affects the constrained variables directly, so again trade taxes should be used only if the constraint involves trade itself.

We must distinguish the best responses to distortions or quantity constraints from second-best responses to distortions. If first-best policies to correct domestic distortions are not available, as may be the case if distortions are due to monopolistic practices, if administrative considerations make uniform taxation of different commodities necessary, or if political considerations make first-best policies unacceptable, there may be second-best responses involving other policies. We study these issues in section 3.

Throughout this chapter, as noted above, we look at trade policy from the point of view of a single country. A very important question of trade policy involves several countries, however. That is the question of customs unions. It turns out that the question of welfare effects of customs unions can be seen as a simple extension of earlier analyses of single-country problems. At the end of the chapter, therefore, we look at how two countries trading with each other and with the rest of the world can gain from co-ordinating their trade and tax policies.

## 1. OPTIMUM TARIFFS AND DOMESTIC TAXES

In this section, the policy variables are tariffs and domestic commodity taxes or transfers. These can be chosen without any subsidiary constraints, subject only to technical feasibility. The objective is maximum welfare in one country, the home country. Since welfare in the rest of the world is not a concern, the home country's gain from improving its terms of trade is relevant. So is interpersonal distribution as entailed by the welfare function. In Chapter 3 we saw how domestic taxes could be deployed to make free trade Pareto superior to autarky. This is sufficient but not necessary for welfare improvement. However, we shall see that domestic taxes retain their major role of adjusting interpersonal distribution.

The rest of the world presents the home country with a net excess demand vector $M$ as a function of prices $P$. These are the prices the home country trades at, and are properly called its trade prices or border prices. They may differ from the prices faced by consumers and producers in other countries, since there may be tariffs and taxes that prevail there. However, since we are taking any such matters as fixed, it is convenient by a slight abuse of language to refer to $P$ as world prices. In general, their equilibrium levels will be influenced by demand and supply from the home country. The function $M(P)$ will be homogeneous of degree zero and will satisfy $P.M(P) = 0$, reflecting an assumption that there are no international transfers of purchasing power. When we are considering the special case where the home country is small, $P$ will be fixed, and any $M$ satisfying $P.M = 0$ will be available to the home country.

Given a system of tariffs and taxes in the home country, an equilibrium will be established. This will involve adjustment of home and world prices to make the home import demand vector $m$ equal to the foreign supply $-M$. Without denying the direction of economic causation from tariffs to prices, it proves convenient to look at the formal mathematics in a different way. Take $P$ itself as the initial choice variable, as if the home country announces the prices at which it will trade. This fixes the imports it will have, as $m = -M(P)$. Then look for a domestic equilibrium given this $m$. Having found the domestic market-clearing prices, we can take the tariffs to be implicitly determined as the difference between home and foreign prices. Since the two can be normalized independently, there is one degree of freedom or arbitrariness in defining tariffs; this is the well-known feature of 'symmetry between import and export taxes'.

The above step of finding a domestic equilibrium for a given net import vector is most easily carried out in terms of the Meade utility function defined on net imports. This should be clear from the properties of such a function examined in Chapter 3. We also took a preliminary look at the optimum tariff problem in Chapter 5, using this function in the context of one consumer and fixed factor supplies. Here we extend the method to variable factor supplies (which could be interpreted as non-traded goods), and to several consumers with particular domestic tax policies. As usual, we begin with the simplest case and work towards successively more difficult ones.

### The one-consumer case

The relevant Meade utility function was defined in Chapter 3, equation (10). Here we briefly recapitulate its properties. We have

$$\phi(m) = \max_{c,v,x} \{f(c, v) \mid c = x + m, g(x, v) = 0\} \qquad (1)$$

The constraints on the material balances of goods can be eliminated by substituting for $c$ in $f$. Let $\mu$ be the multiplier on the production constraint, and write the Lagrangean as

$$L = f(x + m, v) - \mu g(x, v) \qquad (2)$$

The first-order conditions are

$$f_c(x + m, v) - \mu g_x(x, v) = 0 \qquad (3)$$

$$f_v(x + m, v) - \mu g_v(x, v) = 0 \qquad (4)$$

But $(f_c, f_v)$ are the vectors of marginal utilities of goods and marginal disutilities of factors, so $(f_c, -f_v)$ will be proportional to consumer prices of goods and factors. Similarly, $(g_x, -g_v)$ will be proportional to the producer prices of goods and factors. Thus, (3) and (4) can be interpreted as saying that consumer and producer prices should be equalized, or that all marginal rates of substitution should equal the corresponding marginal rates of transformation. As in Chapter 3, non-traded goods can be handled by interpreting them as factors.

The envelope theorem says that the partial derivatives of the envelope function $\phi$ can be found by differentiating the Lagrangean with respect to $m$ and evaluating at the optimum. Then, from (2),

$$\phi_m(m) = f_c(x + m, v) \tag{5}$$

The partial derivatives $\phi_m$ give us the effects on the maximum achievable utility from marginal increases in the net availability of imports, i.e. of goods to the home country. They can therefore be called the shadow prices of goods there. When a symbol making this aspect explicit is necessary, we shall write them as $\hat{p}$. What (5) then says is that $\hat{p}$ should equal the domestic consumer price vector, and the scale being arbitrary, by (3) it also equals the domestic producer price vector. In more complicated settings that follow, we will find that these three price vectors can in general differ. In the present case there are no distortions and there is only one consumer, so domestic taxation has no function, corrective, or distributive. Hence there is no reason to make different agents in the economy face different prices.

Having determined the domestic equilibrium for given $m$, it is a simple matter to set up the optimum tariff problem. Since $m = -M(P)$, we should choose $P$ to maximize $\phi(-M(P))$. This yields first-order conditions

$$\phi_m(m)^T M_p(P) = 0 \tag{6}$$

In Chapter 5, this was interpreted as a condition of tangency between the home indifference surface and the foreign offer surface. After choosing a numeraire, optimum tariffs were found by means of a general inverse elasticity formula. This chapter adds nothing new in these respects. We only point out that for a small country, the problem is one of maximizing $\phi(m)$ subject to $P.m = 0$ for fixed $P$. This has the solution $\phi_m(m) = \alpha P$ for scalar multiplier $\alpha$. This says that domestic prices should equal foreign prices to within a scale factor, i.e. that free trade is optimum in this case.

The important question is how well these results extend to economies with several consumers. That of course depends on the redistributive policies available. We first consider the case where these are the most powerful ones possible, viz. lump-sum transfers. Then we turn to the case where such transfers are not available, and commodity taxation is used for distributive purposes.

### Tariffs and lump-sum transfers

Suppose the home country has several consumers, indexed by $h$. Writing their consumption vectors for goods as $c^h$, and factor supply

vectors as $v^h$, the utilities are given by $u^h = f^h(c^h, v^h)$. We first
consider an apparently even more general problem, where the $c^h$
and $v^h$ can be directly controlled by the government. As usual in
welfare economics, it will turn out that the optimum can be achieved
indirectly using prices and lump-sum transfers.

The constraints are

$$\sum c^h = x + m, \qquad \sum v^h = v, \qquad g(x, v) = 0$$

The objective function is denoted by $\omega(u^1, u^2, \ldots)$, and is increasing in all arguments. Making as much substitution as possible,
we write the maximization problem, and define the Meade envelope
function as

$$\phi(m) = \max \left\{ \omega(f^1(c^1, v^1), \ldots) \mid g\left(\sum c^h - m, \sum v^h\right) = 0 \right\} \tag{7}$$

The choice variables of the maximization problem are all the vectors
$c^h$ and $v^h$. Following the argument used in Chapter 3, we can verify
that the function $\phi$ is increasing, and that it is quasi-concave if $\omega$
is quasi-concave in the utilities and each utility $u^h$ is concave in
$(c^h, v^h)$. We omit the details since they are not of immediate importance; the interested reader should refer to Gorman (1959).

The Lagrangean is

$$L = \omega(f^1(c^1, v^1), \ldots) - \mu g\left(\sum c^h - m, \sum v^h\right) \tag{8}$$

and the first-order conditions are

$$\omega_h f_c^h - \mu g_x = 0 \tag{9}$$

$$\omega_h f_v^h - \mu g_v = 0 \tag{10}$$

for all $h$, where $\omega_h \equiv \partial\omega/\partial u^h$. These have interpretations similar to
(3) and (4) of the one-consumer case. The producer price vector is
$(g_x, -g_v)$ as before. The marginal utilities of goods and factors of
consumer $h$, and hence the vector of prices that must be presented
to him if he is to make the appropriate choice, is given by $(f_c^h, -f_v^h)$.
We see from (9) and (10) that it must equal the producer price
vector to within a scalar multiple, $\omega_h$. This can differ from one consumer to the next. But since it is an arbitrary choice in any case,
that is immaterial. We can therefore say that all consumers and
producers should face the same prices for goods and factors, say
$\hat{p}$ and $\hat{w}$. Having found these, and knowing the optimum choices
$c^h$ and $v^h$, all we need to do in order to achieve a decentralized

implementation of the plan is to give the consumers transfer incomes $y^h = \hat{p}.c^h - \hat{w}.v^h$.

Suppose we choose a common normalization of prices at the level of producer prices, i.e. $(\hat{p}, \hat{w}) = (g_x, -g_v)$. Consider the choice problem for consumer $h$. We know that for all goods and factors, the ratio of marginal utility to price should have the same value, and the common value is simply the marginal utility of lump-sum income. From (9) and (10), then, the marginal utility of consumer $h$'s lump-sum income is $\mu/\omega_h$. Therefore the marginal impact on welfare of giving an incremental lump-sum to him is that times $\partial \omega/\partial u^h$, i.e. $\mu$. Our lump-sum transfers have equalized the marginal welfare effects of redistribution, which is the well-known property of a full welfare optimum. All this is nothing other than a confirmation of the standard welfare-theoretic propositions for the home country with lump-sum transfers, achieving an equilibrium with fixed $m$.

By the envelope theorem, we have

$$\phi_m(m) = \mu \, g_x \left( \sum c^h - m, \sum v^h \right) \tag{11}$$

As before, the domestic shadow prices of goods must capture the effect on welfare of making available marginal additions to the net quantities, i.e. $\hat{p}$ must equal $\phi_m$ to within a scalar multiple. Then (11) shows that shadow prices of goods are simply the producer prices; by earlier reasoning they equal consumer prices as well. So long as lump-sum transfers are available, therefore, the presence of several consumers does not affect the identity between the three concepts of prices in the home country that we saw in the one-consumer model earlier.

This completes the determination of equilibrium in the home country given $m$. Once again, it is a trivial task to set up the optimum tariff problem; the procedure is exactly the same as in the one-consumer case, as is the result (6). We can therefore say that the task of domestic interpersonal distribution is carried out using lump-sum transfers, leaving tariffs to secure the gains from the change in the terms of trade. In the small-country case, tariffs would have no role.

## Tariffs and commodity taxes

Now we suppose that lump-sum transfers are not available. In the manner explained in Chapter 3, we also assume constant returns to scale in production. Thus there are no pure profits, and the only source of income to consumers is their sale of factor services. We assume that all goods and factors can be taxed at any desired rates.

Under these circumstances, we cannot work as if all the consumers' $c^h$ and $v^h$ could be directly controlled. We have to ensure that they are compatible with choice given prices. For this purpose, we use the general expenditure function introduced in Chapter 2, equation (49), giving the minimum lump-sum income necessary to achieve a target utility at given prices. Let $e^{*h}(p, w, u^h)$ be this function for consumer $h$. Then we know that his choices are given by

$$c^h = e_p^{*h}, \qquad v^h = -e_w^{*h} \tag{12}$$

Also, since the consumer has no lump-sum income, we have the consistency condition

$$e^{*h}(p, w, u^h) = 0 \tag{13}$$

We can use (13) to solve for $u^h$ in terms of $(p, w)$. That gives the indirect utility function $u^h(p, w)$. Substituting this into (12), we have the uncompensated consumer product demand functions $c^h(p, w)$ and factor supply functions $v^h(p, w)$. If some factors do not cause disutility, and are accordingly supplied inelastically in the available quantity, the corresponding component in $v^h$ will be constant; this is a special case in our formulation. The constraints of production and aggregate feasibility are

$$\sum c^h(p, w) = x + m, \qquad \sum v^h(p, w) = v, \qquad g(x, v) = 0 \tag{14}$$

It is convenient to regard the consumer prices $p$ and $w$ as the choice variables. The problem having been solved, $(g_x, -g_v)$ at the optimum will be the producer prices, and commodity taxes will be implicitly defined as the differences.

The objective function is $\omega(u^1, u^2, \ldots)$ as before. Each $u^h$ depends on $(p, w)$ through the indirect utility function. It is convenient to find its properties. Totally differentiating (13), we have

$$e_p^{*h}.dp + e_w^{*h}.dw + e_u^{*h} du^h = 0$$

We know that the partial derivative in the last term is the reciprocal of the marginal utility of income to consumer $h$. Write that as $\lambda_h$; then we have

$$du^h = \lambda_h(-c^h.dp + v^h.dw) \tag{15}$$

Now we are ready to set up the optimum tax problem, and define the associated Meade envelope function. We have

$$\phi(m) = \max_{p, w} \left\{ \omega(u^1(p, w), \ldots) \,|\, g\left(\sum c^h(p, w) - m, \sum v^h(p, w)\right) = 0 \right\} \tag{16}$$

The function is clearly increasing. However, we cannot guarantee its quasi-concavity under any reasonable conditions. Thus its indifference surfaces may fail to be convex, and there may be problems in ensuring that first-order conditions yield true maxima. This is a very common problem in optimum tax theory, and we have no solution to offer.

The Lagrangean is

$$L = \omega(u^1(p, w), \ldots) - \mu g\left(\sum c^h(p, w) - m, \sum v^h(p, w)\right) \quad (17)$$

The first-order conditions are, using (15),

$$-\sum \omega_h \lambda_h c^h - \mu\left\{g_x \sum c_p^h + g_v \sum v_p^h\right\} = 0 \quad (18)$$

$$\sum \omega_h \lambda_h v^h - \mu\left\{g_x \sum c_w^h + g_v \sum v_w^h\right\} = 0 \quad (19)$$

These can be recognized as the standard conditions for optimum commodity taxation. The usual treatment in the literature does not distinguish between goods and factors, and results in just one vector equation for all commodities, as in Sandmo (1976). Explicit treatment of factor taxation is quite straightforward. The actual solution for $p$ and $w$ from (18) and (19) can be quite complicated. However, it is clear that in general $(p, w)$ will not be proportional to $(g_x, -g_v)$, i.e. taxes will have to be levied to maintain the desired difference between consumer prices and producer prices; see Dixit (1979) for some details.

What about the shadow prices of goods, $\hat{p}$? By the envelope theorem, we have

$$\hat{p} \equiv \phi_m(m) = \mu \, g_x\left(\sum c^h(p, w) - m, \sum v^h(p, w)\right) \quad (20)$$

Thus shadow prices of goods equal the producer prices to within an arbitrary scale factor. They need no longer equal the consumer prices.

This has obvious implications for the optimum tariffs. Again we choose $P$ to maximize $\phi(-M(P))$, and obtain (6). However, the relevant domestic prices are now the producer prices. In other words, the foreign offer surface should now be tangential to the domestic production frontier in goods space, or orthogonal to the domestic producer price vector.

This is in fact a special case of a very general principle established in the pioneering rigorous analysis of commodity taxation by Diamond and Mirrlees (1971). It is that, with a full set of commodity taxes optimally deployed, production efficiency is desirable. All marginal rates of transformation should be equalized, although they may not equal the corresponding marginal rates of substitution on account of the taxes. Now trade is just another way by which the home country can transform one set of goods into another, and the foreign offer surface defines the transformation possibilities. The tangency with the frontier of domestic transformation possibilities through production is an immediate corollary.

Combining (6) and (20), we can write the optimum tariff formula for this case as

$$g_x^T M_P(P) = 0 \qquad (21)$$

Rigorously speaking, the whole optimization problem must be solved as one, and the optimum commodity taxes and tariffs determined jointly from (18), (19), and (21). Nevertheless, we can say that the structure of these conditions is such that tariffs are essentially concerned with the terms of trade and domestic taxes with interpersonal distribution. Since $g_x$ itself depends on $p$ and $w$, we cannot solve (21) without having found the optimum commodity taxes. But the fact of orthogonality of domestic producer prices to the foreign offer surface is entirely independent of the specifics of the social welfare function: all one needs to know is that the implied redistributive policies are undertaken. The specific taxes or subsidies needed to achieve a domestic distributive optimum, on the other hand, cannot be found without knowing exactly what trade policy is pursued and what gain it gives, since that affects $\mu$. We shall leave it to the reader to consider whether this explains why Chancellors of the Exchequer (or Finance Ministers) are often more powerful figures than Ministers for Trade.

The case of a small country highlights these points in the most direct way. When $\phi(m)$ is maximized subject to $P.m = 0$ for fixed $P$, we have $g_x = \phi_m(m) = \alpha P$ for a scalar multiplier $\alpha$. In other words, domestic producer prices should equal the given world prices. Consumer prices can differ from their common value. The implied commodity taxes should be levied at the same rates on the two sources of supply, whether domestic products or imports. When the home country cannot improve its terms of trade, there is still no role for tariffs; domestic redistribution is better achieved by means of commodity taxes.

## 2. POLICY RESPONSES TO DISTORTIONS AND CONSTRAINTS

Having examined issues of terms of trade and interpersonal distribution at some length, we now put them aside by assuming a small one-consumer economy. This is done in order to highlight the new questions that are raised by the presence of further constraints on policy. It is not in principle difficult to combine everything into a grand model, but its algebraic complexity obscures all economic understanding.

Constraints may pertain directly to policy instruments, or to economic magnitudes that are affected by them. In this section we consider the latter case; the next section looks at the former.

The policy instruments we consider are tariffs, together with taxes on various domestic economic activities, in particular consumption, production, and factor use. We first clear up a preliminary problem. Let $P$ be the fixed vector of world prices, and suppose domestic prices are normalized in the same units. Express all taxes in the specific form, i.e. per unit of quantity. There are various identities relating prices and tariffs. The price vector for imports just after they have crossed the border equals the sum of the world price vector and the tariff vector. Consider consumption from imports; then the consumer price vector must equal this price vector for imports plus the vector of consumption taxes. Similarly, considering consumption from domestic production, we have consumer prices =, producer prices + production taxes + consumption taxes. These let us express domestic consumer and producer prices in terms of world prices and various taxes:

Consumer prices $= P +$ Tariffs + Consumption taxes,

Producer prices $= P +$ Tariffs $-$ Production taxes.

In most cases, the domestic consumer and producer prices are the sole channels through which policy will affect the economy. With three tax vectors, we have a degree of freedom. For instance, we could restrict ourselves by setting one of the tax vectors at zero, and still achieve the same end by deploying the other two. In fact it is sensible to express policy in the simplest possible way, i.e. use just two instruments, and one if possible. For example, a policy that calls for consumer taxes and producer subsidies at equal rates with tariffs set at zero is more simply and equivalently expressed as a tariff at this rate with the other two taxes set at zero. Of course, a tariff alone will not typically be optimum, and it will be an important part of our analysis to find the circumstances when it is.

The policy is constrained by the trade balance requirement $P.m = 0$, by the production feasibility constraint, and in addition by particular distortions and constraints. We consider different cases according to these added complexities.

## Domestic distortions

We begin by considering product markets. There are three important vectors, the shadow price $\hat{p}$, and the vectors of marginal utilities and marginal costs, respectively $f_c$ and $g_x$. In the one-consumer, small-country case we are considering, we have seen that first-best optimality requires $\hat{p}$ to equal the world prices $P$, and $f_c$ and $g_x$ to equal $\hat{p}$, in each case to within scale factors. If there are no domestic distortions, this will be achieved in a competitive equilibrium with free trade. This ensures that domestic prices equal world prices, and optimal adjustment by domestic consumers and producers make each of $f_c$ and $g_x$ proportional to domestic prices.

Now suppose there are distortions within the domestic production sector. A typical source is an externality: one producer's output affects another's production process, but there is no market to allow them to make and receive payments reflecting the marginal gain or loss thus conferred. In such circumstances, competition and free trade will yield $\hat{p} = P$, and $f_c = \hat{p}$, each up to a scalar multiple, but $g_x$ will differ from $\hat{p}$ in composition as well as scale. The optimum policy in this case is well understood from welfare-economic theory. We have a Pigouvian scheme of corrective taxes or subsidies on domestic production which mimics the desired payments for gains or losses. This makes $g_x$ proportional to $\hat{p}$, and restores the first-best optimum.

However, once we are in a distorted equilibrium, the 'general theory of the second-best' raises the possibility that matters may be improved by introducing yet another distortion somewhere else in the economy. A tariff is one such policy. If it is used instead of the Pigouvian policy, domestic prices become $(P + t)$ where $t$ is the tariff vector. Production distortions keep $g_x$ different from $(P + t)$. On the consumption side, $f_c$ becomes proportional to $(P + t)$, and thereby loses proportionality with $\hat{p} = P$. Thus we have two distortions, but they may be better than one, so this state of affairs may be better than the initial equilibrium with distortions and no policy at all. However, it cannot be first-best, and therefore cannot be as good as the optimum Pigouvian policy in conjunction with free trade.

Similarly, a domestic distortion in consumption is best corrected by a Pigouvian scheme applied to consumption, thereby restoring first-best optimality. The general principle is that the policy should correct, or offset, the distortion directly.

If the distortion is such that in a competitive equilibrium in absence of policy, $f_c$ would be proportional to $g_x$, but the common value would differ from $\hat{p}$, then the corrective Pigouvian policy involves equal changes in $f_c$ and $g_x$, i.e. consumption taxes and production subsidies at equal rates. This, as we have seen, is more simply achieved by means of a tariff. In this case, the distortion essentially involves a common stance of all agents in the domestic economy in relation to the rest of the world. Therefore we may think of it as having its origin in trade. It is difficult to think of examples of this, but if it happens, the best offsetting policy is one of trade taxes.

The reasoning extends to factor market distortions: these are best corrected by factor taxes or subsidies, which should be use-specific if the distortion is between different uses of a common factor. We note in passing that a simple immobility of factors across uses need not be a distortion at all; if immobility is a technical constraint, or is due to costs of moving, it is simply a special model, for example the Ricardo–Viner model, and no corrective policy is called for.

The reasoning extends easily to a large country as well. Instead of free trade, the first-best involves an optimum tariff. Once this is imposed, and domestic shadow prices $\hat{p}$ suitably different from world prices $P$ are found, it is desirable to keep $f_c$ and $g_x$ proportional to $\hat{p}$. In face of distortions, this is best done by appropriate Pigouvian taxes and subsidies in consumption and production. These may in exceptional cases work out at rates which can be implemented more directly by tariffs, but in general the role of tariffs is confined to improving the terms of trade. Extensions to several consumers are also easy. There is no new feature at all if domestic redistribution is carried out through lump-sum transfers. With commodity taxes, there is an optimum relation between $f_c$ and $g_x$, while $g_x$ is to be kept proportional to $\hat{p}$. The role of Pigouvian taxation is to restore these relations. For closed economies, this is shown in Sandmo (1975).

Readers who wish to pursue the usual treatment of policy responses to domestic distortions will find a survey in Bhagwati (1971). His analysis of the product market closely parallels ours. He uses marginal rates of substitution and transformation, i.e. relative prices, instead of vectors of marginal utilities and costs, i.e. prices arbitrary as to scale. His domestic rate of substitution (DRS) corresponds to our $f_c$, his domestic rate of transformation (DRT) to our $g_x$, and his foreign rate of transformation (FRT) to our shadow prices $\hat{p}$.

Having examined distortions amenable to full correction by

Pigouvian policy, we turn to constraints which rule out attainment of the first-best, by confining some quantities away from their optimum levels. In such cases no policy can achieve the first-best, but we can find the optimum policy response to the additional constraint. We find a principle similar to the one above: we should use the policy that affects the constrained variables most directly.

## Constraints involving imports

First suppose that the quantities of net imports of certain goods are required to be fixed. This may arise from ceilings on imports dictated by political or strategic considerations, or a ceiling on exports agreed by a country fearing retaliation, or trade agreements under which a country is obliged to buy at least certain minimum amounts from other countries.

Divide the set of goods into two, distinguished by superscripts 1 and 2. Suppose the vector $m^1$ of net imports of goods in category 1 is fixed. Only $m^2$ remains to be chosen, and the budget constraint is $P^1.m^1 + P^2.m^2 = 0$. With no other additional constraints, once $m = (m^1, m^2)$ is chosen, domestic equilibrium will be determined as before, and we can use the Meade utility function, now written as $\phi(m^1, m^2)$. It remains to determine the trade policy by solving the problem

$$\max_{m^2} \{\phi(m^1, m^2) \mid m^1 \text{ fixed, } P^1.m^1 + P^2.m^2 = 0\}$$

The Lagrangean is

$$L = \phi(m^1, m^2) - \alpha(P^1.m^1 + P^2.m^2) \qquad (22)$$

where $\alpha$ is a positive scalar multiplier. This gives the first-order conditions

$$\phi_2(m^1, m^2) - \alpha P^2 = 0 \qquad (23)$$

where we have denoted the vector of partial derivatives of $\phi$ with respect to $m^2$ by $\phi_2$. Choose a normalization so that $(\phi_1/\alpha, \phi_2/\alpha)$ is the whole vector of domestic prices of goods. Then we see that the optimum can be achieved by keeping the domestic prices of category 2 goods equal to their world prices, i.e. by allowing free trade in those goods. The prices of category 1 goods are then found from the requirements that the constraints be satisfied. These entail appropriate tariffs or subsidies on trade in those goods. The policy of concentrating tax policies on the sources of the additional constraints is an instance of the general principle enunciated earlier.

We can in fact say more about the policies required for category 1 goods. By the envelope theorem, the rate at which the maximum attainable utility changes in response to a change in the target quantities of net imports of these goods can be found by evaluating the partial derivatives of $L$ with respect to $m^1$ at the optimum,

$$\phi_1(m^1, m^2) - \alpha P^1 = \alpha\{\phi_1(m^1, m^2)/\alpha - P^1\}$$

If the component of this for a particular good is positive, we will say that the constraint is holding the net imports of it at too low a level. This may be because of a ceiling on imports, or a floor on exports. In either case, this corresponds to the domestic price of that good being kept above its foreign price. This means a suitable tariff if the good is being imported, or a subsidy if it is being exported. In view of the nature of the constraint, this makes eminently good sense.

The other type of constraint involving imports that we consider is on the value of goods in a particular category. With notation as above, suppose we are required to keep $P^1 . m^1 = k$ for some given $k$, and then naturally $P^2 . m^2 = -k$. Then we are to maximize $\phi(m^1, m^2)$ subject to these two constraints. The Lagrangean is

$$L = \phi(m^1, m^2) - \alpha_1(P^1 . m^1 - k) - \alpha_2(P^2 . m^2 + k) \qquad (24)$$

where $\alpha_1$ and $\alpha_2$ are the multipliers, which will be positive since $\phi$ is increasing. The first-order conditions are

$$\phi_1(m^1, m^2) = \alpha_1 P^1, \qquad \phi_2(m^1, m^2) = \alpha_2 P^2 \qquad (25)$$

These require us to keep the domestic prices of each category of goods proportional to their world prices, but with possibly different factors of proportionality. Let us see what this implies, by looking at the response of maximized utility to a change in the constraining $k$. By the envelope theorem, the derivative is simply $(\alpha_1 - \alpha_2)$. If an increase in $k$ raises utility, the constraint is holding down the value of net imports of category 1 goods below what is ideal. In this case, we have $\alpha_1 > \alpha_2$. Suppose we normalize domestic prices so that those for category 2 goods equal their world prices. Then the domestic prices of category 1 goods will be above their world prices by the proportion $(\alpha_1 - \alpha_2)/\alpha_2$, the same for all these goods. This will be achieved by levying an *ad valorem* tariff on all the imported goods in this category, and an *ad valorem* subsidy on all those exported, at the same rate. Goods of category 2 are subject to free trade. Once again, the general principle of using policies which directly affect the constraining variables is illustrated.

## Constraints on domestic production and consumption

We next consider constraints on the levels of production and consumption of particular goods in the home economy. Simple examples are floors on the production of a particular good for strategic reasons, or ceilings on consumption for moral reasons. A more complicated example is where the country wishes to have 95% self-sufficiency in a particular good, say good 1, so the constraint is $x_1 \geq 0.95c_1$. We take a general case where the constraint is given by an implicit equation $h(c, x) \leq 0$. This can cover even more complicated circumstances. For example, with fixed factor supplies, we may have a 'general second-best' constraint which prevents the equalization of marginal rates of substitution and transformation between two goods. This will be of the form $(\partial f/\partial c_1)/(\partial f/\partial c_2) = k(\partial g/\partial x_1)/(\partial g/\partial x_2)$ with $k \neq 1$, which can be cast in our general form.

We now need a slight modification of the Meade utility function. The additional constraint affects the domestic equilibrium for given $m$, and must therefore be taken into account in our definition of this function. Thus we have

$$\phi(m) = \max_{c,x,v} \{f(c, v) \mid c = x + m, g(x, v) = 0, h(c, x) \leq 0\}$$
(26)

In setting up the Lagrangean, it is then simpler to leave the commodity balance equation as a separate constraint, with its own vector of multipliers. These multipliers will give us the effect on maximum utility of additional availability of goods, i.e. they will be the domestic shadow prices of goods, $\hat{p}$. Let $\mu$ be the multiplier on the production constraint as before, and write $\theta$ for that on the additional constraint. Then

$$L = f(c, v) - \hat{p}.(c - x - m) - \mu g(x, v) - \theta h(c, x)$$
(27)

The first-order conditions are

$$f_c - \hat{p} - \theta h_c = 0$$
(28)

$$\hat{p} - \mu g_x - \theta h_x = 0$$
(29)

$$f_v - \mu g_v = 0$$
(30)

The envelope theorem gives

$$\phi_m(m) = \hat{p}$$
(31)

This accords with the usual interpretation of domestic shadow prices of goods, since an increase in net imports is just one way of increasing their domestic availability.

Now choose the normalization so that consumer prices are $(f_c, -f_v)$, and producer prices $(\mu g_x, -\mu g_v)$. Equations (30) are then simple: consumer prices of factors should equal their producer prices, i.e.

factor allocation should be efficient. Since factors are not involved in the additional constraints we have again an example of matching policy to constraints. With $c$ and $x$ involved in the constraint, (28) and (29) give us the policy concerning them: (28) tells us how consumer prices of goods should differ from their shadow prices, and (29) tells us the corresponding result for producer prices. The general formula is best understood through examples.

First consider the case where the consumption of good 1 is being held to a level below a fixed quantity $k$, i.e. $h(c, x) = c_1 - k$. Then $h_x = 0$, and (29) gives equality of producer prices and shadow prices. The same follows from (28) for consumer prices of all goods other than the first, for which we have the consumer price above the shadow price by the amount $\theta$. The policy indicated is free trade, no production taxes, and a specific tax at rate $\theta$ on the consumption of good 1 alone. The reader can similarly verify that the optimum policy involves suitable production taxes alone for the case where the constraint involves production quantities alone.

Next consider the case of 95% self-sufficiency mentioned above, for which $h(c, x) = 0.95c_1 - x_1$. Again, all components of $h_c$ and $h_x$ other than the first are zero, so no taxes on any other goods are needed. For the first good, we have $\partial f/\partial c_1 = p_1 + 0.95\theta$, and $\mu\, \partial g/\partial x_1 = p_1 + \theta$. The consumer price being above the shadow price indicates a consumption tax at the specific rate $0.95\theta$. The producer price being above the shadow price indicates a production subsidy at rate $\theta$. The value of $\theta$ must be found appropriately to satisfy the constraint. Again we have a combination of policies involving the variables that enter the constraint.

It should be noted that the optimum given a constraint of less than 100% self-sufficiency cannot be achieved through tariffs alone. We could of course, by appropriate choice of trade taxes, achieve $x_1 = 0.95c_1$; but the above result says that there are better ways of achieving the desired degree of self-sufficiency. The reason is simply that producer subsidies and consumer taxes can achieve the same thing with a smaller absolute distortion in the quantities $c_1$ and $x_1$ as compared to the first-best optimum.

### Factor market distortions

Finally, we consider additional constraints that arise from an inability to allocate factors in the best possible way. This may arise from use-specific market imperfections; the usual example is the exercise of monopoly power by labour unions in one sector. We offer a very general treatment that can encompass this and other types of constraints.

Here it is necessary to make the process of factor allocation explicit. We have usually been subsuming factor allocation into the formation of a revenue function $r(p, v)$, or an aggregate transformation frontier $g(x, v) = 0$. Both of these assume efficient allocation. When that is no longer the case, we have to go behind the veil of such envelope functions. We do this by supposing that there are two processes of transformation of inputs into outputs, given by functions $g^1(x^1, v^1) = 0$ and $g^2(x^2, v^2) = 0$. When they are both in operation, total input use is $v^1 + v^2$, and total output is $x^1 + x^2$. Thus there are no externalities; we have considered them earlier. The generalization to several processes is easy; it is not even necessary for each process to have positive inputs and outputs of all factors and goods.

If $\hat{p}$ is the vector of shadow prices of goods, the efficient production plan will maximize the value of output, $\hat{p} \cdot (x^1 + x^2)$, subject to the two production constraints and given a total vector of factor quantities, $v$. Let $\mu_1$ and $\mu_2$ be the multipliers for the production constraints, and let $\hat{w}$ be the shadow prices of the factors. Then the Lagrangean is

$$L = \hat{p} \cdot (x^1 + x^2) - \mu_1 g^1(x^1, v^1) - \mu_2 g^2(x^2, v^2) - \hat{w} \cdot (v^1 + v^2 - v)$$

and first-order conditions are

$$\hat{p} = \mu_1 g_x^1(x^1, v^1) = \mu_2 g_x^2(x^2, v^2)$$
$$\hat{w} = -\mu_1 g_v^1(x^1, v^1) = -\mu_2 g_v^2(x^2, v^2) \qquad (32)$$

On choice of normalization, these can be achieved very simply by having producers in both processes face prices $\hat{p}$ for goods and $\hat{w}$ for factors. Then the corresponding marginal rates of transformation in the two will be equalized.

Additional constraints can prevent this. Take a very general form of such a constraint, $h(v^1, v^2) = 0$. With two goods, one produced in each process, for example, the function $h$ might give a weighted difference between the marginal rates of input substitution in the two, with unequal weights. Then $h = 0$ prevents the equalization of the two rates, and yields an inefficient allocation.

To determine the optimum policy under these circumstances, we again define the Meade utility function incorporating all the constraints. We have

$$\phi(m) - \max\{f(c, v) \mid c = x^1 + x^2 + m, v = v^1 + v^2,$$
$$g^1(x^1, v^1) = 0, g^2(x^2, v^2) = 0, h(v^1, v^2) = 0\} \qquad (33)$$

Let $\theta$ be the multiplier on the additional constraint. Then we can write the Lagrangean as

$$L = f(c, v) - \hat{p}.(c - x^1 - x^2 - m) - \hat{w}.(v^1 + v^2 - v)$$
$$- \mu_1 \, g^1(x^1, v^1) - \mu_2 \, g^2(x^2, v^2) - \theta h(v^1, v^2) \qquad (34)$$

This yields first-order conditions

$$f_c - \hat{p} = 0, \qquad f_v + \hat{w} = 0 \qquad (35)$$

$$\hat{p} = \mu_1 \, g_x^1(x^1, v^1) = \mu_2 \, g_x^2(x^2, v^2) \qquad (36)$$

$$\hat{w} = -\mu_1 \, g_v^1(x^1, v^1) - \theta \, h_1(v^1, v^2) = -\mu_2 \, g_v^2(x^2, v^2) - \theta \, h_2(v^1, v^2) \qquad (37)$$

where we have denoted the vectors of partial derivatives of $h$ with respect to $v^1$ and $v^2$ respectively by $h_1$ and $h_2$. Finally, the envelope theorem gives (31) again:

$$\phi_m(m) = \hat{p}$$

The interpretations are immediate. By (31) there should be free trade, by (35) there should be no consumption taxes, and by (36) there should be no production taxes on goods. The only taxes are on factors, and can be found from (37). Factor users in sector 1 should face prices $-\mu_1 g_v^1 = \hat{w} + \theta h_1$; this can be achieved by levying taxes on the use of factors in process 1, the vector of tax rates being $\theta h_1$. Similarly, the use of factors in process 2 should be taxed at a vector of rates $\theta h_2$. The optimum policy thus leaves all other transactions untaxed, but taxes factors at use-specific rates, chosen to reflect the effect of each factor use on the additional constraint, and the shadow price associated with that constraint.

To sum up, our analysis of optimum policies subject to additional constraints has in each case confirmed the general principle that the optimum choices of instruments should be such as to affect the constrained variables directly. Only if the constraints concern trade flows directly, as in the case of product-specific trade agreements, does that call for the use of trade taxes. Readers will find further details in Bhagwati (1971).

### Effective protection

As a final example, we consider a case where intermediate inputs of produced goods are required in production, and policy is concerned with levels of gross outputs. In other words, we find the best way of providing effective protection to industries. The comparative statics of effective tariffs in Chapter 5 assumed fixed coefficients of intermediate inputs. That special assumption is not needed for the welfare analysis here.

Suppose gross output $\xi_j$ of good $j$ can be produced using a vector of intermediate inputs, $\eta^j$, and a vector of primary inputs, $v^j$, according to the production function

$$\xi_j = g^j(\eta^j, v^j) \tag{38}$$

The factor allocations must satisfy

$$\sum_j v^j = v$$

If a vector $m$ of net imports is available, the equation of material balance for goods is

$$c = \xi - \sum_j \eta^j + m$$

Our aim is to choose a plan of production, consumption and factor supply, to maximize $f(c, v)$ subject to these, and an additional constraint,

$$h(\xi) = 0$$

The outcome is the Meade envelope function $\phi(m)$ for this problem.

It is no longer necessary to write down all the first-order conditions. Mostly, they are the conditions of competitive pricing. The exception arises for the gross output vector $\xi$, due to the additional constraint. As usual, let $\hat{p}$ be the vector of shadow prices of goods, and $\mu_j$ the multipliers on (38) for each $j$. Then $\hat{p} = \phi_m(m)$ as usual, whereas $\mu$ is the vector of shadow prices associated with the gross outputs of the various sectors. If $\theta$ is the multiplier on the additional constraint, the two are related by

$$\hat{p} = \mu + \theta h_\xi$$

If such an optimum is to be achieved, all other agents in the economy should face prices $\hat{p}$, but producers in their role of sellers of gross output should receive prices $\mu$. Note that in their role as buyers of intermediate goods, they should pay prices $\hat{p}$. The way to achieve this is to leave everyone facing prices $\hat{p}$, but tax the very operation of production activities at rates $\theta h_\xi$ per unit level of such operation.

This is hardly surprising. If we are concerned about the gross outputs, i.e. activity levels, this is best taken care of by subsidizing them directly. In other words, the best way to provide effective protection is not protection from imports at all.

It may be thought strange to use an aggregate utility function in dealing with a problem that is suggested by concern about factor use and factor prices in particular uses. However, this is again in order to make the general point forcefully. If domestic redistribution is desired, the best way to achieve it is through lump sum transfers, the next best way is through commodity taxation, and it is only if all these fail that tariffs have any role.

It is not in principle difficult to find such a 'third-best' tariff policy. Since the general formula is uninstructive, we leave this to the reader.

## 3. PARTIAL REFORMS OF POLICIES

The next topic is that of constraints on policy itself. If the optimum cannot be achieved at once, for example due to political problems of changing a tax structure too suddenly, we wish to find directions of gradual reform. If some policies are not available, for example if use-specific factor taxes are too subtle an instrument to be practicable, we wish to know whether other policies can yield some improvement on the distorted *status quo*. A general theory of this kind of problem is not very instructive, since there are numerous conceivable combinations of constraints and distortions. We select two examples, in each of which we examine the role of tariffs in securing some improvement in a distorted equilibrium when the optimum responses of curing the distortion are not available. The first concerns product market distortions, and the second those in factor markets.

When the question is no longer one of finding optimum policies, we cannot take the route of doing the optimization and then interpreting the multipliers as shadow prices and calculating taxes from them. We have to formulate the distorted equilibrium explicitly, and examine its comparative statics in response to the permissible small change in policy. Therefore the best techniques for describing equilibrium and doing comparative statics—the expenditure and revenue functions employed in Chapters 3 and 5—come back to replace the Meade envelope functions suited to optimization analysis.

### Product market distortions

We consider a small one-consumer economy, with fixed factor supplies. As in our earlier comparative static exercises, in the knowledge that only relative prices matter, we take one good to be the numeraire, and label it 0. Let $P$ be the fixed vector of world prices of the other $n$ goods. Suppose there is a vector $t$ of tariffs. In addition, let there be a non-tariff wedge given by a vector $\alpha$ between the consumer price and the domestic price of imports, and a similar distortion $\beta$ as regards the producer price. Thus the consumer price vector is $(P + t + \alpha)$, and the producer price vector $(P + t + \beta)$. The national income identity equates the consumer's expenditure to the producer revenue plus the revenue generated by the tariffs and other distortions. Now tariff revenue is $t.(c - x)$, and revenue from distortions in consumption and production is respectively $\alpha.c$ and $-\beta.x$; since we have expressed production distortions as raising domestic producer prices above import prices, they are like subsidies. Thus we have

$$e(1, P + t + \alpha, u) = r(1, P + t + \beta, v) + (t + \alpha).e_p - (t + \beta).r_p$$
$$(39)$$

This determines $u$, and the other quantities in equilibrium can then be inferred.

Consider the comparative static effect of changing $t$, $\alpha$, and $\beta$. Taking total differentials in (39), we have

$$e_u \, du = (t + \alpha).e_{pp}(dt + d\alpha) - (t + \beta).r_{pp}(dt + d\beta)$$
$$+ (t + \alpha).e_{pu} \, du$$

But by homogeneity,

$$e_u = e_{0u} + (P + t + \alpha).e_{pu}$$

Substituting, we have

$$(e_{0u} + P.e_{pu}) \, du = (t + \alpha).e_{pp}(dt + d\alpha) - (t + \beta).r_{pp}(dt + d\beta)$$
$$(40)$$

The coefficient on the left-hand side is the sum of the income effects for all goods, weighted by the world prices. This can be shown to be positive under conditions related to the stability of equilibrium; see Hatta (1976) or Dixit (1975). We assume that to be the case. Then utility changes can be easily found in terms of policy changes. There are several immediate conclusions.

First, we see that an equiproportionate reduction in all distortions improves welfare. Set $dt = -t \, dk$, $d\alpha = -\alpha \, dk$, and $d\beta = -\beta \, dk$, where $dk$ is a positive amount. Then the right-hand side in (40) is

$$\{-(t + \alpha).e_{pp}(t + \alpha) + (t + \beta).r_{pp}(t + \beta)\} \, dk$$

since $e$ is concave and $r$ is convex, each quadratic form is positive semi-definite, so $du \geq 0$. This proves the result, which is an example of a very general principle in welfare economics.

Next suppose that $\alpha$ and $\beta$ are fixed and cannot be changed. Starting from a position of no tariffs, a slight change $dt$ yields the right-hand side in (40) as

$$(\alpha \cdot e_{pp} - \beta \cdot r_{pp})\, dt$$

The coefficient vector is typically non-zero, therefore tariffs have a role to play when there are distortions that cannot be removed by the direct optimum Pigouvian policy. We can calculate the second-best policy of such tariffs. For utility to be at a maximum, $du = 0$, so the coefficient of $dt$ on the right-hand side in (40) must be zero. This gives

$$(t + \alpha)^T e_{pp} - (t + \beta)^T r_{pp} = 0$$

or

$$t^T = -(\alpha^T e_{pp} - \beta^T r_{pp})(e_{pp} - r_{pp})^{-1} \qquad (41)$$

But we suspect this is too complicated to comfort simplistic adherents of tariffs.

## Factor market distortions

When discussing distortions in factor markets, it is not possible to work with an aggregated revenue function for the economy. That presumes efficiency in production, which is no longer valid when there are distortions in factor allocation. To handle this case, we must disaggregate production. As an illustration that suffices to explain the issues, we consider a case where there are two production sectors with a wedge between factor returns in the two sectors. We retain the assumption of a one-consumer economy having fixed total factor supplies $v$ and facing fixed world prices $(1, P)$. For a vector $t$ of tariffs, the domestic prices of the non-numeraire goods are $p = P + t$. This establishes a one-to-one relation between $p$ and $P$; therefore we simplify notation by taking $p$ to be the choice variable, and finding the tariff vector implicitly as $(p - P)$.

Let $r^1(1, p, v^1)$ and $r^2(1, p, v^2)$ be the revenue functions for the two sectors. The factor allocations $v^1$ and $v^2$ must sum to $v$. An efficient allocation would maximize the total revenue subject to this constraint, and that would be achieved by equating the vectors of value marginal products, $r_v^1$ and $r_v^2$. We could then regard the resulting sum of revenues as a function of $p$ and $v$, thus obtaining a single revenue function for the economy, and reconciling the present approach with our earlier one. With a distortion that specifies a discrepancy between the marginal product vectors, this cannot be done usefully. We examine the equilibrium explicitly for one illustrative case, where there is a fixed vector $\theta$ indicating the distortion, i.e. where the allocations must satisfy

$$r_v^2(1, p, v^2) = r_v^1(1, p, v^1) + \theta \qquad (42)$$

Given $p$, the equilibrium allocation of factors is found by solving this together with $v^1 + v^2 = v$. Since we have already chosen a numeraire, there is no further arbitrariness involved in the choice of $\theta$. The conventional treatment of factor market distortions specifies a multiplicative rather than an additive discrepancy between the two marginal products; we comment on this at the end.

To complete the determination of equilibrium, we append the national income identity determining $u$:

$$e(1, p, u) = r^1(1, p, v^1) + r^2(1, p, v^2) + (p - P).m \qquad (43)$$

where the vector of net imports, $m$ is given by

$$m = e_p(1, p, u) - r_p^1(1, p, v^1) - r_p^2(1, p, v^2) \qquad (44)$$

i.e. demand minus the sum of the supplies from the two sectors.

To find the comparative static effect of changing tariffs, we disturb this equilibrium by changing $p$. First we find the induced change in the factor allocation from (42):

$$r_{vv}^2 \, dv^2 + r_{vp}^2 \, dp = r_{vv}^1 \, dv^1 + r_{vp}^1 \, dp$$

Since $dv^2 = -dv^1$, this yields

$$(r_{vv}^2 + r_{vv}^1) \, dv^2 = -(r_{vp}^2 - r_{vp}^1) \, dp$$

The matrices $r_{vv}^1$ and $r_{vv}^2$ are each negative semi-definite, but under constant returns to scale each would be singular, since their respective products with $v^1$ and $v^2$ would be zero. Even then, unless by coincidence $v^2$ is proportional to $v^1$, the sum of the two matrices will be negative definite and therefore non-singular. We assume this to be so, and write the solution as

$$dv^2 = -(r_{vv}^2 + r_{vv}^1)^{-1}(r_{vp}^2 - r_{vp}^1) \, dp \qquad (45)$$

We illustrate this in some simple cases. First consider the Ricardo–Viner model with two goods and only one mobile factor. Suppose $\theta$ is positive, i.e. the value marginal product in sector 2 exceeds that in sector 1. Total revenue could be increased by shifting some of the mobile factor from sector 1 to sector 2, i.e. sector 2 is too small relative to the efficient allocation. Now consider an increase in the price of the non-numeraire good, $p$. If it is produced in sector 2, this raises the marginal product in sector 2 more than that in sector 1, i.e. $r_{vp}^2 > r_{vp}^1 = 0$. Then (42) is violated, the left-hand side being too large. In order to restore equilibrium, the left-hand side must be decreased and the right-hand side increased; since there are diminishing returns to the factor in each use, this is done by shifting it from sector 1 to sector 2. Since $(r_{vv}^2 + r_{vv}^1) < 0$, that is what (45) indicates. Incidentally, we see that in the case just outlined, an increase in $p$ is causing a shift of the factor allocation in a direction towards the efficient one, i.e. increasing the size of the sector which was initially judged too small. That has obvious implications for the effect of tariffs in the presence of such a distortion when it cannot be cured by Pigouvian policies.

Next we consider the two-by-two Heckscher–Ohlin model. Suppose the non-numeraire good is produced in sector 2. A change in its price has no effect on marginal products in sector 1, i.e. $r_{vp}^1 = 0$, while $r_{vp}^2$ has positive components. To find the inverse needed in (45), note that for any two-by-two matrix $A = (a_{ij})$, we have

$$\begin{pmatrix} a_{11} & a_{12} \\ a_{21} & a_{22} \end{pmatrix}^{-1} = \frac{1}{a_{11}a_{22} - a_{21}a_{12}} \begin{pmatrix} a_{22} & -a_{12} \\ -a_{21} & a_{11} \end{pmatrix}$$

Now each $r_{vv}^j$ has negative entries on the diagonal and positive ones off it. Therefore the sum has the same sign pattern, and in addition has a positive determinant. Therefore the inverse has all its entries negative. With the minus sign for the whole expression, then, $\mathrm{d}v^2$ given by (45) is the product of a matrix with positive entries and a vector with positive components, i.e. $\mathrm{d}v^2$ is a positive vector. Thus a rise in the price of the non-numeraire good draws both factors towards that sector  The desirability of this is going to depend on the sign pattern of the distortion vector $\theta$. If it is positive, it is going to be desirable to draw both factors towards sector 2, and the policy of raising the price of the non-numeraire good will be a desirable one.

To see the utility effects explicitly, we have the total differential of (43):

$$e_p.\mathrm{d}p + e_u\,\mathrm{d}u = r_p^1.\mathrm{d}p + r_v^1.\mathrm{d}v^1 + r_p^2.\mathrm{d}p + r_v^2.\mathrm{d}v^2$$
$$+ m.\mathrm{d}p + (p - P).\mathrm{d}m$$

Using (43) and (42), this simplifies to

$$e_u\,\mathrm{d}u = \theta.\mathrm{d}v^2 + (p - P).\mathrm{d}m \qquad (46)$$

In particular, if we consider the effect of a small departure from free trade so that the initial equilibrium has $p = P$, (46) shows that the factor reallocation effect is the dominant one up to the first order. Substituting from (45), we find

$$e_u \, du = -\theta \cdot (r^2_{vv} + r^1_{vv})^{-1}(r^2_{vp} - r^1_{vp}) \, dp \qquad (47)$$

We leave it as an exercise to the reader to examine how this provides formal proofs of the indications we gave from the Ricardo–Viner and Heckscher–Ohlin models.

For sizeable departures from free trade, we have to take into account the effects of the volume of trade in (46). Differentiating (44), we have

$$dm = e_{pp} \, dp + e_{pu} \, du - r^1_{pp} \, dp - r^1_{pv} \, dv^1 - r^2_{pp} \, dp - r^2_{pv} \, dv^2$$

$$= (e_{pp} - r^1_{pp} - r^2_{pp}) \, dp + e_{pu} \, du - (r^2_{pv} - r^1_{pv}) \, dv^2 \qquad (48)$$

If $p$ is chosen optimally for second-best policy when $\theta$ must be accepted as fixed, we must have $du = 0$ for all small changes $dp$. Using this in (47) and (48), and using (45) to determine $dv^2$, we have the first-order condition

$$(p - P)^T \{ e_{pp} - r^1_{pp} - r^2_{pp} + (r^2_{pv} - r^1_{pv})(r^2_{vv} + r^1_{vv})^{-1}(r^2_{vp} - r^1_{vp}) \}$$

$$= \theta^T (r^2_{vv} + r^1_{vv})^{-1}(r^2_{vp} - r^1_{vp}) \qquad (49)$$

This is in appearance very much like the optimum tax formulae in the theory of public finance. The matrix on the left-hand side is a general substitution matrix, taking into account the factor reallocation effects of price changes. We can therefore interpret it in terms of substitution effects on tariff revenue being made proportional to corresponding effects on welfare.

The conventional treatment using distortions in multiplicative form poses some problems. The corresponding matrix on the left-hand side is not symmetric or negative definite. This is due to possible conflict between two different concepts of factor intensity, one based on physical proportions and the other based on value shares. This leads to some 'paradoxical' results, which are examined by Jones (1971b). See also Schweinberger (1979).

# 4. CUSTOMS UNIONS

In this section we consider policy from the point of view of a group of countries, rather than one country. Consider the case where two countries decide to co-ordinate their policies in relation to trade with the rest of the world. This suffices to raise all the relevant issues. In fact there is little that is new by way of either principles or techniques.

We denote variables pertaining to the two countries by lower case letters, distinguished by superscripts 1 and 2. The rest of the world presents them with a net supply function $-M(P)$. Consider an initial equilibrium where the two countries' policies are not co-ordinated, and may consist of an arbitrary set of tariffs and domestic taxes. Suppose $P$ is the equilibrium vector of world prices; then the two countries' net import vector $m^1$ and $m^2$ satisfy $m^1 + m^2 = -M(P)$.

Now suppose the two decide to co-ordinate policies. First consider an extreme case where this extends to their having an agreed objective function, defined over the utilities of all the consumers in the two countries, and being able to maximize it subject only to the constraints of production feasibility in each country, and factor immobility across countries. Then we can set up the kind of first-best problem that led to the Meade utility function in one country with several consumers and lump-sum transfers. We ask how the countries can make the best possible use of a given total vector of net imports $m$. This will entail all consumers and all producers facing the same prices, and the optimum interpersonal distribution being achieved by lump-sum transfers. In a sense, we can regard the initial unco-ordinated equilibrium, in which consumers and producers in the two countries will typically face different prices, as being riddled with consumption or production distortions, and the new first-best optimum as removing these. In this way, the two countries can improve upon the *status quo* even if they arrange matters so that the prices $P$ at which they trade with the rest of the world remain unchanged. This is the idea of a tariff-compensating customs union as defined by Ohyama (1972); his union 'sets its common external tariffs so as to preserve the same volume and composition of net trade with the rest of the world as occurred before it was formed', and 'fully co-ordinates distributional policies inside the union'. There might be further gains by changing $P$; that is the optimum tariff problem for the union as a whole.

However, this extent of co-ordination is extreme, both in stipulating an agreed welfare function, and in allowing lump-sum transfers in the pursuit of maximizing it. One can foresee severe problems if this leaves consumers in one country better off and those in another worse off, and requires international transfers in order to do so. We therefore ask if the countries can improve upon the *status quo* in the Pareto sense, by the use of tariffs and commodity taxes alone. Along the lines of the analysis of Chapter 3 where autarky and free trade for one country were compared, we find an answer in the affirmative.

Suppose that in the initial situation, consumers in country $i$ faced prices $p^i$ for goods and $w^i$ for factors, and chose quantities $\bar{c}^i$ and $\bar{v}^i$. Suppose producers there produced net outputs $\bar{x}^i$ of goods. Suppose $P$ was the vector of world prices, yielding net supplies $-M(P)$, so that

$$\bar{c}^1 + \bar{c}^2 - \bar{x}^1 - \bar{x}^2 = -M(P) \tag{50}$$

Now the two countries co-ordinate their tax policies. Consider the following policy defined by the resulting price vectors. (There will be a resulting tariff vector common to the two countries, and commodity tax vectors different in the two, that can be determined from the price vectors.):

The world price vector will be left at $P$, as will the consumer prices $(p^i, w^i)$. Recall that there are no lump-sum transfers; so the consumers' budget lines are unchanged. Then the consumers will make the same choices $(\bar{c}^i, \bar{v}^i)$.

We will, however, alter the production pattern. Consider the set of all aggregate feasible net outputs, i.e. the set $S$ defined by

$\{x \mid$ there exist $x^1$ and $x^2$ such that each $(x^i, \bar{v}^i)$ is technically feasible in country $i$, and $x = x^1 + x^2\}$

Clearly the point $\bar{x}^1 + \bar{x}^2$ is in this set. However, it will typically not be on the efficient frontier of the set. Since we are assuming convex technologies in the two countries as always, the set $S$ is convex. Therefore there is a supporting hyperplane at any point on its frontier. In other words, if $x^*$ is on the frontier, there is a price vector $p^*$ such that $x^*$ maximizes the value $p^* . x$ over the choice of $x$ in the set $S$. If $x^* = x^{*1} + x^{*2}$ with $x^{*i}$ feasible in country $i$, each $x^{*i}$ must be maximizing the value $p^* . x^i$ over all feasible $x^i$ in that country, otherwise $p^* . x^*$ could be improved upon. This shows that if an aggregate output vector is efficient, there must be a common vector of producer prices for goods in the two countries. Accordingly, to the extent that producer prices in the two countries differ in the *status quo*, and to the extent that their separate production frontiers allow transformation, they can increase outputs of all goods.

Take any point $x^*$ on the frontier of $S$, to the north-east of $\bar{x}^1 + \bar{x}^2$. Let $p^*$ be the supporting prices, and make these the common producer prices for goods in the two countries. Each will have its implied prices for factors, $w^{*i}$. Then the state of affairs can be achieved through common tariffs $(p^* - P)$, consumer taxes $(p^i - p^*)$ on goods, and $(w^{*i} - w^i)$ on factors in country $i$.

Comparing (50), we see that there is a private sector surplus of every good. By Walras's Law, there will be just enough of a surplus of aggregate net revenue from all the taxation and tariffs to allow the governments to buy up these surpluses, and thus achieve a general equilibrium. The government purchases can then be thrown away. The resulting equilibrium is exactly as good as the old one. As before, to the extent that there are genuine gains from changing the production pattern, it will be possible to lower consumer prices of goods in both countries. This can be tailored to use up the surpluses of goods beneficially, making the new equilibrium actually Pareto superior.

It may surprise readers familiar with the established literature on customs unions, e.g. Lipsey (1970), that we have not used the concepts of trade creation and trade diversion. The reason is that we have looked at customs unions from a welfare point of view rather than from the point of view of comparative statics. The usual comparison is between the *status quo* and a union with external tariffs fixed at *arbitrary*, exogenous levels. It is the possibility that the external tariffs are set at unsuitable levels that can produce harmful effects through trade diversion. In our analysis, we *choose* the external tariffs so as to seek an improvement. Our result can then be interpreted as saying that harmful effects of integration can be avoided by appropriate choices of external tariffs. Once this is done, we are left with the benefits of production specialization within the union; this is analogous to the conventional idea of gains through trade creation. These gains are larger, the more different are the pre-union producer prices in the member countries. This also finds an echo in the literature.

This demonstration of a possible gain for a tariff-compensating customs union with limited powers and the stringent aim of Pareto improvement still leaves a lot of scope for further betterment. The point $x^*$ can typically be chosen from a segment of the frontier. Gains from altering $P$ have yet to be explored. There may be even further gains from allowing factor mobility, unless factor prices happen to be equalized. Finally, we can enlarge the group of countries, indeed to the whole world, which is a special case of the above analysis with $M(P)$ identically zero.

## NOTES

Among the textbooks we have been citing, issues of trade and welfare are discussed by Samuelson (1976, ch. 35), Caves and Jones (1976, chs. 2, 3, 11, 12),

Södersten (1971, chs. 2, 19, 21) and Takayama (1972, chs. 15, 17) at increasing levels of mathematical detail. Caves and Johnson (1968) is again a source of important classic articles.

Our treatment of optimum tariffs owes much to the modern theory of taxation. In particular, the influence of Diamond and Mirrlees (1971) is clear. The result on optimum tariffs with lump sum taxes can also be seen as an adaptation of Guesnerie (1975), if his 'uncontrolled firms' are interpreted as the rest of the world; we thank Peter Wagstaff for pointing this out.

For a treatment in the spirit of Meade (1955), see Smith (1979).

The standard geometry of policy responses to distortions and constraints is surveyed by Bhagwati (1971), and follows classic articles by Corden (1957) and Bhagwati and Ramaswami (1963). See Magee (1973) for a survey of the theory of factor market distortions. Several second-best problems are studied by Ohyama (1972); this article has influenced many of our concerns, although we have used different methods. Issues of second-best responses and partial policy reforms were pioneered by Haberler (1950). Our approach follows Dixit (1975), Hatta (1976) and related work on public finance.

# CHAPTER 7

# MONEY AND THE BALANCE OF PAYMENTS

It is common in elementary textbooks to introduce balance of payments adjustment as a manifestation of real disequilibrium. If relative prices are not compatible with clearance of all goods markets, as can happen when enough nominal prices and exchange rates are sticky, then the real imbalances will be reflected in payments imbalances. Each country will, given its competitive assumption that it can transact at the going market prices, plan to remain on its budget constraint, but since all these trades are not mutually compatible in disequilibrium, each will in fact end up violating the constraint.

An example will clarify this. Suppose that in a pure exchange of goods, the equilibrium price ratio between UK and Japan would be 62.5 bottles of whisky per television set. Now suppose the UK price of whisky is sticky at £4 per bottle, and the Japanese price of TV sets at 100,000 yen per set. This will be compatible with equilibrium at an exchange rate of 400 yen/£. But suppose this rate is also sticky at a value of 450. Then the Japanese can exchange each TV set for only 55 bottles of whisky, and the UK needs to offer only 55 bottles to acquire one TV set. Given a stability condition, called the Marshall–Lerner condition, there will be a world excess demand for TV sets and an excess supply of whisky. If trade is attempted under these prices, we will observe a UK balance of payments deficit: If they could sell all their whisky they would operate on their budget constraint, but in the prevailing state of real disequilibrium this plan fails to materialize. Correspondingly, the Japanese sell more TV sets than they plan, thus running down their stocks and running up a surplus on the balance of payments.

However, this is an unconvincing story. It is hard to accept that payments imbalances must always be accompanied by, or are reflections of, a disequilibrium in real exchange. Even within the logic of the model, it is unsatisfactory that features which were no part of the original story of exchange, namely stocks, have to be grafted on if the state of real disequilibrium is to be actually achieved. Further, this is done without considering the consequences of stocks for the future, both on production plans and therefore on supply, on financial settlements, and on income and wealth and therefore on demand. If we are to study a phenomenon with essential inter-temporal aspects, we should do so in a model which explicitly includes the appropriate intertemporal links. When that is done, we have the added advantage that payments imbalances can be logically separated from real disequilibria. Inequalities between countries' current expenditures and outputs can be a part of the general possibility of claims and liabilities against the future, and this can happen consistently with the clearance of world markets in goods at every instant.

In other words, payments imbalances need not reflect real disequilibria, they can simply reflect international differences in the demand for future versus present consumption. As an example, suppose consumers in Japan at the margin are willing to forgo more current consumption to increase future consumption than is the case for the UK consumers. Both parties could then gain from trade in the commodities 'consumption today' and 'consumption tomorrow', just as they gain from trading two standard goods if the autarky price ratio differs between the two countries. As a result, a competitive equilibrium will involve trade in present and future consumption. The way in which that comes about, is by Japan running an export surplus today, in exchange for claims on UK goods produced in the future. In that way, surpluses and deficits on the balance of trade can be seen simply as an extension of commodity trade to trade in claims on production at different dates

This is not to say that the theory of the balance of payments is no more than an extension of standard trade theory to trade in claims on the future. A number of important questions arise because payments imbalances occur in conjunction with, or as a result of, real disequilibria. For example, if lack of price flexibility causes domestic unemployment and an effective demand failure, the result could be an effective excess demand for claims on the future, and thus a balance of payments surplus. Policies correcting for this would have the opposite effect—domestic unemployment would be reduced, but the trade surplus could turn into a deficit. In a sense, problems of this type are more interesting than the questions arising from trade imbalances which reflect equilibrium trade in claims on present versus future production, and we shall investigate balance of payments problems in such a context in the next chapter. The point is only that there is an equilibrium aspect to payments imbalances as well; and that can usefully be studied in isolation from the complications of real disequilibria. That is the purpose of this chapter.

As was shown in Chapter 3, there are no formal problems involved in reinterpreting our basic model of trade to include intertemporal trade as well, so all arguments relating to characteristics of equilibrium, comparative statics and welfare in the basic trade model apply to intertemporal trade as well as to trade in any particular time period. We simply distinguish goods available at different dates as different commodities. Their prices are expressed on a comparable basis, as would be the case if all contracts—including contracts for future sales and purchases—were made at the initial date. If we stick to that interpretation, all prices would be in present values as of that date. There would be only one budget constraint, saying that the value of contracts for present and future sales would have to be at least as great as the value of contracts for present and future purchases. In such a context, the price vector $p$ of the home country could be interpreted as a set of present value price vectors $(p_t)$, where $p_t$ is the price vector of contracts with delivery date $t$. The expenditure and revenue functions would capture the intertemporal consumption and production plans, and the sale and purchase contracts entered into at the initial date would be given by these plans. Writing $m = (m_t)$ for the set of import vectors planned, i.e. for purchase contracts less sales contracts with delivery date $t$, the budget constraint would imply $p \cdot m = \sum_t p_t \cdot m_t \leq 0$. The individual terms $p_t \cdot m_t$ would then be the present values of the trade deficits at the different dates. In this way, the general theory set out in Chapter 3 can be seen to embody a model of the balance of trade.

Even though it provides an explanation of the balance of trade, however, this is not a particularly satisfactory framework for discussing the balance of payments. In particular, in spite of the mention of time, such a model with perfect futures markets provides too static a framework: trade imbalances will be mere parts of complete and compatible plans made at the outset. Moreover, there are no payments in the ordinary sense in such a model. There are claims, but these are claims for specific goods at specific dates, not general financial assets. For a theory of the balance of payments it is preferable to have assets which are broad stores of purchasing power, and which can be associated with national and international payments as we know them in practice.

Rather than simply spelling out the implications of a model with perfect forward markets, therefore, we shall look at the balance of payments in the context of Hicksian temporary equilibria. At each instant, agents have access to markets for spot commodities and assets. The assets are held for the sake of commodities they will buy in spot markets at later dates, so the demand for assets is influenced by the expectations about commodity prices in the future. The expectations need not be consistent across consumers, and some or all of them may turn out to be wrong when the future unfolds. Such a model gives rise to a much wider range of possibilities than one would find in a model with perfect forward markets. Moreover, in the case of perfect foresight (or rational expectations if there is uncertainty), a sequence of Hicksian temporary equilibria coincides with the equilibrium which would obtain with perfect forward markets, so the latter is in a sense embodied in the model we shall consider.

The kinds of assets available will clearly play a major role in a Hicksian equilibrium. With uncertainty, the availability and characteristics of assets are of particular importance, as the extensive literature on stock market equilibria shows. A proper treatment of uncertainty is beyond our scope, so we shall assume at least *subjective* certainty. (As noted above, agents could well turn out to be wrong in their subjectively certain expectations. That has economic implications, but it does not cause analytic difficulties.) In that case, the only important distinction is between financial and real assets. To make things simple, we shall only consider the former, so the only asset is a financial one, call it money.

In the classical treatment of international payments there is only one kind of money common to both countries, viz. gold. A country in trade surplus acquires claims on the other, and these are held in the form of gold. In other words, there is an inflow of gold to a country at a rate equal to its trade surplus. Correspondingly, a deficit country has a gold outflow. As a result, the story goes, prices and costs rise in the surplus country and fall in the deficit country. This raises demands for the products of the latter and lowers that for products of the former, until a balance of trade is established. That is the specie-flow mechanism first pointed out by Hume.

According to the so-called monetary approach to the balance of payments, there is a similar mechanism at work in a world where each country has its own fiat money, and where each country's residents are allowed to hold only its money as an asset. Suppose the exchange rate, i.e. the relative price of the two monies, is held fixed by the governments. Unless this is at a level which balances trade, one country's residents will wish to acquire claims on the other. They must, however, hold these in their own country's money. The authorities will supply this money in exchange for foreign money, and themselves hold the equivalent claims on the other country in the form of foreign exchange reserves. Now there will be an inflow of money supply in a country at a rate equal to its trade surplus, or (what is algebraically the same thing) a drop at a rate equal to its trade deficit. This leads to an adjustment process much like the specie-flow mechanism.

The effects of the specie-flow mechanism could be modified by the government through an active money supply policy. In fact, we could imagine that the authorities deliberately changed the money supply further so as to offset, or sterilize, the effects of the trade imbalance. Some would argue that complete sterilization is impossible in practice. In principle, however, there is no reason to rule out sterilization. But the possibility of offsetting monetary policy does not make the automatic adjustment mechanism less important. An understanding of how the adjustment mechanism works is interesting in its own right, and it is of obvious importance when deciding whether or not sterilization should be attempted. Most of this chapter is therefore devoted to a discussion of the monetary approach within a general equilibrium framework. In particular, we shall be concerned with the question of whether the automatic adjustment mechanism leads to a stable long-term equilibrium.

The monetary approach is only one of several approaches to the balance of payments. Another is the so-called elasticities approach, which is concerned mainly with the effects of changes in the exchange rate. This is associated with the Marshall–Lerner condition, which says that a devaluation will be successful if the sum of the price elasticities of imports to the two countries is greater than unity. It might appear that this is entirely unrelated to the questions posed, and the answers provided, by the monetary approach. That turns out not to be the case. At the end of the chapter, we show that if real and financial decisions can be separated, i.e. if consumers have utility functions that are separable in present and future consumption, the Marshall–Lerner condition must be satisfied if the specie-flow mechanism is to provide a stable long-term equilibrium. In fact, therefore, the monetary and elasticities approaches to the balance of payments are closely interrelated.

## 1. THE SMALL COUNTRY CASE

We begin by describing consumer and producer behaviour in the country under study, the home country. There are $n$ spot commodities with a price vector $p$ relative to money as the numeraire. We do not consider storage or money-holding by producers, so they have the familiar revenue function $r(p, v)$ and supplies $r_p(p, v)$.

Consumers demand spot commodities and money. Money is labelled 0. It is important to remember that it is held not for its own sake but for the sake of commodities that it will buy in the future. It would be convenient to handle this by considering a demand for real balances $c_0$ with price $p_0$. To see under what circumstances such a decomposition is possible, consider a two-period maximization problem for a typical consumer. He has a utility function $u(c^1, c^2)$ defined over the vectors of consumption today and tomorrow, $c^1$ and $c^2$. He faces given spot prices today, $p^1$. Assume that he has point expectations regarding future spot prices, and express these in present-value terms as $p^2$. Denote by $y^1$ his initial money holdings plus his income in the current period, and by $y^2$ his expected income in period 2 in present-value terms. Assume that his income expectations are fixed in real terms, so that $y^2$ is linearly homogeneous in the expected future price vector $p^2$. He will then maximize his utility subject to the budget constraint $p^1.c^1 + p^2.c^2 = y^1 + y^2$. The quantities demanded today, and the quantities planned for consumption tomorrow, can then be found by forming the expenditure function over $p^1$, $p^2$, and $u$, and setting expenditure equal to income:

$$e(p^1, p^2, u) = y^1 + y^2(p^2)$$

where the partial derivatives of $e$ with respect to $p^1$ give commodity demands today, and the derivatives with respect to $p^2$ give the planned demands tomorrow.

To see how this can be used to derive a demand for real balances, subtract $y^2(p^2)$ from both sides of the equality, and define the new function $e^*(p^1, p^2, u) = e(p^1, p^2, u) - y^2(p^2)$. We then have

$$e^*(p^1, p^2, u) = y_1$$

The partial derivatives of $e^*$ with respect to $p^1$ are still consumption demands today. The derivatives with respect to $p^2$ are

$$\partial e^*/\partial p_i^2 = \partial e/\partial p_i^2 - \partial y^2/\partial p_i^2$$

i.e. planned future consumption of good $i$ less the derivative of expected nominal income with respect to the expected price of good $i$. The latter should, if consumers have rational expectations, equal the consumer's share in expected production of good $i$ in period 2. Thus, in a one-consumer economy, the partial derivatives of $e^*$ with respect to period 2 prices should be the planned (or expected) excess demands for goods in period 2.

We know that the expenditure function is linearly homogeneous in the vector of prices, so we must have $e_1^*. p^1 + e_2^*. p^2 = e^* = y^1$, where $e_1^*$ and $e_2^*$ is shorthand notation for the partial derivatives of $e^*$ with respect to period 1 and period 2 prices. Consequently,

$e_2^* . p^2 = y^1 - p^1 . c^1$, so $e_2^* . p^2$ is the amount of income (money) carried forward to the next period. The question of whether money
demand can be decomposed into a real balance demand and a price
of real balances, therefore, is equivalent to whether $e_2^* . p^2$ can be
decomposed.

In order for this to be possible, $e^*$ must be separable in the two
price vectors. In particular, we must be able to write $e^*$ as a function
of $p^1$, $u$, and some scalar aggregate of expected period 2 prices, call
it $\xi(p^2)$, where it is natural to require $\xi$ to be linearly homogeneous
in $p^2$. If that is the case, i.e. if $e^* = e^*(p^1, \xi(p^2), u)$, we see that

$$e_2^* . p^2 = e_\xi^* \xi_p . p^2 = e_\xi^* \xi(p^2)$$

where $e_\xi^*$ and $\xi$ are scalars, so that $e_\xi^*$ can be regarded as a demand
for real cash balances, and $\xi(p^2)$ can be seen as the price of real
balances.

The exact conditions under which we can aggregate $p^2$ in the
expenditure function are given by the Leontief aggregation theorem.
In our context, that condition says that the ratio of planned excess
demands for any pair of goods in the future must be independent
of prices today and of the level of utility. That is a very restrictive
condition indeed. Seen in conjunction with our assumption that the
consumer has subjectively certain point expectations regarding
future prices, rather than probability distributions over these prices,
it means that it is quite unlikely that the concepts of real balances
and a price of money can be defended in practice. Both because the
concepts are widely used in theories of the balance of payments
and because they simplify our analysis substantially, however, we
shall assume the aggregation condition to be satisfied.

We therefore assume that expected future prices can be represented by a price of real balances, call it $p_0$ (which equals $\xi(p^2)$),
so that the demand for real cash balances, call it $c_0$, is a meaningful
concept. We subsume all planned future commodity demands in
$c_0$, and let $p_0$ reflect all relevant price expectations. We can then
suppress the time notation, to let $p$ (without a superscript) denote
spot commodity prices today, and $c$ (without a superscript) commodity demands today. To avoid money illusion, we assume that
future price expectations reflect current spot prices in a linearly
homogeneous fashion; i.e. $p_0$ is some function of $p$

$$p_0 = \psi(p) \tag{1}$$

where $\psi$ is homogeneous of degree one in $p$.

Under these assumptions, then, the consumer will have an expenditure function defined over the price of real balances, current spot

prices of commodities, and the level of utility. This will be a reduced-form expenditure function of the type $e^*$ above, but for ease of notation we shall denote it simply by $e(p_0, p, u)$. This has all the standard properties of expenditure functions, so the derivative with respect to $p_0$ gives the compensated demand function for real cash balances, and the partial derivatives with respect to $p$ give the commodity compensated demand functions.

There is a single consumer in the economy, so his current income will be the current value of production, i.e. $r(p, v)$. In addition, we assume that he has an initial endowment of money, denoted $l$. His total expenditures, including cash balances brought forward to the next period, must equal current income plus initial money holdings, so we shall have

$$e(p_0, p, u) = l + r(p, v) \qquad (2)$$

with $c_0 = e_0$, and $c = e_p$. Note that the left-hand side of (2) is homogeneous of degree one in current prices given the expectations function (1), but the right-hand side is not, on account of the fixed nominal endowment of money. This makes the scale of prices determinate in the model.

## Equilibrium

Now consider this as a small country facing fixed prices $P$ denominated in the large foreign country's currency. Let $\epsilon$ be the exchange rate expressed as the home price of the foreign currency (so a devaluation of the home currency will increase $\epsilon$). Then $p = \epsilon P$ is also fixed. By assumption the home country faces perfectly elastic foreign net supplies, so it can carry out all desired commodity transactions. The balance of trade surplus in terms of the home currency, written as $b$, is simply the value of the net excess supplies of commodities. Thus

$$b = p.(r_p - e_p)$$

But by homogeneity $r_p . p = r$ and $e_0 p_0 + e_p . p = e$. We can therefore write $b$ as

$$b = r - (e - p_0 e_0)$$

Using (2) and $c_0 = e_0$, we therefore have

$$b = p_0 c_0 - l \qquad (3)$$

To interpret this, recall that $p_0 c_0$ is the stock of money the consumer wants to carry forward to the next period. His initial stock is $l$, so $(p_0 c_0 - l)$ is the amount of money he wants to accumulate during the current period. The conventional monetary approach term for the initial excess demand for money is 'hoarding', so $(p_0c_0 - l)$ is the desired hoarding. In the absence of other domestic sectors, consumers can only increase their money holdings by accumulating claims on foreigners. In equilibrium, therefore, desired hoarding must equal the increase in net claims on the rest of the world, i.e. the surplus on the balance of trade. That is what (3) says.

But if domestic consumers are not allowed to hold foreign money directly, the increase in money holdings implicit in (3) cannot take the form of foreign currency. Instead, the government must take foreign currency in exchange for domestic money, so the government must issue an additional amount of domestic money equivalent to the increase in domestic consumers' desired claims. We must therefore assume that the government issues an additional amount of money

$$\Delta l = b \tag{4}$$

where the prefix $\Delta$ denotes an increment.

We should pause here to reflect on the time dimension of transactions. Money is a stock, while production, consumption, and the balance of trade are flows, so time must enter into the problem in an essential way. The best way to think of it is in terms of transactions (production and consumption) taking place during the time period in question, decisions on production and consumption taking place at the beginning of the time period, and financial settlements occurring at the end of the period. In that case, all real transactions will occur before financial settlements, so any balance of trade surplus will not have monetary implications until the end of the period. In other words, the increase in domestic money supply implied by (4) will not have implications for real transactions in the current period; it will only affect the stock of money carried forward to the next, and real transactions then and in later periods. Such an interpretation permits us to interpret $\Delta l$ as an increment with respect to time, and thus to look at some dynamic implications. In doing so, we regard the exchange rate as fixed except when explicitly stated otherwise.

### Monetary dynamics

The next period, or round of transactions, will begin with the money supply $(l + \Delta l)$. This will produce a new value of $b$, and the process will continue. In the case of deficits, it must be assumed that the government's foreign exchange reserves do not run out; this we do. A long-run equilibrium, defined as a state where the money supply does not change, will be characterized by $b = 0$, i.e. balanced trade. The process will converge to a long-run equilibrium if $b$ is a decreasing function of $l$, for then $l$ will be increasing to the left of such an equilibrium and decreasing to the right of it. To investigate this, let $y$ denote the total amount of money at the consumer's disposal in the current period—i.e. his initial stock of money plus current income. In other words, we let $y = (l + r)$. We can then use equation (2) to define $u$ as a function of $p_0$, $p$, and $y$, and use this to solve for real balance demand as $c_0 = c_0(p_0, p, y)$. This gives the demand for real balances as a function of the price of real balances, the prices of all current consumption goods, and the total amount of money at the consumer's disposal. If we let $c_{0y}$ denote the partial derivative of $c_0$ with respect to $y$, differentiation of (3) gives us

$$\partial b/\partial l = p_0 c_{0y} - 1 \qquad (5)$$

To interpret this, consider the interpretation of $p_0 c_{0y}$. It is the marginal propensity to carry forward money to the next period, so it is the share of a money gift received in the current period that the consumer would want to carry forward to purchase consumer goods in later periods. Thus, $p_0 c_{0y}$ is our analogue of the marginal propensity to save. Making the reasonable assumption that it is less than one, which corresponds to assuming that spot commodities as a whole are a normal good, (5) shows that $\partial b/\partial l$ is negative, which is what we need for stability of the long-run equilibrium. In other words, we have a self-adjusting mechanism for achieving a balance of trade in this model.

### Effects of policies

We can very easily use this model to examine the consequences of some policy changes. Active monetary policy, i.e. a change in $l$, has an effect on the short-run equilibrium that can be found from (5). Such a policy could be used for correcting a trade imbalance without waiting for the adjustment mechanism to work itself out. On the other hand, suppose $l$ is increased starting from an initial long-run equilibrium. The short-run impact of this will be to open up a trade deficit, as (5) shows. But this will be followed by a gradual decrease of $l$ as the foreigners' claims on domestic residents are met from the reserves and accompanied by retirement of equivalent amounts of home money. Ultimately the original level of $l$ will be restored, and trade balanced again.

We can also introduce government expenditure in the form of a vector $g$ of commodities purchased by the government. This will merely add an amount $p.g$ to the trade deficit. The effect on $l$ is twofold. The trade deficit causes it to fall as explained above. On the other hand, with no taxes introduced, and no other assets which the government can sell to the home consumers, it will have to finance its expenditure by printing money. The two exactly cancel out. The net effect is as if the government buys its vector of commodities abroad using its foreign exchange reserves, bypassing the domestic economy.

Finally, consider exchange rate changes. Using the variable $y$ defined above, write (3) as

$$b = p_0 \, c_0(p_0, p, l + r(v, v)) - l$$

It is instructive to write this in terms of the exchange rate and prices expressed in the foreign country. We do that by substituting $\epsilon P$ for $p$, and using $p_0 = \psi(p) = \psi(\epsilon P) = \epsilon \psi(P)$ by the assumption that price expectations are homogeneous of degree one in current prices. This gives us

$$b = \epsilon \psi(P) \, c_0(\epsilon \psi(P), \epsilon P, l + r(\epsilon P, v)) - l$$

But $r$ is linearly homogeneous in prices, and demand is homogeneous of degree zero in all prices and income, so we can divide through by $\epsilon$ on both sides to obtain

$$b/\epsilon = \psi(P) \, c_0(\psi(P), P, l/\epsilon + r(P, v)) - l/\epsilon \qquad (6)$$

The left-hand side here is the home country's trade surplus measured in terms of the foreign currency. That clearly is the relevant measure of the trade surplus from the point of view of the home country, as it measures the real value (in terms of purchasing power for commodities) of the net increase in claims on the other country. The right-hand side of (6) involves only the ratio $l/\epsilon$, i.e. the value of the domestic money supply measured in units of foreign currency. It follows that an increase in $\epsilon$ (i.e. a devaluation) has exactly the same effect on the real trade surplus as a reduction in the domestic money supply. But we have already seen that a reduction in the domestic money supply will lead to an increase in $b$, and the effect of $l$ on $b/\epsilon$ is obviously the same as that on $b$ at fixed $\epsilon$. Thus, a devaluation will improve the trade balance in real terms.

This effect is, however, an impact effect only. It enables us to say that a devaluation of a suitable size can eliminate an initial deficit without our having to wait for the money supply adjustment mechanism to work itself out. It also implies that if we start from a position of initial long-run equilibrium, a devaluation will open up a trade surplus. However, if the exchange rate is left at its new level, the money supply will increase in response to the surplus, producing a new long-run equilibrium with balanced trade. The new long-run equilibrium must have the same $l/\epsilon$ as the old one, so the money supply will have increased in the same proportion as the devaluation. In other words, the value of the domestic money supply in units of foreign currency will remain unchanged as we move from one long-run equilibrium to another.

As our model includes an explicit measure of consumer utility, it is tempting to look at the effect of exchange rate changes on utility as well. Using homogeneity, we can write (2) in the form

$$e(\psi(P),\, P,\, u) = l/\epsilon + \pi(P,\, v) \qquad (7)$$

The foreign price vector $P$ being fixed, we see that $u$ is an increasing function of $l/\epsilon$, so in the short run a revaluation would appear to give higher utility while a devaluation would lower utility. However, that is a deceptive result. The simple explanation for the positive effect of a revaluation on utility is that a revaluation worsens the trade balance, thereby enabling consumers to buy greater amounts of commodities. But a worsening of the trade balance involves depletion of foreign exchange reserves (or a slower accumulation of reserves), and the value of these reserves is not taken into account in measuring consumer utility. If we regard foreign exchange reserves as being (indirectly) owned by consumers, we would find that the utility effect of a revaluation vanished even in the short run. The reason is that a revaluation only shifts consumption from future periods to the present; and at the margin, the consumer is indifferent between allocating extra income to present or future consumption. Thus, one should avoid welfare assessments based on the above model.

## Non-traded goods

So far, we have assumed that all goods are tradeable. We could reinterpret the model as a reduced form of a more complete model including non-tradeables, the markets for non-tradeables being cleared in the background. Such a procedure could be dangerously deceptive, however. The price and income derivatives in the reduced form would be complicated combinations of the basic behavioural derivatives in the complete model, and could easily be ambiguous in sign even with reasonable behaviour. In particular, therefore, if the above is taken as a reduced form model, there is no *a priori* assurance that the trade surplus will be a decreasing function of the money supply, or that devaluation will have a positive impact effect on the trade balance.

To see the problems involved, consider the simple extension of the model to include non-tradeables. Let $q$ be the vector of domestic prices of non-tradeables. These enter the revenue function and the expenditure function. Note, however, that with rational expectations they will not enter the price expectations function $\psi(p)$: we recall that the derivatives of the reduced-form expenditure function with respect to future prices are the expected (or planned) *excess* demands for goods in the future. As the markets for non-tradeables will clear in equilibrium, a consumer with rational expectations will not expect excess demands for these goods in the future, so expectations regarding the prices of non-tradeables are irrelevant. Moreover, as the economy is small, there is no basis for expecting future prices of tradeables to depend on present prices of non-tradeables. A rational consumer, therefore, will not let $p_0$ be affected by the prices of non-traded goods.

We therefore have the budget constraint

$$e(p_0, p, q, u) = l + r(p, q, v) \tag{8}$$

where $p_0$ and $p$ are determined by given international prices and the exchange rate, and where the price vector of non-tradeables is determined by the domestic market clearing conditions

$$e_q = r_q \tag{9}$$

To find the effects of an increase in the domestic money supply, note from (8) that $e_u\,du = dl$. Using this, and differentiating (9), we get the effect on the prices of non-traded goods:

$$dq = -(e_{qq} - r_{qq})^{-1}(e_{qu}/e_u)\,dl \tag{10}$$

where $(e_{qu}/e_u)$ is the vector of income demand derivatives of non-tradeables, call it $z_y$, and $(e_{qq} - r_{qq})$ is the substitution matrix for non-tradeables, call it $z_q$.

The effect on the balance of trade could be found by differentiating an expression like (3). It is more convenient to use the direct definition of the trade surplus, however. Using $b = p.(r_p - e_p)$, we get

$$db = p.\{(r_{pq} - e_{pq})\,dq - (e_{pu}/e_u)\,dl\}$$

where $(e_{pu}/e_u)$ gives the income demand derivatives of tradeables, equal to $c_y$. This also equals the derivatives of imports with respect to money income, $m_y$. Next, $(e_{pq} - r_{pq})$ is the matrix of compensated cross-price derivatives between tradeables and non-tradeables, call it $m_q$. Using the abbreviated notation and substituting from (10), we obtain

$$db/dl = p.m_q(z_q^{-1})z_y - p.c_y \tag{11}$$

The second term in (11) is the marginal propensity to spend money on tradeables today, and corresponds to $(1 - p_0 c_{0y})$ in (5). The introduction of non-tradeables has added the complicated first term, which involves the compensated cross-price derivatives $m_q$. To see how these create problems, consider the case of two goods; one tradeable and one non-tradeable. In that case, all terms in (11) are scalars. $z_q$ is clearly negative. With normality, $z_y$ is positive, so the first term is negative provided $m_q$ is positive; i.e. provided tradeables and non-tradeables are substitutes. Provided the two goods are substitutes, therefore, $db/dl$ is negative, as it must be if the money adjustment process is to give a stable long-run equilibrium.

Unfortunately, there is no reason to expect the two goods to be substitutes. Recall that $m_q = (e_{pq} - r_{pq})$. With only two goods, $r_{pq}$ must be negative—that follows from $r_{pp} > 0$ and the homogeneity of supply functions. It could well be that $e_{pq}$ is negative as well, however, as there are more than two goods offered to the consumer— in addition to tradeables and non-tradeables today, he can consume tradeables and non-tradeables in later periods. In extreme cases, therefore, tradeables and non-tradeables today could be complementary to such a degree that $m_q$ becomes negative and dominates in (11). That case, which corresponds to non-tradeables and real cash balances being strong substitutes, could therefore make $(db/dl)$ positive; the implication being that the impact effect of a devaluation would be a worsening of the trade balance, and the money adjustment process leading the economy away from a long-run equilibrium.

In the two-good case we could rule out the possibility of an unstable long-run equilibrium by assuming all goods to be substitutes—i.e. by assuming $e_{pq} > 0$. That turns out to be a sufficient condition for stability in the general case as well. To see this, note from (11) that a sufficient condition for $(db/dl) < 0$ is that the vector $m_q(z_q^{-1})z_y$ is non-positive. If all goods are normal, $z_y$ is positive. If all goods are substitutes, $m_q$ is also positive—an increase in the price of any non-tradeable will increase demand for any tradeable. Finally, the inverse matrix $z_q^{-1}$ will have all non-positive elements. That can be seen by using the following inversion lemma like the one in Mirrlees (1969):

'If a square matrix $A$ has the following properties: (i) its off-diagonal elements are all non-negative, and (ii) there exists a non-negative vector $u$ such that $Au$ is strictly negative, then the matrix $A$ is non-singular, and its inverse has all its elements non-positive.'

The matrix $z_q$ satisfies these conditions. It is a square matrix. By the assumption that all goods are substitutes, its off-diagonal elements are all non-negative—an increase in the price of one non-tradeable will increase demand for all other non-tradeables. Finally, the compensated excess demand functions for non-tradeables, $z(p_0, p, q, u)$, are homogeneous of degree zero in all prices, so

$$z_0 p_0 + z_p p + z_q q = 0$$

which means that

$$z_q q = -z_0 p_0 - z_p p \ll 0$$

so long as the elasticity of substitution between tradeables and other commodities is strictly positive and all goods are substitutes. Since the price vector $q$ is non-negative, therefore, $z_q$ satisfies the conditions of the inversion lemma.

In the case of substitutes, therefore, all elements in the matrix $m_q$ are non-negative; those in $z_q^{-1}$ are non-positive. In addition, with normality, all elements in the vector $z_y$ are positive. It follows that $m_q(z_q^{-1})z_y$ is non-positive, so the first term in (11) is negative. $(db/dl)$ will then unambiguously be negative, so stability is ensured.

Of course, the assumption that all goods are substitutes is a strong one. The fact that it is sufficient, but not necessary, for stability is therefore reassuring. Still, the importance of substitutability should make us cautious when it comes to assuming that the monetary adjustment process will lead us to a long-run equilibrium.

### Extensions to many assets

As noted in the introduction, it is difficult to think in terms of more than one financial asset in a world of subjective certainty. If we allowed for uncertainty, however, we could represent this in a reduced form by letting consumers have preferences defined directly over quantities held of different assets (i.e. assets with different state-contingent payoffs), as in Sandmo (1977). Assets traded internationally at parametric prices would then be just like traded commodities, and net imports of such assets would correspond to voluntary net capital outflows. Non-tradeable assets could be equilibrated out just like the corresponding commodities, but with the same doubtful implications for long-run stability. Such an extension of the model can safely be left to the reader.

## 2. GENERAL EQUILIBRIUM AND COMPARATIVE STATICS

We now turn to a discussion of the full-fledged international equilibrium corresponding to a world of two countries of comparable

212 THEORY OF INTERNATIONAL TRADE

size. The difference from the preceding section is that prices are now endogenous, so changes in money supply or exchange rates will have implications both for the price level and for relative prices. To discuss such an equilibrium, we revert to the simple case where all goods are tradeables. The only non-tradeable commodities are factor inputs, and they are assumed to be inelastically supplied. Using our notation of corresponding lower and upper case letters for the home and foreign countries, we then have two budget conditions

$$e(p_0, p, u) = l + r(p, v) \tag{12}$$
$$E(P_0, P, U) = L + R(P, V) \tag{13}$$

the expectations functions

$$p_0 = \psi(p) \tag{14}$$
$$P_0 = \Psi(P) \tag{15}$$

the relation between the price vectors and the exchange rate

$$p = \epsilon P \tag{16}$$

and, finally, the world goods market clearing conditions

$$e_p + E_P = r_p + R_P \tag{17}$$

We can think of (12)–(17) as describing a short-run equilibrium with a fixed exchange rate. In that case, $\epsilon$, $l$, and $L$ are given. There are $(2n + 4)$ equations, one each from (12) to (15) and $n$ each from (16) and (17). There are also $(2n + 4)$ unknowns, namely the $(2n + 2)$ prices $p_0$, $p$, $P_0$, and $P$, and the two utility levels $u$ and $U$. The numeraire for each country has already been chosen (viz. the local currency), and since we have not yet introduced the money market equilibrium conditions, there are no redundant equations either.

The trade surplus for each country measured in its own currency is the value of its net excess supply of goods. As in the previous section, we can use homogeneity properties of the expenditure and revenue functions to express these in terms of the desired levels of hoarding:

$$b = p_0 e_0(p_0, p, u) - l \tag{18}$$
$$B = P_0 E_0(P_0, P, U) - L \tag{19}$$

In fact we could calculate one of the two surpluses given the other, since

$$b + \epsilon B = p.(r_p - e_p) + \epsilon P.(R_P - E_P) \qquad \text{by definition}$$
$$= p.(r_p - e_p + R_P - E_P) \qquad \text{using (16)}$$
$$= 0 \qquad \text{using (17)}$$

This should come as no surprise, as $b$ is the excess demand for money in the home country, and $\epsilon B$ is the excess demand for money in the foreign country expressed in units of the home currency. Thus $(b + \epsilon B)$ is the world excess demand for money. But if all other markets are cleared, we know by Walras's law that the money market will be cleared as well, so the result is merely a reflection of Walras's law for the whole world economy. We restate it for future reference:

$$b + \epsilon B = 0 \tag{20}$$

As noted in the previous section, however, national money markets cannot be cleared by consumers accumulating claims on the rest of the world. Given our institutional assumption that consumers are allowed to hold domestic currency only, the claims and liabilities resulting from the trade imbalances in each country are held or discharged by the governments out of their foreign exchange reserves, and the country's residents acquire or give up corresponding claims on money, their own government's debt. This leads to changes in money supplies given by

$$\Delta l = b \quad (= p_0 c_0 - l) \tag{21}$$

$$\Delta L = B \quad (= P_0 C_0 - L) \tag{22}$$

At the end of the current transactions period, therefore, the money supplies are $(l + \Delta l)$ and $(L + \Delta L)$, which we see are just the amounts $p_0 c_0$ and $P_0 C_0$ that the residents of the respective countries wish to carry forward to the next period. Equilibrium in the domestic money markets is therefore also assured.

## Implications of homogeneity

Some properties of the short run equilibrium with fixed exchange rate can be seen at once by a slight reformulation. Using homogeneity, we multiply the foreign budget and the demand functions by $\epsilon$ to write the equilibrium conditions as

$$e(\psi(p), p, u) = l + r(p, v) \tag{23}$$

$$E(\Psi(p), p, U) = \epsilon L + R(p, V) \tag{24}$$

$$e_p(\psi(p), p, u) + E_P(\Psi(p), p, U) = r_p(p, v) + R_P(p, V) \tag{25}$$

These $(n + 2)$ equations determine $p$, $u$, and $U$ given $l$ and $\epsilon L$. Note the homogeneity property that if we change $l$ and $\epsilon L$ together in the same proportion, a re-scaling of $p$ in the same proportion with no change in $u$ and $U$ will preserve equilibrium. Correspondingly from (18), $b$ will be a function homogeneous of degree one in $l$ and $\epsilon L$. We could similarly have written the equilibrium system in terms of the foreign prices $P$; these would then be determined with homogeneity in terms of $l/\epsilon$ and $L$, and $B$ would be a function homogeneous of degree one in these variables.

For future reference, it is convenient to write the trade surpluses directly as functions of the money supplies—i.e. to write the reduced form expressions for $b$ and $B$ directly as

$$b = b(l, \epsilon L) \tag{26}$$

$$B = B(l/\epsilon, L) \tag{27}$$

where both, as we have just noted, are homogeneous of degree one in their arguments.

From these observations we can derive, not quite comparative static properties, but some relations between comparative static effects. For example, the short-run effect of a devaluation on the home country's trade balance with money supplies constant is the same as that of an increase in the foreign country's money supply with the home money supply and the exchange rate constant. Specifically, a devaluation improves the trade balance if and only if a rise in the foreign money supply improves it too. Similarly, a rise in $\epsilon$ holding $l$ and $L$ constant has the same effect on $B$ as a reduction in $l$ holding $\epsilon$ and $L$ constant. But from (20), the sign of this is opposite that of the effect on $b$ of a reduction in $l$ holding $\epsilon$ and $L$ constant. In other words, a devaluation improves the trade balance for the home country if and only if an increase in its own money supply worsens it. These are intuitively appealing results, but we have not yet confirmed or refuted the simple guesses as to the actual signs of any of these effects. That turns out to be related to stability.

## Money supply adjustment

As the money supplies in the two countries change from one period to the next, we move to a new short-run equilibrium with its own prices and trade surpluses, and the process continues. The money supply changes in the two countries are connected, for (20) yields $\Delta l + \epsilon \, \Delta L = 0$, and therefore $l + \epsilon L$ is constant. This is just the world money supply measured in terms of the home currency: call it $l^*$. We state this for future reference:

$$l + \epsilon L = l^* \tag{28}$$

Now consider the adjustment process, for sake of definiteness from the standpoint of the home money supply. The trade surplus

$b$ is at its short-run equilibrium level given by (26). Further, the two arguments are related, since (28) holds with a fixed $l^*$. Therefore we have

$$\Delta l = b(l, l^* - l) \qquad (29)$$

If the right-hand side of this is a decreasing function of $l$ at an equilibrium point defined by $b = 0$, then that point will be locally stable under the adjustment process. Since this is a process in one dimension, moreover, if there are multiple equilibria they must be alternately stable (with the right-hand side of (29) decreasing through them) and unstable (with it increasing). Therefore, if this expression is decreasing whenever $b = 0$, we can conclude that the long-run equilibrium will be unique and globally stable under our adjustment process. The derivative of the right-hand side with respect to $l$ is simply $b_1 - b_2$, where these are the partials of the function $b$ with respect to its two arguments. But the homogeneity property of $b$ enables us to apply Euler's theorem to it:

$$l\, b_1(l, \epsilon L) + \epsilon L\, b_2(l, \epsilon L) = b(l, \epsilon L)$$

In particular, when $b = 0$, we see that the partials $b_1$ and $b_2$ must have opposite signs. Then $b_1 - b_2$ can be negative only through having $b_1$ negative and $b_2$ positive. In other words, our condition for stability is that the trade balance should be worsened by an increase in the home money supply and improved by an increase in the foreign money supply.

When we put this together with our earlier observations we have a correspondence result connecting comparative statics and dynamics: the money supply adjustment process will be stable in convergence to a long-run equilibrium if and only if a devaluation can improve the trade balance in the short run. Once again, we have not actually said whether or under what conditions these things will both be true; we return to this point in the next section.

## Long-run equilibrium

For the moment we will assume stability and consider properties of long-run equilibria with fixed exchange rates. Now $\epsilon$ and the total world money supply $l^*$ are given, but the individual country money supplies $l$ and $L$ are variable. Our system of equations (12) to (17) is augmented by two unknowns, and by two equations, one of which is (28), and the other is the trade balance condition for either country, $b = 0$ or $B = 0$. If the process of evolution of short-run equilibria is stable, it will converge to a long-run equilibrium.

We can define a long-run equilibrium in any case, but it loses much of its interest if the stability property is lacking.

Suppose we start in a position of such an equilibrium, with an exchange rate $\epsilon$, a home money supply $\bar{l}$, and a foreign money supply $\bar{L}$. Suppose the relevant government now alters one of these. An increase in the home money supply, for example, will open up a trade deficit in its impact effect. In course of time, this will reduce the money supply at home and increase that abroad, until a new long-run equilibrium is established. We wish to know how the new long run values $l$ and $L$ depend on the policy changes in $\bar{l}$, $\bar{L}$, and $\epsilon$. First we observe that all these policy changes alter the world money supply $l*$ according to the relationship

$$l* = \bar{l} + \epsilon\bar{L} \tag{30}$$

All other changes can be expressed in terms of $l*$. The adjustment of $l$ and $L$ is connected by (28), and in each short run we have expressed $b$ as a function of $l$ and $\epsilon L$. In particular, the new long run level of $l$ must satisfy the trade balance condition, thus

$$b(l, l* - l) = 0 \tag{31}$$

Our assumption of stability makes the left-hand side of this a decreasing function of $l$, therefore a unique equilibrium value is defined given $l*$. In fact the equilibrium $l$ is proportional to $l*$, since doubling the two together will preserve equilibrium by virtue of the homogeneity of $b$. Correspondingly $\epsilon L$ will also be proportional to $l*$. Therefore a 1% increase in $l*$ will raise the long-run equilibrium $l$ and $\epsilon L$ each by 1%. Now (23) to (25) must continue to hold in the long run as well as in the short run, and it was shown in that connection that such a change will raise all components of $p$ by 1%, leaving $u$ and $U$ unaffected. In other words, an increase in the world money stock simply causes balanced inflation all round in a neutral manner. As each country's money supply contributes a part to the world money supply, each has an inflationary impact but a smaller one. We see from (30) that a 1% increase in the home money supply will increase that for the world by $(\bar{l}/l*)\%$, and the corresponding figure for the foreign country will be $(\epsilon\bar{L}/l*)\%$.

A devaluation of 1% by the home country will raise the world money supply measured in terms of its currency by $(\epsilon\bar{L}/l*)\%$, which will raise $p$, the prices in terms of its currency, by the same proportion. However, the prices in terms of the foreign currency are $P = p/\epsilon$, so they will increase by $(\epsilon\bar{L}/l*) - 1\%$, i.e. fall by $(\bar{l}/l*)\%$. This can be seen as a reflection of the fact that the world money supply in terms of the foreign currency, $(\bar{l}/\epsilon) + \bar{L}$, has fallen by this proportion.

## Flexible exchange rates

It is possible to reinterpret our model in terms of flexible exchange rates. When changes in $\epsilon$ preserve trade balances in each period, there are no changes over time in the money supplies. Therefore $l$ and $L$ are both given. We merely add to the system (12) to (17) one unknown, namely $\epsilon$, and one equation for trade balance, which can be either (18) or (19) set equal to zero. There is no distinction between the short run and the long run in this case, at least in the sense of monetary dynamics.

Finally, consider comparative statics with a flexible exchange rate. Here we are given $l$ and $L$, while $\epsilon$ is to be determined. Using the earlier expressions (26) and (27) for the trade balances in terms of the money supplies, we can write the equilibrium condition in the form

$$b(l, \epsilon L) = 0 = B(l/\epsilon, L) \qquad (32)$$

From this it is obvious that an increase in the home money supply will depreciate the home currency by an equiproportionate amount, while a rise in the foreign money supply will cause it to appreciate by the proportion of that change.

For the purpose of this section, the only properties of demand that we needed were ones of homogeneity. The reason was that even though prices could change, such changes as actually occurred were all proportional ones. Since homogeneity is preserved in reduced forms, we can generalize this section to allow non-tradeable commodities, as the reader can verify by writing out the two-country version of the model with non-tradeables outlined in section 1. Again, when we look at stability conditions we will find that they do not generalize so readily.

## 3. STABILITY OF THE LONG-RUN EQUILIBRIUM

The difficult question of whether a sequence of short-run equilibria with trade imbalance and money supply change evolves towards a long-run equilibrium with balanced trade can no longer be postponed. We saw in the previous section that several short-run comparative static effects were linked—the trade balance responded in the same qualitative manner to a devaluation, a decrease in the home money supply, and an increase in the foreign money supply—and all these were in turn linked to the question of stability of the long-run equilibrium. Here we examine the whole issue by studying the response of the trade balance to money supply changes at a fixed exchange rate. We consider two cases separately, as they involve different economic assumptions and mathematical features.

## The one-good case

In our first case there is only one tradeable good. Now $p$ and $P$ are scalars, linked by $p = \epsilon P$ with $\epsilon$ fixed. The expectation functions can be written

$$p_0 = kp, \qquad P_0 = KP \qquad (33)$$

where $k$ and $K$ are positive constants. The revenue functions are simply

$$r(p, v) = pf(v), \qquad R(P, V) = PF(V) \qquad (34)$$

where $f$ and $F$ are the production functions. Writing demands as functions of prices and total income including money endowments, the trade balances are

$$b = p_0 \, c_0(p_0, p, l + pf(v)) - l \qquad (35)$$

$$B = P_0 \, C_0(P_0, P, L + PF(V)) - L \qquad (36)$$

Finally, the condition for clearance of the world market for the one tradeable good is

$$c(p_0, p, l + pf(v)) + C(P_0, P, L + PF(V)) = f(v) + F(V) \qquad (37)$$

As the money supplies change, so do the equilibrium prices, and we can calculate the response by taking total differentials in (37). The total change in $c$, for example, is

$$dc = (\partial c / \partial p_0)k \, dp + c_p \, dp + c_y(dl + f(v) \, dp)$$

However, since $c$ is homogeneous of degree zero in its arguments,

$$(\partial c / \partial p_0)kp + c_p p + c_y(l + pf(v)) = 0$$

Substituting, we have

$$dc = c_y(dl - dp(l/p))$$

With a similar expression for the foreign country, total differentiation of (37) yields

$$c_y(dl - dp(l/p)) + C_Y(dL - dP(L/P)) = 0 \qquad (38)$$

Assuming only that $c_y$ and $C_Y$ are positive, i.e. the good is normal in both countries, we see that as the money supply in either country increases, the prices in both countries increase. Moreover, the increases are all in a smaller proportion, i.e. all the elasticities are between 0 and 1. For example

$$\frac{l}{p}\frac{\partial p}{\partial l} = \frac{lc_y}{lc_y + LC_Y}$$

Now let only the home money supply change, and let us find the impact on the home trade surplus starting from a position of balance. Taking total differentials in (35), we have

$$db = c_0 k\,dp + p_0(c_{00}k\,dp + c_{0p}\,dp + c_{0y}\,dl + c_{0y}f(v)\cdot dp) - dl$$

By homogeneity of $c_0$,

$$c_{00}kp + c_{0p}p + c_{0y}(l + pf(v)) = 0,$$

therefore

$$db = c_0 k\,dp + p_0(c_{0y}\,dl - lc_{0y}\,dp/p) - dl$$

At the initial point, $b = 0$, so $c_0 kp = l$ and

$$db = (1 - p_0 c_{0y})(l\,dp/p - dl)$$

Then

$$\frac{db}{dl} = -(1 - p_0 c_{0y})\left(1 - \frac{l}{p}\frac{\partial p}{\partial l}\right) \qquad (39)$$

Given our assumption that the tradeable good is normal in demand, the marginal propensity to hold money must be less than one, making the first parenthesis on the right-hand side in (39) positive. The same assumption led to the result that the elasticity in the expression in the second parenthesis is less than one, therefore that expression is positive as well. This makes $db/dl$ negative, proving the desired stability of the long-run equilibrium and all the attendant comparative static results for the short run.

### The gross substitutes case

In the case of a small country with non-tradeables, we saw previously that an assumption that all goods were substitutes was sufficient to ensure stability of the money adjustment mechanism. Generally, it is well known in micro-economic theory that the complexities and ambiguities of comparative statics and stability of general equilibrium can be avoided by making the strong assumption that all commodities are gross substitutes. This requires the excess demand for each commodity to respond negatively to its own price, and non-negatively to all other prices. This assumption proves useful in the present context as well. Of course we have to assume that in each country, goods and money are also gross substitutes.

Write the excess demand for goods in the home country as a vector function of the prices and the money supply, thus subsuming the separate determination of supplies and demands:

$$m(p, l) = c(\psi(p), p, l + r(p, v)) - r_p(p, v)$$

Our assumption is that the matrix of derivatives $m_p = (\partial m_j / \partial p_k)$ has negative entries along the diagonal and non-negative ones everywhere else. Also, $m_l = c_y$ is the vector of the income derivatives of the demands for goods. We assume all goods to be normal, so this vector is strictly positive. Finally, $m$ is homogeneous of degree zero in its arguments, so

$$m_p p + m_l l = 0$$

or

$$m_p p = -m_l l \ll 0 \qquad (40)$$

The foreign country has a similar structure of excess demands.

Now consider the world market clearance for the goods. We can without loss of generality choose the currency units in the two countries so that the fixed exchange rate is unity; then $p = P$ and some expressions are simplified. We have

$$m(p, l) + M(p, L) = 0 \qquad (41)$$

Taking total differentials and using $m_l = c_y$ etc. we find

$$-(m_p + M_P)\,\mathrm{d}p = c_y\,\mathrm{d}l + C_Y\,\mathrm{d}L \qquad (42)$$

At this point we can use the inversion lemma which we applied earlier to the small country with non-tradeables.

With gross substitutes, each of $m_p$ and $M_P$ has negative elements along the diagonal and positive elements off it, and hence so does their sum. Further, using (40) and its analogue for the foreign country

$$(m_p + M_P)p = -c_y l - C_Y L \ll 0$$

so from the inversion lemma, $(m_p + M_P)^{-1}$ has all non-positive elements.

Therefore we can solve (42) to write

$$\mathrm{d}p = -(m_p + M_P)^{-1}(c_y\,\mathrm{d}l + C_y\,\mathrm{d}L) \qquad (43)$$

and notice that the coefficients of $\mathrm{d}l$ and $\mathrm{d}L$ on the right-hand side are each the product of a non-singular, non-negative matrix and a positive vector, and therefore positive. In other words, an increase in the money supply of either country raises all prices in both. This is the kind of result that follows from the assumption of gross substitutes and would not be valid otherwise.

As we saw before, the trade surplus in each country simply equals the excess demand for money (which is met through the supply adjustment process). Let us write the excess demand functions for nominal money in the two countries as $h(p, l)$ and $H(P, L)$, subsuming in this the effects of expectations. The gross substitutes assumption is that excess demands respond non-negatively to other prices, hence the vectors $h_p$ and $H_P$ are non-negative. Comparing these functions with expressions like (35) and (36), we also see that $h_l = -(1 - p_0 c_{0y})$ and $H_L = -(1 - P_0 C_{0Y})$ are negative under our assumption of normalcy. Finally, each is homogeneous of degree one in its arguments.

It is then easy to see what happens to the trade balance. Taking total differentials in $b = h(p, l)$, we have

$$\mathrm{d}b = h_p\,\mathrm{d}p + h_l\,\mathrm{d}l$$

$$= -h_p(m_p + M_P)^{-1}(c_y\,\mathrm{d}l + C_Y\,\mathrm{d}L) + h_l\,\mathrm{d}l \qquad (44)$$

using (43). If we consider a change in the foreign money supply only, therefore, we find

$$\mathrm{d}b/\mathrm{d}L = -h_p(m_p + M_P)^{-1}C_Y \qquad (45)$$

which is immediately seen to be positive. But we recall that we can write $b = b(l, \epsilon L)$, with $b_1 l + b_2 \epsilon L = b = 0$ at a point of balanced trade. Thus, at a point of balanced trade, (45) implies $\mathrm{d}b/\mathrm{d}l$ negative, and thus stability.

The gross substitute case therefore yields the desired result. With gross substitutes, we can also accommodate non-tradeables, provided we are willing to assume that *all* commodities—tradeables, non-tradeables, and money—are gross substitutes. Having shown the general procedure for the small country case, we can safely leave the generalization in this case to the reader.

As pointed out earlier, however, the assumption of gross substitutes is very hard to justify on any grounds, so the above result is of limited interest. It shows that if the long-run equilibrium is unstable, it must be due to complementarities. Beyond that, it does not really shed light on the conditions that have to be satisfied for money adjustment process to equilibrate the trade balance, or for a devaluation to have a positive impact effect on the trade surplus.

In the general case, therefore, we cannot be sure that the long-run equilibrium will be stable. Moreover, we cannot deduce *necessary* conditions for stability with simple economic interpretations. We can, of course, note that a necessary and sufficient condition for long-run stability is that the right-hand side of (45) must be positive, but that is hardly instructive. To arrive at more precise necessary and sufficient conditions for stability, we must look at more restrictive models. We turn now to a discussion of one such model, viz. a special case of the general model in which real and financial decisions are separable. That gives us the framework of the traditional elasticities approach to the balance of payments, and is therefore of interest in its own right. Moreover, it turns out that necessary and sufficient conditions for stability can be given simple interpretations in such a context.

## 4. THE ELASTICITIES APPROACH

Apparently, the so-called elasticities approach to the balance of payments is qualitatively different from the monetary approach. The essence of the former is that the effect of a devaluation depends on the price derivatives of the import demand functions and export supply functions for goods. In particular, it is argued that a devaluation will be successful if and only if the sum of the import demand elasticities for the two goods exceeds one. That is the Marshall–Lerner condition, and it has obvious implications for the stability of a long-run equilibrium with a money adjustment mechanism. In the general equilibrium framework above, a devaluation is equivalent to a reduction in the domestic money supply. If the Marshall–Lerner condition is necessary and sufficient for a devaluation to be successful in our general equilibrium model, therefore, it is also a necessary and sufficient condition for the trade surplus to be a decreasing function of the domestic money supply, and thus a necessary and sufficient condition for stability of the long run equilibrium. Our task in this section, therefore, is to see whether the elasticities approach can be consistent with general equilibrium, and whether the Marshall–Lerner condition is related to stability of such an equilibrium in the long run.

We should then first note that the elasticities approach implicitly assumes that we can separate real and financial decisions. If separation is not possible, any condition on the effects of changes in exchange rates or money supplies will involve at least cross-price effects between the demands for goods and the demands for assets, so simplifications involving only derivatives with respect to goods prices will in general be impossible. As a result, we should discuss the elasticities approach within a more restrictive model where such separation is possible. That means that demands must be generated by a utility function which is separable in real cash balances on the one hand, and the vector of current consumption on the other; i.e. that there are separate functions $u^0$ and $u^1$ such that

$$u = u^0(c_0, u^1(c))$$

Note that this is much stronger than the separability condition needed to define real cash balances in the first place. That required the composition of planned excess demands in the future to be independent of current prices. We now in addition require the marginal rates of substitution between any pair of goods consumed today to be independent of real cash balances brought forward, and thus independent of future consumption. In other words, to formulate a utility function like the one above, we must not only be able to lump together all future consumption vectors in one scalar aggregate—we must also be able to do the same with the vector of current consumption.

The separable utility function is to be maximized subject to the budget constraint

$$p_0 c_0 + p.c = l + r(p, v)$$

This problem can be solved in two stages: Given $c_0$, we can choose $c$ so as to maximize $u^1(c)$ subject to $p.c = l - p_0 c_0 + r(p, v)$. The resulting choices will be functions of $(p, l - p_0 c_0)$, and homogeneous of degree zero in the arguments. Then the sub-utility $u^1$ will be a function of these, and it will remain to choose $c_0$ to maximize $u^0(c_0, u^1)$.

It is convenient to do all of this using the shorter route of Meade utility functions employed in earlier chapters. Note that $u^1$ is a function only of the consumption of goods, and thus a function of production plus imports, so $u^1 = u^1(x + m)$. We can therefore define the Meade utility function

$$\phi^1(m) = \max_x u^1(x + m) \qquad \text{subject to } x \text{ being feasible}$$

just as in previous chapters. The import demands for goods can then be found by maximizing $\phi^1(m)$ subject to $p.m = l - p_0 c_0$, giving us import demand functions $m = m(p, l - p_0 c_0)$. The demand for real balances can then be found by maximizing $u^0(c_0, \phi^1)$.

Doing this, and noting that $l - p_0 c_0 = -b$ (the trade surplus), we can express the demand functions for imports as functions of goods prices and the trade surplus, and express the desired trade surplus (desired hoarding) as a function of prices and initial cash balances. In other words, we have $m = m(p, b)$—where $m$ is homogeneous of degree zero in its arguments—and $b = h(p, l)$—where $h$ is homogeneous of degree one in its arguments since it pertains to nominal magnitudes. It should be emphasized that we allow $h$ to depend on the prices in an arbitrary manner, and do not restrict it to be a function of a scalar price index for the goods. That would require $u^1$ homothetic in $c$, a restriction that is unnecessary for our purpose.

## Properties of excess demand functions

We need some specific properties of the demand functions for imports and net claims. Note first that we will have

$$h_l = p_0 c_{0y} - 1 \tag{46}$$

as before, so with normal demands for goods, $h_l$ will be negative. Next, by homogeneity, writing $h_p$ for $\partial h / \partial p$, we have

$$h_p p + h_l l = b \tag{47}$$

As for the excess demand functions for goods, we must have $p . m = -b$, so

$$p . m_b = -1 \tag{48}$$

The terms on the left-hand side are minus the marginal propensities to spend on the goods out of the budget that has been allocated to them. They will therefore relate to the basic propensities according to the relation

$$p_i c_{iy} = -p_i m_{ib}(1 - p_0 c_{0y})$$

so when all goods are normal, all the $m_{ib}$ will be negative. Finally, from homogeneity we have

$$m_p p + m_b b = 0 \tag{49}$$

## Equilibrium and effects of monetary expansion

Using the import demand equations and substituting in the equations for desired accumulation of claims, we see that equilibrium in the world goods markets is given by

$$m(p, h(p, l)) + M(p, H(p, L)) = 0 \tag{50}$$

We have here set the exchange rate equal to one, as we wish to focus on the effects of a change in the supply of money. (50) gives us $n$ equations to determine the $n$ prices of goods as functions of the domestic and foreign money supplies. As before, we shall only be concerned with the effects of changes in the money supply in the neighbourhood of a long-run equilibrium where $b = 0 = B$, so when looking at effects of changes in $l$ or $L$, we shall evaluate the derivatives of (50) for $h = 0 = H$.

We can at once note a sufficient condition for an increase in the domestic supply of money to reduce the domestic trade surplus, and thus a sufficient condition for stability of the long-run equilibrium: Differentiating (50) totally, we have

$$(m_p + M_P)\, \mathrm{d}p + m_b\, \mathrm{d}h + M_B\, \mathrm{d}H = 0$$

But $h = b = -B = -H$ in equilibrium, so in equilibrium $\mathrm{d}H = -\mathrm{d}h$, so the above can be written as

$$(m_p + M_P)\, \mathrm{d}p + (m_b - M_B)\, \mathrm{d}h = 0$$

If the marginal propensities to spend out of the budget allocated to goods consumption are the same in the two countries, i.e. if $(m_b = M_B)$, we must therefore have

$$(m_p + M_P)\, \mathrm{d}p = 0 \tag{51}$$

But evaluated at a point of balanced trade, i.e. at a point where $b = 0$, we know from (49) that $m_p p = 0$, and similarly for the foreign country $M_P p = 0$. The condition (51) will therefore be satisfied for $\mathrm{d}p = vp$, where $v$ is some scalar. That means that relative prices will remain unchanged—the only effect of a change in money supplies will be a change in the level of prices. But that essentially brings us back to the one-good case discussed in section 3, in which we showed that the long-run equilibrium is stable. A sufficient condition for long run stability is therefore that the marginal propensities to spend on any good out of the budget allocated to consumption be the same in the two countries.

The more interesting case is where the marginal propensities differ between the countries. In that case, a change in the domestic supply of money will have effects on relative prices, and thus on the terms of trade. The elasticities approach can be seen as an attempt at finding the exact restrictions that must be placed on the price derivatives of the import demand equations in order for this terms of trade effect not to offset the direct effect of monetary expansion on the balance of payments. There will be meaningful restrictions of this type in the general case, but they have immediate economic interpretations only in the case of two goods. We shall therefore concentrate on the two-good case.

From (50), the general effect of an expansion in the domestic supply of money on prices is given by

$$(m_p + m_b h_p + M_P + M_B H_P) \, \mathrm{d}p = -m_b h_l \, \mathrm{d}l$$

Writing that out in full for the two-good case, using $m_i$ to denote import demand for good $i$, and $m_{ij}$ for its derivative with respect to the price of good $j$; and using similar notation for $M$, $h$, and $H$, we get

$$\begin{bmatrix} m_{11}+M_{11}+m_{1b}h_1+M_{1B}H_1 & m_{12}+M_{12}+m_{1b}h_2+M_{1B}H_2 \\ m_{21}+M_{21}+m_{2b}h_1+M_{2B}H_1 & m_{22}+M_{22}+m_{2b}h_2+M_{2B}H_2 \end{bmatrix} \begin{bmatrix} \mathrm{d}p_1 \\ \mathrm{d}p_2 \end{bmatrix}$$
$$= \begin{bmatrix} -m_{1b}h_l \, \mathrm{d}l \\ -m_{2b}h_l \, \mathrm{d}l \end{bmatrix} \quad (52)$$

The matrix on the left-hand side here is a messy one. The patient reader can work it out, to find that at an initial point of balanced trade, it is non-singular (i.e. has a non-zero determinant) if and only if the marginal propensities to spend $m_{1b}$ and $M_{iB}$ differ between the countries. As we have already seen that they must differ for relative prices to change, that is hardly surprising. We assume that to be the case, so that the matrix is non-singular.

Beyond that, we do not really have to worry about the matrix. It is the matrix of excess demand derivatives in the goods markets. If the short run equilibrium which clears these markets is to be attained through a stable tâtonnement process, its determinant must be positive. (See Arrow and Hahn (1971, ch. 12, section 5)). The reader familiar with phase diagrams can verify this by considering the two-good tâtonnement process $\Delta p_i = \zeta_i(p_1, p_2)$, where $\zeta_i(p_1, p_2)$ is the excess demand function for good $i$. By drawing the corresponding phase diagram, he will discover that a condition for stability is $\zeta_{11}\zeta_{22} > \zeta_{21}\zeta_{12}$, i.e. that the determinant of the excess demand price derivatives be positive. Our entire exercise is clearly uninteresting if goods markets are unstable, so we can safely assume that the determinant is positive. We denote it by $D$, and thus have $D > 0$.

Further interpretations of (52) are possible using the properties of the demand functions given by (46)–(49). Writing these out for the two-good case, and simplifying notation by choosing units of commodities so that the initial prices are unity, we have for an initial point of $b = 0$,

$$h_1 + h_2 = -h_l l \qquad \text{(homogeneity of } h\text{)} \qquad (53)$$

$$m_{1b} + m_{2b} = -1 \qquad \text{(sum of income derivatives)} \qquad (54)$$

$$m_{11} + m_{12} = 0 = m_{21} + m_{22} \qquad \text{(homogeneity of } m\text{)} \qquad (55)$$

$$m_1 + m_2 = 0 \qquad \text{(balanced trade)} \qquad (56)$$

In addition, we know that $p_1 m_1 + p_2 m_2 = -b$, so $m_1 + p_1 m_{11} + p_2 m_{21} = 0$, and similarly for the derivatives with respect to $p_2$. Again choosing units so that prices are one, therefore, we have

$$m_1 + m_{11} + m_{21} = 0 = m_2 + m_{12} + m_{22} \qquad (57)$$

Identical conditions apply to the foreign country.

We can use these to simplify (52) in terms of elasticities. Suppose that in the initial equilibrium with trade balance, the home country is importing good 1, so $m_1 > 0$. The numerical value of the elasticity of import demand with respect to the price of imports is then $-p_1 m_{11}/m_1$, abbreviate it as $\lambda$. Using (55), (56), and (57) we then have

$$m_{11} = -\lambda m_1, \qquad m_{12} = \lambda m_1, \qquad m_{21} = (\lambda - 1)m_1,$$

$$m_{22} = -(\lambda - 1)m_1$$

Similarly, for the foreign country which is importing good 2, let $\Lambda$ be the price elasticity of import demand—i.e. let $\Lambda = -P_2 M_{22}/M_2$. Then we get the corresponding expressions

$$M_{11} = -(\Lambda - 1)M_2, \qquad M_{12} = (\Lambda - 1)M_2,$$

$$M_{21} = \Lambda M_2, \qquad M_{22} = -\Lambda M_2$$

Also, $m_1 = -m_2$ by the home country's balanced trade, and $-m_2 = M_2$ by the equilibrium condition for the market for good 2, so $m_1 = M_2$. Write $\tau$ for the common level of $m_1$ and $M_2$, so $\tau$ is positive and measures the volume of trade. In this notation, we then have

$$m_{11} + M_{11} = m_{22} + M_{22} = -\tau(\lambda + \Lambda - 1)$$

$$m_{12} + M_{12} = m_{21} + M_{21} = \tau(\lambda + \Lambda - 1)$$

We can substitute this into (52), and use the resulting set of equations to solve for $dp_i$ as functions of the change in the domestic money supply $dl$. Doing that is messy, but not difficult, so it can safely be left to the reader if he is not willing to take the solution on trust. We get

$$\begin{bmatrix} dp_1 \\ dp_2 \end{bmatrix} = -\left(\frac{h_l}{D}\right) \begin{bmatrix} \tau(\lambda + \Lambda - 1) + H_2(m_{1b}M_{2B} - m_{2b}M_{1B}) \\ \tau(\lambda + \Lambda - 1) - H_1(m_{1b}M_{2B} - m_{2b}M_{1B}) \end{bmatrix} dl$$

$$(58)$$

where we recall that $D$ is the (positive) determinant of the matrix of price derivatives of excess demands.

To find the effects on the trade surplus, we can use $db = -dB$, so

$$db = -H_1\,dp_1 - H_2\,dp_2$$

Using (58) and observing that the second terms in the price effects cancel when multiplied by $H_1$ and $H_2$ respectively, we therefore have

$$db = (1/D)h_l(H_1 + H_2)\tau(\lambda + \Lambda - 1)\,dl$$

or, using (53)—i.e. $H_1 + H_2 = -H_L L$

$$db = -(1/D)h_l H_L L\tau(\lambda + \Lambda - 1)\,dl \qquad (59)$$

Both $h_l$ and $H_L$ are negative by normality. $D$ is positive by stability of the goods markets. $\tau$ is positive by definition. Consequently (59) says that $db/dl$ is negative if and only if $\lambda + \Lambda > 1$, i.e. if and only if the sum of the import elasticities for the two countries is greater than one. In other words, the Marshall–Lerner condition must be satisfied if the impact effect on the trade surplus of domestic money expansion is to be negative. The implication is that the Marshall–Lerner condition must be satisfied for the impact effect of a devaluation to be positive, and for the money adjustment mechanism to lead to a stable long-run equilibrium.

From (58) we can also find the relative price effect of a devaluation or an expansion in the domestic money supply: It is given by

$$d(p_1/p_2) = dp_1 - dp_2 \quad \text{since} \quad p_1 = p_2 = 1 \quad \text{initially}$$

$$= -(h_l/D)(H_1 + H_2)(m_{1b}M_{2B} - m_{2b}M_{1B})\,dl$$

$$= Lh_l H_L(m_{1b}M_{2B} - m_{2b}M_{1b})\,dl/D$$

Noting that $m_{2b} = -(1 + m_{1b})$ and similarly for $M_{2B}$ we therefore get the result

$$d(p_1/p_2)/dl < 0 \qquad \text{if and only if} \quad m_{1b} > M_{1B}$$

Recall that the home country is importing good 1, and the effects of a devaluation are like those of a reduction in the domestic money supply. Therefore a devaluation worsens the home country's terms of trade if and only if the marginal propensity to spend on good 1 out of the budget allocated to goods is smaller at home than abroad. This is very similar to the condition governing the effect of a transfer of goods on the terms of trade in our model of Chapter 5 which did not involve money.

If we compare these results with the results from models involving real disequilibria, as outlined in the introduction to this chapter, we find an important difference. In those models, a devaluation worked by worsening the commodity terms of trade, i.e. the Marshall–Lerner condition also ensured that the devaluing country's terms of trade deteriorated. In the monetary model, that need not be the case.

## Extensions

The Marshall–Lerner condition is a condition relating to two goods, and cannot, therefore, apply to a world of many goods. Nor is it generally possible to derive similar simple conditions for the general case—one can get conditions involving elasticities, but they cannot be reduced to forms with simple interpretations. Nor can a similarly simple condition be derived for the effect of monetary expansion or exchange rate changes from a position of unbalanced trade. Again, one gets a condition involving elasticities, but it is neither so elegant nor so easily interpreted as the Marshall–Lerner condition. The conditions under which the Marshall–Lerner condition applies should therefore be regarded as a very special case. It is instructive because it sheds qualitative light on what is involved in the general case. To our mind, it is also appealing because it demonstrates that there is a relationship between the monetary approach to the balance of payments and the neoclassical approach with its emphasis on price elasticities.

## NOTES

As with comparative advantage, there seems little point in tracing the classical gold-flow mechanism back to Hume, or the elasticities approach back to Marshall. An elementary exposition of the specie-flow mechanism is in Samuelson (1976, ch. 33); see also the introduction to Frenkel and Johnson (eds.) (1976). The mechanism relying on disequilibrium in the goods market is in Caves and Jones (1976, ch. 17) and Södersten (1971, ch. 13). Pearce (1970, chs. 2–4) uses features of both approaches.

An early model integrating money in a micro-economic trade context was developed by Hahn (1959) who, however, considered only short run equilibrium. The importance of the monetary adjustment process was recognized by Mundell, Johnson, and others, and this became the cornerstone of the new (or revived) monetary approach to the balance of payments. Many seminal articles in this line are collected in Frenkel and Johnson (eds.). Although some of the claims of its proponents have been severely criticized, for example by Hahn (1977), the crucial importance of the adjustment process is now widely accepted. Many who take the monetary approach also embrace macro-economic monetarism by believing that the demand function for money has a particularly simple form, or depends on very few strategic variables. More general micro-economic approaches can be found in Kemp (1970), Takayama (1972), and Anderson and Takayama (1977).

This chapter relies on all of the above. The small country model is essentially that of Johnson and the one-good model that of Dornbusch (both in Frenkel and Johnson), but the functional forms are more general. The rest is based on Anderson and Takayama, with some differences of order and notation.

# CHAPTER 8

# TRADE AND PAYMENTS WITH FIXED PRICES

The monetary approach to the balance of payments, as expounded in the previous chapter, is essentially a Walrasian equilibrium theory of international trade involving financial assets. If one country has a trade surplus, this is because its aggregate consumption plans fall short of aggregate production plans in the current period, while the opposite is true for the rest of the world. Thus any payments imbalance is a planned imbalance—not planned by any central agency, but consistent with the optimum plans of all consumers and producers. And there is an obvious analogy between payments imbalances and trade in goods. That enables a country to consume more of one good than it produces in return for consuming less of another. Payments imbalances enable a country to trade excess saving today against excess consumption later, or vice versa.

The monetary approach can, therefore, be seen as an extension of the standard model of trade, allowing for trade in claims on future production in addition to trade in current goods; the only difference is that the former claims are held in the form of financial assets instead of futures contracts for specific goods. As such, the approach is valuable. For example, it points out that trade imbalances need not indicate market failure—on the contrary, such imbalances can be evidence of gains from intertemporal trade. To counter the popular belief that any trade imbalance is a disequilibrium indicating a need for action, such a model can be very valuable indeed.

However, one should recognize that the monetary approach gives one extreme view of the processes involved. It assumes perfectly flexible prices of goods and factors, and therefore instantaneous attainment of equilibrium on all these markets. It has been argued that such an assumption is particularly inappropriate in the short-run context in which issues concerning trade imbalances are commonly raised. Trade imbalances and related questions of exchange rates are often connected with problems of unemployment and inflation: both of which are outside the scope of Walrasian equilibrium theory. The Keynesian tradition that short-run market clearance occurs through quantity rationing at sticky prices might be deemed more relevant to such settings. Even without complete endorsement of this alternative, some of the issues it raises and some of the links it points out are worth consideration. That is the object of this chapter.

To see what is involved, recall that in Chapter 7, we found two equivalent expressions for the trade surplus, one being the excess of domestic holdings of financial assets over the (initial) supply of these assets, and the other the excess of the value of current production over that of current consumption; thus

$$b = p_0 c_0 - l = p . x - p . c$$

The equivalence of the two followed from accounting identities of budget balance, independently of any assumptions concerning equilibrium. What followed additionally from the assumption of instantaneous price flexibility was the equality between actual values and planned values of the various quantities. For example, $p . x$ was the maximum value of output at the equilibrium prices with the given factor quantities, and this entailed full employment. It was then often—but not always—most convenient to focus on the first expression for $b$, viz. the excess of the demand for money over its initial supply.

If prices are fixed at levels different from the short-run market-clearing ones, not all the agents' plans can be realized. If a market fails to clear, the amount supplied or demanded, whichever is smaller, must be rationed among the agents on the other side. Such quantity constraints will affect the choices of these agents in other markets. The decisions concerning supply or demand in one market, taking into account any quantity constraints encountered in other markets, are called *effective* demands or supplies, in contrast to the *notional* ones which take into account only the prevailing prices and the income or production possibilities. When we step outside the setting of Walrasian or flexible-price equilibria, the effective demand and supply govern matters. If unemployment prevails, for example, consumption and money-holding decisions will be affected. Even if we adopt the first expression for the trade surplus, we will have to interpret $c_0$ as the effective demand for real balances. More importantly, when the failure of some markets for goods or factors to clear affects the others, such chain reactions can be more easily traced if we use the second, or real, expression for the trade surplus. This is not a denial of the importance of financial sectors in allowing the very possibility of holding claims against the future, or of the ubiquitous interaction among all parts of the economy, but simply a matter of convenience in using one technique of analysis rather than another.

Unemployment is only one of several possibilities in a world of sticky prices. Producers may face a sales constraint, i.e. their actual sales may be determined by demand at a level smaller than they would wish given the ruling prices. This will have repercussions on their demand for factors, and thence on the demand for commodities. Yet other possibilities are cases where consumers are unable to buy their planned quantities of goods. If such a state prevails only on markets for non-traded goods, they may increase their demand for tradeables, so that the rationing in domestic product markets generates an effective trade deficit. If all goods are in short supply, there may be forced saving, which can force an accumulation of claims on the rest of the world.

As should be apparent, one could make a long catalogue of possibilities with fixed prices. If we limit ourselves to two countries, each having a market for one factor and one non-tradeable good, and let there be one tradeable good, we have five markets each of which could have flexible or fixed prices, making 32 distinct possible combinations. Each market which fails to clear could be in excess supply or excess demand, thus multiplying the classifications with fixed prices. It is clearly beyond the scope of one chapter to investigate all of these combinations. We limit ourselves, first by assuming that all goods are tradeable. In this context, the device of netting out non-tradeables and working with a reduced form model does not work since Walrasian equilibrium conditions in the markets for non-tradeables are not available. Models with non-tradeables have been developed by Neary (1978) and Steigum (1978). Excluding non-tradeables, we have eight possible combinations of fixed and flexible prices. Of these, we examine only two: first combining sticky factor prices with flexible goods prices, and the second where all prices are sticky. In the first case, domestic factor markets clear by quantity adjustments, and the resulting effective excess demand for goods in the world is reduced to zero by price adjustment. In the second case, there is quantity adjustment even on the goods market.

The models we present are very much in the tradition of Barro and Grossman (1976) and Malinvaud (1977). As we wish to focus on payments issues, however, we simplify some other aspects. Most important is the assumption of inelastic factor supplies: this means that unemployment has only income effects and no substitution effects in determining the effective demands for commodities and money holdings. Further, unlike Malinvaud or Dixit (1978), we assume that profits are instantaneously distributed to the consumer. Both of these assumptions are compatible with the framework of the previous chapter, and that is indeed their attraction here, since they enable a closely parallel treatment.

Consider the case where product prices are flexible. For the home country, we can still write as in the previous chapter

$$e(p_0, p, u) = l + r(p, v) \tag{1}$$

$$p_0 = \psi(p) \tag{2}$$

$$m = e_p(p_0, p, u) - r_p(p, v) \tag{3}$$

$$b = p_0\, e_0(p_0, p, u) - l \tag{4}$$

To recapitulate, (1) is the equation between expenditure and disposable income, both including money, (2) expresses the expected future price level as a function of current prices, (3) gives the excess demand vector for goods, and (4) is the financial expression for the trade surplus. Similar equations hold for the rest of the world.

The new feature arises in the factor markets. In the previous chapter, full employment was assumed. Then $r$ and its derivatives were to be evaluated at the fixed supply quantities $v$, and the equilibrium factor prices were given by $w = r_v(p, v)$. This is no longer necessarily so. Consider the case of one factor. If $w$ is fixed at a level that leaves the factor in excess supply, actual employment is determined from the inverse factor demand equations $w = r_v(p, v)$, and the revenue function in (1) is to be evaluated for this quantity. If there is excess demand for the factor, then $r$ is to be evaluated at the supply quantity. The price is fixed below what the producers would be willing to pay, but this only affects the distribution of the product among types of income, and that is irrelevant given our assumptions of one consumer and instantaneous profit distribution.

The case where product prices are also sticky is more difficult. It may not be possible to achieve the maximum value of output as expressed in (1); instead, we may have to use $p \cdot x$ with $x$ determined by demand on the right-hand side. Depending on the levels at which the various prices are fixed, different cases may arise. We shall not attempt an exhaustive catalogue. Rather, we shall restrict ourselves to the ranges of factor and product prices which correspond to general excess supply—output is constrained by actual sales and labour use is constrained by demand—often called the Keynesian unemployment case. This is the case which has received much attention in the simple trade multiplier analyses, and we can relate the new developments in models of fix-price equilibria to that tradition. This clarifies the role of some *ad hoc* procedures that are often invoked without much thought. It is also hoped that the reader will be able to apply the same methods to analyse other cases of interest.

# 1. SMALL COUNTRY WITH STICKY WAGES

We begin by considering a small country with factor prices fixed in the short run, facing Walrasian international product markets. Thus we assume that world product prices are given, and that there are no quantity constraints restricting the sales or purchases of goods by this country. The model is a somewhat simplified version of Dixit (1978); for an extension with non-traded goods, see Neary (1978).

### The balance of trade

Product demand and supply in a country facing no product market constraints are given by equations (1)–(4) above. In addition, with international product prices $P$ and an exchange rate $\epsilon$, we have

$$p = \epsilon P \tag{5}$$

where the price vector $P$ is exogenous in the small country case. Substituting (2) and (5) into (1) and (4), we then find that the balance of trade is determined by the two equations

$$e(\psi(\epsilon P), \epsilon P, u) = l + r(\epsilon P, v)$$
$$b = \psi(\epsilon P)e_0 - l \tag{6}$$

We can use the first of these to solve for utility as a function of prices and disposable income. Substituting that into the latter equation, we get the trade balance expressed in terms of the uncompensated demand for money. Using homogeneity, we can then—just as we did in Chapter 7—write the trade balance as

$$\frac{b}{\epsilon} = \psi(P) c_0\left(\psi(P), P, \frac{l}{\epsilon} + r(P, v)\right) - \frac{l}{\epsilon} \tag{7}$$

This is exactly the same expression as the one we had in Chapter 7. There is, however, an important difference of interpretation: in Chapter 7, $v$ was factor supply. Here it is actual employment, which can fall short of supply when wages are sticky.

### The labour market

We shall concentrate on only one factor, called labour. Total labour supply is fixed at $\bar{v}$. The wage rate is fixed at $w$. If labour demand, at $w$, falls short of $\bar{v}$, actual employment is determined by demand. If demand exceeds $\bar{v}$, firms will be rationed, and actual employment will be $\bar{v}$. As for labour demand, the absence of sales constraints makes that equal to notional labour demand, which is found along conventional lines: $r_v(p, v)$ gives the demand price of labour for output prices $p$ and employment level $v$, so it is the inverse demand function for labour. Assuming $r_v(p, v)$ strictly decreasing in $v$, it can be inverted to give labour demand as a function of the wage rate.

We therefore have two possibilities. One is that the price-wage configuration can be such as to produce unemployment. The actual employment level is then given by

$$r_v(p, v) = w \tag{8}$$

Alternatively, prices and wages can be such that (8) gives $v > \bar{v}$. Labour will then be rationed. To make things simple, we assume that labour is rationed in an efficient manner—i.e. that it is rationed in such a way as to maximize $p.x$. With rationing we shall then have $p.x = r(p, \bar{v})$, and actual employment equal to $\bar{v}$.

It is useful to express employment in terms of international product prices. Recalling that $r_v$ is homogeneous of degree one in $p$, we have

$$r_v(\epsilon P, v) = \epsilon r_v(P, v)$$

so if there is unemployment, $v$ will be given by

$$r_v(P, v) = w/\epsilon \tag{9}$$

while $v = \bar{v}$ if $r_v(P, \bar{v}) \geq w/\epsilon$. Thus the exchange rate will affect the level of employment. In addition to the real balance effect, therefore, exchange rate changes will have an independent effect on production.

### External and internal balance

We can use this simple model to illustrate the problems of maintaining full employment and balanced trade in a small, open economy. To do so, let us depict the equations for the trade balance and the employment level in $(w, \epsilon)$ space. First, use equation (9) to trace the $(w, \epsilon)$ combinations consistent with full employment—i.e. the combinations of $w$ and $\epsilon$ such that labour demand equals labour supply. They are obviously given by

$$w/\epsilon = r_v(P, \bar{v}) \tag{10}$$

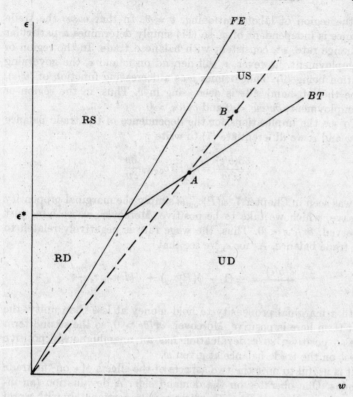

U—unemployment
R—labour rationing
S—trade surplus
D—trade deficit

**Figure 8.1**

As $P$ and $\bar{v}$ are given, this determines a unique $(w/\epsilon)$-ratio; so the combination of wages and rate of exchange consistent with a Walrasian labour market equilibrium is simply a ray through the origin, such as the $FE$ line in Figure 8.1. Moreover as $r_{vv} < 0$, we shall have unemployment to the right of that ray, and labour rationing of firms to the left of it.

Consider next the combinations of $w$ and $\epsilon$ that would produce balanced trade. From (7), these are given by

$$\psi(P)\, c_0\!\left(\psi(P),\, P,\, \frac{l}{\epsilon} + r(P, v)\right) = \frac{l}{\epsilon} \tag{11}$$

In the region of labour rationing, $v = \bar{v}$. In that case, the trade balance is independent of $w$, so (11) simply determines a particular exchange rate, $\epsilon^*$, consistent with balanced trade. In the region of unemployment, however, $v$ will depend on $w$ and $\epsilon$, the governing relation being (9). That defines $v$ as a decreasing function of $(w/\epsilon)$, since the left-hand side is decreasing in $v$. Thus, in the region of unemployment, $\partial v/\partial w < 0$ and $\partial v/\partial \epsilon > 0$.

To see the implications for the dependence of the trade balance on $w$ and $\epsilon$, we differentiate (7) to write

$$\frac{\partial (b/\epsilon)}{\partial w} = \psi(P)\, c_{0y}\, r_v\, \frac{\partial v}{\partial w}$$

As was seen in Chapter 7, $\psi(P)c_{0y}$ is simply the marginal propensity to save, which we take to be positive. Moreover, as we have just observed, $\partial v/\partial w < 0$. Thus, the wage rate is negatively related to the trade balance. As for $\epsilon$, we see that

$$\frac{\partial (b/\epsilon)}{\partial \epsilon} = \frac{l}{\epsilon^2}(1 - \psi(P)c_{0y}) + \psi(P)c_{0y}\, r_v\, \frac{\partial v}{\partial \epsilon}$$

With a marginal propensity to hold money at less than unity, the first term here is positive. Moreover, $\partial v/\partial \epsilon > 0$, so the second term is also positive; so a devaluation has an unambiguously positive effect on the trade balance at given $w$.

It is useful to note the two aspects of the effects of $\epsilon$ on the trade surplus. One operates on the demand side. A devaluation (an increase in $\epsilon$) raises all domestic prices equiproportionately with world prices fixed. This causes a reduction in the supply of real balances, and therefore reduces demand. This is captured in the first term in the above expression, and the same effect would arise in the Walrasian model of Chapter 7. The second effect is on the output side: the higher domestic prices make it desirable to expand production, which raises income and therefore the demand for money. This is shown in the second term, and is an effect peculiar to a model with variable employment.

Now we can combine the effects of $w$ and $\epsilon$ on the trade surplus to examine the locus of balanced trade in the unemployment region. If we start at a point on this locus and raise $w$, a trade deficit would ensue, and $\epsilon$ would have to be raised to restore balance and return to the curve. Thus the combinations of $\epsilon$ and $w$ consistent with balanced trade in the region of unemployment form an upward-sloping curve. Moreover, that curve must be less steep than the $FE$-curve. To see why, consider a proportionate increase in $w$ and $\epsilon$.

Such an increase would leave $(w/\epsilon)$ unchanged, and so have no effect on employment. The only effect on the trade balance would be the real balance effect

$$\frac{l}{\epsilon}(1 - \psi(P)c_{0y})\frac{d\epsilon}{\epsilon}$$

which is positive. Starting from a position of balanced trade, therefore, a proportional increase in $w$ and $\epsilon$ would produce a surplus. Since $b = 0$ at $A$, we would have $b > 0$ at $B$, so the balanced trade locus must be below the $AB$ ray. It follows that the balanced trade locus must be a curve such as $BT$ in Figure 8.1. Above that locus, we shall have a trade surplus; below it, a trade deficit.

That gives us four possible regions—unemployment and trade deficit (UD), unemployment and trade surplus (US), labour rationing and trade deficit (RD), and labour rationing and trade surplus (RS).

## Macroeconomic policies

The macroeconomic policy implications of this model are fairly obvious, but nevertheless quite interesting. In particular, demand management has no effect on employment—as is apparent when one recalls that employment is given by (9)—whereas exchange rates have an effect. This seems to question the conventional wisdom that one should use exchange rates to achieve external balance, and demand management to maintain full employment. In fact, the converse combination could seem appealing: if $w$ is inflexible above its Walrasian equilibrium level, one could devalue sufficiently to create full employment. That would create a surplus on the balance of trade, which could be eliminated by e.g. expansionary monetary policy. (Note that an increase in $l$ worsens the balance of trade, just as in the Walrasian model of Chapter 7.)

This does not mean, however, that all conventional wisdom would induce policies that were bound to fail. Thus, suppose the exchange rate is allowed to float, so as to equilibrate the foreign exchange market. In a situation of unemployment, $v$ and $\epsilon$ will then be given by (9) and (11). Consider now a change $dl$ in $l$, and the corresponding changes in $\epsilon$ and $v$. Let $s_y$ be shorthand for the marginal propensity to hold money ($= \psi(P)c_{0y}$). We then have

$$(1 - s_y)\frac{l}{\epsilon}\frac{d\epsilon}{\epsilon} + s_y\, r_v\, dv = (1 - s_y)\frac{1}{\epsilon}\, dl$$

$$\frac{w}{\epsilon}\frac{d\epsilon}{\epsilon} + r_{vv}\, dv = 0$$

Using the latter to solve for $(d\epsilon/\epsilon)$ in terms of $dv$, and substituting into the former, we get

$$\left(s_y\, r_v - (1 - s_y)\, \frac{l}{w}\, r_{vv}\right) dv = (1 - s_y)\, \frac{1}{\epsilon}\, dl$$

As $r_{vv} < 0$, the coefficient on the left is positive. The expansionary monetary policy will therefore increase employment in the case of a flexible exchange rate.

We have not spoken of demand management through fiscal policy, as the model is not very suitable for its analysis. With all goods tradeable at constant world prices, any government demand merely shows up in the trade deficit, with no effect on the domestic economy. If non-tradeables were the object of government demand, matters would be different; see Neary (1978).

### Trade policy

Trade restrictions are often recommended in countries experiencing a combination of unemployment and trade deficit. Such policies can never be first-best: as we have just seen, the money supply $l$ and the exchange rate $\epsilon$ can be manipulated simultaneously to achieve the Walrasian equilibrium, and tariffs can do no more. Nevertheless, it is instructive to analyse the effects of tariffs. We do this keeping the exchange rate fixed, choosing units so that $\epsilon = 1$.

Tariffs enable the country to keep its prices $p$ different from the prices $P$ for the rest of the world. In the small country case, in fact, $P$ is constant, and a choice of tariffs is immediately equivalent to a choice of $p$. It is then possible to use tariffs to replicate the effects of an exchange rate change. Raising all components of $p$ equiproportionately above those of $P$, for example, corresponds to raising $\epsilon$ above 1, i.e. a devaluation. Such a policy means levying tariffs on imports, and giving subsidies on exports, at equiproportionate rates. This will be a special case of the general analysis below.

The equilibrium is described by equations like (1)–(4) and (8), the only new feature being the inclusion of the tariff revenue on the right-hand side of the national income equation (1). We restate the conditions for immediate reference

$$e(p_0, p, u) = l + r(p, v) + (p - P).m \tag{12}$$

$$m = e_p(p_0, p, u) - r_p(p, v) \tag{13}$$

$$p_0 = \psi(p) \tag{14}$$

$$r_v(p, v) = w \tag{15}$$

which determine $u$, $v$, $m$ and $p_0$ given $l$, $w$, and $p$, and then the trade balance can be calculated as

$$b = p_0 \, e_0(p_0, p, u) - l \qquad (16)$$

The initial equilibrium has $p = P$. We find the effects of a change $dp$ by taking total differentials. At the same time, we allow a change $dl$ in $l$, as it makes the interpretation of some of the effects of the tariffs more transparent.

Differentiating (12), we have

$$e_0 \, dp_0 + e_p.dp + e_u \, du = dl + r_p.dp$$
$$+ r_v \, dv + (p - P).dm + m.dp$$

Using (13), three terms in this vanish. Further, from the initial condition on $p$, another term vanishes. This leaves

$$e_u \, du = dl - e_0 \, dp_0 + r_v \, dv \qquad (17)$$

Next, from (15), we have

$$r_{vp}.dp + r_{vv} \, dv = 0$$

or

$$dv = (-1/r_{vv})r_{vp}.dp \qquad (18)$$

Since $r_{vv} < 0$, the expression in the parentheses is positive. Finally,

$$db = e_0 \, dp_0 - dl + p_0(e_{00} \, dp_0 + e_{0p}.dp + e_{0u} \, du)$$

Substituting from (17), we have

$$db = e_0 \, dp_0 - dl + p_0(e_{00} \, dp_0 + e_{0p}.dp)$$
$$+ (p_0(e_{0u}/e_u))(dl - e_0 \, dp_0 + r_v \, dv)$$

By equation (45) of Chapter 2, $e_{0u}/e_u = c_{0y}$, so $p_0(e_{0u}/e_u)$ is simply $s_y$, the marginal propensity to hold money. We are assuming that it lies between 0 and 1. Then we have, using (18), the expression

$$db = -(1 - s_y)(dl - e_0 \, dp_0) + p_0(e_{00} \, dp_0 + e_{0p}.dp)$$
$$+ s_y(-r_v/r_{vv})r_{vp}.dp \qquad (19)$$

We now examine the effects of tariffs on the trade balance by considering three groups of terms in this expression. First, there is a positive contribution to the trade balance if $dl < e_0 \, dp_0$. This can be thought of as a real balance effect, or an absolute price effect. Note that $dp_0 = \psi_p.dp$. In the case of a pure devaluation, with all components of $p$ increasing equiproportionately, we can be sure that $dp_0 > 0$, while $dl = 0$. There are several other ways in which the expected price level could be raised faster than the increase in the money supply (if any). This lowering of the real balances lowers current demand by a fraction $(1 - s_y)$ of itself, producing a corresponding improvement in the trade balance. However, this seems hardly in the realm of practical policy. No one would seriously advocate the use of tariffs on the grounds that they reduce overall purchasing power. The corresponding price-raising effect of a pure devaluation is often strenuously resisted; there is no reason to believe a different response to tariffs. It can in fact be argued that we should concentrate on the *relative* price effects of tariffs by assuming that consumers are compensated for the *absolute* effects on their real balances, i.e. setting $dl = e_0 \, dp_0$.

The second group of terms concerns substitution in demand. This is in general ambiguous. In the case of a pure devaluation, for example, we have $dp = p \, d\epsilon$ for a scalar $d\epsilon$, and therefore $dp_0 = p_0 \, d\epsilon$ by homogeneity. Then

$$p_0(e_{00} \, dp_0 + e_{0p} . dp) = p_0(e_{00} p_0 + e_{0p} . p) \, d\epsilon = 0$$

by homogeneity of $e_0$. The effects of relative price changes can clearly work either way.

The third term, concerning the production and employment effect, is clearly the most interesting, and it is in terms of such impacts that practical arguments for tariffs are often put. Comparing (18) and (19), the drift of the argument is clear. At fixed $w$, a set of tariffs that increase employment will increase income, some of which will be held in the form of money, contributing to an improvement of the trade balance. The effect of a devaluation is clear: with $dp = p \, d\epsilon$, we have

$$dv = (-1/r_{vv})r_{vp} . p \, d\epsilon = (-1/r_{vv})r_v \, d\epsilon$$

by homogeneity of $r_v$. This is positive for $d\epsilon > 0$. If we are to use selective tariffs, however, we must take care to ensure that $r_{vp} . dp > 0$. This is simple in case the production side is like the Ricardo–Viner model. Then every component of $r_{vp}$ is positive, and it is enough to have every component of $dp$ positive, i.e. levy tariffs on all imports and offer subsidies to all exports at arbitrary rates. In the Heckscher–Ohlin case, $r_{vp}$ has a positive component for the good which is relatively more labour-intensive, and a negative component for one which is relatively less labour-intensive; it is then sufficient to match the signs of the components of $dp$ to these.

Our conclusion is that carefully calculated selective tariffs can help the trade balance and employment, but there is nothing that a pure devaluation could not do as well or better.

Incidentally, (17) shows that utility is increased if real balances rise ($dl > e_0\, dp_0$) or if employment rises. However, recall that this is a short-run model, and therefore subject to the caveats mentioned in Chapter 7: the long-run effects of a current deficit are not taken into account, and the expectations generated by $\psi$ may be mistaken.

## 2. INTERNATIONAL EQUILIBRIA

We are now in a position to examine complete international equilibria in a world where product prices are flexible, and domestic factor prices are sticky. We abandon the assumption of given output prices, and replace it by standard market clearing conditions. With two countries, we then get the familiar conditions

$$e(p_0, p, u) = l + r(p, v) \tag{20}$$

$$E(P_0, P, U) = L + R(P, V) \tag{21}$$

$$p_0 = \psi(p) \tag{22}$$

$$P_0 = \Psi(P) \tag{23}$$

$$p = \epsilon P \tag{24}$$

$$e_p + E_P = r_p + R_P \tag{25}$$

For given $v$, $V$, and $\epsilon$, these determine current output prices and future price expectations. The trade balance is

$$b = p_0\, e_0 - l \tag{26}$$

Although we generally take $\epsilon$ to be fixed, the case of a flexible exchange rate can be immediately allowed by setting $b = 0$ in (26) and using this to determine $\epsilon$.

Finally, we have the determination of $v$ and $V$, as the minima of the amounts available and demanded, i.e.

$$v = \min(\bar{v}, v') \text{ where } r_v(p, v') = w \tag{27}$$

$$V = \min(\overline{V}, V') \text{ where } R_V(P, V') = W \tag{28}$$

Unfortunately, this general system does not yield any simple or clear insights. We shall therefore limit ourselves to the one-good case. Then $p$ and $P$ are the current price levels, and (25) is the aggregate product market clearing condition for the one good for the world.

## Stability

As we have a single market, the condition for a tâtonnement process to be stable is simply that the excess demand function is downward-sloping. To see what this implies, use (20) and (25) to solve for consumption as a function of price and disposable income:

$$c = c(\psi(p), p, l + r(p, v)) \tag{29}$$

Note that, with one good, $\psi_p$ is a constant. Note, moreover, that we can use (27) to solve for $v$ as a function of $p$ and $w$: with one good, $r(p, v)$ is simply $pf(v)$, so notional labour demand is given by

$$f_v(v) = w/p$$

If this gives $v > \bar{v}$, there will be labour rationing. Otherwise, the marginal productivity condition above determines employment. Consequently, if we denote by $\omega$ the physical marginal product of labour at full employment,

$$\omega \equiv f_v(\bar{v})$$

we shall have

$$v(p, w) = \begin{cases} \bar{v} & \text{for } (w/p) \le \omega \\ f_v^{-1}\left(\dfrac{w}{p}\right) & \text{for } (w/p) \ge \omega \end{cases} \tag{30}$$

as illustrated in Figure 8.2.

Using this, we can find the excess demand functions for the world product market. The import demand function for the home country is

$$m(p, l, w) = c(\psi(p), p, l + r(p, v(p, w))) - r_p(p, v(p, w)) \tag{31}$$

and similarly for the rest of the world. Observe that

$$m_l = c_y \tag{32}$$

while

$$m_w = c_y r_v v_w - r_{pv} v_w$$

But $r_{pv}$ is simply $\partial x/\partial v$—i.e. $f_v(v)$. With unemployment, that is equal to $(w/p)$; so we have

$$m_w = \left(c_y w - \frac{w}{p}\right) v_w = -\frac{w}{p} v_w(1 - pc_y)$$

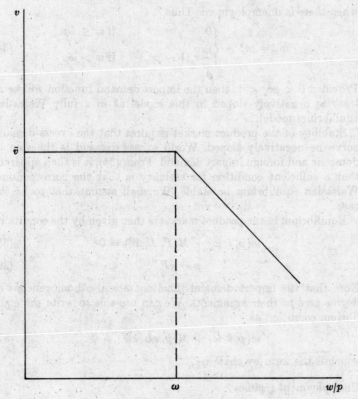

**Figure 8.2**

If there is labour rationing, $v_w = 0$. Thus

$$m_w = \begin{cases} 0 & \text{if } w \le \omega p \\ -\dfrac{w}{p} v_w (1 - pc_y) & \text{if } w > \omega p \end{cases} \tag{33}$$

Finally, observe that

$$m_p = (c_0 \psi_p + c_p + c_y r_p - r_{pp}) + (c_y r_v - r_{pv}) v_p$$

The first parenthesis here is the standard excess demand price derivative common to fully Walrasian equilibrium models—call it $m_p^*$. The second term is zero when there is labour rationing. It can be written as

$$(c_y r_v - r_{pv}) = -\frac{w}{p} (1 - pc_y)$$

when there is unemployment. Thus,

$$m_p = m_p^* - \begin{cases} 0 & \text{if } w \leq \omega p \\ \dfrac{w}{p} v_p(1 - pc_y) & \text{if } w > \omega p \end{cases} \tag{34}$$

Provided $0 < pc_y < 1$, then the import demand function will be at least as negatively sloped in this model as in a fully Walrasian equilibrium model.

Stability of the product market requires that the excess demand curve be negatively sloped. World excess demand is the sum of domestic and foreign import demand. From (34), it is then apparent that a sufficient condition for stability is that the corresponding Walrasian equilibrium be stable. We shall assume that to be the case.

Equilibrium in the product market is then given by the conditions

$$m(p, l, w) + M(P, L, W) = 0 \tag{35}$$

$$p = \epsilon P \tag{36}$$

Note that the import demand functions are also homogeneous of degree zero in their arguments. We can use this to write the equilibrium condition as

$$m(p, l, w) + M(p, \epsilon L, \epsilon W) = 0 \tag{37}$$

which is the form we shall use.

### Unemployment regimes

Unemployment in this model is a consequence of sticky wages. To find combinations of unemployment and labour rationing possible, therefore, equilibria should be projected in $(w, W)$-space. We shall do that for a given exchange rate, and for given values of money supplies.

Consider first the fully Walrasian equilibrium. In that equilibrium, (37) holds. In addition, notional demand equals supply in the domestic labour markets; so $w/p = f_v(\bar{v}) \equiv \omega$, so $w = \omega p$. The same goes for the foreign labour market, so if $\Omega$ is the full-employment marginal product of labour abroad, we must have $W = \Omega P$: or $\epsilon W = \Omega \epsilon P = \Omega p$. Thus, the price level in a fully Walrasian equilibrium is given by

$$m(p, l, \omega p) + M(p, \epsilon L, \Omega p) = 0 \tag{38}$$

Denoting this by $\hat{p}$, the Walrasian wage rates will be $\hat{w} = \omega \hat{p}$, and $\hat{W} = \Omega \hat{p}/\epsilon$.

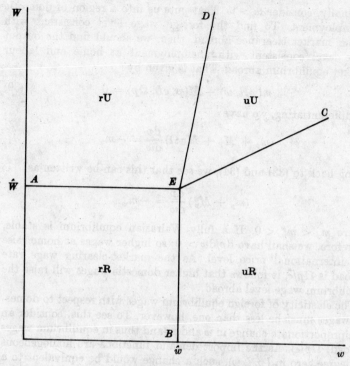

r—labour rationing at home
R—labour rationing abroad
u—unemployment at home
U—unemployment abroad

**Figure 8.3**

Next, consider $w < \hat{w}$. For a given output price, a lower $w$ will simply create domestic labour rationing, having no effect on product demand and supply. There will therefore be no shift in the import demand curve, and thus no change in the product price. As a result, a reduction in $w$ below $\hat{w}$ has no effect on the market-clearing price of labour abroad. Thus, for $w \leq \hat{w}$, the foreign labour market is cleared for $W = \hat{W}$; $W < \hat{W}$ will create labour rationing abroad, while $W > \hat{W}$ creates unemployment. That gives us the borderline $AE$ in Figure 8.3. Above $AE$ there will be unemployment abroad; below it, labour rationing. Similar reasoning gives us the $BE$-locus. To the left of this, there is labour rationing at home; to the right, unemployment.

Finally, consider $w > \hat{w}$. That puts us into a region of domestic unemployment. To find the foreign wage level consistent with labour market clearance abroad, then, we should find the output price level consistent with unemployment at home and labour market equilibrium abroad. That is given by

$$m(p, l, w) + M(p, \epsilon L, \Omega p) = 0 \qquad (39)$$

so, differentiating, we have

$$(m_p + M_P + M_W \Omega) \frac{\mathrm{d}p}{\mathrm{d}w} = -m_w$$

Going back to (33) and (34), we see that this can be written as

$$(m_p + M_p^*) \frac{\mathrm{d}p}{\mathrm{d}w} = -m_w$$

where $m_p < m_p^* < 0$. If a fully Walrasian equilibrium is stable, therefore, we shall have $\mathrm{d}p/\mathrm{d}w > 0$; so higher wages at home raise the international price level. As the market-clearing wage rate abroad is $\Omega p/\epsilon$, it follows that higher domestic wages will raise the equilibrium wage level abroad.

The elasticity of foreign equilibrium wages with respect to domestic wages must be less than one, however. To see this, consider an equiproportionate change in $w$ and $p$ (and thus in equilibrium wages abroad, $\Omega p/\epsilon$). As the import demand functions are homogeneous of degree zero in $(p, l, w)$, such a change would be equivalent to a reduction in $l$ and $L$, and would therefore produce excess supply. It follows that we must have $\mathrm{d}p/p < \mathrm{d}w/w$; so the foreign wage level must rise proportionately less than domestic wages.

To the right of $E$, therefore, the equilibrium wage locus abroad will be upward-sloping; but the slope must be less than the slope of a ray from the origin to any point on the locus. We therefore get a locus like $EC$. Again, above it, there will be unemployment abroad; below it, labour rationing.

Once more, we could do the same for the home country; finding its equilibrium wage level as a function of exogenously given wages abroad. That would give us the $ED$-locus. It is upward-sloping for the same reason that $EC$ is upward sloping; and it is steeper than corresponding rays from the origin because of the homogeneity argument. With these loci, the various combinations are clear: sufficiently high wages produce general unemployment; while sufficiently low ones produce labour rationing both at home and abroad. High wages at home and low ones abroad will give unemployment at home and labour rationing abroad; and vice versa.

## Devaluations and the trade balance

The home country balance of trade in this one-good model is simply $(-pm)$. We can project this in $(w, W)$ space as well. To do so, we must look separately at the various regimes. Consider first the $(u, U)$ regime. Here, price is given by

$$m(p, l, w) + M(p, \epsilon L, \epsilon W) = 0 \tag{40}$$

while balanced trade requires

$$m(p, l, w) = 0 \tag{41}$$

To find the combinations of domestic and foreign wage levels consistent with balanced trade, we simply differentiate (40) and (41) totally. From (41) that gives us

$$dp = -\frac{m_w}{m_p} dw$$

while (40), observing (41), gives us

$$dp = -\frac{M_W}{M_P} \epsilon \, dW$$

Therefore balanced trade requires the following relation between $dw$ and $dW$:

$$\frac{m_w}{m_p} dw = \frac{M_W}{M_P} \epsilon \, dW \tag{42}$$

So the balanced trade locus is upward sloping in the $(w, W)$-space when there is unemployment in both countries. We therefore get a locus like $FG$ in Figure 8.4. To the left of this locus, the home country will have a payments surplus; to the right a deficit.

What the locus looks like in other regions, depends on where the point $G$ is. As drawn, we move from the (u, U) region to the (u, R)-region. In that region, price is given by

$$m(p, l, w) + M(p, \epsilon L, \Omega p) = 0 \tag{43}$$

while balanced trade requires $m = 0$, and so $M = 0$; i.e.

$$M(p, \epsilon L, \Omega p) = 0 \tag{44}$$

This uniquely determines $p$; which means that (43) determines a unique $w$ consistent with a trade balance. Consequently, the balanced-trade locus becomes a vertical line in the (u, R)-region. Had $FG$ moved into the (r, U)-region—as indicated by $F'G'$—we should have

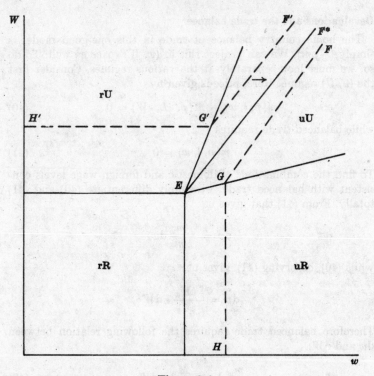

**Figure 8.4**

a horizontal line in that region. In general, therefore, the balanced trade locus looks like $FGH$ or $F'G'H'$ in Figure 8.4.

This framework enables us to look at some comparative statics issues. We shall not attempt a comprehensive catalogue of cases. Rather, we shall look at a few, leaving the rest to the reader.

Suppose first that we have labour market equilibrium in both countries, so wages are given by the point $E$. Suppose also that balanced trade is given by the $F'G'H'$ locus, so the home country at $E$ is running a balance-of-payments deficit. It might then attempt a devaluation. To see what effects such a devaluation would have, consider the Walrasian equilibrium condition

$$m(p, l, \omega p) + M(p, \epsilon L, \Omega p) = 0$$

As $M_L > 0$, a higher $\epsilon$ creates excess demand, so $p$ would rise; so $\hat{w} = \omega p$ would rise. As for $\hat{W}$, it equals $\Omega p/\epsilon$; so the change in equilibrium wages abroad depends on

$$d\hat{p}/\hat{p} - d\epsilon/\epsilon$$

Suppose $d\hat{p}/\hat{p} = d\epsilon/\epsilon$. Then, as $M$ is homogeneous of degree zero, $dM = 0$. We get $dm < 0$, however, as $l$ is unchanged. Consequently, we should get excess product supply. It follows that we must have

$$d\hat{p}/\hat{p} < d\epsilon/\epsilon$$

and so $d\hat{W} < 0$. A devaluation in the home country, therefore, will raise the domestic equilibrium wage and lower the equilibrium wage abroad; so it will shift the fully Walrasian equilibrium in a southeasterly direction; as indicated by the shift from $E$ to $E'$ in Figure 8.5. As a result, a devaluation will create labour market rationing at home, and unemployment in the rest of the world.

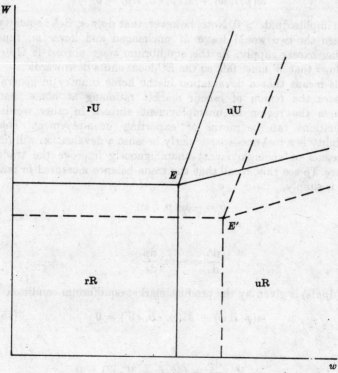

Figure 8.5

This can easily be generalized, in that a devaluation shifts all regions in a southeasterly direction. That is obvious as regards the (r, R)-region. As for the (u, U)-region, that is defined by two loci: (1) the locus corresponding to labour market equilibrium at home and unemployment abroad, and (2) the locus with unemployment at home and equilibrium abroad. The former is defined by

$$m(p, l, \omega p) + M(p, \epsilon L, \epsilon W) = 0$$

so, for given $W$, we have

$$(m_p^* + M_P)\,\mathrm{d}p + (M_L L + M_W W)\,\mathrm{d}\epsilon = 0$$

As $M_L$, $M_W > 0$, it follows that $\mathrm{d}p/\mathrm{d}\epsilon > 0$. The equilibrium wage at home is $\omega p$, so the equilibrium wage at home will rise. In other words, locus $ED$ in Figure 8.3 will shift to the right.

Similarly, locus $EC$ in Figure 8.3 is given by

$$m(p, l, w) + M(p, \epsilon L, \Omega p) = 0$$

which implies $\mathrm{d}p/\mathrm{d}\epsilon > 0$. Note, however, that $\mathrm{d}p/p < \mathrm{d}\epsilon/\epsilon$: equality between the two would leave $M$ unchanged and lower $m$, thus creating excess supply. As the equilibrium wage abroad is $\Omega p/\epsilon$, it follows that $W$ must fall, so the $EC$-locus shifts downwards.

This means that a devaluation in the home country in general increases the region of labour market rationing at home, and increases the region of unemployment abroad. In other words, devaluations can be means of 'exporting' unemployment. This possibility is a real one—particularly because a devaluation will (in the region of unemployment) unambiguously improve the trade balance. To see this, recall that the trade balance measured in real units is simply

$$b = -m(p, l, w)$$

so

$$\frac{\mathrm{d}b}{\mathrm{d}\epsilon} = -m_p \frac{\mathrm{d}p}{\mathrm{d}\epsilon}$$

But $(\mathrm{d}p/\mathrm{d}\epsilon)$ is given by the product market equilibrium condition

$$m(p, l, w) + M(p, \epsilon L, \epsilon W) = 0 \tag{45}$$

so

$$(m_p + M_P)\frac{\mathrm{d}p}{\mathrm{d}\epsilon} + (M_L L + M_W W) = 0$$

so

$$\frac{db}{d\epsilon} = \left(\frac{m_p}{m_p + M_P}\right)(M_L L + M_W W) > 0$$

Thus, a deficit country has real incentives to devalue; and such a devaluation can produce employment problems abroad.

## Effects of monetary policy

Expansionary monetary policy will have the effects one should expect on employment. To see this, consider the Walrasian equilibrium

$$m(p, l, \omega p) + M(p, \epsilon L, \Omega p) = 0$$

Clearly, if $l$ or $L$ is increased, the effect will be to raise $p$, and thus to increase the equilibrium wage rates in both countries. We leave to the reader the exercise to show that the $EC$-locus shifts upwards, and the $ED$-locus outwards. As a result, expansionary monetary policy will increase the size of the region with labour market rationing, and reduce the likelihood of unemployment. We saw in section 1 that a small country cannot alleviate domestic unemployment by expansionary monetary policy so long as the exchange rate is fixed; now we see that a large country can do so.

Such a policy will, however, worsen the trade balance. To see that, consider the case of unemployment in both countries (similar results are easily obtained for the other regimes). We have, from (45),

$$(m_p + M_P)\frac{dp}{dl} + m_l = 0 \tag{46}$$

so

$$\frac{db}{dl} = -m_l + \frac{m_p}{m_p + M_P}m_l$$

$$= -\left(\frac{M_P}{m_p + M_P}\right)m_l < 0 \tag{47}$$

Thus, expansionary monetary policy at home will increase employment but worsen the trade balance, while the rest of the world will gain both in terms of employment and payments.

## Money flows and the transfer problem

From the above, we can find the effects of a transfer of purchasing power from one country to another, such as would come about through the money flow mechanism. Again, we restrict attention to the region of unemployment in both countries, leaving straight-forward generalizations to the reader.

Consider therefore a transfer of money from the home country to the rest of the world. As the rate of exchange is fixed, we set it equal to 1, in which case we get $dL = -dl$, where $dL$ is the transfer. By (45), such a transfer will induce a price change $dp$ given by

$$(m_p + M_P)\,dp + m_l\,dl + M_L\,dL = 0$$

i.e. using $dl = -dL$,

$$(m_p + M_P)\,dp = (m_l - M_L)\,dL \qquad (48)$$

Recalling, from (32), that $m_l = c_y$, $M_L = C_Y$, we therefore see that a transfer will raise the world price level if, and only if, the marginal propensity to consume is higher abroad than at home. As employ-ment will rise only if $p$ increases, this means that the money flow mechanism will lead to higher employment only if surplus countries have higher marginal propensities to consume than deficit coun-tries. If the converse is true, the mechanism will create additional unemployment.

Nevertheless, the mechanism *will* eliminate payments imbalances in this model (although, had we had many commodities, instability problems of the kind considered in Chapter 7 could have arisen). To see this, note from (47) that

$$db = -\left(\frac{M_P}{m_p + M_P}\right)m_l\,dl + \left(\frac{m_p}{m_p + M_P}\right)M_L\,dL$$

so for $dl = -dL$, we have

$$db = \left(\frac{M_P m_l + m_p M_L}{m_p + M_P}\right)dL \qquad (49)$$

As $dL > 0$ if the home country has a payments deficit, and since the parenthesis in (49) is positive, it follows that the trade balance will improve in the deficit country when the mechanism works.

To see what (48) and (49) imply, consider an example: suppose we are in a fully Walrasian equilibrium, in which the home country suffers a trade deficit. Suppose, moreover, that the marginal pro-pensity to consume is higher at home than abroad. Then, by (48), the changes in money supplies brought about by the deficit, will move the countries into the region of unemployment. On the other hand, by (49), the countries will move towards balanced trade. In other words, the specie flow mechanism will, in this example, restore payments equilibrium; but it will create labour market disequilibrium.

Finally, note that all of this applies equally well to straightforward gifts. It can therefore be used to analyse the Keynesian approach to the transfer problem. By (48), the price level—and thus employment levels—will rise if, and only if, the recipient has a higher consumption propensity than the donor. And by (49), it will always improve the donor's trade balance, and worsen that of the recipient. Note, however, that a gift will worsen the donor's *current* balance (the trade balance less net gifts). If $g$ is the value of net gifts, the current balance is $(b - g)$. From (49) it is easily seen that $db/dg < 1$.

## 3. ALL PRICES STICKY

So far, we have assumed that product prices are flexible, so that international product markets clear without rationing. In this section, we replace that assumption by an assumption of fixed product prices and rationing in the goods markets. That brings us much closer to the familiar income-expenditure models of open economies, and can thus enable us to study the implications of the so-called absorption approach to the balance of payments. Our explicit attention to fixed prices in these quantity-adjustment equilibria often enables us to consider comparative static issues that are ignored by the usual 'Keynesian' models.

A large number of regimes are possible in a world with sticky product prices and sticky wages in each country. For example, we could have consumers rationed in the labour market at home, producers rationed in the labour market abroad, and producers rationed in international product markets. Seven other regimes are possible. We shall not investigate all of these, nor try to project them in price space. Rather, we shall pick out one regime, and study that in some detail. The regime we choose is that of what Malinvaud calls Keynesian unemployment—i.e. the regime where consumers are rationed in labour markets (so there is unemployment) and producers are rationed in product markets (so there is an effective demand failure).

There is a particular problem about modelling rationing in a trade context, viz. the problem of how rations are distributed between countries. A similar problem exists, of course, in models of closed economies, where rations must be distributed among consumers, or firms. In closed-economy models, however, the problem can be solved—at least in a technical sense—by assuming a single consumer or firm. That obviously is no solution in a trade context, so the question of how rations are distributed must be faced.

Income-expenditure models 'solve' the problem of allocating rations by introducing the concept of an import demand function. This must not be confused with the net excess demand function for goods that we have been using, viz. $m = e_p - r_p$. It is simply a rule, which comes into operation when effective demand falls short of potential output, and dictates what proportion of a country's demand will be allocated to home firms. Thus it can be seen as a separate *ad hoc* construct existing side by side with the consumption function. Such an import demand function has no theoretical foundation, and while there seems to be some empirical support for it, it should be regarded as an expedient device to handle rationing, rather than as a satisfactory solution to the problem of allocating rations.

To make things simple, and to facilitate comparisons with traditional models, we use the same construction. In particular, we assume that of domestic demand, a fraction $\gamma$ goes to domestic firms, and $(1 - \gamma)$ to foreign firms. This distribution is taken to be the same for all goods; although it is not hard in principle to allow different fractions, there seems little gain in analytical purchase on the problem so long as these are exogenously specified. With this assumption, the conventional marginal propensity to import, i.e. the increase in spending on imports resulting from a marginal unit increase in income, is simply $(1 - \gamma)$ times the marginal propensity to consume. Similarly, a fraction $\Gamma$ of foreign demand goes to foreign firms and $(1 - \Gamma)$ comes to the home country; thus the foreign country's marginal propensity to import is $(1 - \Gamma)$ times its marginal propensity to consume.

### The small country case

As usual, it is convenient to start by considering a small country. Ordinarily, 'small' would refer to an inability to affect world prices. In the context of a quantity-adjusting equilibrium with fixed prices, this is not enough. We must require that the country has no appreciable influence on quantities in the rest of the world. In particular, consumption demand $C$ in the rest of the world is an exogenous variable in this problem. So are the world prices $P$, and once the exchange rate $\epsilon$ is fixed, domestic prices $p = \epsilon P$.

Our concern is an equilibrium with general excess supply. Thus we assume that the producers are unable to sell as much as they would like, while consumers can buy the goods they wish to. On the other hand, firms get all the labour they want, but consumers cannot supply all they want. Consumers' demand for goods and firms' demand for labour is then an effective demand, in each case conditional on the quantity constraint in the other market.

First consider the production side. As firms are rationed, actual production is determined by actual demand. The actual demand for domestic goods is the sum of two parts, $\gamma c$ coming from home consumers, and $(1 - \Gamma)C$ from foreign ones. Thus we have

$$x = \gamma c + (1 - \Gamma)C \tag{50}$$

This also determines employment. Production of good $j$ is $x_j = f_j(v^j)$ where $v^j$ is employment in that sector. Inverting the production functions and adding, we have total employment. In fact we are more interested in changes. In sector $j$, output and employment changes are related by $\mathrm{d}x_j = f_j'(v^j)\,\mathrm{d}v^j$. Solving for $\mathrm{d}v^j$ and adding,

$$\mathrm{d}v = \sum_j (1/f_j')\,\mathrm{d}x_j \tag{51}$$

Since producers cannot sell all they would like, we must have $f_j'(v^j) \geq w/p_j$, with equality if the constraint is only just binding. In that special case, (51) simplifies to

$$\mathrm{d}v = \left(\sum_j p_j\,\mathrm{d}x_j\right)\Big/ w = p.\mathrm{d}x/w \tag{52}$$

Turning to the demand side, we note that consumers are not rationed in the goods market. However, their actual real income equals their actual wage income plus the actual profit income (which we are assuming to be instantaneously distributed), i.e. the value of actual output. Therefore the demand side of the economy can be described in the now familiar fashion:

$$e(p_0, p, u) = l + p.x \tag{53}$$

$$c = e_p(p_0, p, u) \tag{54}$$

As usual, let $y$ denote the right-hand side of (53). Now it will be possible to solve for $u$ using (53), and substitute in (54) to express $c$ as a function of $p_0$, $p$, and $y$. On doing this, and substituting from (50), we can express the equilibrium condition compactly as

$$y = l + (1 - \Gamma)p.C + \gamma\, p.c(p_0, p, y) \tag{55}$$

This is very similar to the conventional national income equilibrium equation of an income-expenditure model. However, there are two points of difference. First, the conventional aggregates are replaced by a more detailed system of effective demand functions based on choice-theoretic considerations, thus making it clear where and in what form prices appear. Secondly, $y$ is different from the usual measure of national income in that it includes the money stock. If it is desired to have a measure excluding this, we should use $(y - l)$; call this $\bar{y}$. Then we can rewrite (55) as

$$\bar{y} = (1 - \Gamma)p.C + \gamma\,p.c(p_0, p, \bar{y} + l) \qquad (56)$$

We can think of $\bar{y}$ as a measure of national product, and it can be related to employment. If output changes at fixed prices, we have $d\bar{y} = p.dx$. If the initial point is such that sales constraints are only just binding, (52) immediately gives

$$dv = d\bar{y}/w \qquad (57)$$

If the initial point is not of this special kind, the more general relation (51) must be used. Remembering that $(1/f_j') \leq p_j/w$, we see that the employment effects are then smaller than those indicated by (57). In what follows, we consider only the effects on income; the reader can look at employment using these remarks.

The stage is now set for some comparative static analyses. First suppose the exogenous demand in the rest of the world undergoes a shift. Taking total differentials in (55), we have

$$dy = (1 - \Gamma)p.dC + \gamma\,p.c_y\,dy$$

or

$$dy = (1 - \Gamma)p.dC/(1 - \gamma p.c_y) \qquad (58)$$

This is the familiar export multiplier formula. The numerator is the value of the change in exports. In the traditional income-expenditure format, the denominator would be the sum of the marginal propensities to save and to import. The former is $(1 - p.c_y)$ and the latter is $(1 - \gamma)p.c_y$ in our notation, and their sum is $(1 - \gamma p.c_y)$, which is just the denominator in (58).

We can also obtain the effect on the trade balance. This is now more conveniently written in real terms, i.e. as the value of exports less that of imports. Thus

$$b = (1 - \Gamma)p.C - (1 - \gamma)p.c(p_0, p, y) \qquad (59)$$

Differentiating,

$$db = (1 - \Gamma)p.dC - (1 - \gamma)p.c_y\,dy$$
$$= \frac{1 - p.c_y}{1 - \gamma p.c_y}(1 - \Gamma)p.dC \qquad (60)$$

Thus the trade balance improves, but by a smaller amount than the rise in exports, due to the induced rise in import demand.

The reader can similarly work out the effects of an increase in $l$. We do this slightly differently, taking advantage of the new feature of the above model as compared to a traditional income-expenditure model, namely our explicit consideration of prices. Having included prices explicitly, we can consider the effects of price changes systematically. In particular, we look at exchange rate changes. The traditional income-expenditure treatment proceeds by making the exchange rate an argument of the export and import functions in an *ad hoc* way. In contrast, we use the relation $p = \epsilon P$, and use homogeneity of the demand and expectation functions, to express 'national income' $y$ and the trade balance $b$ in terms of the foreign currency. The method should be familiar from earlier use in Chapter 7 and this chapter; the result is

$$y/\epsilon = l/\epsilon + (1 - \Gamma)P.C + \gamma\, P.c(\psi(P), P, y/\epsilon) \qquad (61)$$

$$b/\epsilon = (1 - \Gamma)P.C - (1 - \gamma)P.c(\psi(P), P, y/\epsilon) \qquad (62)$$

This highlights the fact that exchange rate changes in this context work essentially through real balance effects. A devaluation, i.e. an increase in $\epsilon$, has the same effects as a decrease in $l$ on the foreign currency measures of income and the trade balance. Taking total differentials, we have

$$\mathrm{d}(y/\epsilon) = \mathrm{d}(l/\epsilon) + \gamma\, P.c_y\, \mathrm{d}(y/\epsilon)$$

i.e.

$$\mathrm{d}(y/\epsilon) = \mathrm{d}(l/\epsilon)/(1 - \gamma P.c_y) \qquad (63)$$

Then

$$\mathrm{d}(b/\epsilon) = -(1 - \gamma)P.c_y\, \mathrm{d}(y/\epsilon)$$

$$= -(1 - \gamma)P.c_y\, \mathrm{d}(l/\epsilon)/(1 - \gamma P.c_y) \qquad (64)$$

Thus an increase in the money supply at a fixed exchange rate raises income and worsens the trade balance. Conversely, with a fixed money supply, a devaluation lowers income and improves the trade balance, both measured in world prices. Assuming that the sales constraints are only just binding at the initial point, the effects on employment are easily found. From (52), we have $w\, \mathrm{d}v = p\,.\mathrm{d}x$. Then $(w/\epsilon)\, \mathrm{d}v = P.\mathrm{d}x = \mathrm{d}(\bar{y}/\epsilon)$, which in turn equals $\mathrm{d}(y/\epsilon) - \mathrm{d}(l/\epsilon)$. Using (63), we have

$$(w/\epsilon)\, \mathrm{d}v = \mathrm{d}(\bar{y}/\epsilon) = \gamma P.c_y\, \mathrm{d}(l/\epsilon)/(1 - \gamma P:c_y) \qquad (65)$$

An increase in the money supply raises employment, and a devaluation lowers it. This last result is unusual, and is due to the fact that this model has a rigid relation between the trade balance and national income, as was seen in the process of deriving (64). It might be said that the model allows only expenditure-reducing policies, and no expenditure-switching ones. In many simple models the latter are introduced by means of *ad hoc* devices such as letting the export volume depend on the exchange rate. In our context this would mean making $\Gamma$ a function of $\epsilon$. That may be a realistic assumption, but not one well founded in choice theory. We prefer to bring the problem to the readers' attention and leave it.

We have considered a particular kind of price change in our analysis of devaluation. But more general changes in world prices can be studied using (61) and (62). The algebra of the general case is not interesting, and we leave it to the reader to examine special examples that arise in contexts of applications.

## An international equilibrium

Having examined domestic equilibrium in a small country, it is straightforward to describe international equilibrium with two countries. The simplest method is to use (55), relate $C$ to the conditions in the foreign country, and add a similar equation for that country. This results in the pair of equations

$$y = l + \gamma \, p \cdot c(p_0, p, y) + (1 - \Gamma)p \cdot C(P_0, P, Y) \qquad (66)$$

$$Y = L + \Gamma P \cdot C(P_0, P, Y) + (1 - \gamma)P \cdot c(p_0, p, y) \qquad (67)$$

All prices are fixed, but of course they are fixed in such a way that $p = \epsilon P$. These two equations determine $y$ and $Y$.

The solution is illustrated in Figure 8.6. First consider the home-country equilibrium locus $ee$ defined by (66). To find its slope, take total differentials of that equation, yielding

$$dy = \gamma \, p \cdot c_y \, dy + (1 - \Gamma)p \cdot C_Y \, dY$$

or

$$(1 - \gamma p \cdot c_y) \, dy = (1 - \Gamma)p \cdot C_Y \, dY \qquad (68)$$

Therefore $ee$ is an upward-sloping locus. Similarly, differentiating (67), we have along the foreign country equilibrium locus $EE$,

$$(1 - \gamma)P \cdot c_y \, dy = (1 - \Gamma P \cdot C_Y) \, dY \qquad (69)$$

It is easily checked that $EE$ is steeper than $ee$. To see this, choose units so that $\epsilon = 1$ and $p = P$. Then the expressions in the paren-

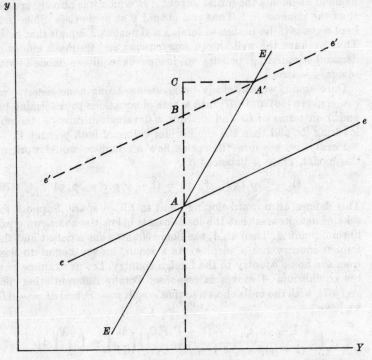

**Figure 8.6**

theses on the right-hand sides of (68) and (69) are respectively $(1 - \Gamma)P.C_Y$ and $(1 - \Gamma P.C_Y)$, of which the latter is greater so long as the marginal propensity to consume, $P.C_Y$, is less than one. Similarly, the expression in the parentheses on the left-hand side of (68) is greater than that of (69). Therefore the slope $dy/dY$ along (68) is smaller than that along (69).

Figure 8.6 can be used for simple comparative statics. For example, consider an increase in the domestic money supply. For each fixed $Y$, this increases the $y$ defined by (66), i.e. shifts $ee$ upwards. In fact, since fixing $Y$ fixes $C$, we can use the small-country result (63) to calculate the magnitude of the shift, and we know that it exceeds the amount of the increase in $l$. This initial rise in $y$ raises demand for foreign goods, hence $Y$, and so on. The ultimate equilibrium occurs at $A'$, the point of intersection of $EE$ with the new home country locus $e'e'$. The expansionary monetary policy raises income levels in both countries. The secondary effect $BC$ on domestic demand augments the initial impact $AB$, which was already greater than the increase in $l$. Thus real output $\bar{y}$ at home rises. Since $L$ is kept constant, the change in foreign real output $\bar{Y}$ equals that in $Y$. Thus we have the well-known repercussion and feedback effects of demand-stimulating policies in income-expenditure models with several countries.

Once again, we can study price effects. Using homogeneity, we can convert (66) and (67) into a pair of equations to determine $y/\epsilon$ and $Y$ in terms of $l/\epsilon$ and $L$. Now a devaluation raises $\epsilon$, thereby lowering $l/\epsilon$, and then the equilibrium values of both $y/\epsilon$ and $Y$.

Finally, we see how the specie flow mechanism would work on this model. Trade is balanced if

$$(1 - \Gamma)p.C(P_0, P, Y) = (1 - \gamma)p.c(p_0, p, y) \tag{70}$$

This defines an upward-sloping locus in $(Y, y)$ space. Suppose for sake of definiteness that the locus passes below the short-run equilibrium point $A$. Then at $A$, the home country has a deficit and the foreign country has a surplus. As a result, money begins to flow from the home country to the foreign country. Let us examine how the equilibrium $A$ moves in response. Totally differentiating (66) and (67), with the units chosen so that $\epsilon = 1$, $p = P$, and $dl = -dL$, we have

$$\begin{pmatrix} 1 - \gamma p.c_y & -(1 - \Gamma)P.C_Y \\ -(1 - \gamma)p.c_y & 1 - \Gamma P.C_Y \end{pmatrix} \begin{pmatrix} dy \\ dY \end{pmatrix} = \begin{pmatrix} -1 \\ 1 \end{pmatrix} dL$$

Call the determinant of the matrix on the left-hand side $D$. The fact that $EE$ is steeper than $ee$ ensures $D > 0$. Then we have the solution

$$dy = -\{(1 - P.C_Y)/D\}\, dL$$
$$dY = \{(1 - p.c_y)/D\}\, dL \tag{71}$$

So the specie flow mechanism lowers the expenditure level in the home country, and raises that in the foreign country. The point $A$ moves to the south-east, i.e. towards the locus of trade balance. Therefore the mechanism is stable. Again, the total effect on world expenditure is given by

$$dy + dY = \{(P.C_Y - p.c_y)/D\}\, dL$$

which depends on the relative marginal propensities to save in the two countries.

We leave to the reader a similar comparative static exercise. Consider an exogenous increase in $\gamma$, for example arising from an anti-import campaign in the home country. The effects are obvious: $y$ and $b$ rise, while $Y$ falls. Thus a country suffering from unemployment and a trade deficit can alleviate both problems by import restrictions, but only by worsening both problems in the foreign country. As with competitive devaluations, this raises fears of competitive import controls.

The whole analysis appears considerably simpler than that of Chapter 7. There, in each short-run equilibrium, we had to determine the market-clearing prices for goods. Changes in these prices from one equilibrium to another could cause considerable difficulties in proving stability of the specie flow mechanism, and strong assumptions such as gross substitutes had to be invoked. Here, the whole problem is removed by the assumption of fixed prices. However, we have not considered the difficulties inherent in quantity-adjusting equilibria of determining whether there is effective excess supply or effective excess demand in various markets at the set prices. We have simply assumed a state of general excess supply to prevail. Further work along these lines will have to consider other regimes, and possible transitions from one to another during the course of evolution of the economy.

Another line for further work that is indicated concerns the incorporation of other financial assets. We have extended the basic income-expenditure model by considering choice and prices explicitly. Much of the literature on the balance of payments, on the other hand, has been concerned with extensions to incorporate interest rates and capital flows. Integration of these aspects into a logically satisfactory treatment of fixed-price equilibria must be an important item on the programme of future developments.

## NOTES

Conventional expositions of Keynesian income-expenditure models of trade and payments can be found in Södersten (1971, ch. 15) or Caves and Jones (1977, chs. 18–20). More advanced treatments can be found in Mundell (1968, chs. 14–18) and Turnovsky (1977, Part II). We have criticized these approaches for their lack of attention to the modelling of constrained choice. An offsetting advantage is their detailed examination of interest rates and financial capital movements. Further work on the fix-price equilibrium method to incorporate these aspects must be an important item of future research.

References to the literature on fix-price equilibrium models occur at the relevant points in the text.

Multi-country Keynesian multiplier models have obvious analogues in the literature on regional economics.

# CHAPTER 9

# SCALE ECONOMIES AND IMPERFECT COMPETITION

The models of trade considered in Chapters 1–6 were all concerned with the theory of comparative advantage and its ramifications. In this chapter we return to questions of trade, but with the important difference that we now look at trade in the context of economies of scale. It is well-known and fairly obvious that scale economies create potential gains from trade—it simply reflects Adam Smith's observation that the division of labour is limited by the extent of the market. It is also quite apparent that scale economies matter empirically. In particular, the large volume of intra-industry trade—estimated at 50% of world trade by Grubel and Lloyd (1975)—can only be understood within the context of product differentiation and economies of scale. Both theoretically and empirically, therefore, there is a strong case for explicit analysis of the importance of non-convexities for trade.

It is not easy to give a precise treatment of trade based on scale economies. The difficulties relate to the market structure under which such trade will occur. Perfect competition is in general incompatible with economies of scale, so some form of imperfect competition will prevail. For descriptive purposes, one must then choose among the numerous alternative ways in which imperfect competition can be modelled; and the conclusions one arrives at will in general depend on the particular specification chosen. To arrive at a general theory of trade with imperfect competition is therefore impossible; the most one can hope for is a catalogue of special models. The same goes for welfare assessments. Because of imperfect competition, the gains from trade may not materialize; conceivably there could even be a loss from trade due to an increase in certain distortions. Again, whether trade will be beneficial depends on the market structure under which trade occurs. Rather than deriving general propositions regarding gains from trade, therefore, one must settle for a discussion of special cases.

As we see it, there are three major issues relating to trade in a world of economies of scale and imperfect competition. The first is directly related to market structure: will trade, by expanding the total market, increase competition and thus reduce monopolistic distortions? The set answer is yes. The implication is that there should be a double gain from trade: it should result in longer production runs and thus lower average cost, and it should reduce mark-ups of price over marginal cost. In section 1, we set up a standard model of Nash–Cournot equilibrium in an industry with free entry. It turns out that the set answer is correct under a wide set of assumptions.

The second important issue relates to product selection. It is commonly asserted that trade is advantageous because an expansion of the market leads to the introduction of products that would otherwise not be produced. As a descriptive proposition, that is only partly true. With imperfect markets, it can well be that certain product types disappear as the market expands; although there is a tendency for the total number of goods to increase. As a normative proposition, the popular view may well be completely wrong. Again the reason is imperfect competition. Thus, consider a monopolist examining the profitability of alternative products. Roughly speaking, in so doing he neglects the consumer surplus associated with the products. Consequently, a market outcome is biased against product types with a high ratio of consumer surplus to profit. It is possible that the integration of two economies through trade increases such a bias, thereby lowering welfare for some or all consumers. Section 2 provides an example of this. The special case chosen is for illustration, but it is suggestive of the general conditions under which such losses might arise.

With regard to market structure and product selection, trade is simply a vehicle for market expansion; country labels as such being of minor importance. In sections 1 and 2, therefore, we do not consider international trade explicitly. In section 3 we do. There, we consider the determinants and characteristics of international trade in a world with economies of scale, product differentiation, and imperfect competition. In particular, we look at a model with two production sectors. One is perfectly competitive, producing a homogeneous output. The other is an industry with Chamberlinian monopolistic competition, where there is a potentially large number of product varieties, where the producer of each variety realizes that he faces a downward-sloping demand curve and attempts to exploit this monopoly power, and where there is unrestricted entry. Such a model enables us to study both trade in product varieties (intra-industry trade) and trade in the two commodity groups (inter-industry trade). It also enables us to re-examine some of the questions looked at in earlier chapters, such as the question of factor price equalization.

# 1. TRADE AND COMPETITION

Economies of scale produce natural monopolies or oligopolies even if there are no formal barriers to entry. The reason is simply that the number of firms that can produce profitably in an industry with scale economies is limited, so even with unrestricted entry we should expect the industry to have an oligopolistic equilibrium. The larger the market, however, the more firms there should be room for, and the smaller should be the monopoly power exercised by any one firm. The expansion of the market brought about by international trade should therefore make an industry more competitive.

To see whether that is in fact so, we consider an industry producing a homogeneous product with increasing returns to scale. There is unrestricted entry, and the output of each firm is given by a Nash–Cournot equilibrium. To make things simple, we assume that all firms have the same technology, and the equilibrium is perfectly symmetric. Having established the equilibrium, we look at the effect on price, outputs, and the number of firms of expanding the economy by increasing the number of consumers. Thus, we do not consider trade explicitly, but take the opening up of trade as equivalent to increasing the number of consumers in the economy. Correspondingly, we temporarily abandon our notation of upper and lower case letters for foreign and home magnitudes, and instead use upper case letters for total and lower case ones for per capita magnitudes.

## Demand

There are $H$ identical consumers. Each consumes two goods—the good produced in the industry in question, and a numeraire good. The latter can be used either for consumption or as an input in the production of the other commodity. Each consumer has an endowment of the numeraire good, and his consumption of the numeraire is his endowment less his expenditure on the other good, plus his share in the profits generated by the oligopoly. Since consumer expenditure less profit equals the cost of producing the good, this means that per capita consumption of the numeraire good is per capita endowment less per capita cost of production in the oligopolistic industry. Without loss of generality we can set per capita endowments equal to zero, in which case consumption of the numeraire is simply minus the cost of producing the good in the oligopolistic industry.

Let $c_0$ denote consumption of the numeraire good per capita, and $c$ (without a subscript) per capita consumption of the good produced in the oligopolistic industry. We let the utility function take the particularly simple form

$$u = g(c) + c_0 \tag{1}$$

The consumer budget constraint is

$$c_0 + pc = y \tag{2}$$

where $p$ is the price of the non-numeraire good, and $y$ is lump-sum income received by the consumer. In equilibrium, $y$ will equal profit per capita, so $(pc - y)$ will be cost per capita of producing the non-numeraire good. It is sometimes convenient to write the utility function in terms of consumption and costs, so letting $B$ denote total production costs in the oligopolistic industry, we can write utility as

$$u = g(c) - B/H \tag{3}$$

From (1) and (2) we get the inverse demand function for the non-numeraire good

$$p = g'(c) \tag{4}$$

### Industry equilibrium

Let $X_j$ be production by firm $j$. We assume the cost of producing the good to consist of a fixed cost, $f$, and a constant marginal cost, $b$. Total cost of production for firm $j$ is therefore $(f + bX_j)$. It is convenient to write this in terms of per capita magnitudes, so let us define $x_j$ as production per capita by firm $j$. Its output level is then $Hx_j$, and its costs $(f + bHx_j)$. Total production per capita in the industry is

$$c = \sum_k x_k \tag{5}$$

so profits of firm $j$ are

$$\Pi_j = H\left\{ g'\left(\sum_k x_k\right)x_j - bx_j \right\} - f \tag{6}$$

If production is profitable at all, the firm chooses its output level so as to maximize (6), taking the output levels of all other firms as given. That gives the familiar first-order condition

$$g' + x_j g'' - b = 0$$

which we can rewrite in terms of the demand elasticity: Let $\epsilon$ be the inverse elasticity of market demand; i.e.

$$\epsilon \equiv -cg''(c)/g'(c)$$

The first-order condition can then be written as

$$g'(c)(1 - \epsilon x_j/c) - b = 0 \qquad (7)$$

The second-order condition turns out to be of considerable importance for our exercise. Without deriving it formally, we simply state that it can be written as

$$2(c/x_j) - \epsilon + \gamma - 1 > 0 \qquad (8)$$

where $\gamma$ is the elasticity of $\epsilon$ with respect to $c$; i.e. $\gamma = \epsilon'c/\epsilon$.

A Nash–Cournot equilibrium obtains when equations like (7) hold for all firms in the industry simultaneously. It is apparent that there is a solution with the same volume of production for all firms, i.e. perfect symmetry. Call the common value of production per capita $x$. We then have $(x_j/c) = (x/c) = (1/n)$, where $n$ is the number of active firms in the industry. Using this, we can restate the first- and second-order conditions (7) and (8) as

$$g'(nx)\left\{1 - \frac{\epsilon(nx)}{n}\right\} - b = 0 \qquad (9)$$

$$2n - \epsilon + \gamma - 1 > 0 \qquad (10)$$

We shall not be concerned with problems of existence and uniqueness for such an equilibrium. We ought to be concerned with stability, however, as comparative statics exercises are rather pointless if the equilibrium is unstable. As shown in Seade (1978), a necessary condition for the above equilibrium to be stable is

$$n - \epsilon + \gamma > 0 \qquad (11)$$

We shall assume that this condition holds.

Provided a stable equilibrium exists, production per firm per capita is determined by (9). It is only determined for a given number of active firms, however. With unrestricted entry, we therefore need one further condition to make the equilibrium determinate. The condition we choose is that entry by another firm should make the industry unprofitable. In other words, we compute profits per firm in equilibrium as a function of the number of active firms. As the number of consumers is irrelevant for this exercise, we might as well do it on a per capita basis. Call profits per firm per capita $\pi(n)$. To determine $n$, we require

$$\pi(n) \geq 0 \qquad \pi(n + 1) < 0$$

In order for this to produce a stable long-run equilibrium, $\pi(n)$ must be monotonically decreasing in $n$. That is in fact the case, provided the conditions above are satisfied. The derivation is so tedious that we leave it to the reader.

Because $\pi(n)$ is decreasing in $n$, we can find the equilibrium number of firms by finding the real number which makes profits equal to zero, i.e. by finding $n$ such that

$$\pi(n) = g'(nx)x - bx - f/H = 0 \tag{12}$$

The actual number of active firms in the industry will then be given by the integer part of $n$ as defined by (12). Together, therefore, (9) and (12) determine $x$ and $n$.

## Effects of a larger market

An expansion of the market is taken to be equivalent to increasing the number of (identical) consumers, i.e. to an increase in $H$. Looking at the equilibrium conditions (9) and (12), we see that the number of consumers only enters into the latter. A larger market will have no effect on price or per capita production unless it affects the number of active firms. Moreover, we see from (12) that the size of the market works through fixed cost per capita. By lowering fixed cost per capita, a larger population leads to higher profit, and thus encourages entry to the industry. There are then two possible cases. One is the case where an increase in $H$ does not affect the integer part of $n$ as defined by (12), i.e. where the expansion of the market is not substantial enough to make room for an additional firm. In that case, the number of active firms will remain unchanged, so from (9) output per capita and price will remain unchanged. The other case is the case where the integer part of $n$ as defined by (12) *does* change, so both price and output levels per capita will be affected. For international trade, it is the latter case which is interesting, since trade leads to substantial changes in market size.

In tracing out the effects of market expansion, we shall treat $n$ as if it were a real number defined by (12). For descriptive purposes, the error this introduces is unimportant. We shall establish that an increase in $H$ increases $n$ and increases $nx$ ($= c$), thus lowering $p$. All of these results hold when the integer constraint is taken into consideration as well. When we come to welfare implications of market expansion, however, the integer constraint is very important, so we shall then have to be more careful.

Consider a change $dH$ in the total number of consumers, and the corresponding changes $dx$ and $dn$ in $x$ and $n$ as defined by (9) and (12). Differentiating (9) logarithmically, we get

$$-\epsilon \frac{dn}{n} - \epsilon \frac{dx}{x} - \frac{\epsilon/n}{1 - \epsilon/n} \left\{ \gamma \frac{dn}{n} + \gamma \frac{dx}{x} - \frac{dn}{n} \right\} = 0$$

Cancelling and rearranging, we then obtain

$$\frac{dx}{x} = \frac{1 - (n - \epsilon + \gamma)}{n - \epsilon + \gamma} \frac{dn}{n} \tag{13}$$

Note that this holds exactly, whether the integer constraint on the number of active firms is binding or not. We cannot determine the sign of $(dx/dn)$ from (13), however. Stability implies that the denominator is positive, but the numerator can have either sign.

To differentiate (12) it is convenient to rewrite it as

$$g'(nx) = b + \frac{f}{Hx}$$

Differentiating this logarithmically, we get

$$\epsilon \frac{dn}{n} + \epsilon \frac{dx}{x} = \frac{f/Hx}{b + f/Hx} \left\{ \frac{dx}{x} + \frac{dH}{H} \right\}$$

But $f/Hx = (g' - b)$, and $(b + f/Hx) = g'$, so using (9) and rearranging we get

$$\frac{dn}{n} + \left( 1 - \frac{1}{n} \right) \frac{dx}{x} = \frac{1}{n} \frac{dH}{H} \tag{14}$$

Substituting from (13) for $(dx/x)$ then gives us

$$\frac{dn}{n} = \frac{n - \epsilon + \gamma}{2n - \epsilon + \gamma - 1} \frac{dH}{H} \tag{15}$$

The numerator here is positive by the stability condition (11), and the denominator is positive by the second-order condition (10). As should be expected, therefore, the number of active firms in the industry increases as the market expands.

Note that the percentage increase in $n$ will be smaller than the percentage increase in $H$, as the denominator in (15) equals the numerator plus $(n - 1)$. Thus, the real number of firms consistent with zero profits increases less than proportionally with the size of the economy. The integration of two economies should therefore lead to a reduction in the total number of firms in the two economies, when compared to autarky equilibria in the two countries. That is an attractive result, with obvious implications for welfare (it implies lower fixed costs per capita). Unfortunately, the constraint that the number of firms must be an integer may alter it. As an example, suppose the initial equilibrium involves 2 firms, but that the real number of firms as defined by the zero profit condition is 2·99. A small expansion of the economy will then make room for one more firm, in which case the increase in the number of active firms will be proportionally greater than the increase in the size of the economy.

Consumption per capita is $c = nx$. To see what happens to it when the economy expands, note from (13) that

$$\frac{\mathrm{d}n}{n} + \frac{\mathrm{d}x}{x} = \left\{ 1 + \frac{1 - (n - \epsilon + \gamma)}{n - \epsilon + \gamma} \right\} \frac{\mathrm{d}n}{n}$$

$$= \frac{1}{n - \epsilon + \gamma} \frac{\mathrm{d}n}{n} \tag{16}$$

Provided the Nash–Cournot equilibrium is stable, therefore, an expansion of the market will increase consumption per capita of the non-numeraire good. It follows that an expansion of the market will lower the price of the non-numeraire good; i.e. that it will reduce the oligopolistic mark-up of price over marginal cost. A larger market therefore reduces monopoly power.

### Implications for welfare

To see how an extension of the market affects welfare, we must look at the effect on utility per capita. We recall that utility per capita could be written as $u = g(c) - pc + y = g(c) - B/H$, where $y$ is total industry profit per capita, and $B$ are total costs of production. We clearly have $y = n\pi$, and $B = nHbx + nf$. Utility per capita will therefore be

$$u = g(nx) - g'(nx)nx + n\pi \tag{17}$$

or, alternatively

$$u = g(nx) - bnx - nf/H \tag{18}$$

From (17), we see that if profits remain unchanged as the economy expands, the utility effect depends on the effect on aggregate industry output. If industry output per capita increases, as (16) shows that it will, utility per capita will increase. Thus, if the zero profit condition holds exactly both before and after market expansion (i.e. if $n$ as defined by the zero-profit condition (12) happens to be an integer both before and after the increase in $H$), there will be an unambiguous welfare gain from a larger market. From (18) we see that the same is true if the expansion of the market is insufficient to cause new entry. In that case, $n$ is unchanged. By (9) we then know that $x$ will also remain unchanged, so we are left with the effect that fixed cost per capita decreases.

An even stronger result can be obtained by inspection of (18). We know that $nx$ increases as the market expands. As $(g' - b) > 0$. this is a source of a utility gain. Provided the term $(nf/H)$ does not increase, therefore, per capita utility will increase when the market expands. In other words, a sufficient condition for market expansion to be advantageous is that $n/H$ does not increase, i.e. the number of firms does not increase by a greater proportion than the number of consumers. As we have seen, however, there is no reason to expect this condition to be satisfied. Because the number of firms must be an integer, it could well be that $(n/H)$ increases as the market expands. If that is the case, one can easily construct examples in which per capita utility declines as the market expands. We leave that to the reader.

## 2. PRODUCT SELECTION

Having examined the effects of trade on competition, we now turn to the effects of trade on product selection. When there are scale economies, there will always be products for which demand is insufficient to make production profitable. By expanding the market, trade will lessen the importance of scale economies, so trade should lead to an increase in the number of product varieties offered to the consumer. Nevertheless, it could well be that some products disappear as the market expands. That can easily be seen if we think of economies of scale in terms of fixed costs. In autarky, products with relatively low fixed costs will be produced. As the market expands through trade, products with higher fixed costs will be introduced. If high-fixed-cost varieties and low-fixed-cost varieties are substitutes, the effect could well be such a substantial drop in demand for the autarky varieties that these disappear. Even though the total number of product varieties should increase when the market expands, therefore, some products could well disappear.

The question of how trade affects the total number of product varieties will be discussed in section 3. Here we shall look at the effects of trade on the *types* of goods produced. General issues relating to product selection in imperfect markets have recently been examined by Spence (1976) and Dixit and Stiglitz (1977). They find that biases arise when producers are not able to capture the consumer surpluses associated with their goods. The market test of profitability operates to the relative disadvantage of goods which have a high ratio of consumer surplus to revenue. The analysis needs to be handled carefully, taking into account the full general equilibrium aspects such as interactions in demand, but the general idea is a robust one. Recent work by Dixit and Stiglitz (1979) has examined how these biases depend on the size of the economy. They find no necessary connection. If a larger economy entails the selection of a good, or group of goods, with a lower consumer surplus, then utility can be lower for some or even all consumers in a larger economy.

To see what is involved, we shall consider an example of product selection in a completely monopolized market. That is not a very natural assumption in the context of trade, as we saw in the preceding section. We make it for simplicity only. Similar results can be obtained, but with much greater analytic difficulty, for the case where each product type is handled by a separate producer, and the various producers are in less than perfect collusion.

## Demand

We retain the essential features of demand as set out in section 1, except that there are now two potential products from the non-numeraire sector. There are $H$ identical consumers, each with a utility function defined over consumption of the numeraire good and two other potential goods labelled 1 and 2. The utility function takes the simple form

$$u = c_0 + g(c_1, c_2) \qquad (19)$$

where the function $g$ is increasing and concave, with $g(0, 0) = 0$. The goods are substitutes, which in this case requires $g_{12} < 0$. The numeraire good is treated as before, so $c_0$ will be simply minus production costs for the other two goods.

As there is only one producer, consumption per capita of a particular good equals that producer's production per capita of the good. For consistency of notation, we let $x_i$ be production per capita of good $i$, and substitute $x_i$ for $c_i$ in the following. The inverse demand functions then become

$$p_i = g_i(x_1, x_2) \qquad i = 1, 2 \qquad (20)$$

**Production**

For each good $i$, the total cost of production depends on the total output $X_i$ according to the relation

$$B_i = \delta_i f_i + b_i X_i \tag{21}$$

where $f_i$ is the fixed cost of producing at all, $b_i$ the constant marginal cost, and $\delta_i$ is 1 if $X_i$ is positive and 0 if $X_i$ is zero, thus providing a short-hand way of indicating that the fixed cost can be avoided by shutting down production.

The producer seeks to maximize his total profit $\Pi$. As $X_i = H x_i$, this is given by

$$\Pi = H\{x_1\, g_1(x_1, x_2) + x_2\, g_2(x_1, x_2) - b_1 x_1 - b_2 x_2\}$$
$$- \delta_1 f_1 - \delta_2 f_2 \tag{22}$$

Notice that optimum quantities of the two goods given decisions to produce them can be found simply by maximizing the expression in brackets. Using these quantities, we can then examine whether production yields positive profit. In other words, we first maximize the excess of revenue over variable costs, and then see whether this surplus is enough to cover fixed costs. We have to consider four separate cases, corresponding to the active production of neither, either or both of the products, and then compare the outcomes to examine the policy which is best for the producer. For each, we can also evaluate the utility of each consumer. This is quite simply related to the profit per capita, $\pi$, in that

$$u = s + \pi \tag{23}$$

where $s$ is the consumer surplus, given by

$$s = g(x_1, x_2) - x_1\, g_1(x_1, x_2) - x_2 g_2(x_1, x_2) \tag{24}$$

Begin with the case where neither of the monopolized products is being produced. With $x_1 = x_2 = 0$, we have $\pi = 0$, and also $s = 0$ since $g(0, 0) = 0$. Thus $u = 0$.

Next look at the case where only type 1 is being produced. The quantity, $\bar{x}_1$, say, is determined by the first-order condition

$$g_1(\bar{x}_1, 0) + \bar{x}_1\, g_{11}(\bar{x}_1, 0) = b_1 \tag{25}$$

Let $\pi_1$ be the profit per capita, $s_1$ the consumer surplus, and $u_1$ the utility for each consumer in this case. Write $a_1$ for the excess of revenue over variable costs per capita. Then we have

$$a_1 = \bar{x}_1(g_1(\bar{x}_1, 0) - b_1) \tag{26}$$

$$\pi_1 = a_1 - f_1/H \tag{27}$$

$$s_1 = g(\bar{x}_1, 0) - \bar{x}_1\, g_1(\bar{x}_1, 0) \tag{28}$$

$$u_1 = \pi_1 + s_1 \tag{29}$$

In the case where only good 2 is produced, the corresponding quantities $\bar{x}_2$, $a_2$, $\pi_2$, $s_2$, and $u_2$ are defined analogously.

Finally, when both types are being produced, the quantities $(\hat{x}_1, \hat{x}_2)$ are determined from the first-order conditions

$$g_1(\hat{x}_1, \hat{x}_2) + \hat{x}_1\, g_{11}(\hat{x}_1, \hat{x}_2) + \hat{x}_2\, g_{21}(\hat{x}_1, \hat{x}_2) = b_1$$
$$g_2(\hat{x}_1, \hat{x}_2) + \hat{x}_1\, g_{12}(\hat{x}_1, \hat{x}_2) + \hat{x}_2\, g_{22}(\hat{x}_1, \hat{x}_2) = b_2 \tag{30}$$

Write $\hat{a}$ for the excess of revenue over variable costs, $\hat{\pi}$ for the profit, $\hat{s}$ for the consumer surplus, and $\hat{u}$ for the utility, all per capita, in this case. We have

$$\hat{a} = \hat{x}_1(g_1(\hat{x}_1, \hat{x}_2) - b_1) + \hat{x}_2(g_2(\hat{x}_1, \hat{x}_2) - b_2) \tag{31}$$

$$\hat{\pi} = \hat{a} - (f_1 + f_2)/H \tag{32}$$

$$\hat{s} = g(\hat{x}_1, \hat{x}_2) - \hat{x}_1\, g_1(\hat{x}_1, \hat{x}_2) - \hat{x}_2\, g_2(\hat{x}_1, \hat{x}_2) \tag{33}$$

$$\hat{u} = \hat{\pi} + \hat{s} \tag{34}$$

### Effects of trade

This completes the description of the various possibilities. Now let us examine which of the cases will actually occur for any specified value of $H$, and how this choice will vary with $H$. Then we can examine the consequences for utility.

The analysis is most easily conducted by showing profits per capita as a function of $1/H$. For each individual case, this is a linear function. For each fixed $H$, the most profitable choice will be made. Thus the actual profit per capita will be the upper envelope of the separate profit functions, and at each point the function which is uppermost indicates the product selection of the monopolist.

The case where neither product is produced simply has zero profit per capita all along. In the case where only type 1 is produced,

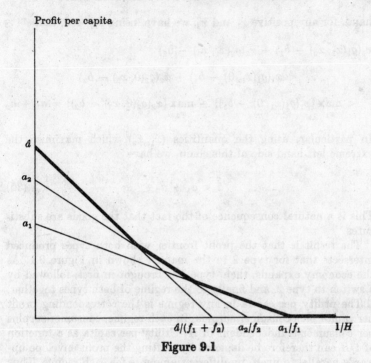

**Figure 9.1**

the function has a vertical intercept of $a_1$, and declines with a slope of $f_1$ to a horizontal intercept of $a_1/f_1$. Similarly for type 2, we have the intercepts $a_2$ and $a_2/f_2$. Label the products so that $f_1 < f_2$. In order to avoid uninteresting cases where one of the types totally dominates the other over the entire range where both are profitable, we assume $a_1 < a_2$ and $a_1/f_1 > a_2/f_2$. Then, as Figure 9.1 shows, in very small economies, i.e. for very large $(1/H)$, neither type will be produced. For somewhat larger economies, type 1 will be introduced, and later still, this will give way to the type with the higher fixed cost.

The introduction of both types together depends on the relation between $â$, $a_1$, and $a_2$, and this can be established using the assumptions made so far. Note first that $â$ is obtained by maximizing the excess of all revenues over variable costs without restriction, while each of $a_1$ and $a_2$ is obtained by maximizing the same expression while restricting one of the two quantities to be zero. Therefore $â$ must be greater than each of $a_1$ and $a_2$ taken singly. On the other hand, for any positive $x_1$ and $x_2$, we have, using $g_{12} < 0$, that

$$x_1(g_1(x_1, x_2) - b_1) + x_2(g_2(x_1, x_2) - b_2)$$

$$< x_1(g_1(x_1, 0) - b_1) + x_2(g_2(0, x_2) - b_2)$$

$$< \max_{x_1} \{x_1(g_1(x_1, 0) - b_1)\} + \max_{x_2} \{x_2(g_2(0, x_2) - b_2)\} = a_1 + a_2$$

In particular, using the quantities $(\hat{x}_1, \hat{x}_2)$ which maximize the extreme left-hand side of this chain, we have

$$\hat{a} < a_1 + a_2 \tag{35}$$

This is a natural consequence of the fact that the goods are substitutes.

The result is that the profit frontier with both types produced intersects that for type 2 in the manner shown in Figure 9.1. As the economy expands, then, type 1 is brought in first, followed by a switch to type 2, and finally to the regime of both types together.

The utility per capita in any regime is the corresponding profit per capita plus consumer surplus. In each regime, consumer surplus per consumer is independent of $H$. Utility per capita as a function of $1/H$ can therefore be depicted by shifting the profit envelope upwards parallel to itself, by different amounts for each regime. Thus utility will be discontinuous at the points where regimes switch.

However, there is no necessary relation between $s_1$, $s_2$, and $\hat{s}$. It is clear that there need be no relation between $s_1$ and $s_2$, and hence the switch from type 1 to type 2 may be an improvement or a worsening from the point of view of each consumer. More disturbingly, $\hat{s}$ may be less than $s_2$, thus making the introduction of a new variety a Pareto worsening. The point is that with the introduction of type 1 in the last switch, the output of type 2 goes down since the types are substitutes. If this causes a greater loss of surplus for type 2 than the gain of surplus for type 1, there may be a net loss.

### An example

To illustrate these points in the sharpest way, we develop an example where one of the products has no consumer surplus at all. Suppose the utility function is

$$u = x_0 + \beta \min (x_1 + x_2, \mu) + \alpha x_1^\theta \tag{36}$$

where $\alpha$, $\beta$, $\mu$, and $\theta$ are constants, with $\theta < 1$. The inverse demands are

$$
\begin{aligned}
p_1 &= \alpha\theta x_1^{\theta-1} + \beta && \text{if } x_1 + x_2 < \mu \\
&= \alpha\theta x_1^{\theta-1} && \text{if } x_1 + x_2 > \mu
\end{aligned}
\tag{37}
$$

and

$$
\begin{aligned}
p_2 &= \beta && \text{if } x_1 + x_2 < \mu \\
&= 0 && \text{if } x_1 + x_2 > \mu
\end{aligned}
\tag{38}
$$

To visualize this, think of the two goods as being perfect substitutes for some primary purpose, where a total amount $\mu$ leads to satiation, but there is constant marginal benefit up to this point. In addition, type 1 has a secondary use; call it prestige value. There is no surplus from the primary use. Thus the demand for type 2 is of the reservation price kind. Type 1 has a demand containing an element of this aspect, as well as an ordinary demand relative to its secondary use.

Consider the case where only type 1 is being produced. The marginal revenue is

$$
\begin{aligned}
MR_1 &= \alpha\theta^2 x_1^{\theta-1} + \beta && \text{if } x_1 < \mu \\
&= \alpha\theta^2 x_1^{\theta-1} && \text{if } x_1 > \mu
\end{aligned}
$$

Assume $b_1$ lies in the interval $(\alpha\theta^2\mu^{\theta-1}, \alpha\theta^2\mu^{\theta-1} + \beta)$. Then the profit-maximizing output will be $\mu$, and we will have

$$
a_1 = \alpha\theta\mu^\theta + (\beta - b_1)\mu
\tag{39}
$$

$$
s_1 = \alpha(1 - \theta)\mu^\theta
\tag{40}
$$

The case where only type 2 is produced is simple. Output is $\mu$, price is $\beta$, and

$$
a_2 = (\beta - b_2)\mu
\tag{41}
$$

$$
s_2 = 0
\tag{42}
$$

With both types produced, output of the two together will be $\mu$. Using this and maximizing profit with respect to the first, we find its output $\hat{x}_1$ given by

$$
\hat{x}_1 = (\alpha\theta^2/(b_1 - b_2))^{1/(1-\theta)}
\tag{43}
$$

For the solution to be acceptable, this must be well-defined and less than $\mu$, which requires

$$
b_1 - b_2 > \alpha\theta^2\mu^{\theta-1}
\tag{44}
$$

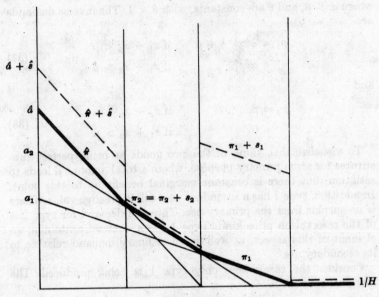

**Figure 9.2**

We have already assumed that $b_1$ by itself exceeds the right-hand side, so it is possible to satisfy (44) provided $b_2$ is sufficiently small. Note that our assumption of $a_1 < a_2$ automatically ensures (44).

With both types produced, we have

$$\hat{a} = (\alpha\theta\hat{x}_1^{\theta-1} + \beta - b_1)\hat{x}_1 + (\beta - b_2)(\mu - \hat{x}_1) \qquad (45)$$

$$\hat{s} = \alpha(1 - \theta)\hat{x}_1^{\theta} \qquad (46)$$

It is now clear that, with $f_1 < f_2$, the switch from type 1 to type 2 is going to reduce the surplus from a positive value to zero. This is going to lower utility as the economy expands. When both types are introduced, the surplus recovers to $\hat{s}$. However, $\hat{s} < s_1$ since $\hat{x}_1 < \mu$. Therefore, whether utility recovers to a high level on the introduction of both types or not depends on how large this difference is, and on how far profit per capita has increased during the traverse of the type 2 regime. Figure 9.2 illustrates a very adverse case. The profit frontier is shown as a heavy solid line, and the utility per capita as a line with dashes.

Similarly, we can build an example where type 2 has a large amount of consumer surplus while type 1 has none. Then the switch from type 1 to type 2 increases utility, but on the reintroduction of 1, the output of 2 falls, lowering the surplus and therefore utility across the switch point. The details are very similar to those of the above example and are left to the reader.

Let us return to a closer examination of the earlier case. In the interpretation given, type 1 is a low-fixed-cost, high surplus product, while type 2 is a high-fixed-cost, low surplus one. In a small economy, only the first is viable, while in a somewhat larger economy, or with the opening of trade, the second ousts it. The surplus for type 1 was interpreted as due to its prestige value, so the utility loss came from the replacement of hand-crafted prestige products by mass-produced utilitarian ones. With identical consumers, the loss was felt by everyone. However, other interpretations are possible, where only one group of consumers value the prestige aspect, and these are made worse off by growth or trade, while others do not value the prestige and can be better off. Such conclusions, although not based on such models, have been recently expounded in various guises by Scitovsky (1976) and Hirsch (1976). Dixit and Stiglitz (1979) give some formal analysis of the problem from the angle of heterogeneous consumers.

# 3. PRODUCT DIFFERENTIATION AND INTRA-INDUSTRY TRADE

In the preceding two sections, trade was merely a vehicle for market expansion. For analysing the implications of this, we did not have to consider trade explicitly. For many purposes, however, we need explicit models of trade in the context of scale economies and imperfect competition. In particular, if we are to study the determinants of intra-industry trade, we must have explicit trade models. The same is true if we are to understand how trade based on scale economies interacts with trade based on comparative advantage. The model set out in this section is an example of an explicit theory of trade with product differentiation, economies of scale and imperfect competition.

The model is based on Norman (1976), but has several similarities with Krugman (1978a, b). It attempts to explain trade within an industry consisting of close substitute products with similar technologies, as well as trade of the products of this industry for outputs of other industries. We relate the determinants of the two kinds of trade to the underlying reasons for trade, and show how intra-industry trade can be explained by product differentiation while conventional explanations apply to inter-industry trade. The basic model is kept extremely simple to allow explicit solutions which bring this aspect to the forefront. Some questions of generalizations are discussed at the end.

## Demand

We simplify the demand side by using the stock assumption of international trade theory, viz. identical and homothetic preferences for all consumers in both countries. Then the aggregate commodity demands can be derived from a similar utility function. Two kinds of goods enter into the utility function. One, labelled 0, is a numeraire good intended to embody all goods other than the ones in the industry on which we wish to focus, the other kind being goods of that industry. These are assumed to be differentiated, so that the elasticity of substitution between any pair of them is finite. The product varieties are indexed $1, 2, \ldots$; but we assume perfect symmetry so that it does not matter which label a particular product type bears. We take a special form of the utility function, where utility is Cobb–Douglas in the quantity of the numeraire good and a scalar measure of consumption of differentiated products, this scalar measure being a constant-elasticity-of-substitution function in the quantities of each product type.

As the total number of consumers in the two countries will be fixed, we can set world population at 1 without loss of generality. In that case, we do not have to distinguish between total and per capita quantities, so we let $c_0$ and $c_k$ $(k = 1, 2, \ldots)$ denote the respective (total or per capita) quantities of the numeraire and the differentiated goods. The utility function is then

$$u = \left( \sum_k c_k^\beta \right)^{\alpha/\beta} c_0^{1-\alpha} \qquad (47)$$

where we can regard the term in parentheses as a measure of consumption of differentiated products. In order for the product varieties to be imperfect substitutes, we must have $\beta < 1$. On the other hand, we need $\beta > 0$ for the differentiated products to be good enough substitutes to warrant the label 'product group': The elasticity of substitution between any pair of differentiated products is $1/(1 - \beta)$. Thus, if $\beta < 0$, the elasticity of substitution is less than unity. But given our Cobb–Douglas specification, the elasticity of substitution between differentiated goods and the numeraire good is unity, so if $\beta < 0$, the differentiated goods and the numeraire good are closer substitutes than are the differentiated goods among themselves. We therefore require $0 < \beta < 1$. In addition, we need

$0 < \alpha < 1$ for our canonical representation of the utility function to be concave.

World demands can be found by maximizing the utility function subject to the budget constraint

$$c_0 + \sum_k p_k c_k = y \qquad (48)$$

where the $p_k$ are prices, and $y$ is the total of factor income and profits for the world. It is easy to find the inverse demand functions for the differentiated goods:

$$p_j = \alpha\, c_j^{\beta - 1}\, y/z \qquad (49)$$

where

$$z = \sum_k c_k^\beta \qquad (50)$$

The demand for the numeraire is

$$c_0 = (1 - \alpha)y \qquad (51)$$

Note that these demand functions pertain to the world as a whole. Each country's quantities can be found by multiplying world demands by that country's share in world income.

## Production

The numeraire good is produced under constant returns to scale in a perfectly competitive market. There are economies of scale in the production of the differentiated products, and the market structure is one of Chamberlinian monopolistic competition. Production functions are the same for all product varieties. The potential range of varieties is assumed to be so large that only a finite subset of the range is actually produced. The number of differentiated goods produced will therefore be determined by the entry condition for the industry. The two countries have identical technologies.

The numeraire good has a unit cost function $b(w)$ of factor prices. In principle, factor prices can be different in the two countries, although we shall investigate the possibility of their equalization through trade. Reverting to our home and foreign country notational convention, let $w$ be the vector of factor prices in the home country and $W$ that in the foreign country. We assume for the moment that both countries produce the numeraire good, so we have the zero-pure-profit conditions

$$b(w) = 1 = b(W) \qquad (52)$$

As for the differentiated products, each product type has a total cost function $f(.)h(.)$, where $f$ depends on factor prices and $h$ on the output quantity. Thus the production functions are homothetic; in particular the factor proportions are independent of the output level. This is restrictive, but has the merit of highlighting certain aspects of the question of factor price equalization and thereby providing the point of departure for further analyses. There are significant economies of scale, i.e. $h(x)/x$ is decreasing over the relevant range of output levels $x$.

Production of each product variety in such an industry will be undertaken by only one producer, since a potential entrant can always do better by introducing a new product variety than by sharing in the production of an existing product type. We assume that the number of varieties produced is large enough to make oligopolistic interactions negligible, so that we have a monopolistically competitive industry. Each producer attempts to maximize profit given the inverse demand function facing him, and treating the outputs of others as fixed and world income as beyond his control. Entry occurs until the marginal firm is just breaking even; with symmetry this implies zero profit all around.

We can find the elasticity of the inverse demand function for the producer of good $j$ from (49) and (50). From (49) we have

$$\frac{c_j}{p_j}\frac{\partial p_j}{\partial c_j} = (\beta - 1) - \frac{c_j}{z}\frac{\partial z}{\partial c_j}$$

The second term here is the indirect effect, through total industry output, that an increase in the quantity of one product type has on the price of that variety. Using (50) we see that this effect is

$$\frac{c_j}{z}\frac{\partial z}{\partial c_j} = \beta\frac{c_j^\beta}{z} = \beta\frac{c_j^\beta}{\sum_k c_k^\beta}$$

This is clearly inversely related to the total number of product varieties in existence; in fact, in a symmetric equilibrium, it is simply $\beta$ times the inverse of the number of product varieties. Under our assumption of large numbers, therefore, this term will be negligible. The elasticity of inverse demand can then be approximated by $(1 - \beta)$ in absolute value, so the marginal revenue for the producer of product type $j$ is $\beta p_j$. For profit maximization, this will be equated to marginal cost. In the home country, marginal cost is $f(w)h'(x_j)$, so if product type $j$ is produced there, we shall have

$$\beta p_j = f(w)h'(x_j) \tag{53}$$

We shall consider only long-term equilibria, i.e. equilibria in which no producer has incentives to enter or leave the industry. If the differentiated products are produced in the home country at all, this means that there must be zero pure profits in the industry, i.e. the number of product types must be such that average revenue equals average cost:

$$p_j = f(w)h(x_j)/x_j \tag{54}$$

Dividing (53) by (54), we find

$$\beta = x_j h'(x_j)/h(x_j)$$

This must be true for all products $j$ that are produced. In particular, it must hold regardless of factor prices, so long as differentiated products are produced at all in the country we are looking at. Provided the right-hand side is a monotonic function of $x_j$, the equation will have a unique solution. The implication is that all product varieties in existence will have the same output level, the common value of $x$ being defined by

$$\beta = x h'(x)/h(x) \tag{55}$$

This result depends crucially on homotheticity in production. The special form of the utility function is less important; for much more general functions, the left-hand side will be a function of $x$ alone, which is all that matters. The convenience of the result lies in the fact that it allows us to concentrate on the number of products in the industry.

### General equilibrium

We assume that each country is active in the production of at least one variety from the industry. Then we have equations like (53) and (54) in each country for at least one $j$. Using (55), all these can be summarized into the following

$$\beta p = f(w)h'(x) = f(W)h'(x) \tag{56}$$

$$px = f(w)h(x) = f(W)h(x) \tag{57}$$

Note that given (55), only one of (56) and (57) can be regarded as independent. Given (55) and (56), for example, we can derive (57).

Next we have the equilibrium conditions in the factor markets. We know that the cost-minimizing factor inputs are the derivatives of the appropriate cost functions with respect to factor prices. Let $x_0$ be the home production of the numeraire good and $n$ the number of differentiated products produced in the home country; let $X_0$

and $N$ be the corresponding entities for the foreign country. Strictly speaking, $n$ and $N$ must be integers, which causes problems attaining an exact balance in factor markets. The fact that we have assumed the total number of product types to be large (i.e. $(n + N)$ large) does not solve this problem. Nevertheless, we shall regard both $n$ and $N$ as real numbers. In places where the integer constraint matters, however, we shall point out how. With both as real numbers, we have the equilibrium conditions

$$x_0\, b_w(w) + n\, f_w(w)h(x) = v \tag{58}$$

$$X_0\, b_w(W) + N\, f_w(W)h(x) = V \tag{59}$$

where $v$ and $V$ are the vectors of factor endowments.

Finally, we require that the world output levels be compatible with equilibrium in the goods markets. Noting that world income is factor income alone, since profits vanish in a Chamberlinian equilibrium, total income is $(w.v + W.V)$. Substituting in (49) and (51), we have

$$p = \alpha(w.v + W.V)/\{x(n + N)\} \tag{60}$$

$$x_0 + X_0 = (1 - \alpha)(w.v + W.V) \tag{61}$$

If $m$ is the number of factors in each country, we have in (58)–(61) $(2m + 2)$ equations, of which one is redundant by Walras's law. To complete the determination of equilibrium, we append (52) and (55)–(57), which contribute five more independent equations, making $(2m + 6)$ in all. These suffice to determine the $(2m + 6)$ unknowns $p$, $x$, $n$, $N$, $x_0$, $X_0$, $w$, and $W$, subject to the usual caveats concerning existence and uniqueness.

It is instructive to regard the equilibrium formally in a different light. Let (55) fix $x$, and then think of the industry under consideration as producing just one good, viz. the number of products. This is produced at constant unit cost $\phi(\ ) = f(\ )h(x)$, and sold competitively at price $\rho = px$. The equilibrium conditions then become

$$b(w) = 1 = b(W) \tag{62}$$

$$\phi(w) = \rho = \phi(W) \tag{63}$$

$$x_0 b_w(w) + n\phi_w(w) = v \tag{64}$$

$$X_0 b_w(W) + N\phi_w(W) = V \tag{65}$$

$$x_0 + X_0 = (1 - \tilde{\alpha})(w.v + W.V) \tag{66}$$

$$n + N = \alpha(w.v + W.V)/\rho \tag{67}$$

These are formally exactly like the conditions for a competitive equilibrium in a two-good economy with each good produced in both countries. We will have to be careful when it comes to assessing the welfare consequences of trade, since this short-hand description treats all product varieties essentially in an additive way, whereas they are in fact imperfect substitutes. But as far as descriptive aspects are concerned, this approach has some immediate implications. We begin with the most important of these, which leads to our drawing a distinction between inter-industry and intra-industry trade.

### Inter-industry trade

The model gives an account of the trade between the numeraire good and the aggregate quantity of differentiated goods. Further, given identical technologies and preferences in the two countries, the mechanism is exactly like that of the conventional factor-abundance model. For example, if the differentiated goods are more capital-intensive, the more capital-abundant country will have a comparative advantage in them in the sense examined in Chapter 3. We can then establish the Rybczynski propositions concerning changes in the supplies of differentiated goods as a result of factor endowment changes, and other comparative static results. This can by now be safely left to the reader.

### Intra-industry trade

However, the important new feature of this model is intra-industry trade. Suppose the home country accounts for a fraction $\lambda$ of world income. With homothetic preferences, it consumes a fraction $\lambda$ of the world output of each good, $c_0 = \lambda(x_0 + X_0)$, and $c = \lambda x$ for each of the $(n + N)$ differentiated goods produced. Its production is $x_0$ for the numeraire good and $x$ for each of $n$ varieties of the differentiated goods. Without loss of generality, suppose that the home country is a net exporter of differentiated goods. Suppose it produces the first $n$ of these by choice of labelling. Define $\sigma = n/(n + N)$, so $\sigma$ is the home country's share in world production of differentiated products. For the home country, net imports of the numeraire are $c_0 - x_0 = \lambda X_0 - (1 - \lambda)x_0$. Its exports of varieties $1, 2, \ldots, n$ are $(1 - \lambda)x$ each, and its imports of varieties $(n + 1), \ldots$ $(n + N)$ are $\lambda x$ each. Total trade is balanced, i.e.

$$\lambda X_0 - (1 - \lambda)x_0 = np(1 - \lambda)x - Np\lambda x$$

Gross exports of differentiated goods are of value

$$npx(1 - \lambda) = (n + N)px\sigma(1 - \lambda)$$

while net exports of differentiated goods are

$$npx(1 - \lambda) - Npx\lambda = (n + N)px\{\sigma(1 - \lambda) - (1 - \sigma)\lambda\}$$
$$= (n + N)px(\sigma - \lambda)$$

Remember that we have chosen labels so that the home country is a net exporter of these goods, i.e. $\sigma > \lambda$. For the foreign country, gross exports of differentiated goods are similarly seen to be $(n + N)px(1 - \sigma)\lambda$. For the world as a whole, then, the value of gross trade $T_G$ is

$$T_G = (n + N)px\{\sigma(1 - \lambda) + (1 - \sigma)\lambda\} \tag{68}$$

and that of net trade, $T_N$, is

$$T_N = (n + N)px(\sigma - \lambda) \tag{69}$$

The difference is intra-industry trade $T_I$. Simplifying, we see

$$T_I = 2(n + N)px\lambda(1 - \sigma) \tag{70}$$

These expressions have some immediate implications for the pattern of trade. The simplest is a confirmation of our earlier observation that net trade (i.e. the net exchange of differentiated goods for the numeraire good) is explained by conventional comparative advantage. In the formula for net trade, this boils down to the fact that the share of the home country in the production of differentiated goods is larger than its share of world income. If the countries were identical, we would have $\lambda = \sigma = \frac{1}{2}$ and no net trade. More generally, if the two were scaled replicas of each other, we would have $\lambda = \sigma$ and no net trade.

Next, gross trade is not related to comparative advantage as such, but to a correlation between comparative advantage and country size. Fixing $(n + N)px$ and varying $\lambda$ and $\sigma$ in (68), we find that the expression in the brackets takes on its maximum value when $\lambda = 0$ and $\sigma = 1$, i.e. when a small country has great comparative advantage in the production of differentiated goods.

Turning to intra-industry trade, we see from (70) that it will be more important when $\lambda$ is large and when $\sigma$ is small. Since we have $\sigma > \lambda$, this means that intra-industry trade will be at its height when each of these is nearly $\frac{1}{2}$. In other words, if the two countries are of a similar size, and have no clear comparative advantage across industries, then we will see the predominant pattern of trade as one of intra-industry trade. Movements of factors, transmission of technology, and convergence of tastes are all shifts which are conducive to such a state of affairs.

It is possible to relate our model to the work of Grubel and Lloyd (1975), and express their ratio index of intra-industry trade in terms of our $\sigma$ and $\lambda$. As that does not yield any further insights, we leave it as an exercise for the reader.

The assumption of symmetry between the differentiated goods has a further implication that the matter of which country produces which good can be settled in an arbitrary manner. The total volume of trade is determinate, but its pattern is not. These observations concerning intra-industry trade may be seen as a partial confirmation of the views of Linder (1961).

## Factor price equalization

Let us turn to the question of factor prices. We assumed an equilibrium where each country produced both kinds of goods. In the manner of conventional theory briefly discussed in Chapter 2, we could then ask whether the price-equals-unit-cost conditions uniquely fix factor prices, i.e. whether (62) and (63) must yield $w = W$ for given $\rho$. With two factors and no factor-intensity reversals, such would be the case. Better still, we could follow the general equilibrium approach of Chapter 4, making endogenous the question of specialization and the determination of output prices. If there is an equilibrium with trade in goods but with equal factor prices, it must be an equilibrium of an integrated world with factors as well as goods traded. Conversely, given the factor prices $\hat{w}$ of such an integrated equilibrium, these will serve as equalized factor prices following trade in goods alone, provided the world outputs can be decomposed into feasible $x_0$, $X_0$, $n$, and $N$ satisfying the separate factor-market equilibrium conditions (64) and (65) for the two countries. With two factors, we can examine this in a diagram similar to those used in Chapter 4. In Figure 9.3, we show the unit factor input vectors $b_w(\hat{w})$ and $\phi_w(\hat{w})$ of the integrated equilibrium in directions $OA_1$ and $OA_2$. The lengths $OC_1$ and $OC_2$ mark off the amounts needed to produce the total outputs, $(x_0 + X_0)$ of the numeraire good and $(n + N)$ varieties of differentiated goods in amounts $x$ each. The coordinates of $O'$ relative to $O$ give the total world factor endowments. Then we know that if the factor endowments of the home country measured relative to $O$ (and simultaneously those of the foreign country relative to $O'$) lie outside the parallelogram $OC_1O'C_2$, it will be impossible to achieve such a decomposition. Then our assumption of completely non-specialized production will not be valid, and factor-price equalization will not occur. Inside the parallelogram, there is a slight new problem. Not all the points

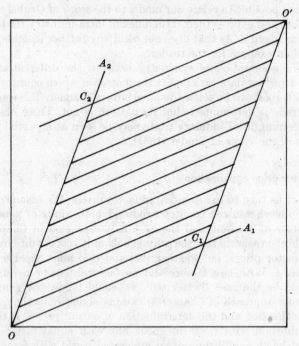

**Figure 9.3**

there are feasible, given the requirement that the number of differentiated goods must be an integer, and each must be produced in the fixed amount $x$. Therefore we mark off along $OC_2$ all integer multiples of $\phi_w(\hat{w})$, the factor requirement of each variety. The numeraire good being assumed perfectly divisible, we draw from these points lines parallel to $OA_1$. For home factor endowments lying on any of this family of parallel lines, we can determine a part of the total world production to be undertaken at home while achieving exact clearing of factor markets. Within the parallelogram but off these lines, such exact equilibrium is not possible. However, so long as the number of products is large, any point in the parallelogram will be relatively close to one of the lines, and we will be justified in thinking of an approximate equilibrium with diversified production and factor price equalization.

The generalization of these arguments to the case of $m$ factors and $(n-1)$ industries of differentiated goods is in principle clear. In so far as the likelihood of factor price equalization depends on

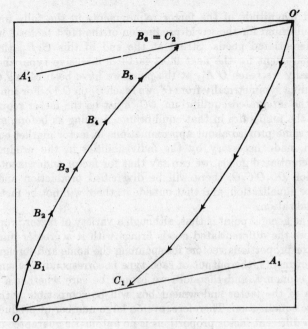

**Figure 9.4**

the relative numbers of goods and factors, what is then at stake is the number of *industries* with differentiated products, and not the total distinguishable number of commodities. This may be of some interest to those who believe that there are 'obviously' more goods than factors in the world.

## Unequal factor proportions

As demonstrated, this result depends on the assumption that all product types in the industry have the same factor proportions. This may be a reasonable assumption for some industries, but one would like to know how robust the result is. To answer this question, consider an example where the differentiated goods are graded by relative factor intensities. Suppose for sake of clarity of exposition that there are two factors, and that the numeraire good is more factor-1 intensive than any of the differentiated goods. Form the box of world factor endowments as in Figure 9.4. Let $OA_1$ be the direction of factor proportions of the numeraire good as usual, and let $O'A_1'$ be the parallel direction from $O'$. Let $OB_1$ be the direction and magnitude of the factor requirements in the fully integrated equilibrium for the world production of the most factor-2 intensive differentiated goods. String at the end of this $B_1 B_2$, the factor requirement for the next most factor-2 intensive type, and so on. Finally we reach $O' A_1'$, at the point we have been calling $C_2$. Proceeding symmetrically from $O'$, we reach $C_1$ on $OA_1$. For consistency of the integrated equilibrium, $OC_1$ must be the factor requirement for the numeraire in that equilibrium. Arguing as before, and with the same proviso about approximations in factor market equilibration made necessary by the indivisibilities in the production of differentiated goods, we can say that for factor endowments in the region $OC_1 O' C_2 O$, there will be diversified production and factor price equalization, and that outside it, there will not be factor price equalization.

The general point is that, although a variety of factor proportions across the differentiated goods brings with it a greater number of factor proportions vectors for spanning the home and foreign factor endowments, the output of each type is correspondingly smaller in the economy, and therefore we cannot be sure whether a greater area of the factor endowment box will be compatible with factor price equalization. Therefore, even a large number of product types with different factor proportions is no automatic guarantee of equal factor prices. Recall that we reached the same uncertain conclusion in Chapter 4 when we increased the number of goods without classifying them into industries. With some differences caused by scale economies and imperfect competition, the present verdict is analogous.

## Other asymmetries

Having departed from the symmetry assumption of the formal model in one respect, we take this opportunity to say something about cases where differentiated goods do not enter preferences in a symmetric way. Precise models are difficult to specify, but some likely conclusions stand out. The asymmetry may pertain to product types or to countries. Consider first the case where goods can be ordered along a chain labelled $1, 2, 3, \ldots$. Preferences shift systematically along the chain, and goods farther apart are poorer substitutes than ones closer together in labels. The case most favourable to large intra-industry trade, as well as to a large shift in the pattern of production towards differentiated goods after the opening of trade, is the one where each country's preferences are strongest where its comparative cost advantage is weakest along the chain. In isolation, each country would not find it worthwhile to devote much of its resources to the production of relatively high cost and weakly desired differentiated goods. With the possibility of trade, each will be able to produce the types of differentiated goods desired by the other. On the other hand, if preferences match comparative cost advantage with respect to differentiated goods, there will be little intra-industry trade. There may be net trade of differentiated goods for the numeraire good depending on conventional comparative advantage.

The above discussion took the pattern of preferences over the spectrum of differentiated goods to be exogenous. But it could depend on income, thus giving rise to endogenous explanations of intra-industry trade. For example, suppose mass-produced varieties of goods are relatively capital intensive. On the other hand, a capital abundant country has a higher real income per head of population, which is at the margin more heavily spent on the hand-crafted varieties. This would be a case compatible with a large volume of intra-industry trade.

### Gains from intra-industry trade

To conclude this section, we return to the symmetric case and examine the welfare aspects of trade. To concentrate on the new feature of intra-industry trade, it is best to consider the simple case where this is the only kind of trade. As we saw before, this occurs when each country is a scaled replica of the world. Suppose the home country has a fraction $\lambda$ of the population and of each primary factor of production. We can determine the autarky equilibrium of the home country by methods similar to those employed at the beginning of the section. The output of each differentiated good will be governed by (53) and (54), and will therefore be the same, $x$, for all of them, and given by (55). Factor and output market conditions will then imply that the numeraire output, and the number of varieties produced, are each proportional to the size of the economy. When the two economies are allowed to trade, the output of each variety will remain unchanged, but the total numbers will increase. The gain from trade has its source here.

Suppose that the trading world would have $\hat{n}$ varieties of differentiated goods and an output $\hat{x}_0$ of the numeraire good. Recall that units are chosen so that world population equals 1. The consumption levels per capita are $\hat{x}_0$ for the numeraire good and $x$ for each of the $\hat{n}$ differentiated goods. Substituting in (47), each consumer's utility is

$$\hat{u} = (\hat{n}x^\beta)^{\alpha/\beta}\,\hat{x}_0^{1-\alpha}$$

Now consider the countries in isolation. In the home country, there would be $\lambda$ consumers, an amount $\lambda \hat{x}_0$ of the numeraire good, and $\lambda \hat{n}$ varieties of differentiated goods each in quantity $x$. Per capita consumption levels would be $\hat{x}_0$ for the numeraire good and $x/\lambda$ for each of $\lambda \hat{n}$ varieties of differentiated goods. Therefore the utility of each home consumer under autarky would be

$$u = (\lambda \hat{n}(x/\lambda)^\beta)^{\alpha/\beta} \, \hat{x}_0^{1-\alpha}$$
$$= \lambda^{\alpha(1-\beta)/\beta} \, \hat{u}$$

Similarly, in the foreign country, utility of each consumer would be

$$U = (1-\lambda)^{\alpha(1-\beta)/\beta} \, \hat{u}$$

Since $\beta < 1$, each of $u$ and $U$ is less than $\hat{u}$. We see the essential role played by product differentiation. Total consumption of differentiated products per capita is the same in autarky as under free trade—it is $\hat{n}x$ under free trade, and $(\lambda \hat{n})(x/\lambda) = \hat{n}x$ in autarky. The gain arises because the consumer gets a larger number of product varieties, and a proportionally smaller amount of each variety; and with convex preferences, the consumer prefers this.

## 4. CONCLUDING REMARKS

This chapter may leave the reader with an agnostic attitude to trade. We have shown that trade is likely to provide greater product variety and a reduction in monopolistic distortions. Both are advantageous. On the other hand, trade may increase biases in product selection, and it may encourage the establishment of too many firms in oligopolistic industries. As a result, one cannot assert that there are unambiguous gains from trade in a world of scale economies and imperfect competition. There are *potential* gains from trade in the presence of economies of scale, but with imperfect markets there is no assurance that these gains will be reaped in practice.

That may seem a sad note on which to end a book on the theory of international trade. We do not think so, however. The models and conclusions of this final chapter show that there is still a lot to be done before we have a satisfactory theory of international trade. Earlier chapters also pointed out several directions of further research, and potential applications of the techniques illustrated in this book. From the point of view of research, at least, that is an encouraging conclusion. Readers who had invested a great deal of effort in studying the book would have been much sadder if we had succeeded in tying everything together, and making international trade theorists redundant.

## NOTES

The literature on international trade under imperfect competition is very sparse. Caves and Jones (1977, ch. 9) discuss the topic, but do not set up formal models. Melvin and Warne (1973) analyse the gains from trade under monopoly in simple models—specifically in models where trade completely eliminates monopolistic distortions, and where trade does not affect domestic monopolies at all. Our discussion in section 1 can be seen as an extension of their work, in that we make market structure endogenous to the problem.

More work has been done on product differentiation in international trade. As noted, both Linder (1961) and Grubel and Lloyd (1975, particularly ch. 6) discuss the determinants of trade in differentiated products. Vernon (1966) can be said to do the same, although his concept of a product cycle is a narrower one. Our approach, however, does not follow these. It is much more closely related to recent literature on the theory of monopolistic competition, such as Spence (1976) and Dixit and Stiglitz (1977).

# MATHEMATICAL APPENDIX

We assume that the reader is familiar with the basic vector and matrix operations and with partial differentiation. Some elementary definitions are given below in order to establish the notation. Relevant results are also stated without proof. Beyond such very elementary levels, too, only sketches of proofs or intuitive justifications are given. At the end of the chapter, references are cited where the matters may be pursued further by interested readers. No attempt is made at comprehensive coverage; our sole aim is to allow readers to follow the developments in the text more easily.

## 1. LINEAR ALGEBRA AND GEOMETRY

**Set-theoretic notation**

A set is a collection of objects or elements having a prescribed property. If $S$ is the set, $x$ a typical object, and $P$ the property, this is written symbolically as

$$S = \{x| \ x \text{ has the property } P\}$$

and read: $S$ is the set of elements $x$ such that $x$ has the property $P$. For example, the set of all numbers that can be expressed as squares of real numbers is

$$S = \{x \mid x = y^2 \text{ for some real number } y\}$$

or more briefly

$$S = \{y^2| \ y \text{ is a real number}\}$$

The fact of an object $x$ being in a set $S$ is denoted by $x \in S$, and read: $x$ is in $S$, or $x$ belongs to $S$.

Given a set of real numbers, we often need to find out the smallest or the largest element of it, when one exists. The smallest square of a real number is zero; this is written as

$$\min_{y} \{y^2| \ y \text{ is a real number}\} = 0$$

and read: the minimum with respect to $y$ of $y^2$ when $y$ is a real number is zero. This minimum is obviously attained when $y = 0$.

$S$ is a *subset* of $T$ if every element of $S$ is also in $T$ but not necessarily conversely; this is written $S \subset T$.

## Vectors and matrices

We will deal with finite dimensional vectors having real components. If a symbol such as $x$ is used to indicate a vector, the components will generally be indicated by placing subscripts on this symbol, as $(x_1, x_2, \ldots, x_n)$. The set of real numbers is the one-dimensional space $R$; the $n$-dimensional space will be written $R^n$.

Vectors represent points in such spaces. Specifically, $x$ denotes the point with coordinates $(x_1, x_2, \ldots, x_n)$ relative to the origin, which is the zero vector $0 = (0, 0, \ldots, 0)$. If $x$ and $y$ are points in $R^n$, then $\frac{1}{2}(x + y)$, i.e. the vector with components

$$(\tfrac{1}{2}(x_1 + y_1), \tfrac{1}{2}(x_2 + y_2), \ldots, \tfrac{1}{2}(x_n + y_n))$$

represents the mid-point of the line segment joining them. More generally, the set

$$\{\lambda x + (1 - \lambda)y \mid 0 \leq \lambda \leq 1\}$$

is the whole *line-segment* joining $x$ and $y$. The *directed line segment* joining $y$ to $x$ is simply the vector indicating the point $x$ relative to a new origin placed at $y$, namely $x - y$.

In $R^n$, $x = 0$ means $x_i = 0$ for all $i$ from 1 to $n$; $x \geq 0$ means $x_i \geq 0$ for all $i$; $x > 0$ mean $x \geq 0$ but $x \neq 0$, i.e. that $x$ has all its components non-negative and at least one positive; $x \gg 0$ means $x_i > 0$ for all $i$; $x \geq y$ means $x - y \geq 0$ etc.

The notation for matrices is generally analogous. An $m$-by-$n$ matrix $A$ will have elements $A_{ij}$ in the $i$th row and $j$th column, for $i = 1, 2, \ldots, m$ and $j = 1, 2, \ldots, n$. However, many important matrices arise from differentiation of functions, and these will have a special notation to be explained shortly.

The *transpose* of a matrix is denoted by the superscript $T$. Thus $B = A^T$ is an $n$-by-$m$ matrix with $B_{ji} = A_{ij}$ for all $i$ and $j$. The *inverse* of a non-singular matrix is denoted by a superscript $-1$. Thus, if $A$ is $n$-by-$n$ and non-singular, then $AA^{-1} = A^{-1}A = I$, where $I$ is the $n$-by-$n$ identity matrix having entries 1 along the diagonal and 0 elsewhere.

## Geometry

Vectors are understood to be columns, i.e. an $n$-dimensional vector $x$ is an $n$-by-1 matrix with elements $x_i$ in the $i$th row.

If $x$ and $y$ are vectors in $R^n$, their *inner product*, written $x.y$, is defined as the matrix product $x^T y$, i.e.

$$x.y = x^T y = \sum_{i=1}^{n} x_i y_i \tag{1}$$

The (Euclidean) *length* of a vector $x$, written $\|x\|$, is defined as

$$\|x\| = (x.x)^{1/2} = \left\{ \sum_{i=1}^{n} x_i^2 \right\}^{1/2} \tag{2}$$

The (Euclidean) *distance* between points $x$ and $y$ is simply the length of the directed line segment joining $y$ to $x$, i.e. $\|x - y\|$.

The geometric significance of the inner product is that two vectors are mutually perpendicular (orthogonal) if and only if their inner product is zero.

Let $S$ be a set of points in $R^n$. Its *complement*, written $S^C$, is the set of points in $R^n$ but not in $S$. A point $x$ in $S$ is called an *interior point* if, for some positive real number $\epsilon$, all points of $R^n$ within distance $\epsilon$ of $x$ are in $S$. The collection of all interior points of $S$ is called its *interior*. A point which is neither in the interior of $S$ nor in that of its complement is called a *boundary point* of $S$ (and also of $S^C$). Thus $x$ is a boundary point of $S$ if, for any $\epsilon > 0$, there are points of $S$ as well as points of $S^C$ within distance $\epsilon$ of $x$. The collection of boundary points of $S$ is called its *boundary*. Figure A.1 illustrates these concepts.

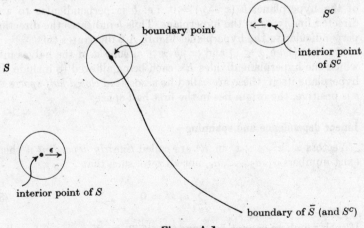

boundary point

$S^C$

interior point of $S^C$

$S$

interior point of $S$

boundary of $\bar{S}$ (and $S^C$)

**Figure A.1**

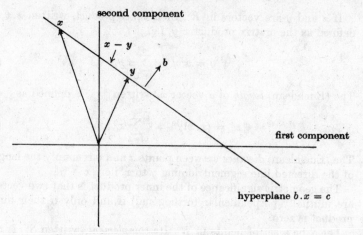

**Figure A.2**

A set may or may not contain its boundary points. In one dimension, the set $S = \{x \mid 0 \leq x < 1\}$ has the points 0 and 1 as its boundary points, of which it contains only the former. A set which does contain all its boundary points is called *closed*; one which contains none of its boundary points is called *open*. Thus $S$ is closed if and only if $S^c$ is open.

Let $b$ be a non-zero vector in $R^n$ and $c$ a real number (i.e. scalar). The set $\{x \mid b.x = c\}$ is called a *hyperplane*. If $x$ and $y$ are points of the hyperplane, $b.(x - y) = 0$, i.e. $b$ is perpendicular to any directed line lying in the hyperplane. Thus $b$ indicates the direction perpendicular to the hyperplane. Figure A.2 illustrates this.

The sets $\{x \mid b.x \leq c\}$ and $\{x \mid b.x \geq c\}$ consist of the halves into which the hyperplane divides $R^n$, each being allowed to include the hyperplane itself; these are called its associated *closed half-spaces*. If $c$ is positive, the origin lies in the first half-space.

### Linear dependence and spanning

Vectors $x^1, x^2, \ldots, x^k$ in $R^n$ are called *linearly dependent* if there exist numbers $\alpha_1, \alpha_2, \ldots, \alpha_k$, not all zero, such that

$$\sum_{j=1}^{k} \alpha_j \, x^j = 0 \tag{3}$$

If such numbers cannot be found, i.e. if (3) implies $\alpha_j = 0$ for all $j$,

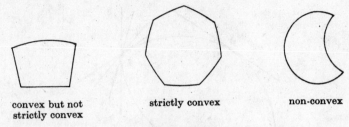

convex but not
strictly convex

strictly convex

non-convex

**Figure A.3**

then the vectors are called *linearly independent*. In the $n$-dimensional space, there are sets of $n$ linearly independent vectors, but any set containing $(n + 1)$ or more vectors must be linearly dependent. In fact this could be made the definition of *dimension*.

Let $x^1, x^2, \ldots, x^k$ be vectors in $R^n$. A vector $y$ in $R^n$ will be said to be *spanned* by $x^1, x^2, \ldots, x^k$ if there exist numbers $\alpha_1, \alpha_2, \ldots, \alpha_k$ such that

$$y = \sum_{j=1}^{k} \alpha_j x^j \qquad (4)$$

The set of all vectors spanned by $x^1, x^2, \ldots, x^k$ is called the *subspace spanned* by them. If the vectors are linearly independent, this subspace has dimension $k$. In such a case, the vectors $x^1, x^2, \ldots, x^k$ are said to form a *basis* for the subspace; further, for any vector $y$ in the subspace, the expression (4) is unique, and the scalars $\alpha_j$ are called the components of $y$ relative to this basis.

**Convex sets**

A set $S$ in $R^n$ is called *convex* if, whenever $x$ and $y$ are in $S$, the line segment joining them, i.e. the set $\{\lambda x + (1 - \lambda)y \mid 0 \le \lambda \le 1\}$, is entirely contained in $S$. The set is called *strictly convex* if all points of the line segment other than the end points, i.e. the points $\{\lambda x + (1 - \lambda)y \mid 0 < \lambda < 1\}$, are interior points of $S$. Figure A.3 illustrates.

This definition can run into problems if the set $S$ can be contained in a space of dimension smaller than that of the whole space. For example, a circular disc in three-dimensional space has no interior points at all – any point on the disc has points outside the disc arbitrarily close to it – but one would want to call it a strictly convex set. Since we shall not meet such cases in our applications, we do not pursue this matter. For a rigorous treatment, see Arrow and Hahn (1971, p. 70).

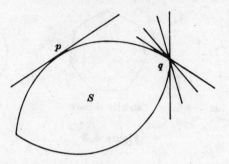

**Figure A.4**

Note that a non-convex set is *not* called concave; there is no such thing as a concave set.

We will need the following important result for convex sets: *The supporting hyperplane*: If $S$ is a convex set and $p$ a boundary point of $S$, then there exists a hyperplane (not necessarily unique) containing $p$ such that $S$ lies entirely in one of its closed half spaces. Such a hyperplane is called a supporting hyperplane. Figure A.4 illustrates this, and also indicates how at a point like $q$ where the set $S$ has a corner, the supporting hyperplane can be non-unique.

In view of the evident geometric sense of this property, we omit a formal proof. We likewise omit further results and extensions since these are not needed for our immediate purpose

The algebra is easy to state. Let the equation of the hyperplane be $b.x = c$. For it to contain $p$, we must have $c = b.p$. Therefore the result can be written as follows: If $S$ is a convex set and $p$ a boundary point of it, then there exists $b \neq 0$ such that $b.x \leq b.p$ for all $x$ in $S$.

## 2. FUNCTIONS AND DIFFERENTIATION

**Functions**

A function $f$ defined over a set $S$ and taking values in a set $T$ will be indicated by $f: S \rightarrow T$. Its value at a point $x$ of $S$ will be written $f(x)$. The set $S$ will be called the *domain*; typical elements of it will be called *arguments* or *independent variables* of $f$. We will usually be concerned with cases where $S$ is part or all of $R^n$, and $T$ is $R^m$, often $R$.

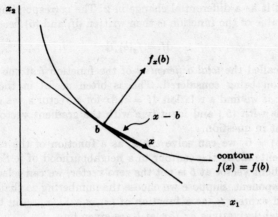

**Figure A.5**

## Differentiation

Let $f: R^n \to R$, and let $x$ be the (vector) independent variable. The partial derivative with respect to the $j$th component is denoted by $\partial f/\partial x_j$, or more often by $f_j$. This has the advantage of highlighting the fact that each partial derivative is itself a function $R^n \to R$. Thus its value at a point $x = b$ can be written in our notation as $f_j(b)$. The totality of these partial derivatives for $j = 1, 2, \ldots, n$ form a vector-valued function which will be written as $f_x$. The $f_x(b)$, the value at $x = b$, is called the *gradient vector* of $f$ at $b$, and has components $f_j(b)$.

The first-order Taylor approximation to $f$ around $b$ is

$$f(x) \simeq f(b) + \sum_{j=1}^{n} f_j(b)(x_j - b_j)$$

$$= f(b) + f_x(b) \cdot (x - b) \qquad (5)$$

Figure A.5 shows the set of points $x$ where $f(x) = f(b)$; this is called a *contour* of $f$. Let $x$ be a point on the contour close to $b$. To the order of approximation in (5), then, we have $f_x(b) \cdot (x - b) = 0$, i.e. the gradient vector indicates a direction perpendicular to the contour at $b$.

In much applied work, it is convenient to regard the approximation in (5) as exact for $(x - b)$ infinitesimally small. This can be given a rigorous foundation, but for our purpose, that is not necessary. In this context it is customary to write $dx$ for $(x - b)$, and speak of it as a differential change in $x$. The corresponding change in the value of the function is then written $df$, and (5) becomes

$$df = f_x(b) . dx \tag{5'}$$

This is called the *total differential* of the function $f$ at the point of evaluation being considered. This is often useful in the reverse context: if we find a relation $df = z . dx$ for a vector $z$, we can compare this with (5') and identify $z$ with the gradient vector of $f$ at the point in question.

If $f_j(b) \neq 0$, we can solve the $x_j$ as a function of the remaining components along the contour in a neighbourhood of $b$. So long as the gradient vector at $b$ is not the zero vector, we can select a non-zero component. Suppose we choose the numbering so that it is the $n$th, and express $x_n$ as a function of $(x_1, x_2, \ldots, x_{n-1})$ in this way. Its partial derivatives $\partial x_n/\partial x_j$ at $b$ are given by

$$\partial x_n/\partial x_j = -f_j(b)/f_n(b) \quad \text{for } j = 1, 2, \ldots, (n-1) \tag{6}$$

This is the *Implicit Function Theorem*, again to the extent of rigour needed for our applications. Correspondingly, (6) is called the formula for differentiation of implicit functions.

Sometimes it is convenient to partition the independent variables of a function into two or more classes, e.g. fixed and variable inputs in a production function. Let $f: R^{m+n} \to R$, and let the arguments be written $(x, y)$ with $x$ in $R^m$ and $y$ in $R^n$. The partial derivatives $\partial f/\partial x_i$ will be written as $f_{x_i}$, or even $f_i$ if no confusion is likely, while $\partial f/\partial y_j$ will be $f_{y_j}$, or even $f_j$ if it is clear to which variables the subscript applies. The first kind will be collected into a vector function $f_x: R^{m+n} \to R^m$, and the second into $f_y: R^{m+n} \to R^n$. The gradient vector at $x = a$ and $y = b$, for example, will be $(f_x(a,b), f_y(a, b))$. Where one argument, e.g. $y$, is one-dimensional, $f_y$ will be an ordinary partial derivative $\partial f/\partial y$.

A vector-valued function $f: R^n \to R^m$ will have component functions generally denoted by superscripts as $f^i: R^n \mapsto R$; thus, for $x$ in $R^n$, $f^i(x)$ is the $i$th component of $f(x)$. The partial derivatives $f_j^i$ will be collected over $j$ into the vector function $f_x^i$, and then over $i$ into the matrix function $f_x$. Thus the value at $x = b$, $f_x(b)$, is an $m$-by-$n$ matrix with element $f_j^i(b)$ in the $i$th row and $j$th column.

Suppose that the independent variables of $f: R^n \to R$ are themselves values of functions $g^j: R^m \to R$. Then let $g$ be the vector-valued function with component functions $g^j$, and form the composite function $h: R^m \to R$ as follows:

$$h(y) = f(x) \quad \text{where } y \text{ is in } R^m \text{ and } x = g(y)$$

i.e. $h(y) = f(g(y))$. Then the partial derivatives of $h$ can be related to those of $f$ and $g$ by the *chain rule* of differentiation

$$\partial h / \partial y_i = \sum_{j=1}^{n} (\partial f / \partial x_j)(\partial g^j / \partial y_i)$$

which in our notation becomes the matrix product

$$h_y(y)^T = f_x(g(y))^T g_y(y) \qquad (7)$$

Multiplying both sides by $dy$ gives us the chain rule for total differentials.

Back to $f: R^n \to R$. The second-order partial derivatives $\partial^2 f / \partial x_i \, \partial x_j$ will be written as $f_{ij}$, and formed into an $n$-by-$n$ matrix function $f_{xx}$. The value at $x = b$, $f_{xx}(b)$, is a matrix with $f_{ij}(b)$ as the element in the $i$th row and $j$th column. If $f$ is twice continuously differentiable, the cross-partial derivatives are equal, and then the matrix is symmetric i.e.

$$f_{ij}(b) = f_{ji}(b) \qquad \text{for all } i, j, \text{ or } f_{xx}(b)^T = f_{xx}(b) \qquad (8)$$

The second-order Taylor approximation to $f(x)$ around $x = b$ is

$$f(x) \simeq f(b) + \sum_{j=1}^{n} f_j(b)(x_j - b_j) + \tfrac{1}{2} \sum_{i=1}^{n} \sum_{j=1}^{n} f_{ij}(b)(x_i - b_i)(x_j - b_j)$$

$$= f(b) + f_x(b) \cdot (x - b) + \tfrac{1}{2}(x - b)^T f_{xx}(b)(x - b) \qquad (9)$$

Comparing this with (5), the additional term is called the second-order term. The particular structure proves to be important in problems of maximization. The following sub-section paves the way for this.

## Quadratic forms

Let $M$ be an $n$-by-$n$ symmetric matrix, and let a function $q: R^n \to R$ be defined as the inner product $y \cdot My$, or

$$q(y) = y^T M y \qquad \text{for } y \text{ in } R^n \qquad (10)$$

Such a function is called a *quadratic form*. The form is called *negative semi-definite* if $q(y) \leq 0$ for all $y$ in $R^n$, *negative definite* if $q(y) < 0$ for all non-zero $y$ in $R^n$.

The test for these properties is as follows. Pick any $k$ rows of the matrix, and the $k$ columns with the same numbering, for example $k = 3$, and the first, third, and sixth row and column. The $k$-by-$k$ matrix formed by elements in these rows and columns is called a principal minor of size $k$. For $M$ to be negative semi-definite, each principal minor of size $k$ should have a non-positive determinant for $k = 1, 3, 5, \ldots$ and a non-negative determinant for $k = 2, 4, 6, \ldots$. For negative definiteness, it is further required that the inequalities indicated should all hold strictly, i.e. such a minor of size $k$ should have a determinant of sign $(-1)^k$.

A square symmetric matrix $M$ is called negative (semi-)definite if the quadratic form it defines according to (10) has this property. It is called positive (semi-)definite if $-M$ is negative (semi-)definite; the readers can derive the tests using those stated above.

## Concave functions

Let $D$ be a convex subset of $R^n$, and consider a function $f: D \to R$. It is called *concave* if the set $S$ in $R^{n+1}$ defined by

$$S = \{(x, y) \mid x \in D, y \in R, y \le f(x)\}$$

is convex. The idea is that the graph of a concave function traps a convex set underneath it. Whether the function is increasing or decreasing is immaterial. Figure A.6 illustrates three cases where $D$ is a subset of $R$, and one where $D$ is a subset of $R^2$.

To test the concavity of $f$, we take any two points $(x', y')$, $(x'', y'')$ in $S$ and any number $\lambda$ satisfying $0 \le \lambda \le 1$, and see whether the point $(\lambda x' + (1 - \lambda)x'', \lambda y' + (1 - \lambda)y'')$ is in $S$. We have chosen $x'$, $x''$ in $D$, which is a convex set, so $\lambda x' + (1 - \lambda)x''$ is in $D$. It remains to see whether

$$\lambda y' + (1 - \lambda)y'' \le f(\lambda x' + (1 - \lambda)x'')$$

By definition of $S$, we have $y' \le f(x')$ and $y'' \le f(x'')$. The most severe test we seek therefore occurs when $y' = f(x')$ and $y'' = f(x'')$. This gives us an alternative characterization of concavity: $f$ is concave if, for any $x'$, $x''$ in $D$, and any $\lambda$ satisfying $0 \le \lambda \le 1$, we have

$$\lambda f(x') + (1 - \lambda)f(x'') \le f(\lambda x' + (1 - \lambda)x'') \tag{11}$$

Figure A.7 illustrates this for $D \subset R$. The intuitive idea is that the chord joining any two points on the graph of the function should lie everywhere below, or at most on, this graph.

This suggests a strengthening: call $f$ *strictly concave* if, for distinct $x'$, $x''$ in $D$, and $0 < \lambda < 1$,

$$\lambda f(x') + (1 - \lambda)f(x'') < f(\lambda x' + (1 - \lambda)x'') \tag{12}$$

In Figure A.6, for example, the function in case (a) is concave but not strictly concave; those in cases (b) and (d) are strictly concave.

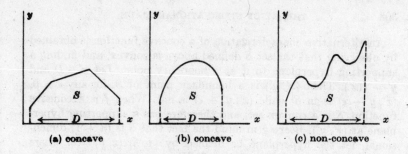

(a) concave       (b) concave       (c) non-concave

(d) concave

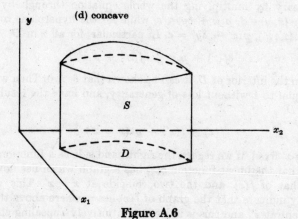

**Figure A.6**

$f(x'')$

$f(\lambda x' + (1-\lambda)x'')$

$\lambda f(x') + (1-\lambda)f(x'')$

$f(x')$

$x'$    $\lambda x' + (1-\lambda)x''$    $x''$

**Figure A.7**

An alternative characterization of a concave function is obtained by observing that the set $S$ defined above is convex, and finding a supporting hyperplane to it at a boundary point. Let $x' \in D$ and $y' = f(x')$. Then $(x', y')$ is a boundary point of $S$: for any $\epsilon > 0$, $(x', y' - \epsilon)$ is in $S$ while $(x', y' + \epsilon)$ is not. When $f$ is a concave function, $S$ is a convex set, and therefore has a supporting hyperplane at $(x', y')$. Bearing in mind the fact that $S$ is $(n + 1)$-dimensional, let the hyperplane be defined by $(p, \delta).(x, y) = c$, where $p \in R^n$ and $\delta \in R$, i.e. $p.x + \delta y = c$. We can always choose $\delta \geq 0$, if necessary by multiplying the whole equation through by $-1$. Then for $(x, y) \in S$, $p.x + \delta y \leq c$, while for the hyperplane to pass through $(x', y')$, $p.x' + \delta y' = c$. In particular, for all $x$ in $D$,

$$\delta f(x) + p.x \leq \delta f(x') + p.x'$$

If $x'$ is in the interior of $D$, it can be shown that $\delta > 0$. Then we can set it equal to 1 without loss of generality, and have the result: for all $x$ in $D$,

$$f(x) \leq f(x') + p.(x - x') \qquad (13)$$

Holding $x'$ fixed, if we regard the right-hand side as a function $g(x)$, we see that the linear function $g(x)$ has a graph which lies nowhere below that of $f(x)$, and the two coincide at $x = x'$. This would normally indicate that the graph of $f(x)$ lies nowhere above that of its tangent at $x'$, and this is indeed an intuitively appealing characterization of concavity. However, we know that there need not be a unique supporting hyperplane to a convex set at a boundary point where the set has a corner. Correspondingly, the graph of $f(x)$ will not have a unique tangent at $x'$ if the graph has a kink there, i.e. if the function fails to be differentiable. Figure A.8 illustrates the cases. We can say that a supporting hyperplane is a generalized tangent.

To see this more precisely, choose $x$ different from $x'$ only in the $j$th component, with $x_j = x'_j + h$. Then (13) becomes

$$f(x) - f(x') \leq p_j h$$

Dividing by $h$,

$$(f(x) - f(x'))/h \leq p_j \qquad \text{if } h > 0$$
$$\geq p_j \qquad \text{if } h < 0$$

Next take limits as $h$ goes to zero. The limit of the ratio on the left-hand side as $h$ goes to zero through positive values is by definition the 'right-handed' partial derivative of $f$ with respect to the $j$th

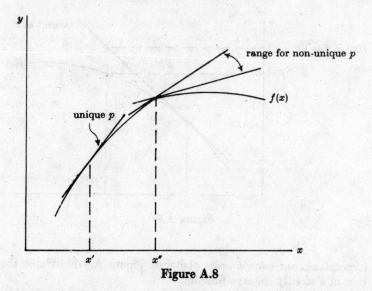

**Figure A.8**

argument at $x'$; write it as $f_{j+}(x')$. The limit from negative values of $h$ is similarly the 'left-handed' partial derivative $f_{j-}(x')$. Therefore

$$f_{j-}(x') \geq p_j \geq f_{j+}(x') \tag{14}$$

Accordingly in Figure A.8, the slopes of the graph to the left and right of a kink point such as $x''$ provide limits to the range in which the slope of a supporting line can lie. If the function is differentiable, the two one-sided partial derivatives are equal, each being simply the partial derivative $f_j(x')$, and then (14) collapses to $f_j(x') = p_j$, or collecting such equations over $j$, we have

$$p = f_x(x') \tag{15}$$

For a differentiable function, therefore, we have another characterization of concavity: $f$ is concave if, for any $x$, $x'$, we have

$$f(x) \leq f(x') + f_x(x') \cdot (x - x') \tag{16}$$

i.e. any first-order Taylor approximation is an overestimate of the corresponding change in the value of the function. For a strictly concave function, this overestimation is strict whenever $x$ and $x'$ are distinct. A function which is concave but not strictly concave can have a graph that coincides with its tangent or supporting

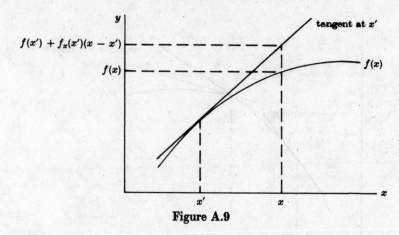

**Figure A.9**

hyperplane, but cannot cross above it. Figure A.9 illustrates the case of a strictly concave function.

Now consider a concave function that is twice differentiable. Compare the first- and second-order Taylor approximations (5) and (9). If the former is to be an overestimate, the added terms in the latter must be non-positive, and negative in the case of a strictly concave function. In other words, for all $x$ and $x'$ we must have

$$(x - x')^T f_{xx}(x')(x - x') \leq 0 \qquad (17)$$

for a concave function, while a strictly concave function must have the same expression negative for distinct $x$ and $x'$. This means that a concave function requires the matrix $f_{xx}(x')$ to be negative semi-definite. In particular, letting $x$ and $x'$ differ only in the $j$th component, we see that a concave function requires $f_{jj}(x') \leq 0$ for all $j$ and all $x'$. For a function of one (scaler) variable, the requirement is simply that the sign of the second derivative be non-positive, i.e. that the first derivative be non-increasing. If the various conditions hold in the strict sense, e.g. if $f_{xx}(x')$ is everywhere negative definite, or in the case of a scalar argument, $f''(x')$ is negative, then the function is strictly concave.

This gives us the common economic setting in which the property of concavity arises. If $x$ is input and $f(x)$ is output, the first derivative has the interpretation of marginal product, and concavity then corresponds to this marginal product being non-increasing, while strict concavity has it diminishing. The case of a kink in the graph is one where the marginal product drops suddenly as a point is

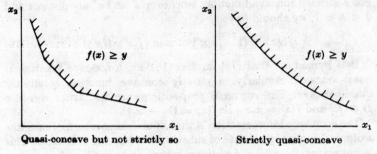

Quasi-concave but not strictly so          Strictly quasi-concave

**Figure A.10**

crossed; then a unique marginal product at the point itself cannot be defined, but bounds for it can be established by reference to the marginal products of the last and the next doses of the input.

A function $f: D \to R$ is called *convex* (resp. strictly convex) if the function $g: D \to R$ defined by $g(x) = -f(x)$ for all $x$ in $D$ is concave (resp. strictly concave). The various characterizations using chords, tangents and their generalizations, and second-order derivatives, can be developed similarly and are left to the reader.

A result concerning composite functions is sometimes useful: If $f: D \to R$ is concave, and $g: R \to R$ increasing and concave, then the composite $h: D \to R$ defined by $h(x) = g(f(x))$ is concave.

### Quasi-concave functions

Once again, let $D$ be a convex set in $R^n$, and consider $f: D \to R$. For $y$ in $R$, the set in $R^n$ defined by $\{x \mid f(x) \geq y\}$ is called an *upper contour set* of $f$. In other words, an upper contour set consists of one contour and all higher ones. A function is called *quasi-concave* if all its upper contour sets are convex; *strictly quasi-concave* if they are all strictly convex. Figure A.10 illustrates these ideas by showing typical upper contour sets.

Quasi-concavity is thus a rigorous formulation of the economic concept of a diminishing marginal rate of substitution along an isoquant or an indifference curve.

To express the convexity of an upper contour set algebraically, we require that whenever $f(x') \geq y$ and $f(x'') \geq y$, and $0 \leq \lambda \leq 1$, we have $f(\lambda x' + (1 - \lambda)x'') \geq y$. This is equivalent to requiring, for all $x'$, $x''$ in $D$ and $0 \leq \lambda \leq 1$,

$$f(\lambda x' + (1 - \lambda)x'') \geq \min\left(f(x'), f(x'')\right) \tag{18}$$

For a strictly concave function, whenever $x'$ and $x''$ are distinct and $0 < \lambda < 1$, we should have

$$f(\lambda x' + (1 - \lambda)x'') > \min (f(x'), f(x'')) \qquad (19)$$

It is immediate that (11) implies (18), i.e. a concave function is quasi-concave. Similarly, a strictly concave function is strictly quasi-concave. The converse propositions are not true; consider $D \subset R^2$ and $f(x) = x_1 x_2$, or $f(x) = (x_1 + x_2)^2$.

The economic interpretation is that diminishing returns guarantee a diminishing marginal rate of substitution, but not vice versa. This is important for utility functions, where for a model of consumer choice we require only the latter property.

The lower contour sets of a function are defined in the obvious way, and (strict) quasi-convexity is defined as the (strict) convexity of all lower contour sets.

The quasi-concavity of composite functions is easily established: If $f: D \to R$ is quasi-concave and $g: R \to R$ is increasing, then the composite $h: D \to R$ defined by $h(x) = g(f(x))$ is quasi-concave. The analogous result for strictly quasi-concave functions is also true. Economically, quasi-concavity of utility is preserved under increasing transformations.

## Homogeneous functions

In this section we take the domain of the functions to be the non-negative orthant of $R^n$, written $N^n$ and defined as $\{x \mid x \in R^n, x \geq 0\}$. It is possible to establish similar results in more general settings, but that is unnecessary for our purpose.

A function $f: N^n \to R$ is called *homogeneous of degree* $k$, if, for all $x$ in $N^n$ and all non-negative $\lambda$, we have

$$f(\lambda x) = \lambda^k f(x) \qquad (20)$$

The economic significance of this concept is focused on two cases. When $k = 1$, (20) becomes $f(\lambda x) = \lambda f(x)$. If we regard $x$ as a vector of inputs and $f(x)$ as outputs, this is the idea of constant returns to scale: changing all input quantities proportionately changes output in the same proportion. When $k = 0$, (20) is $f(\lambda x) = f(x)$. Here the value of the function is independent of the scale of the vector $x$, but depends only on the relative proportions of its components. This corresponds to the irrelevance of absolute levels of all prices and money income together in determining the demand for a commodity. Incidentally, a function that is homogeneous of degree one is often called *linearly homogeneous*.

A very important property of homogeneous functions is given by *Euler's Theorem*: If $f$ is homogeneous of degree $k$, and $x \gg 0$, we have

$$\sum_{j=1}^{n} f_j(x)x_j \equiv f_x(x) \cdot x = k f(x) \qquad (21)$$

To prove this, we fix $x$, regard both sides in (20) as functions of $\lambda$, and differentiate with respect to $\lambda$, using the chain rule on the left-hand side. Then set $\lambda = 1$ to obtain (21).

For the case $k = 1$, Euler's Theorem has the economic interpretation of the Wicksteed Imputation Theorem. Let $x$ be a vector of inputs and $f(x)$ the output, and let constant returns to scale prevail. Suppose factor markets competitive, so that the equilibrium price of each input in terms of the output equals its marginal product. Then the total payment to factors, $\sum f_j(x)x_j$, will exactly exhaust the output, $f(x)$.

It is useful to know what happens to homogeneous functions upon differentiation. If $f$ is homogeneous of degree $k$, each of its partial derivatives $f_j$ is homogeneous of degree $(k - 1)$. Sometimes a function is homogeneous in a subset of its arguments. If $f(x, y)$ is homogeneous of degree $k$ in the first set of variables, i.e. $f(\lambda x, y) = \lambda^k f(x, y)$, then each $f_{x_i}$ is homogeneous of degree $(k - 1)$ in $x$, but each $f_{y_j}$ is homogeneous of degree $k$ in $x$.

The following useful theorem relates homogeneity and convexity: If $f: N^n \to R$ is quasi-concave, non-negative valued, and homogeneous of degree $k$ for $0 \leqslant k < 1$, then it is concave.

## Homothetic functions

A function $f: N^n \to R$ is called homothetic if, for all $x'$, $x''$ in $N^n$ satisfying $f(x') = f(x'')$, and for all non-negative $\lambda$, we have $f(\lambda x') = f(\lambda x'')$. Figure A.11 illustrates this. The requirement is that all contours of $f$ should be radial scale replicas of one another.

If the value of $f$ increased in the same proportion along these contours, the function would be homogeneous of degree one. But that is not needed for homotheticity. This is economically relevant for utility functions. Homogeneity of degree one, i.e. constant returns to scale, is not a meaningful property for an ordinal utility scale. However, the property that indifference between two consumption bundles should be preserved if each is magnified or shrunk in the same proportion is a meaningful one.

However, there is a close connection between homotheticity and homogeneity. If $f: N^n \to R$ is homothetic and increasing in its

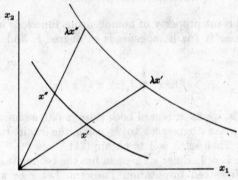

**Figure A.11**

arguments, then we can find $g: N^n \to R$ which is homogeneous of degree one, and $h: R \to R$ which is increasing, such that $f$ is the composite defined by $f(x) = h(g(x))$.

To see this, fix an $\bar{x} \gg 0$, and define $g$ by the following rule: For any $x$, choose $\lambda$ such that $f(\lambda\bar{x}) = f(x)$, and then set $g(x) = \lambda$. Since $f(\lambda\bar{x}) = f(x)$ implies $f(\mu\lambda\bar{x}) = f(\mu x)$ by homotheticity, we have $g(\mu x) = \mu g(x)$, i.e. $g$ is homogeneous of degree one. Further, from the way $g$ is defined, $g(x') = g(x'')$ if and only if $f(x') = f(x'')$, i.e. the contours of the two coincide. Since they are both increasing, each must be an increasing transform of the other.

In other words, given a homothetic utility function, we can find another ordinal scale which is homogeneous of degree one to represent the same indifference map.

## 3. OPTIMIZATION

It should be emphasized that the following is a very sketchy account of the theory. Only brief proofs or intuitive explanations are given. A condition called the constraint qualification is omitted altogether since it poses no problems in the particular applications in the book.

### Lagrange's method

Let $f: R^n \to R$ be a scalar-valued function, $g: R^n \to R^m$ a vector-valued function with component functions $g^i: R^n \to R$, $m < n$, and $c \in R^m$. Consider the following maximization problem with equality constraints: choose $x \in R^n$ to maximize $f(x)$ subject to $g(x) = c$. In our set-theoretic notation, this will be written as

$$\max_{x} \{f(x) \mid g(x) = c\}$$

Lagrange's Method proceeds with the solution as follows. Introduce auxiliary variables called *Lagrange multipliers* $\lambda \in R^m$, and define a function $L: R^{n+m} \to R$, called the *Lagrangean*, by

$$L(x, \lambda) = f(x) - \lambda^T(g(x) - c)$$

$$= f(x) - \sum_{i=1}^{m} \lambda_i(g^i(x) - c_i) \tag{22}$$

Then the solution $x$ and the multipliers $\lambda$ satisfy the following conditions

$$L_x(x, \lambda) \equiv f_x(x) - \lambda^T g_x(x) = 0 \tag{23}$$

$$L_\lambda(x, \lambda) \equiv c - g(x) = 0 \tag{24}$$

The conditions are called the *first-order necessary conditions*: they involve first-order derivatives of the Lagrangean, and are necessarily satisfied at a solution point. They provide $(m + n)$ equations, which as a rough check are right for the determination of the $(m + n)$ numbers involved in $x$ and $\lambda$. We shall not pursue the matter of existence of a solution—this will never be a problem in the applications that interest us in this book—but we will look at the issue of sufficiency of such conditions to determine an optimum later in a more general context.

The optimum choice $x$, the corresponding Lagrange multipliers $\lambda$, and the maximum value $v = f(x)$ are all functions of $c$. In particular, we have the important result providing an interpretation of the Lagrange multipliers:

$$\lambda_i = \partial v / \partial c_i \quad \text{or} \quad \lambda = v_c(c) \tag{25}$$

Thus each Lagrange multiplier gives us the effect on the maximand of altering the right-hand side of the corresponding constraint by a marginal unit. Therefore it can be interpreted as the shadow price or shadow valuation placed on its constraint, i.e. the maximum amount in terms of the objective function value that the solver of the problem would be willing to pay if that would secure a marginal unit relaxation of the constraint. For a consumer maximizing utility subject to a budget constraint, for example, the Lagrange multiplier on the budget constraint gives the marginal utility of the exogenous money income appearing on the right-hand side. For a firm minimizing the cost of producing a given target level of output, the multiplier is simply the marginal cost (of output).

### Envelope theorem

More generally, let $\theta$ be a vector of parameters appearing in the objective function and the constraint functions. Consider the problem of maximizing $f(x, \theta)$ subject to $g(x, \theta) = 0$. (Note that our earlier problem can be cast in this form by moving the $c_i$ to the left-hand side and redefining the functions $g^i$, with the $c_i$ relabelled $\theta_i$.) The Lagrangean is defined as

$$L(x, \lambda, \theta) = f(x, \theta) - \lambda^T g(x, \theta) \tag{26}$$

The first-order necessary conditions are

$$L_x(x, \lambda, \theta) \equiv f_x(x, \theta) - \lambda^T g_x(x, \theta) = 0 \tag{27}$$

$$L_\lambda(x, \lambda, \theta) \equiv -g(x, \theta) = 0 \tag{28}$$

Writing $v(\theta)$ as the value $f(x, \theta)$ when $x$ is optimally chosen, we have

$$v_\theta(\theta) = L_\theta(x, \lambda, \theta) \tag{29}$$

evaluated at the optimum choices of $x$ and $\lambda$. This last result is known as the *envelope theorem*, or the *envelope property*, and accordingly the function $v$ is sometimes called the *envelope function* of the problem.

The practical importance of this result should be clear. If we were to differentiate $v(\theta) = f(x, \theta)$ directly, remembering that the optimum $x$ itself depends on $\theta$, we would have to use the chain rule, and then determine the dependence of $x$ on $\theta$ using the complicated conditions (27) and (28). But the general result says that the outcome of doing all this is quite simple, and can be obtained indirectly by taking the *partial* derivative of the Lagrangean with respect to $\theta$, and evaluating it at the optimum $x$ and $\lambda$.

The special case where the parameters $\theta$ affect only the objective function is even simpler. Now $g_\theta$ is identically zero, and (29) reduces to

$$v_\theta(\theta) = f_\theta(x, \theta) \tag{30}$$

In other words, we need only count the direct effect of the parameters on the maximand, neglecting the indirect effect through induced change in the optimum choice $x$. This can be explained quite simply. Consider the case of a single parameter. Let $\bar{\theta}$ be a particular value of it, and $\bar{x}$ the corresponding optimum choice of

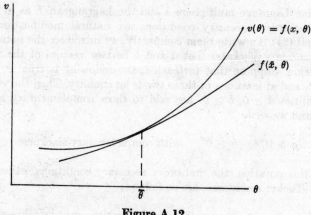

**Figure A.12**

the variables. Since the parameter does not affect the constraint
functions, $\bar{x}$ remains a feasible choice for all parameter values. For
any $\theta$, by selecting $\bar{x}$, it is always possible to attain the value
$f(\bar{x}, \theta)$ for the objective function. But this need not be the best
procedure for that $\theta$. If we make the best choice $x$, in order to
maximize the value of the function, we will then have $f(x, \theta) \geq$
$f(\bar{x}, \theta)$. Since $\bar{x}$ is the best choice for $\bar{\theta}$, the relation will hold as an
equality for $\theta = \bar{\theta}$. If we depict the two sides of the inequality as
functions of $\theta$, the relation between them will be shown in Figure
A.12. Assuming the functions to be differentiable at $\bar{\theta}$, their slopes
will be equal; this is just the envelope result (30). Further, their
curvatures will stand in a definite relation: $v(\theta) = f(x, \theta)$ with $x$
chosen optimally will be more convex, or less concave, than $f(\bar{x}, \theta)$
with $\bar{x}$ fixed. We will return to such second-order properties in a
more general context shortly.

### Kuhn–Tucker theory

Here we consider maximization subject to inequality and sign
constraints. This is important in economic applications because it is
sometimes desirable to retain slack in some constraints in economic
optimization, and many variables in these problems are naturally
restricted to be non-negative. Let $f: N^n \to R$, $g: N^n \to R^m$, and
$c \in R^m$; it is not necessary here to place any restrictions on the relative magnitudes of $m$ and $n$. Consider the problem of choosing $x$ to
maximize $f(x)$ subject to $g(x) \leq c$. Note that restricting the domain
to $N^n$, we have automatically imposed constraints $x \geq 0$.

Define Lagrange multipliers $\lambda$ and the Lagrangean $L$ as in (22). The first-order necessary conditions are natural modifications of (23) and (24). To write them compactly, we introduce the notion of *complementary slackness*. Let $a$ and $b$ be two vectors of the same dimension. Suppose that for each $i$, the following is true: $a_i \geq 0$, $b_i \geq 0$, and at least one of these two is an equality. Then the vector inequalities $a \geq 0$, $b \geq 0$, are said to show complementary slackness, and we write

$$a \geq 0, \quad b \geq 0 \quad \text{with complementary slackness}$$

With this notation, the first-order necessary conditions, called the Kuhn–Tucker conditions, are as follows:

$$L_x(x, \lambda) \leq 0, \quad x \geq 0 \quad \text{with complementary slackness}$$
$$(31)$$

$$L_\lambda(x, \lambda) \geq 0, \quad \lambda \geq 0 \quad \text{with complementary slackness}$$
$$(32)$$

To explain these, consider (31) first. By definition of complementary slackness, for each component $j$, we have $\partial L/\partial x_j \leq 0$ and $x_j \geq 0$, with at least one equality. For example, if $x_j > 0$, then $\partial L/\partial x_j$ must equal zero, i.e. if the non-negativity constraint is not binding, we have a condition exactly like the corresponding component condition in (23) where sign constraints were absent. The modification arises when the non-negativity constraint is binding, i.e. $x_j = 0$. Then the component of (31) must be left as $\partial L/\partial x_j \leq 0$. This is a natural condition for maximization to occur at the end of the range of the permissible values of the variable, namely that the function should start to decrease as we move away from the end-point.

The interpretation of (32) is assisted by recalling the shadow price interpretation of the Lagrange multipliers. Writing a component of (32) as $c_i - g^i(x) \geq 0$, $\lambda_i \geq 0$, with at least one equality, we have the conclusion that if $g^i(x) < c_i$, then $\lambda_i$ must equal zero. Now remember that $\lambda_i$ is the increase in $f(x)$ that is achievable following a marginal unit increase in $c_i$. Since an increase in $c_i$ leaves the old optimum choice feasible, the maximum value cannot decrease; this is reflected in the non-negativity of $\lambda_i$. But if a constraint is not binding, a further relaxation of it gains nothing, and therefore $\lambda_i$ must be zero for such a constraint. This is the interpretation of complementary slackness.

## Sufficiency and uniqueness

Consider the problem of maximizing $f(x)$ subject to $x \geq 0$, $g(x) \leq c$ as in the previous section. We have two results that enable us to be sure we have found a solution.

*Sufficiency theorem*: If $f$ is concave and each $g^i$ is convex, and if $x$ and $\lambda$ satisfy (31) and (32), then $x$ is optimum in the weak sense that no feasible choice can yield a higher value of the objective function.

This is quite easy to establish, and the argument provides a useful recapitulation of the concepts defined earlier. With $f$ concave and each $g^i$ convex, and each $\lambda^i$ non-negative, an inspection of (22) shows that $L$ is concave as a function of $x$. Let $x'$ be any feasible choice, i.e. satisfying $x' \geq 0$, $g(x') \leq c$. Let $x$ be feasible and satisfy (31) and (32). We show that $f(x') \leq f(x)$.

Consider the first-order Taylor approximation to $L$ around $x$. By concavity, as in (16) but with the roles of $x$ and $x'$ interchanged, we have

$$L(x', \lambda) \leq L(x, \lambda) + L_x(x, \lambda).(x' - x)$$

Now

$$L(x', \lambda) = f(x') - \sum_{i=1}^{m} \lambda_i(g^i(x') - c_i)$$
$$\geq f(x')$$

since $\lambda_i \geq 0$ and $g^i(x') \leq c_i$ for each $i$, while

$$L(x, \lambda) = f(x) - \sum_{i=1}^{m} \lambda_i(g^i(x) - c_i)$$
$$= f(x)$$

since one of $\lambda_i \geq 0$ and $g^i(x) \leq c_i$ is an equation for each $i$.

Next, $L_x(x, \lambda).x' \leq 0$ since each component of $L_x(x, \lambda)$ is $\leq 0$ while $x' \geq 0$. Finally, $L_x(x, \lambda).x = 0$ since complementary slackness ensures that each term in the inner product is zero. Using all these results in the above Taylor approximation, the conclusion emerges.

This result is behind several of the arguments in Chapter 2. Sometimes, as in the maximization of an ordinal utility function, we cannot rely on concavity. However, the following uniqueness result often applies. When the optimum choice is unique, knowing that it must satisfy the necessary conditions, we can conclude that if we have found a solution to (31) and (32), we have found the optimum.

*Uniqueness theorem*: If $f$ is strictly quasi-concave, and each $g^i$ is convex, then the maximizing choice of $x$ is unique.

To see this, suppose two feasible choices $x'$ and $x''$ yield the same value $f(x') = f(x'') = v$, and that it is the maximum feasible value. By feasibility, $x' \geq 0$, $x'' \geq 0$, and for each $i$, $g^i(x') \leq c_i$, $g^i(x'') \leq c_i$. Then $\frac{1}{2}(x' + x'') \geq 0$, and by convexity of each $g^i$,

$$g^i(\tfrac{1}{2}(x' + x'')) \leq \tfrac{1}{2}g^i(x') + \tfrac{1}{2}g^i(x'') \leq \tfrac{1}{2}c_i + \tfrac{1}{2}c_i = c_i,$$

so $\frac{1}{2}(x' + x'')$ is feasible. But by the strict quasi-concavity of $f$,

$$f(\tfrac{1}{2}(x' + x'')) > \min\left(f(x'), f(x'')\right) = \min(v, v) = v$$

This contradicts the hypothesis that $v$ is the maximum feasible value.

## Typology of solutions

The conditions (31) and (32) for maximization with inequality constraints contain $(n + m)$ equations, since each pair of component inequalities is guaranteed to have one equation by complementary slackness. Call a particular pattern of inequalities and equations to emerge from (31) and (32) a *regime*. The determination of the regime that prevails in the solution is of course a part of the whole problem of maximization. Thus, for the first component in (32), we have to find out whether $g^1(x) = c_1$ or $\lambda_1 = 0$ (or indeed both, a possibility allowed by complementary slackness). If we alter the problem by changing some parameters, the solution may move from one regime to another. For example, if $c_1$ is increased starting from low levels, we may first have a phase where the constraint is binding, and then for large $c_1$ move into a phase where the constraint is slack so that the shadow price is zero. At the transition point, we will have both $g^1(x) = c_1$ and $\lambda_1 = 0$.

A general theory of the selection of a regime and of transitions from one regime to another would be fruitless. In particular contexts, we will have occasion to observe some crucial transitions and their consequences.

The selection of a regime is essentially the determination of which constraints are binding and thus may be regarded as equality constraints, and which ones are slack and may be forgotten. Once this has been done, the maximization problem is exactly like the earlier one with equality constraints. The envelope theorem giving the results of parametric variations developed earlier for the case of equality constraints thus extends to the case of inequality constraints so long as the parametric variation does not cause a transition from one regime to another. If such a transition occurs, new problems, including those of a failure of differentiability at the boundary, arise.

## Concavity of envelope functions

Consider the general problem of maximization subject to inequality constraints involving parameters. We wish to examine the curvature of the envelope function in its dependence on the parameters. There are two results in this regard that have useful applications for our purpose, one where the parameters enter only into the objective function, the other where they only enter into the constraints.

Let $\theta$ be a general vector of parameters, and first consider the problem of maximizing $f(x, \theta)$ subject to the constraints $g(x) \le 0$. Let $v(\theta)$ be the envelope function. We show that, if $f$ is convex as a function of $\theta$ for each fixed $x$, then $v$ is convex.

This is essentially the result of Figure A.12, but we can offer a simple general proof for the case of inequality constraints, without placing any restrictions on the functions $g$. Let $\theta'$ and $\theta''$ be any two values of the parameter vector, and let $\lambda$ be a number with $0 \le \lambda \le 1$. Let $\bar{x}$ solve the maximization problem when the parameter vector takes on the value $\lambda\theta' + (1 - \lambda)\theta''$. By the convexity of $f$ in $\theta$,

$$v(\lambda\theta' + (1 - \lambda)\theta'') = f(\bar{x}, \lambda\theta' + (1 - \lambda)\theta'')$$

$$\le \lambda f(\bar{x}, \theta') + (1 - \lambda)f(\bar{x}, \theta'')$$

The constraint functions being independent of the parameters, $\bar{x}$ remains feasible for parameter values $\theta'$ and $\theta''$. Since the maximum value of the objective function can be no less than any feasible value we have $f(\bar{x}, \theta') \le v(\theta')$ and $f(\bar{x}, \theta'') \le v(\theta'')$. With $\lambda$ and $(1 - \lambda)$ both non-negative, $\lambda f(\bar{x}, \theta') + (1 - \lambda)f(\bar{x}, \theta'') \le \lambda v(\theta') + (1 - \lambda)v(\theta'')$. Putting this together with the earlier inequality, we have

$$v(\lambda\theta' + (1 - \lambda)\theta'') \le \lambda v(\theta') + (1 - \lambda)v(\theta'')$$

as required. The formal steps are really a paraphrase of the informal argument of Figure A.12: it is always possible to keep $x$ fixed and vary $\theta$ alone, securing $f(x, \theta)$ which is already convex. If $x$ is chosen optimally, the result can be no worse.

A particularly important case is where $f$ is linear in $\theta$, as is the case when the parameters are prices and the objective is cost or value.

Next consider a case where the parameters affect only the constraints. Let the objective function be $f(x)$. We will express the constraints somewhat more generally, by requiring that the combined vector $(x, \theta)$ should lie in a specified set $S$ in $R^{n+p}$, where $n$ is the number of variables and $p$ that of the parameters. An obvious special case is where the set is defined by functional inequalities, as with $g: R^{n+p} \rightarrow R^m$, $S = \{(x, \theta) \mid g(x, \theta) \leq 0\}$.

We prove that if the set $S$ is convex, and $f$ is concave, then the envelope function $v(\theta)$ giving the maximum of $f(x)$ subject to $(x, \theta) \in S$ is a concave function. For a set defined by functional inequalities as above, it is sufficient for its convexity to have each component function $g^i$ convex.

The reasoning is again simple. Let $\theta'$ and $\theta''$ be any two parameter values, and let $x'$ and $x''$ be the corresponding optimum choices. Then $(x', \theta')$ and $(x'', \theta'')$ are in $S$, and $v(\theta') = f(x')$, $v(\theta'') = f(x'')$. Let $\lambda$ satisfy $0 \leq \lambda \leq 1$. Since $S$ is a convex set, $(\lambda x' + (1 - \lambda)x''$, $\lambda \theta' + (1 - \lambda)\theta'')$ is in $S$, i.e. $\lambda x' + (1 - \lambda)x''$ is a feasible choice of the variables for parameter values $\lambda \theta' + (1 - \lambda)\theta''$. Since the optimum value can be no less than any feasible value,

$$v(\lambda \theta' + (1 - \lambda)\theta'') \geq f(\lambda x' + (1 - \lambda)x'')$$

$$\geq \lambda f(x') + (1 - \lambda)f(x'') \qquad \text{since } f \text{ is concave}$$

$$= \lambda v(\theta') + (1 - \lambda)v(\theta'')$$

which completes the proof.

## Minimization

Since minimization of $f(x)$ is achieved by maximization of $-f(x)$, a separate account of the theory of minimization is unnecessary. Interested readers can re-cast the various conditions and results above for minimization problems. With some care taken when replacing concavity by convexity etc., there should be no difficulties in doing so.

## 4. APPLICATIONS: COST AND REVENUE FUNCTIONS

In this section we put several of the above concepts and results to work, and construct two functions that are used repeatedly in the book. Some of this material is duplicated in Chapter 2 for readers who have skipped the Mathematical Appendix. But for those who have worked through it, the continuity from theory to application seemed useful, and the recapitulation in Chapter 2 will do no harm.

### The cost function

The principles of the mathematical theory are unchanged, but we alter the symbols to suit the convention in each economic application. Let $v$ be a vector of factor inputs, and $x$ a scalar output, related to the inputs by a production function $f$. Let $w$ be the vector of input prices, and consider the cost-minimization problem

$$\min_{v} \{w.v \mid f(v) = x\}$$

Here $v$ are the choice variables, and the factor prices $w$ and the target output level $x$, the parameters. The envelope function is the resulting minimum cost expressed as a function of the parameters, say $c(w, x)$. This is called the *cost function* dual to the production function $f$. Our aim is to examine its properties.

The simplest observation is that for fixed $x$, the cost function is homogeneous of degree one in $w$. This follows from the fact that input prices do not affect feasibility of input quantities. So let $v'$ be the optimum choice for $w'$, and let $\lambda$ be a positive number. Since $v'$ remains feasible when the parameter values are $\lambda w'$, we have $c(\lambda w', x) \le (\lambda w').v' = \lambda w'.v' = \lambda c(w', x)$. The reverse inequality is established when we start with the optimum choice for $\lambda w'$, and thus $c(\lambda w', x) = \lambda c(w', x)$. Since $w'$ could be arbitrary, the result follows.

The economic argument behind this result is that an equiproportionate change in all input prices does not create any incentives for substitution of one input by another. The optimum input mix remains unchanged; all that happens is that its cost changes equiproportionately with prices.

To derive further properties as corollaries of our earlier general theorems, let us express the problem as a maximization problem:

$$-c(w, x) = \max_{v} \{-w.v \mid -f(v) + x \le 0\} \tag{33}$$

Introducing a Lagrange multiplier $\lambda$, the Lagrangean is

$$L = -w.v - \lambda(-f(v) + x)$$

By the envelope theorem, we have $-c_x = L_x$ evaluated at the optimum. Hence $c_x = \lambda$, which confirms the interpretation of the multiplier as a shadow price: it gives the effect on cost of a marginal unit change in the target output level, i.e. marginal cost. Next, $-c_w = L_w = -v$ evaluated at the optimum. In other words, the optimum input choices $v$ can be found simply by differentiating the cost function with respect to factor prices. The optimum input choices for given factor prices and output levels are of course the conditional factor demand functions for a fixed output, written as $v(w, x)$. Thus we have

$$v(w, x) = c_w(w, x) \qquad (34)$$

Since $c$ is homogeneous of degree one in $w$, the conditional factor demand functions are homogeneous of degree zero in $w$, which confirms the earlier assertion that an equiproportionate change in all input prices does not change the optimum input mix.

Continue to fix $x$, and consider $c$ as a function of $w$. We next examine its concavity, noting that $w$ does not affect the constraints of the problem in (33). For fixed $v$, the objective function is linear, and therefore convex (although only just) in $w$. Therefore the envelope function $-c$ is convex in $w$, i.e. $c$ is concave in $w$. The argument is essentially that of Figure A.12, modified for the minimization problem. If there were only one input combination $v$ that could produce the fixed output target $x$, i.e. if fixed coefficients ruled in production, there would be no choice left in the cost-minimization problem and we would have a linear cost function $c(w, x) = w.v$ for fixed $v$. If there is any substitution possible, this is used in order to reduce cost, so the cost function increases less than linearly with factor prices, i.e. it is concave. If $v'$ is the optimum choice for a particular $w'$, then, the linear function $w.v'$ serves as a supporting hyperplane for the concave function $c(w, x)$: the two coincide at $w'$, and the latter has a lower value elsewhere. If $c$ is differentiable, the coefficient vector $v'$ of the hyperplane is simply the derivative vector of $c$ at the point of contact, i.e. $v' = c_w(w', x)$. The general statement of this is in (34).

If we differentiate each factor demand with respect to the price of that factor in (34), we have

$$\partial v_i / \partial w_i = \partial^2 c / \partial w_i^2 \leq 0$$

by concavity. Thus we can sign the substitution effect of the own-price change on a factor demand.

Some other consequences of the homogeneity of the cost function are developed in Chapter 2.

In the work so far, we have not had to impose any restrictions on the production function at all, whether homogeneity, concavity or even quasi-concavity. If the production function is quasi-concave, it can be shown that the cost function is fully dual in the sense that given a cost function satisfying the above properties, it is possible to work back to a unique production function. In actual applications, we will usually wish to characterize competitive equilibria, and will work with concave production functions to ensure a solution to the problem of competitive profit-maximization. Then we can legitimately employ the cost function as a fully equivalent characterization of production.

Sometimes we will also assume constant returns to scale in production, i.e. we will assume $f$ to be homogeneous of degree one. In such a case, the cost function takes a particularly simple form. For any $x$, we can write

$$c(w, x) = \min_{v} \{w.v \mid f(v) = x\}$$

$$= x \min_{v} \{w.(v/x) \mid f(v/x) = 1\}$$

by homogeneity

$$= x \min_{y} \{w.y \mid f(y) = 1\}$$

in terms of new variables $y = v/x$

$$= x \, \bar{c}(w), \qquad \text{say} \tag{35}$$

where $\bar{c}(w)$ is simply the minimum cost of producing one unit of output when factor prices are $w$. Call it the *unit-cost function*. Then the cost for $x$ units is simply $x$ times the unit cost, which is a very natural consequence with constant returns to scale. Now average cost and marginal are each equal to the unit cost.

## The expenditure function

Consider a consumer facing prices $p$ and having money income $m$. Write $c$ for the vector of quantities consumed, and $u = f(c)$ for utility, where $f$ is an increasing and strictly quasi-concave function. Then the problem of choosing $c$ to maximize $u = f(c)$ subject to the budget constraint $p.c \leq m$ has a unique solution.

For positive prices, we can equivalently consider the problem achieving a target utility level at minimum expenditure, i.e. of minimizing $p.c$ subject to $f(c) \geq u$. This has an envelope function which tells us the minimum expenditure required to attain the target utility $u$ when the price vector is $p$. It is called the *expenditure function* dual to the utility function $f$, and written $e(p, u)$.

The formal structure of the problem is identical to that of the input cost minimization problem of the previous sub-section. We can therefore write down the properties of the expenditure function by analogy. (1) For fixed $u$, it is homogeneous of degree one in $p$. (2) The partial derivatives $e_p$ yield the optimum quantity choices for attaining the given utility level, i.e. the Hicksian compensated demand functions. (3) For fixed $u$, the expenditure function is concave in $p$; this arises from substitution along an indifference curve, and leads to the result that the own substitution effect of a price change is non-positive. Some other results arise in Chapter 2.

Since we have assumed a strictly quasi-concave utility function, the expenditure function is fully dual in the sense of providing an equivalent characterization of consumer preferences. Since utility is ordinal, no importance can be assigned to homogeneity, but homotheticity of preferences is a meaningful property. If $f$ is homothetic, we have seen that an increasing transform of it, say $g(f)$, is homogeneous of degree one. Then

$$e(p, u) = \min_{c} \{p.c \mid f(c) \geq u\}$$

$$= \min_{c} \{p.c \mid g(f(c)) \geq g(u)\}$$

$$= g(u)\, \bar{e}(p) \tag{36}$$

by an argument repeating that used for homogeneous production functions.

### The revenue function

Now consider a general problem of production where an input vector $v$ produces an output vector $x$ subject to the feasibility requirement that $(x, v)$ lies in a subset $S$ of $N^{n+m}$, where $x$ is in $N^n$ and $v$ in $N^m$. Let $p$ be a vector of output prices, and consider the problem faced by a competitive producer with this technology: choose $x$ to maximize $p.x$ subject to feasibility. The parameters are $p$ and $v$, and the envelope function can be written as

$$r(p, v) = \max_{x} \{p.x \mid (x, v) \in S\} \tag{37}$$

This is called the *revenue function* dual to the production technology. We examine some of its properties.

First keep $v$ fixed and examine the dependence on $p$. The important point is that the parameters $p$ do not affect the constraint. This has several consequences. (a) $r$ is homogeneous of degree one in $p$. The reasoning is the same as that used for the cost function. So is the economic principle: an equiproportionate change in all output prices does not alter the optimum output mix, but only changes its value. (b) By the special case of the envelope theorem derived in (30), the optimum output choices, i.e. supply functions, are given by $r_p = x$. Then the supply functions are homogeneous of degree zero in $p$. (c) $r$ is convex in $p$; this is again the argument of Figure A.12. If $x'$ is the optimum output choice for $p'$, then the linear function $p.x'$ is the supporting hyperplane for $r(p, v)$ at $p'$. (d) On account of the convexity, $\partial x_j/\partial p_j = \partial^2 r/\partial p_j^2 \geq 0$. Other properties are examined in Chapter 2. These include particular problems that arise since $r$ fails to be differentiable at some crucial points.

Next fix $p$ and examine $r$ as a function of $v$. If $S$ is a convex set, we can use our second theorem on the concavity of envelope functions to conclude that $r$ is a concave function of $v$. The partial derivatives $r_v$ give us the effects on the objective function of marginal unit increases in input quantities; they are therefore the shadow prices of the inputs, and become the derived demand prices if inputs are traded in competitive markets.

If there are constant returns to scale in production, it is possible to change the entire scale of any feasible input-output combination, i.e. if $(x, v)$ is in $S$, so is $(\lambda x, \lambda v)$ for any $\lambda \geq 0$. Then $r$ will be homogeneous of degree one in $v$; the reasoning for this is very similar to earlier homogeneity arguments, and is left to the reader.

# REFERENCES

A detailed treatment of linear algebra and calculus that is accessible to economics students is in Chiang (1974) or Glaister (1978). For optimization see Dixit (1976). More thorough mathematical treatments are in Apostol (1967–69), Eggleston (1963) and Panik (1978). Cost and revenue functions are treated exhaustively by McFadden (1978).

# BIBLIOGRAPHY

Anderson, R. K. and Takayama, A. (1977) 'Devaluation, the specie flow mechanism and the steady state'. *Review of Economic Studies*, **44** (2), 347–361.

Apostol, T. M. (1967–69) *Calculus*, Vols. I and II, second edition, Waltham, Mass.: Blaisdell.

Arrow, K. J. and Hahn, F. H. (1971) *General Competitive Analysis*, San Francisco: Holden-Day.

Barro, R. J. and Grossman, H. I. (1976) *Money, Employment and Inflation*, Cambridge University Press.

Batra, R. N. (1973) *Studies in the Pure Theory of International Trade*, London: Macmillan.

Baumol, W. J. (1977) *Economic Theory and Operations Analysis*, fourth edition, Englewood Cliffs, N.J.: Prentice-Hall.

Bhagwati, J. N. (1958) 'Immiserising growth: a geometric note', reprinted in Caves and Johnson (1968).

Bhagwati, J. N. (1964) 'The pure theory of international trade: A survey', *Economic Journal*, **74** (1), 1–84.

Bhagwati, J. N. (1968) 'Distortions and immiserizing growth: A generalization', *Review of Economic Studies*, **35** (4), 481–485.

Bhagwati, J. N. (1971) 'The generalised theory of distortions and welfare', in J. Bhagwati *et al.*, *Trade, Balance of Payments and Growth*, Amsterdam: North-Holland.

Bhagwati, J. N. and Johnson, H. G. (1961) 'A generalized theory of the effects of tariffs on the terms of trade', *Oxford Economic Papers*, **13** (3), 225–253.

Bhagwati, J. N. and Ramaswami, V. K. (1963) 'Domestic distortions, tariffs and the theory of optimum subsidy', reprinted in Caves and Johnson (1968).

Bhagwati, J. N. and Rodriguez, C. (1975) 'Welfare-theoretical analyses of the brain drain', *Journal of Development Economics*, **2** (3), 195–221.

Bliss, C. J. (1975) *Capital Theory and the Distribution of Income*, Amsterdam: North-Holland.

Caves, R. E. and Johnson, H. G. (eds.) (1968) *Readings in International Economics*, London: Allen and Unwin.

Caves, R. E. and Jones, R. W. (1977) *World Trade and Payments*, second edition, Boston: Little, Brown.

Chiang, A. C. (1974) *Fundamental Methods of Mathematical Economics*, second edition, New York: McGraw-Hill.

Chipman, J. S. (1965a) 'A survey of the theory of international trade: Part 1, The classical theory', *Econometrica*, **33** (3), 477–519.

Chipman, J. S. (1965b) 'A survey of the theory of international trade: Part 2, The neo-classical theory', *Econometrica*, **33** (4), 685–760.

Chipman, J. S. (1966) 'A survey of the theory of international trade: Part 3, The modern theory', *Econometrica*, **34** (1), 18–76.

Chipman, J. S. (1972) 'The theory of exploitative trade and investment policies', in L. E. DiMarco (ed.), *International Economics and Development*, New York: Academic Press.

Chipman, J. S. (1974) 'The transfer problem once again', in G. Horwich and P. Samuelson (eds.), *Trade, Stability and Macroeconomics*, New York: Academic Press.

Corden, W. M. (1957) 'Tariffs, subsidies and the terms of trade', *Economica*, **24** (3), 235–242.

Corden, W. M. (1971) *The Theory of Protection*, Oxford University Press.

Corden, W. M. and Gruen, F. H. (1970) 'A tariff that worsens the terms of trade', in I. A. McDougall and R. H. Snape (eds.), *Studies in International Economics*, Amsterdam: North-Holland.

Diamond, P. A. and Mirrless, J. A. (1971) 'Optimal taxation and public production', *American Economic Review*, **61** (1) and (3), 8–27 and 261–278.

Diewert, W. E. (1974) 'Applications of duality theory', in M. Intriligator and D. Kendrick (eds.), *Frontiers of Quantitative Economics*, Vol. II, Amsterdam: North-Holland.

Diewert, W. E. (1978) 'Duality approaches to microeconomic theory', in K. Arrow and M. Intriligator (eds.), *Handbook of Mathematical Economics*, Amsterdam: North-Holland, forthcoming.

Dixit, A. K. (1975) 'Welfare effects of tax and price changes', *Journal of Public Economics*, **4** (2), 103–123.

Dixit, A. K. (1976), *Optimization in Economic Theory*, Oxford University Press.

Dixit, A. K. (1978) 'The balance of trade in a model of temporary equilibrium with rationing', *Review of Economic Studies*, **45** (3), 393–404.

Dixit, A. K. (1979) 'Price changes and optimum taxation in a many-consumer economy', *Journal of Public Economics*, **11** (2), 143–157.

Dixit, A. K. and Norman, V. (1979) 'Comparative advantage and factor prices in the Ricardo-Viner model', in preparation.

Dixit, A. K. and Stiglitz, J. E. (1977) 'Monopolistic competition and optimum product diversity', *American Economic Review*, **67** (3), 297–308.

Dixit, A. K. and Stiglitz, J. E. (1979) 'Product selection and the size of an economy', in preparation.

Dornbusch, R. (1973) 'Devaluation, money and non-traded goods', reprinted in Frenkel and Johnson (1976).

Eggleston, H. G. (1963) *Convexity*, Cambridge University Press.

Frenkel, J. A. and Johnson, H. G. (eds.) (1976) *The Monetary Approach to the Balance of Payments*, London: Allen and Unwin.

Gale, D. (1960) *The Theory of Linear Economic Models*, New York: McGraw-Hill.

Gale, D. and Nikaido, H. (1965) 'The Jacobian matrix and the global univalence of mappings', *Mathematische Annalen*, **159**, 81–93.

Glaister, S. (1978) *Mathematical Methods for Economists*, second edition, Oxford: Blackwells.

Gorman, W. M. (1959) 'Are social indifference curves convex?', *Quarterly Journal of Economics*, **73** (3), 485–498.

Grubel, H. G. and Johnson, H. G. (eds.) (1971) *Effective Tariff Protection*, Geneva: GATT.

Grubel, H. G. and Lloyd, P. J. (1975) *Intra-Industry Trade*, London: Macmillan.

Guesnerie, R. (1975) 'Production of the public sector and taxation in a simple second best model', *Journal of Economic Theory*, 10 (2), 127–156.

Haberler, G. (1950) 'Some problems in the pure theory of international trade', reprinted in Caves and Johnson (1968).

Hahn, F. H. (1959) 'The balance of payments in a monetary economy', *Review of Economic Studies*, 26 (2), 110–125.

Hahn, F. H. (1977) 'The monetary approach to the balance of payments', *Journal of International Economics*, 7 (3), 231–250.

Hatta, T. (1977) 'A theory of piecemeal policy recommendations', *Review of Economic Studies*, 44 (1), 1–21.

Hirsch, F. (1976) *Social Limits to Growth*, Cambridge, Mass.: Harvard University Press.

Johnson, H. G. (1957) 'Factor endowments, international trade and factor prices', reprinted in Caves and Johnson (1968).

Johnson, H. G. (1959) 'Economic development and international trade', reprinted in Caves and Johnson (1968).

Johnson, H. G. (1967a) 'The possibility of income losses from increased efficiency or factor accumulation in the presence of tariffs', *Economic Journal*, 77 (1), 151–154.

Johnson, H. G. (1967b) 'The possibility of factor-price equalisation when commodities outnumber factors', *Economica*, 34 (3), 282–288.

Johnson, H. G. (1971) *The Two-sector Model of General Equilibrium*, London: Allen and Unwin.

Johnson, H. G. (1972) 'The monetary approach to balance-of-payments theory', reprinted in Frenkel and Johnson (1976).

Jones, R. W. (1965) 'The structure of simple general equilibrium models', *Journal of Political Economy*, 73 (4), 557–572.

Jones, R. W. (1967) 'International capital movements and the theory of tariffs and trade', *Quarterly Journal of Economics*, 81 (1), 1–38.

Jones, R. W. (1971a) 'Effective protection and substitution', *Journal of International Economics*, 1 (1), 59–81.

Jones, R. W. (1971b) 'Distortions in factor markets and the general equilibrium model of production', *Journal of Political Economy*, 79 (3), 437–459.

Jones, R. W. (1975a) 'Income distribution and effective protection in a multicommodity trade model', *Journal of Economic Theory*, 11 (1), 1–15.

Jones, R. W. (1975b) 'Presumption and the transfer problem', *Journal of International Economics*, 5, 263–274.

Jones, R. W. and Scheinkman, J. A. (1977) 'The relevance of the two-sector production model in trade theory', *Journal of Political Economy*, 85 (5), 909–935.

Kemp, M. C. (1966) 'The gain from international trade and investment: A neo-Heckscher-Ohlin approach', *American Economic Review*, 56 (4), 788–809.

Kemp, M. C. (1969) *The Pure Theory of International Trade and Investment*, Englewood Cliffs, N.J.: Prentice-Hall.

Kemp, M. C. (1970) 'The balance of payments and the terms of trade in relation to financial controls', *Review of Economic Studies*, **37** (1), 25–31.

Krugman, P. (1978a) 'Increasing returns, monopolistic competition, and international trade; mimeo., Yale University.

Krugman, P. (1978b) 'Scale economies, product differentiation, and the pattern of trade', mimeo., Yale University.

Kuhn, H. W. (1968) 'Lectures on mathematical economics', in G. Dantzig and A. Veinott (eds.), *Mathematics of the Decision Sciences*, Part 2, Providence, R. I.: American Mathematical Society.

Kyle, J. F. (1978) 'Financial assets, non-traded goods and devaluation', *Review of Economic Studies*, **45** (1), 155–163.

Land, A. H. (1959) 'Factor endowments and factor prices', *Economica*, **26** (2), 137–142.

Lerner, A. P. (1936) 'The symmetry between import and export taxes', reprinted in Caves and Johnson (1968).

Lerner, A. P. (1952) 'Factor prices and international trade', *Economica*, **19** (1), 1–15.

Linder, S. B. (1961) *An Essay on Trade and Transformation*, New York: Wiley.

Lipsey, R. G. (1970) *The Theory of Customs Unions*, London: Weidenfeld and Nicholson.

McFadden, D. L. (1978) 'Cost, revenue and profit functions', in M. Fuss and D. McFadden (eds.), *Production Economics: A Duel Approach in Theory and Applications*, Amsterdam: North-Holland.

McKenzie, L. W. (1955) 'Equality of factor prices in world trade', *Econometrica*, **23** (3), 239–257.

Magee, S. P. (1973) 'Factor market distortions, production, and trade: A Survey', *Oxford Economic Papers*, **25** (1), 1–43.

Malinvaud, E. (1977) *The Theory of Unemployment Reconsidered*, Oxford: Blackwells.

Markusen, J. R. and Melvin, J. R. (1979) 'Tariffs, capital mobility, and foreign ownership', *Journal of International Economics*, **9** (3), 395–409.

Meade, J. E. (1952) *A Geometry of International Trade*, London: Allen and Unwin.

Meade, J. E. (1955) *Trade and Welfare: Mathematical Supplement*, Oxford University Press.

Melvin, J. R. (1968) 'Production and trade with two factors and three goods', *American Economic Review*, **58** (5), 1249–1268.

Melvin, J. R. and Warne, R. D. (1973) 'Monopoly and the theory of international trade', *Journal of International Economics*, **3**, 117–134.

Metzler, L. A. (1949) 'Tariffs, terms of trade, and the distribution of national income', reprinted in Caves and Johnson (1968).

Mirrless, J. A. (1969) 'The dynamic non-substitution theorem', *Review of Economic Studies*, **36** (1), 67–76.

Mundell, R. A. (1968) *International Economics*, New York: Macmillan.

Mussa, M. (1974) 'Tariffs and the distribution of income: The importance of factor specificity, substitutability, and intensity in the short and long run', *Journal of Political Economy*, **82** (6), 1191–1203.

Neary, J. P. (1978) 'Non-traded goods and the balance of trade in a neo-Keynesian temporary equilibrium', *Quarterly Journal of Economics*, forthcoming.

Norman, V. (1976) 'Product differentiation and international trade', paper presented at the Summer Research Workshop, Warwick University.

Ohyama, M. (1972) 'Trade and welfare in general equilibrium', *Keio Economic Studies*, 9 (2), 37–73.

Panik, M. J. (1978) *Classical Optimisation: Foundations and Extensions*, Amsterdam: North-Holland.

Pearce, I. F. (1970) *International Trade*, London: Macmillan.

Robinson, R. (1956), 'Factor proportions and comparative advantage', reprinted in Caves and Johnson (1968).

Rybczynski, T. M. (1955) 'Factor endowments and relative commodity prices', reprinted in Caves and Johnson (1968).

Samuelson, P. A. (1947) *Foundations of Economic Analysis*, Cambridge, Mass.: Harvard University Press.

Samuelson, P. A. (1949) 'International factor-price equalisation once again', reprinted in Caves and Johnson (1968).

Samuelson, P. A. (1952) 'The transfer problem and transport costs', reprinted in Caves and Johnson (1968).

Samuelson, P. A. (1953) 'Prices of factors and goods in general equilibrium', *Review of Economic Studies*, 21 (1), 1–20.

Samuelson, P. A. (1971) 'Ohlin was right', *Swedish Journal of Economics*, 73 (4), 365–384.

Samuelson, P. A. (1976) *Economics*, tenth edition, New York: McGraw-Hill.

Sandmo, A. (1975) 'Optimal taxation in the presence of externalities', *Swedish Journal of Economics*, 77 (1), 86–98.

Sandmo, A (1976) 'Optimal taxation: An introduction to the literature', *Journal of Public Economics*, 6 (1), 37–54.

Sandmo, A. (1977) 'Portfolio theory, asset demand and taxation: Comparative statics with many assets', *Review of Economic Studies*, 44 (2), 369–379.

Schweinberger, A. G. (1979) 'The theory of factor price differentials: the case of constant absolute differentials', *Journal of International Economics*, 9 (1), 95–115.

Scitovsky, T. (1976) *The Joyless Economy*, Oxford University Press.

Seade, J. K. (1979) 'The stability of Cournot revisited', Warwick Economic Research Paper No. 121.

Smith, M. A. M. (1979) 'Optimal tariffs, optimal taxes and shadow prices', mimeo., London School of Economics.

Södersten, B. (1971) *International Economics*, London: Macmillan.

Spence, A. M. (1976) 'Product selection, fixed costs and monopolistic competition', *Review of Economic Studies*, 43 (2), 217–235.

Steigum, E. (1978) 'Keynesian and classical unemployment in an open economy', manuscript, Norwegian School of Economics and Business Administration.

Stolper, W. and Samuelson, P. A. (1941) 'Protection and real wages', *Review of Economic Studies*, 9 (1), 58–73.

Suzuki, K. (1976) 'The deterioration of the terms of trade by a tariff', *Journal of International Economics*, 6, 173–182.

Takayama, A. (1972) *International Trade*, New York: Holt, Rinehart and Winston.

Turnovsky, S. J. (1977) 'Macroeconomic Analysis and Stabilization Policy', Cambridge: Cambridge University Press.

Uzawa, H. (1959) 'Prices of the factors of production in international trade', *Econometrica*, **27** (3), 448–468.

Uzawa, H. (1964) 'Duality principles in the theory of cost and production', *International Economic Review*, **5** (2), 216–220.

Varian, H. R. (1978) *Microeconomic Analysis*, New York: Norton.

Vernon, R. (1966) 'International investment and international trade in the product cycle', *Quarterly Journal of Economics*, **80** (2), 190–207.

Woodland, A. D. (1977a) 'A dual approach to equilibrium in the production sector in international trade theory', *Canadian Journal of Economics*, **10** (1), 50–68.

Woodland, A. D. (1977b) 'Joint outputs, intermediate inputs and international trade theory', *International Economic Review*, **18** (3), 517–533.

# INDEX

ABSOLUTE advantage: 4, 84.
Absorption approach to the balance of payments: 255.
Aggregate world demand: 21.
Anderson and Takayama: 230n.
Arrow and Hahn: 77, 226, 301.

BALANCED inflation: 216.
Balance of trade, condition: 22, surplus: 204.
Barro and Grossman: 233.
Baumol: 64.
Bergson-Samuelson social welfare function: 75, 166.
Bhagwati: 28n, 164n, 178, 184, 195n.
Bhagwati and Johnson: 164n.
Bhagwati and Ramaswami: 195n.
Bhagwati and Rodriguez: 164n.
Bliss: 87.
Boundary point: 299.
Budget line: 2.

CAVES and Johnson: 28n; 195n.
CAVES and Jones: 28n, 92n, 163n, 194n, 229n, 263n, 295n.
Chain rule: 305.
Chamberlinian equilibrium: 66, 286.
Chipman: 28n, 52, 125n.
Cobb-Douglas, cost function: 118; demand function: 118.
production function: 104, 140.
technology: 141.
Comparative advantage: 1ff; 93ff.
Compensated (Hicksian) demand function: 60 ff; 325.
Compensated import demand function: 90ff.
Compensated world excess demand: 130.
Complementary slackness: 46, 318.
Concave function: 306.
Conditional factor demand function: 324.

Constant elasticity of substitution 48, 282.
Consumer prices: 68, 176.
Consumer surplus: 266, 274ff.
Consumer taxes: 176.
Convex functions: 311.
Convex sets: 31, 301.
Corden: 160, 195n.
Cost function: 29, 44, 322.
Cost-minimization: 47, 323.
Currency appreciation: 217.
Currency depreciation: 217.
Customs unions: 167, 191ff.

DEMAND functions: 60ff.
Demand functions for factors: 34.
Devaluation: 201.
competitive: 262.
Diamond and Mirrlees: 175, 195n.
Diewert: 64n.
Direct investment: 142ff.
Distortion: 23, 133, 176ff.
Diversification: 18, 51ff, 113–114.
Diversification cone: 52, 121.
Dixit: 64n, 174, 187, 195n, 233, 235.
Dixit and Norman: 40, 64n, 87, 92n, 125n.
Dixit and Stiglitz: 274, 281, 295n.
Domestic distortions: 177.
Dornbusch: 230n.
Dual approach: 26.
Duality: 29.

ECONOMIC efficiency: 50.
Economic growth: 21, 127.
Effective demand: 232.
excess demand: 233.
excess supply: 263.
supply: 232.
Effective protection: 29, 160ff, 184.
Elasticities approach: 201, 222ff.
Elasticity, of demand: 136.
of substitution: 114, 141.
of supply: 136.